GOD'S OTHERS

ALSO BY DAVID PERLSTEIN

Solo Success: 100 Tips for Becoming a $100,000-a-Year Freelancer

GOD'S OTHERS

Non-Israelites' Encounters With God in the Hebrew Bible

DAVID PERLSTEIN

Foreword by Rabbi Martin S. Weiner,
Past President, Central Conference of American Rabbis

iUniverse, Inc.
New York Bloomington

God's Others
Non-Israelites' Encounters With God in the Hebrew Bible

iUniverse books may be ordered through booksellers or by contacting:

iUniverse
1663 Liberty Drive
Bloomington, IN 47403
www.iuniverse.com
1-800-Authors (1-800-288-4677)

ISBN: 978-1-4502-2278-5 (sc)
ISBN: 978-1-4502-2279-2 (dj)
ISBN: 978-1-4502-2280-8 (ebk)

Library of Congress Control Number: 2010905200

Printed in the United States of America

iUniverse rev. date: 06/01/2010

For
Morris and Blanche Perlstein, my past
Carolyn Perlstein, my present
Seth, Yosi and Aaron Perlstein, my future

Choose life.

Deuteronomy 30:19

Contents

FOREWORD

GOD'S OTHERS offers a most engaging volume. Calling upon the text of the Hebrew Bible, the wisdom of ancient rabbinic sages, and a host of medieval and modern commentators of all faiths, this book brings new insights to the fascinating stories of a host of "characters," such as the Pharaoh of Egypt, Ruth and Job, with whom many biblical readers are familiar in a general way. It also reveals portraits of others, such as Hagar, Laban, Balaam, Rahab, Naaman and Cyrus of whom many people have little or no familiarity. They, too, have much to tell us about God's presence in the world.

Most significantly, David Perlstein's sensitive exploration of God's relationship to non-Israelites in the Hebrew Bible leads to challenging guidance for our twenty-first century attitudes towards those who profess "other" faiths. The concluding chapter on building a world of "respect beyond tolerance" presents a worthy goal—and a means by which we may move towards it—for all who are concerned about the future of humanity.

Rabbi Martin S. Weiner
Past President, Central Conference of American Rabbis
San Francisco, California

Introduction

Turn it and turn it again, for everything is in it; reflect on it and grow old and grey in it and do not move away from it, for there is no better way than this.
Mishnah Avot 5:22

These and these are the words of God.
Talmud (Eruvin 13b)

A PROSTITUTE FROM JERICHO revealed "God's others" to me. Rahab, a key character in the Book of Joshua, appears in this volume in chapter six, *Women of Valor*. A non-Israelite, she protects two Israelite spies sent to the city of Jericho. Having heard about the miracles God wrought in freeing the Israelites from Egyptian bondage, she pledges herself to the God of Israel—something of a miracle in itself. After all, it is the Israelites of the Exodus, not Rahab, who experience God first-hand. They, not she, survive the plagues in Egypt. They, not she, walk through the parted waters of the Reed Sea—the direct translation of the Hebrew Yam (sea) Suf (reed). And they, not she, stand amidst the thunder and lightning at Sinai as God reveals the Ten Commandments.

Yet Rahab's response to hearsay is so heartfelt—albeit that fear, too, plays a great role in her decision to protect the spies—and her acknowledgement of God so genuine that Judaism's Sages and commentators sing the praises of this Canaanite woman.

What drew my attention to Rahab? I regularly read the weekly portion of the Torah—the five books from Genesis through Deuteronomy, which constitute the first of three sections of the Hebrew Bible, most commonly referred to by Christians as the Old Testament.[1] However, some years had passed since I'd read the second and third sections—Nevi'im (Prophets) and Kethuvim (Writings). I decided to reexamine these texts and began with the Book of Joshua, which immediately follows Deuteronomy. Rahab's appearance caused the proverbial light bulb to flash—and brightly. I had an epiphany, if I may borrow a word more appropriate to St. Paul on the road to Damascus. The Hebrew Bible, I realized, presents God as having complex, deeply meaningful relationships with non-Israelites, some of them God-fearers, others committed pagans.

Rahab's story moved me to search out other non-Israelites in the Hebrew Bible to whom God appears or speaks directly (often but not always in dreams) or appears indirectly through the working of miracles and wonders. I wanted to discover what such encounters would say about them, about Israel and about God's relationship with all of humanity. I also sensed that "God's others" might provide support "hidden in plain sight" for people seeking to bridge the gaps that often separate adherents of different religious beliefs. We know all to well, as I will discuss next, that some people take the Bible at its most literal and quote cherry-picked verses without context, dividing rather than uniting and thus fostering mistrust and hostility in the name of love.

My re-reading of the Hebrew Bible included a new focus on the Torah, which presents many of "God's others." The biblical narrative makes clear, I learned, that many non-Israelites know God in differing yet profound ways. God takes upon Himself the prerogative to reveal Himself when He will, as He will, to whom He will. (I use the masculine form not because God has a sexual identity but because the Hebrew renders God in the masculine, and this provides a more streamlined term than "He or She" or "[S]He" or similar attempts to achieve gender equality.)

1 The acronym for these three sections is *Tanakh* by which Jews often refer to the Hebrew Bible.

To be sure, the Hebrew Bible presents Israel's relationship with God as special, and this ongoing relationship maintains a crucial position in Jewish thought. But critical to the discussion of *God's Others* is the understanding that the biblical narrative never portrays Israel's relationship with God as exclusive. As descendants of Abraham, Israel possesses great spiritual potential and has been chosen to set an example for the world. As human beings, however, Israelites may—and often do—squander that potential. The Bible portrays this "nation of priests" as subject to the same weakness and corruption as the nations that surround it. The Israelites repeatedly fail to fulfill God's commandments and suffer grave consequences accordingly.

Israel's repeated cycles of accepting God's commandments then abandoning them informs us that coming to terms with the Hebrew Bible's depth and complexity presents significant challenges. In response, Jewish scholarship has pursued a variety of ways to uncover all the meaning contained in the biblical text—and accepted a multiplicity of interpretations and opinions. As a result, an answer to any one question often yields a cascade of additional questions, many defying easy answers. Some questions yield no rational answers at all, taking inquiry into spiritual realms to which some scholars and students adhere and others do not. As a result, moving deeper into the biblical text constitutes an endless journey. While we retain a sense of our objective, every step forward may push that objective tantalizingly into the distance much as the false peak of a mountain draws us upward only to recede as we approach. The more we learn, the less likely it seems that we will master all the nuances of the biblical narrative. Yet our efforts to unravel one mystery after another offer meaningful rewards as our knowledge grows and our horizons expand. Life, as many advised in the sixties, is a journey, not a destination.

A Note on Method and Format

In writing *God's Others*, I have undertaken to do three things.

First and foremost, I retell the stories of non-Israelites who encounter God, and I do so in meaningful detail. Their stories form the crux of this book. To add perspective, I offer two sections as valuable bookends. Part I, *The God of All*, presents a brief overview of the challenges to a civil society posed by claims to exclusive religious truth (chapter one) and the Hebrew Bible's view of monotheism as humanity's natural religious state originating in creation (chapter two). The latter chapter suggests that some of "God's others" inherit monotheistic traditions before the time of Abraham. Part III offers a concluding chapter, *Beyond Tolerance*, addressing the question that naturally arises following a reading of these stories: How can we transform a knowledge of "God's others" into a practical approach promoting respect and tranquility?

Second, I emphasize the biblical text by including numerous verses. Reading about "God's others" cannot substitute for engaging these men and women within the framework of the text itself. The 1999 Jewish Publication Society edition of the Tanakh serves as my source. Based on the 1985 edition, it offers a direct translation from Hebrew to English. (Many biblical editions, particularly—although not exclusively—in the Christian tradition, present translations from Hebrew first to Greek or Latin then to English.) JPS proves eminently readable, and the use of a single translation offers a consistent approach to referencing all the books of the Hebrew Bible and relating incidents and speeches in one book to another. Occasionally, I cite other translations that offer additional insights or raise new questions concerning translation. I hope that the reader, after concluding *God's Others*, will open the Bible in whichever translation is preferred for a first-hand reading or rereading of these stories.

Third, I add context by citing a relevant selection of commentary, both traditional and critical. Traditional Jewish commentary spans the period of the Talmud—roughly 200 BCE to 500 CE—to the present. Normative (rabbinic) Judaism does not read the Torah in isolation. Indeed, it cannot. Textual gaps, along with translation challenges, obscure cultural references and occasional scribal errors, abound. The text serves as a jumping off point for investigation and discussion. Thus the Sages did not always agree with the Law as written. Deuteronomy 19:21, for example, includes the oft-quoted verse, "Nor must you show pity: life for life, eye for eye, tooth for tooth, hand for hand, foot for foot." The Sages looked beyond the literal meaning to interpret this verse as requiring monetary compensation for injuries. Going further, they acknowledged the Torah's instructions invoking the death penalty in cases of intentional murder, adultery, idolatry and other specified violations of the Law then developed legal procedures to make execution nearly impossible.

The Midrash complements Talmudic commentary. Vast and varied collections of stories, midrash (from "to investigate") fill in textual gaps and add depth to characters and events. Some midrash are quite well known. One tells of Abraham, in his ardent monotheism, smashing the idols in the shop of his father, Terach. Many Jews believe this story to be in the Torah. It is not.

Talmud and Midrash represent part of the foundation of Jewish biblical discussion but hardly its entirety. Medieval scholars, such as the Torah's supercommentator, Rashi—who cites Midrash with great frequency and also provides his own interpretations—along with Maimonides, Nachmanides, Ibn Ezra and others add their own views. The tradition of unearthing new truths and wisdom from the biblical text continues today. One cannot understand the Hebrew Bible from the Jewish perspective without referencing this vast body of literature.

Christians and Muslims also have written their own commentaries on the Hebrew Bible. Periodically, I cite passages from the New Testament and the Quran, as well as comments by Christian and Muslim scholars by way of comparison and contrast. I hope that Jewish readers of *God's Others* will find new insights in this material, as I hope that Christian and Muslim readers will discover much to value in Jewish perspectives emphasizing our common humanity.

Further, I include commentary from critical scholars as well as from commentators on a variety of related topics. In the nineteenth century, literary analysts, linguists, historians, archaeologists and anthropologists—most Christian—began to view the Bible as reflective of the peoples, cultures, languages and literature that existed before and during the biblical era. The Documentary Hypothesis, assembled from a variety of earlier sources by the

German scholar Julius Wellhausen (1844-1918), proposed that the Torah is the work of a number of distinct—although unidentified—individuals.[2]

Traditional Jewish scholars reject, or at least look askance at, such work. Orthodox Jewish exegesis accepts the Torah as the literal word of God transmitted to, and written down by, Moses at Mount Sinai. It attributes authorship of the rest of the Bible to human beings whose authors the Talmud delineates, such as Joshua, who is credited not only with writing his own book but the last eight verses of Deuteronomy following Moses' death. The Sages also consider such biblical individuals as Abraham and Sarah, Moses and Zipporah, Samson and Delilah, Job, and Esther to be actual historical figures rather than literary ones.

Judaism's Reform, Conservative and Reconstructionist movements incorporate the critical approach into their textual studies. None disparage the integrity of the biblical narrative or abandon traditional exegesis. Rather, they pursue an additional dimension of understanding based on critical findings simply unavailable to Talmudic, medieval and many later commentators.

It is important to recognize that while traditional and critical scholars have their differences, they share a focus on the biblical narrative and a desire to better understand it. Thus I present critical material in *God's Others* because I strongly believe that it adds to—rather than detracts from—our understanding. As Richard Friedman writes, "For those who hold the Bible as sacred, it can mean new possibilities of interpretation; and it can mean a new awe before the great chain of events, persons, and centuries that came together so intricately to produce an incomparable book of teachings." (Friedman/Who Wrote, 245)

After all, Judaism did not arise in a vacuum. The Mesopotamian world into which Abraham was born and Egypt, which he visited and which strove with Mesopotamia for domination of the ancient Near East, play key roles in the biblical narrative. Judaism represents an immense leap forward in religious thinking, but it is a leap forward

2 Richard Friedman's *Who Wrote the Bible?* presents this subject in comprehensive and very accessible terms.

from something. We cannot help but concede that the patriarchs and the later Israelites were influenced by the cultures that surrounded them. Thus Richard E. Rubenstein warns that Jews, Christians and Muslims alike must be wary of what he terms "the myth of cultural authenticity: the notion, common to many cultures, that a particular civilization developed on its own from original sources rather than being borrowed from or imposed by outsiders." (Rubenstein, 6)

Understanding the tensions between traditional and critical commentary, I have attempted to keep them somewhat separate—much as Jewish law mandates separating meat and dairy products in the same meal, wool and flax in the same garment, and two species of animals under a single yoke. Where a source does not incorporate traditional exegesis, I strive to identify it as critical for clarity's sake. Where a source seems obviously non-traditional, I do not make this identification to avoid slowing the narrative. As my efforts at separation are only partial, I ask some allowance for utilizing these differing but ultimately complementary sources of knowledge.

All this being stated, I wish to emphasize that *God's Others* represents the work of a storyteller. I include references and citations to make these stories more accessible to general readers while leaving more specialized, detailed work to scholars.

Acknowledgements

Four wonderful and learned rabbis have assisted me with their observations. Rabbi Martin Weiner, Rabbi Emeritus at Congregation Sherith Israel in San Francisco and former president of the Central Conference of American Rabbis, helped keep me on course with his detailed comments and continuing encouragement. I am honored that he accepted my invitation to write the foreword. Rabbi Lawrence Raphael, Senior Rabbi at Congregation Sherith Israel; Rabbi Yoel Khan, Senior Rabbi at Congregation Beth El in Berkeley; and Rabbi Melanie Aron, Senior Rabbi at Congregation Shir Hadash in Los Gatos, California all helped me get this project off on the right foot.

Dr. Tamara Cohn Eskenazi, Professor of Bible at Hebrew Union College-Jewish Institute of Religion in Los Angeles, reviewed the story of Ruth, provided guidance and graciously permitted me to cite observations she offered in a private conversation. I value her insights.

Several friends also greatly assisted me, serving as a readers sounding board: Jane Cutler, Ira Fateman, Les Kozerowitz, James Shay and Dan Weiss helped me stay focused on the primary goal of every writer—to communicate clearly and succinctly.

Finally, I must thank my beloved wife, Carolyn, for her continuing support. As one of "God's others," she has helped make ours a Jewish household, raised three Jewish children and encouraged my love of Jewish knowledge and practice.

San Francisco, California

PART I:

THE GOD OF ALL

1
Which Side is God On?

And God created man in His image, in the image of God he created him: male and female he created them.
Genesis 1:27

"Behold I am the Lord, the God of all flesh."
Jeremiah 32:27

In March 1942 following Japan's attack on Pearl Harbor, Joe Louis, the famed "Brown Bomber" and heavyweight champion of the world, spoke at a Navy Relief Society dinner at New York's Madison Square Garden. Explaining why he had recently enlisted in the Army—and as a private at that, having turned down an officer's commission—Louis proclaimed, "We're on God's side."[3] Louis emphasized America's position as a nation of goodness fighting the evils of Imperial Japan, Nazi Germany and fascist Italy.

Louis's widely hailed remark turned a common phrase upside down to present not only a sense of unwavering purpose but of humility. Those who believe in the righteousness of their cause often exclaim that "God is on our side," leaving their opponents in

3 This famed remark was not lost on Bob Dylan, who wrote the song "With God on Our Side" in 1963 during the Cold War just prior to full-scale American military involvement in Vietnam.

defenseless opposition to God's will. Less boastful, the champ's statement still drew a clear line separating the Axis nations from the United States and its allies. No one could question which side represented morality and goodness—if they were Americans, Britons, Frenchmen and even officially atheistic Russians. Yet Japanese, Germans and Italians believed that *they* were on God's side and, conversely, that God was on theirs. Who was right?

A century earlier, in 1862, Abraham Lincoln pondered the difficult issue of human alignment with God's will. In autumn, with the Union continuing to suffer battlefield losses, Lincoln wrote what appears to be something of a meditation: "The will of God prevails. In great contests each party claims to act in accordance with the will of God. Both *may* be, and one *must* be, wrong. God cannot be *for*, and *against* the same thing at the same time." (Safire, 114)

Lincoln, unshakably determined to preserve the Union, expressed considerable doubt rather than certainty regarding the issue of God's intentions. Claiming to know God's will, Lincoln wrote in so many words, is just that—a claim. Moreover, Lincoln pointed out, neither party in a dispute may be on God's side. Such reservation rarely finds expression in today's highly polarized world in which not only condemnations of others but the slaughter of innocents in the name of God occur with bloodcurdling frequency. The inevitable question arises: How can any nation or group truly *know* that it is on God's side? Yet many religious leaders and their followers endlessly promote a challenging mantra: "What I believe is right. If you do not believe what I believe, you are wrong. There is one way and only one way—and that is *my* way."

How shocking—and shockingly familiar—such words have become, whether spoken outright or couched in more polite terms. On the global stage, the theology of exclusive religious truth fuels today's various jihads waged by Islamists with venomous fury against fellow Muslims and "nonbelievers" in the West. Within the United States, claims to exclusive religious truth, sometimes stated with subtlety but with no less surety, underlie deep divisions within American society as some conservative Christians seek to impel, or even compel, others to live according to their own specific beliefs.

Must religious differences based on Jewish, Christian and Muslim scriptures lead us to further mistrust and violence? If we glance at these texts cursorily and refuse to engage in their complexity, the answer most likely will be yes. But a deeper look at the Hebrew Bible—the foundation text of both the Christian Bible and the Quran—offers us another path. The stories of "God's others" demonstrate that no one religion, denomination or sect can rightly claim exclusive religious truth. Many paths to God exist.

Samuel Huntington's posited "clash of civilizations" has stirred much controversy, yet however one wishes to define "civilization"—as a religious, ethnic, cultural or political entity or, perhaps more accurately, as an entity defined by all of these factors—a sense of difference, of "us and them," has gravely altered our world since September 11, 2001. Yet each of the Abrahamic faiths—Judaism, Christianity and Islam—holds sacred that all human beings are created in the image of God. This shared belief should inform us that we have far more in common than we realize.

Universalism and Particularism

Wishing for mutual respect does not ensure its implementation. Certainty exercises a seductively powerful appeal. Certainty makes us feel more comfortable with ourselves, more at ease in a world in which not everyone thinks and acts as we do. Conversely, doubt threatens our place in the world and makes us uneasy. To true believers, doubt is anathema. They know that they, and they alone, are on God's side and thus adhere to a universalistic point of view: Every human being should accept their religious truth, since other beliefs inherently lack legitimacy.

Consequently, those who follow a universalistic religion and claim exclusive truth worship a *particularistic* God. Their God grants favor only to those who follow a single set of rigidly circumscribed beliefs and practices. Thus true believers do not acknowledge different beliefs simply as being different. They condemn them as wrong. Claimants to exclusive religious truth divide the world into "us" and "them." Because "they" betray God's intentions and threaten the righteous, "they" must be converted, contained or eliminated.

What induces so many people to adopt such hostile stances towards others' beliefs rather than dismiss them and go about their business? If my neighbors' beliefs are different from mine, can I not simply ignore them and, if necessary, my neighbors, as well? Surely my neighbors' beliefs have no impact on me as long as my neighbors refrain from forcing me to profess or adhere to them.

In a perfect world, the matter would be resolved in much the way people approach their preferences for ice cream. If I like vanilla and others prefer chocolate, strawberry or banana cream pie, they can freely enjoy their favorite flavors without provoking or fearing a confrontation regarding our "differences." My partiality to vanilla—or peach or green tea—may hold no appeal to a chocolate lover, but we pose no perceived threat to each other.

Religion entails a very different frame of reference. It addresses adherents' beliefs in essential truths rather than inconsequential preferences. Such beliefs inform us about the nature of God, how God expects us to live in this world and, for many of faith, how to define and prepare for the next world. As a result, Jews, Christians and Muslims—in spite of good-faith efforts—often encounter difficult questions in regard to each other that reinforce universalistic perspectives and pose potent obstacles to mutual understanding and acceptance.

Cognitive dissonance becomes the order of the day. Jews cannot believe, as they traditionally do, that prophecy and revelation ended in 586 BCE with the destruction of the First Temple in Jerusalem *and* that Jesus is the Son of God, who brought new prophecy to Israel.[4] Christians cannot conceive of Jesus as God's final revelation *and* accept Muslims' belief that revelation continued—and concluded—with Muhammad. In turn, Muslims have great difficulty reconciling the Quran as God's ultimate revelation, which corrects the errors of the Hebrew and Christian Bibles, and draws Muslims back to the

4 I use the increasingly adopted BCE, the abbreviation for Before the Common Era—and CE, for the Common Era—in place of tracking time by any one religion's calendar. BC (Before Christ) and AD (Anno Domini) are Christian terms.

original monotheism of Abraham, *and* that Jews and Christians are right to reject it. Given distinct views of the opening and closing of the gates of revelation, all three religions cannot possibly be right—if right is an outcome upon which we insist. As Mr. Lincoln might advise, two must be wrong and all three may be in error.

Even when we confirm our rightness—or righteousness—we may be left uneasy. Obviously, we would not hold an incorrect religious belief. Doing so would affront God. Just as obviously, we would believe as others do if they could demonstrate the rightness of their position. The fact that we do not serves as proof that they cannot demonstrate the rightness of their positions. In effect, what we believe is right and worthy by definition. Logically, other beliefs are false.

Here lies the rub. Other religions or streams or sects, through their very existence, torment us. They profess their beliefs—false as they may be—even while we clearly demonstrate by our very faith that we possess the Truth. This suggests the potential weakness of our beliefs and practices. If we possess and profess Truth, it only stands to reason that everyone else should accept it. Yet others, resisting our best efforts, persist in rejecting the Truth.

Such rejection leads to another conundrum. If we take a more liberal position and simply dismiss others as different or merely irrelevant, do we betray ourselves? Do we transform our relationship with God into nothing more than a preference for any of thirty-one—or more—perfectly acceptable flavors? Can we accept a free-market approach to religion that views difference as a good and necessary challenge that ultimately can strengthen, rather than weaken, our beliefs? Jonathan Sacks, Chief Rabbi of Britain, answers affirmatively. "The test of faith," he proposes, "is whether I can make space for difference." (Sacks/Dignity, 201)

This test poses no small challenge. External professions of belief may mask significant internal struggles. We may wonder, consciously or, more likely, subconsciously, whether we are wrong about the most important issues that we will ever confront. Quite possibly, the more we profess our faith—like whistling in a dark graveyard to conceal our fear—the less faith we may actually have. The more we struggle within ourselves, the more we may condemn others.

Common Roots, Common Ground

The stories of "God's others" offer a unique capacity to bring adherents of the three Abrahamic faiths more closely together. Again, we must acknowledge that meaningful differences of opinion exist. Because each religion has developed its own interpretations of the biblical text, let us not address these differences from a position of naiveté. Jews *do* believe that revelation ended with the destruction of the First Temple. Christians *do* believe that what they term the Old Testament points to Jesus as God's continuing—and final—revelation as well as a new covenant with Israel.[5] Muslims venerate Jesus as a great prophet but deny his divinity while believing that the Quran offers humanity God's newest—and final—revelation.

Difficulties stemming from varying beliefs regarding the opening and closing of the gates of revelation likely will never disappear. Yet let us not abandon hope that religious enmity can at least be further reduced if not overcome. A survey by the Pew Forum on Religion and Public Life published in June 2008 concluded that 70 percent of Americans believe that members of other religions can attain eternal life. When some evangelical Christians objected, Pew repeated the survey in August. Sixty-five percent of respondents again averred that members of other religions—any religion—could go to the next life. (Blow) Of course, thirty-five percent indicated that adherents to other religions would not attain eternal life.

We can do more. While dogma is not easily cast aside, Jews, Christians and Muslims of good will all revere the words of Leviticus 19:18, "Love your fellow [neighbor] as yourself." Our challenge is to arrive at a more inclusive definition of "neighbor" and admit that, "we are all different just the same." I explore possible—and I believe

5 The concept of supersession, attributed to St. Paul through his mission to the Gentiles, has been the subject of no little debate. James Carroll, a former Catholic priest, examines Church history and acknowledges the reality of supersession, writing bluntly, "When the priest at the consecration says, 'This is the cup of the New Covenant,' he is pronouncing the Old Covenant superfluous. Its job, after Jesus, is to leave the sanctuary. The Jew's job is to disappear." (Carroll/Constantine, 50)

practical—approaches to this challenge in the concluding chapter, *Beyond Tolerance*.

"God's others" offer an important premise for reconciliation and peace by revealing God's multi-faceted relationships not with just a single nation but with all humanity. To be sure, the Bible, from the Jewish perspective, serves primarily as a religious and political history of Israel. The biblical narrative takes us from God's covenant with Abraham and Sarah to their descendants' evolution into a clan, a people enslaved, twelve populous tribes emerging into freedom and finally a nation rising, falling and ultimately rising again with its return from Babylonian exile in the sixth century BCE. Significantly, however, the Bible does not introduce Abraham until the end of chapter 11 of its first book, Genesis. And only at the beginning of chapter 12 is Abraham's critical role as God's prophet made known.

What fills the first eleven chapters of Genesis? The biblical text focuses not on Israel, which does not yet exist as a people or a nation, but on creation. A single God establishes the world and everything within it. From His creative efforts flow the development of human culture and the nations of the world. These early chapters introduce us to a host of pre-Israelites: Adam and Eve, Cain and Abel, a list of their long-lived progeny, Noah, Noah's descendants, who form the seventy known nations of the world, and the builders of the Tower of Babel. We may be disappointed—but not surprised—that most of the first twenty generations of humanity continually turn away from God, presenting what Abraham Joshua Heschel terms "a story of failure and defiance." (Heschel, 561) These chapters set the stage for the appearance of Abraham and Israel since, as Heschel notes, God did not abandon man but rather searched the earth for someone through whom humanity would be blessed—and found Abraham.

It bears emphasizing that by including these pre-Israelites rather than beginning with Abraham, the Bible pointedly reminds us that all human beings trace their origins to a single Creator and a single set of parents. We are all one family no matter how distantly related. The Mishnah—the Oral Law traditional Jews believe God gave to Moses on Sinai along with the written Torah, passed down through the generations and edited towards the end of the second century

CE—sheds important light on this matter. God created all humanity out of Adam/Eve so that no one could say that his ancestor was greater than anyone else's. (Sanhedrin 4:5) Regrettably, we often act like children clamoring for our divine Parent's total attention at the expense of our siblings. As adults, however, we come to know that parents can love all their children, even if in different ways.

As this underlying biblical theme of the oneness of creation and humanity becomes clearer, we discover a new set of individuals of whom we may never have been aware. Yes, many people know something, no matter how sketchy, of Abraham, Isaac, Jacob, Joseph, Moses, Aaron, Miriam, Joshua, David, Solomon and Esther. But a host of non-Israelites also fills the Bible's pages. They, too, encounter God. While not all are heroes—just as Israel produces its share of villains from Korach to Ahab—they have much to teach us.

That "God's others" must be taken into account reflects Judaism's self-definition as a particularistic religion revering a universalistic God. Jewish tradition understands Judaism to be the right and proper religion only for Jews. The commandments given to the Israelites at Mount Sinai following the Exodus from Egypt bind all Jews for all time—but no one else. In turn, because Judaism is only for Jews, God gives the land of Canaan to the descendants of Abraham, Isaac and Jacob—but *only* Canaan. (God promises to remove the seven Canaanite peoples in due time yet pockets of Canaanites remain in the land.) The Canaanites must forfeit their land not because they are polytheists, which does displease God, but because of what they *do*. Their *actions*, not their beliefs, condemn them. Therefore, professions of monotheism alone do not suffice for Israel. The Bible makes clear that Israel, despite its chosen status, can claim no exemption from the same punishment decreed against the Canaanites if it fails to *act* correctly. Through Moses, God explicitly warns the Israelites tarrying in the wilderness: "So let not the land spew you out for defiling it, as it spewed out the nation that came before you" (Lev. 18:28).

Of great importance, God never commands Israel to conquer peoples outside Canaan and spread a single religion to the surrounding region. To a great degree, Israel moves in the opposite direction, separating itself from the nations. As Reuven Firestone notes, "It is likely that a number of social practices that emerged in the Bible, such as strict dietary laws, did so, at least in part, in order to separate Israelites from social interaction with other peoples. The religion of the Bible certainly would not have placed such an emphasis on separation if it had been interested in mission." (Firestone, 118)

The biblical narrative assigns to Israel only a defensive position regarding its neighbors' religions. As Firestone emphasizes, "Israelite chosenness included no theology or political ideology of mission or conversion, and it generally left others to practice whatever religion they wished as long as it did not impact negatively on the religious or political independence of Israel." (Firestone, 119)

Thus the Bible portrays God as the universalistic God of all humanity, accepting particularistic modes of monotheistic worship by different peoples. As Jonathan Sacks so eloquently observes: "Biblical monotheism is not the idea that there is one God and therefore one gateway to His presence. To the contrary, it is the idea that *the unity of God is to be found in the diversity of creation.*" (Sacks/Dignity, 53)

True, Jews proselytized in the ancient world. The Mishnah (Avot 1:12) quotes Hillel: "Be a disciple of Aaron, loving peace and pursuing peace, loving people and drawing them near to the Torah." But Hillel does not encourage militant efforts at conversion. Rabbi Chaim Stern points out, "The desire of the Pharisees to draw 'all people' near the Torah is a corollary of love, and means: bring them to a fuller knowledge of God." (Stern, 20) With some exceptions, Jews have not emulated the conversion fervor of Christians and Muslims, who historically believed their religions to be universalistic and incumbent upon all peoples.[6] One notable exception took

6 Islam exempts Jews, Christians and other monotheists from the requirement of conversion. The Quran establishes *dhimmi* status for these monotheists, both protecting and restricting them in return for payment of a special tax, the *jizyah*. However, sura 3:85 lends itself to the interpretation that only Islam is the acceptable religious practice for humanity: "He that chooses a religion other than Islam, it will not be accepted from him and in the world to come he will be one of the lost." Whether the Quran accepts or rejects non-Muslims is open to interpretation. As always, one may cite specific verses to support virtually any opinion. Religions, however, tend to define themselves more by the actions they inspire than by the beliefs they espouse.

place in the second century BCE when John Hyrcanus conquered the Idumeans (Edomites), of whom the villainous Herod was a descendant—reinforcing the old adage, "Be careful what you wish for"—and brought them into Judea's political sphere. Jews in the Greek and Roman eras lacked the military might with which to support attempts to convert the majority of non-Jews surrounding them. Following two disastrous rebellions against Rome, many Sages opposed proselytes, suspecting that their conversions were motivated by ulterior or impure motives.

Nonetheless, many non-Jews, known as God fearers, frequently worshipped or studied in synagogues. A number, including some of the Roman elite, converted to Judaism. They did so not through compulsion but by observing Jewish life and finding Jewish values worthy of emulation and adoption.

Ultimately, any active seeking of converts to Judaism had to be abandoned in 315 CE when the emperor Constantine, who made Christianity the state religion of Rome, issued an edict declaring Jewish proselytizing a crime. A century later, Jewish proselytizing became a capital offense. The realities of living in the Diaspora of both Christian Europe and the Muslim world, where seeking converts invited great danger, reinforced Jewish particularism.

It follows that the biblical requirement that Israelite monotheism be practiced only by Israelites left other peoples to maintain and develop their own religious expressions with the hope that they would, of their own free will, come to recognize the One Creator. The only requirement imposed by God on the rest of the world, as the Sages deduced from Genesis, consists of adhering to the Noahide laws given after the Flood. These seven basic laws—as opposed to the 613 commandments by which traditional Jews are bound—are enunciated in the first chapter of this book, *Monotheism: Humanity's Natural Religious State*.

A First Step

Whether a study of "God's others" will lead us to a more open approach to our fellow human beings remains to be seen. Segments of the Muslim world remain at war with each other and with the non-Muslim world. Ultra-orthodox Jews in Israel seek to retain control over lifecycle events such as marriage, divorce and burial to the exclusion of other Jewish streams. In the United States, many conservative Christians continue to oppose liberal religious and secular groups. At the same time, what appears to be a growing atheist movement seeks not simply to moderate religion's impact on society but to prove religion totally false and valueless.

Sadly, those who claim exclusive religious truth are not prone to modifying their beliefs regardless of the case presented to them. Moreover, even the most moderate and open Jews, Christians and Muslims may, from time to time, find themselves uncomfortable with "the other" and speak or act in ways that hurt rather than heal. Nonetheless, I believe that understanding the role played by "God's others" can bring to light more complex truths often displaced or dismembered in the cause of a simple, "pure" faith. In this regard, it is worth remembering that all three Abrahamic religions adhere to monotheism and follow the commandment not to worship idols. As Rabbi Elliot Dorff, one of Judaism's leading ethicists, warns, absolutism in itself is "tantamount to idolatry." (Dorff/Right, 59)

In acknowledging non-Israelites who encounter God in the Hebrew Bible, we restore ourselves to the religious intentions we publicly profess but too often privately cast aside. *God's Others* serves as a call to remember God's proposal to His heavenly court as He engages in the process of creation: "Let us make man in our image, after our likeness" (Gen. 1:26). We must recognize all human beings as bearing God's image and being worthy of our acceptance *as they are*. Wrestling with our prejudices in the biblical text, no matter how difficult this may be, can help us take meaningful steps towards achieving what armies, security services, police, technology and the untold billions of dollars behind them have failed to accomplish. They can help cool the rhetoric of intolerance and hatred, and reduce the violence it so often produces. "God's others" demonstrate that we are all children in a single family, each entitled to our own special relationship with our Creator/Parent and to respect.

2

Monotheism: Humanity's Natural Religious State

Sh'ma Yisrael, Adonai Eloheinu, Adonai echad.
Hear, O Israel! The Lord is our God, the Lord alone.
Deuteronomy 6:4

Thus said the Lord, the King of Israel,
Their Redeemer, the Lord of Hosts:
I am the first and I am the last,
And there is no god but Me.
Isaiah 44:6

Think of it as akin to an urban legend like alligators abounding in Manhattan's sewers or Elvis sighted in an Indian ashram. Many people *know* that monotheism began with Abraham, the first Hebrew patriarch and ancestor of Israel.[7] After all, Abraham's father, Terach, sold idols, which no believing monotheist could do in good conscience. Before Abraham, God had no presence in human

7 Abraham and his wife Sarah are first known by the names Abram and Sarai, which God changes in Genesis 17:5 and 17:15 respectively. Traditional commentators refer to them as Abraham and Sarah, even regarding verses prior to the name change. This book will do so as well. Citations of the biblical text remain as written.

thought and behavior. People worshipped a profusion of nature gods and idols. This is common wisdom. From the Bible's perspective, it is wrong.

Scholars in disciplines such as anthropology, archaeology, mythology, linguistics and the history of religion trace humanity's religious evolution along a path leading from polytheism to monotheism. Human beings have always needed gods, they inform us. If we cannot control a natural environment shattered by earthquakes, hurricanes, tornadoes, floods and drought—not to mention the dark side of the human personality—where do we look for comfort and relief? What brings us hope that we can overcome our fragile existence—if not now, then at some future time?

The Bible, too, understands our need to connect with a power that can ease our fears in a frightening and disorderly world. The Psalmist ponders the limitations inherent in the human condition and declares in awe and wonder:

> When I behold Your heavens, the work of Your fingers,
> the moon and stars that You set in place,
> what is man that You have been mindful of him,
> mortal man that you have taken note of him… (Psalms 8:4-5)

"All advanced societies must come to grips with two issues above all," E.A. Speiser writes in the middle of the twentieth century after technology and the human psyche demonstrate how high—and low—they can take us. "One is the relation of the individual to society. The other is the alignment of both individual and society to nature and the universe." (Goldin, 2)

From an anthropological point of view, it seems only natural that people sought to placate and influence an array of sky and sea gods, earth and tree gods, rain and sun gods, national, local and tribal gods. Ironically, the very origins of these gods eventually led to their downfall. As human creations, the gods took on human personalities and thus human failings—if on a more grand and dramatic scale than our own. The mythologies of ancient peoples from the Babylonians to the Greeks to the Norse offer gods striving with each other just as earthly individuals, clans, tribes and city-states lived in continual conflict. Periods of relative peace offered some respite, but these were few and far between. People looked to their gods for comfort. However, if the gods could overthrow each other or support the overthrow of earthly kings, what measure of security could people count on? An Assyrian Wisdom lament asks, "Who can know the will of the gods in heaven?" (Segal, 78)

Speiser comments, "The outstanding single feature of the cosmos in ancient Mesopotamia was the tenet that no single god is the ultimate source of power and authority; none is truly omnipotent. All the figures of the Mesopotamian pantheon had themselves been created." (Goldin, 3) The gods were not part of the solution; they were part of the problem. Then something happened.

Much secular scholarship points to monotheism's birth in what the philosopher Karl Jaspers termed the Axial Age—approximately 700 to 200 BCE—a period of great upheaval that Karen Armstrong calls "pivotal to the spiritual development of humanity."[8] Armstrong notes, "This age was itself the product and fruition of thousands of years of economic, and therefore social and cultural, evolution, beginning in Sumer in what is now Iraq, and in ancient Egypt." As agriculture evolved from subsistence to surplus, these societies developed sophisticated urban civilizations. "In these altered circumstances, people ultimately began to find that the old paganism, which had served their ancestors well, no longer spoke fully to their condition." Perspectives broadened. "Instead of seeing the divine as embodied in a number of different deities, people increasingly began to worship a single universal transcendence and source of sacredness." (Armstrong/Battle, xiv)

The Bible presents a different view. It plants monotheism's roots at the time of creation. What then of Abraham? He provides

---

8 Regarding Israelite religion, critical scholars point to the Deuteronomist in the time of King Josiah of Judah (reigned 639-609 BCE) as establishing true monotheism through reforms that included the worship of a single God—YHVH—in a single place—the Temple in Jerusalem.

impetus to monotheism more than a thousand years before the Axial Age. But the biblical narrative reveals that Abraham is *not* the first person to know the One God. Monotheism does not begin with him. Abraham's role, as crucial as it is, consists of advancing, rather than introducing, monotheism. The Bible makes clear that an original pair of monotheists precedes Abraham—Adam and Eve. By the time the biblical narrative introduces us to Abraham, humanity appears to have developed a host of monotheistic traditions. Granted, the narrative only hints at these, subtly acknowledging rather than exploring them. When Abraham first appears, most of humanity seems to have abandoned monotheism to indulge in a variety of polytheistic practices. Most—but not all.

Why should human beings naturally be monotheists? Malbim, the nineteenth-century Russian biblical commentator, explains: "The existence and oneness of the Divinity is attained by the direct exercise of men's intellectual functions. The Lord implanted these concepts in him from birth. They are innate ideas." (Leibowitz/Shemot, 305-6) Monotheism quite naturally begins with Adam and Eve. We need only begin our investigation of monotheism at the beginning.

Religious Revolution

The very first verse of Genesis, the first book of the Bible, stands religious thought in the ancient Near East on its head:

> When God began to create heaven and earth—the earth being unformed and void, with darkness over the surface of the deep and a wind from God sweeping over the water..." (Gen. 1:1-2)

Compare the Bible's approach to that of the Enuma Elish, the Babylonian/Akkadian creation epic. The latter tells of the joining of the waters of the rivers (the god Apsu) and the sea (the goddess Tiamat) and concludes with Marduk, the storm-god, splitting Tiamat's dead body to divide the basic matter of the universe into heaven and earth. Other gods then emerge to define the physical components of the earth, its waters and the sky above. Finally, Marduk creates the first man from a mix of dust and the blood of the slain god Kingu.[9]

From a critical approach, the words "When God began to create" shake the foundations of polytheism. The Bible enters new territory by telling us that no other gods provoke or determine nature's ongoing patterns. Nahum Sarna observes that, "the quintessential idea of Israel's monotheism" is that God is "entirely outside of and sovereign over nature."[10] (Sarna/Exodus, 111) Belief in the God of Genesis creates an inevitable gulf between monotheists and polytheists. The scholars Henri and H.A. Frankfort offer, "When we read in Psalm 19 that 'the heavens declare the glory of God; and the firmament sheweth his handiwork,' we hear a voice which mocks the beliefs of Egyptians and Babylonians." (Finegan, 115)

The single God Who created the world also rules it. Humanity once believed that its fate was decided by the constant battling or convening of multiple gods as well as the caprices of a succession of kings who claimed to be gods or gods' instruments. No more. The world before Genesis, according to E.A. Speiser, "lacked a true basis for an ethical approach to life." (Goldin, 4) Mankind's moral and emotional compass was forever shifting. The One God of the Bible changed the way humanity would gauge right and wrong. The biblical narrative portrays God's ways not as arbitrary but as constant—if often difficult to understand. Thus God's ways remain subject to various interpretations but cannot be overthrown. Humanity, Speiser declares, was "liberated from the whims of capricious and unpredictable cosmic powers, and by being freed from the authority of mortal rulers with divine pretensions, mankind was launched on a new course of responsibility, dignity and hope." (Goldin, 15)

---

9 Genesis, like the Enuma Elish and other myths, acknowledges water as the basic building block of creation. Egyptian myths tell of a primeval and chaotic ocean, called Nun, from which the creator god emerged and made dry land. The Sages of the Talmud and later commentators did not concern themselves with the origins of the waters.

10 In the third century BCE, Aristotle posited God as the Unmoved Mover but not the creator of the universe—what Richard E. Rubenstein terms an abstract, passive "deity of sorts." (Rubenstein, 79)

As to Adam and Eve, they enjoy a personal and remarkably intimate relationship with God, Who grants Adam the power to name all the animals, plants a garden in Eden for him, instructs him not to eat from a specific tree and brings forth Eve as his companion and helper.

In a movie or TV show, such activity would foreshadow disaster. We would suspect that everything seems too good to be true. And we would be right. The biblical narrative clearly understands the human condition. It also recognizes our longing for a lost age of innocence, even if such an age never existed. But what we most desire we cannot have. So Adam and Eve play their roles, defying God, as children inevitably defy their parents to establish their individuality and independence. The first humans eat from the Tree of Knowledge of Good and Bad. (Eve takes the rap but Adam takes the fruit from her and eats without a word of questioning or protest.) Paradise is about to be lost.

In spite of this disobedience, God remains accessible. Adam and Eve hear Him "moving about in the garden at the breezy time of day" (Gen. 3:8) when the late afternoon offers some relief from the heat. Such an anthropomorphic portrait of God may make some moderns uncomfortable, but this image reflects the view of the ancients who prized a highly personal relationship between the Creator and His creation.[11] When Adam and Eve become newly aware of their nakedness—and embarrassed by it—they hide. God calls out, inquiring as to their whereabouts. Like a child who cannot imagine his parents seeing through his ruses, Adam reveals their disobedience by answering that they have hidden to cover their flesh. Of course, God knows this. His rhetorical question offers Adam and Eve an opportunity to explain and repent. They fail to seize it. This displeases God. He puts His figurative foot down and informs Eve that serious wrong brings serious consequences:

> "I will make most severe
> Your pangs in childbearing;
> In pain shall you bear children." (Gen. 3:16)

11 James L. Kugel's *The God of Old* offers an excellent discussion of anthropomorphism's role in ancient religion.

To Adam, He says,

> "Cursed be the ground because of you;
> By toil shall you eat of it
> All the days of your life." (Gen. 3:17)

Yet God's relationship with Adam and Eve remains intimate. Angry though He may be, He will not abandon them to shame. God serves as Adam and Eve's personal tailor, making them garments of skins. The first humans know, if not understand, God and His power both to love and punish. Adam and Eve, the biblical text demonstrates, are monotheists by default.

Their sons also understand the concept of the One God with Whom they also maintain a highly personal relationship. Cain and Abel present offerings. God pays heed to Abel's, a firstling from his flock, but not to Cain's, taken from the fruit of the soil but not necessarily the best of his crops. Downhearted, Cain sulks. God notices and offers sound parental advice.

> "Surely if you do right,
> There is uplift.
> But if you do not do right
> Sin couches at the door;
> Its urge is toward you,
> Yet you can be its master." (Gen. 4:7)

This verse underlies a basic Jewish approach to free will, although within Jewish thought, a range of opinions exists about the role of providence. Ours is the power to choose, God informs us. We hold our fate in our hands and must accept responsibility for our actions or suffer the consequences. Thus later in Deuteronomy, Moses warns the Israelites about accepting responsibility for upholding the Torah given at Sinai when they inhabit Canaan:

> See, this day I set before you blessing and curse: blessing, if you obey the commandments of the LORD your God that I enjoin upon you this day; and curse, if you do not obey the commandments

> of the Lord your God, but turn away from the path that I enjoin upon you this day and follow other gods, whom you have not experienced. (Deut. 12: 26-28)

The early stories of Genesis reveal the essential duality of human nature. The Sages respond to Adam and Eve, and Cain and Abel, by declaring that every individual possesses both the good impulse *(yetzer hatov)* and the bad impulse *(yetzer hara)*—recognition of human imperfection rather than sin. Yet our moral weakness need not condemn us. We can overcome the *yetzer hara* and even harness it for good. Thus the Sages explain that the sexual urge leads us to have children and fulfill the commandment to be fruitful and multiply. On the other hand, we cannot obliterate the bad impulse.

Cain, as we know, yields to his *yetzer hara* and murders Abel. God spares Cain's life but punishes him with exile. "Cain left the presence of the Lord and settled in the land of Nod, east of Eden. Cain knew his wife, and she conceived and bore Enoch" (Gen 4:16-17). Cain marries! Yet the biblical text never reveals his wife's identity or from where she comes.[12]

With Abel dead and Cain banished, Adam and Eve's family tree finds extension in a third offspring—Seth. We know nothing of Seth other than that he fathers a son named Enosh, as well as other sons and daughters. No mention is made of Seth's relationship with God. But it is difficult to imagine Adam and Eve failing to inform him about their Creator. We can reasonably assume that Seth had some monotheistic perspective and quite possibly a great deal of knowledge of God, which the biblical narrative simply does not consider important to detail.

Given Cain's taking a wife and Seth's also doing so, the earth starts to become somewhat populous in humanity's second generation. And people know of God, Genesis informs us. "It was then that men began to invoke the Lord by name" (Gen. 4:26).[13] The Hebrew term

12 The Talmud (Sanhedrin 58b) comments that Cain marries his sister. On the other hand, Cain's wife may be a separate creation of God formed to preclude incestuous relationships. We can surmise, but we cannot know.

13 Rashi, drawing on the Midrash, interprets the invoking of God by name as indicating that the generation of Enosh introduced idolatry.

translated as Lord is known as the Tetragrammaton for its four letters and transliterated in English as YHVH. It represents God's mysterious and unpronounceable name. Its inclusion early in Genesis induces the biblical scholar Nahum Sarna to write, "This text takes monotheism to be the original religion of the human race, and the knowledge of the name YHVH to be pre-Abrahamic." (Sarna/Genesis, 40)

Regrettably if inevitably, humanity descends into wrongdoing and idolatry. In response, God seems to conceal himself. Yet some human beings maintain their monotheistic ways. Enoch, the seventh in Adam's line and great-grandfather of Noah "walked with God 300 years" (Gen. 5:22) even if Rashi limits the degree of Enoch's righteousness.

In the ninth generation, Lamech, son of Methuselah, clearly knows of God, creation and history. In naming his son, Noah, he remarks: "This one will provide us with relief from our work and from the toil of our hands, out of the very soil which the LORD placed under a curse" (Gen. 5:29).

Why do the early generations of the Bible turn to polytheism? Let us return to the *yetzer hara*. Free to make choices in order to raise themselves above the level of the animals, humanity likewise remains free to turn away from God. The Talmud (Berachot 33b) explains, "Everything is in the hand of heaven except the fear of heaven." God will not—and perhaps cannot—compel human beings to hold Him in awe and act appropriately.

Human development continues in Genesis, marked by a widespread surrender to the evil inclination that undercuts monotheism and for the most part casts it away. The story of the Tower of Babel offers a prime example of human pride and ensuing tragedy. Men migrate from the east to the land of Shinar (Babylonia). All share a common language. They declare to each other, "Come, let us build us a city, and a tower with its top in the sky, to make a name for ourselves; else we shall be scattered all over the world" (Gen. 11:4).

Humanity seeks a place in the heavens but apparently not so that it can better approach God. Rather, people wish to neutralize His power if not usurp Him. God halts the project by fragmenting their speech into many different languages. Their subsequent division and disharmony represent a self-fulfilling prophecy. The would-be ascent becomes a descent. Humanity loses its universal language. The original knowledge of God and His Oneness apparently suffers serious dilution as people become isolated from each other and, inevitably, from God. As discrete cultures form, different peoples begin first to worship varying concepts of God and then many gods in whose names they commit a multiplicity of abominations.

The Emergence of Polytheism

The medieval commentator Maimonides (1135-1204) in his *Mishneh Torah* proposes a steady decline from monotheism beginning in the days of Enosh (Laws of Idolatry). Men begin to praise the sun, moon and stars since God placed them on high. Next they build temples to these natural objects. Then they make images to worship and place them in their temples, in groves and on mountaintops. Finally, false prophets claim that the stars, planets, sun and moon communicate directly with them about how they are to be worshipped. "As time went on, the awesome and glorious name of God was forgotten from the mouths of all mankind and from their minds and they recognized him not. Thus it came about that all the people of the land, women and children were only acquainted with the image of wood and stone, the sanctuary of stones to which they had been reared from childhood to bow down to, to worship and swear by. The wise men they possessed, that is to say, their priests imagined that there was no other God save the stars and spheres represented by these images, whilst there was no one who recognised the Rock of Eternity, no one would acknowledge Him save a few individuals such as Enoch, Methuselah, Noah, Shem and Eber."

Ten generations after Adam and Eve, humanity has corrupted the earth. Rabbi Arthur Green comments, "The generations of Adam's children, in the biblical tale, live out their exile from paradise without finding a way to maintain or protect God's image in an unprotected world. Murder, idolatry, violent debauchery, false attempts to reach heaven, all mark the vanity of life in those early generations." (Green, 165)

All is not lost, however. God finds one wholehearted person from whom humanity can continue—Noah. But the story of the Flood, so beloved by children for the gathering of animals "two by two," presents no little complexity. Noah's moral position spurs considerable debate. Some Sages, like Resh Lakish, see Noah as particularly righteous given the corruption of his generation. Others, like Rabbi Yohanan, offer a relativistic approach: Noah merely rises above his generation's low standards. They cite Noah making no attempt to warn others of the impending Flood, unlike Abraham who takes God to task for His intention to destroy Sodom and Gomorrah. Tanchuma, a medieval midrash, defends Noah, stating that God warns Noah's generation for 120 years, but it fails to take heed. During the time that Noah builds the ark, people still refuse to change their corrupt ways. Only when the Flood begins do they realize they will perish. Too late! God sends lions to protect the ark from them.

God's relationship with Noah, as with Adam and Eve, is highly personal. He not only tells Noah to build an ark but also provides its dimensions and instructions for bringing aboard pairs of all living creatures.[14] Finally, Noah boards the ark with his unnamed wife—identified in the Midrash as Naamah, sister of Tubal-Cain (B'reishit Rabbah 23:3)—three sons and three unnamed daughters-in-law. He is six hundred years old when the earth is flooded. Only these four couples survive.

Following the Flood, God apparently suffers remorse. He enters into a covenant with Noah and all humanity to follow. Never again will He destroy the world by flood. The rains may fall, but the rainbow will serve as the sign of His agreement to spare humanity another fatal deluge. According to the Talmud (Sanhedrin 56a), God also provides Noah, his family and their descendants with seven laws to guide them. These Noahide laws forbid idolatry, blasphemy, bloodshed,

14 Noah brings each animal aboard the ark both "two by two"— a single pair—and in seven pairs. The latter, according to Rashi (on Gen. 7:2), represents animals that will be designated as ritually clean when the Torah is given at Sinai. In Genesis 8:20, Noah makes a burnt offering of at least one representative of every clean animal and bird. These creatures could not propagate unless he saved more than a single pair.

incest and adultery, and robbery; mandate the establishment of courts of law; and prohibit eating flesh from a living animal. They form the core of monotheistic beliefs to which all humanity must adhere. They are so important, Rashi notes, that Moses repeats them at Sinai along with the Ten Commandments and other ordinances before writing them down.

Humanity flourishes in the postdiluvial world. Genesis 10 delineates seventy nations—the number is symbolic and often employed by the Torah to communicate a large, complete number (in this case the entire world)—that flow from Noah's three sons. This table of nations, according to Nahum Sarna, "affirms, first of all, the common origin and absolute unity of humankind after the Flood; then it tacitly, but effectively, asserts that the varied instrumentalities of human divisiveness are all secondary to the essential unity of the international community, which truly constitutes a family of man.... God's sovereignty extends to every nation; His providence governs them all." (Sarna/Genesis, 69) All humanity descends from Adam and Eve, and Noah. Thus all humanity descends from monotheists.

What then of Eden? It remains only a memory and a longing. The generations descending from Noah drift into various forms of polytheism and idol worship—some temporarily and others permanently. The very survivors of the Flood betray God. When Noah, the first vintner, becomes drunk with wine, one of his sons performs a corrupt act. "Ham, the father of Canaan, saw his father's nakedness..." Gen. 9:22. The Sages deem this a euphemism for having had sex with Noah. In response, Noah curses Ham. He will be "the lowest of slaves" to his brothers.

Post-Flood humanity inherits knowledge of the One God, yet the human heart rejects Him. Although Noah blesses both Japheth and Shem—the latter the antecedent of the Hebrews and Israelites—the *yetzer hara* tightens its grip on the world. God seems forgotten. The Midrash (Sifré on Deuteronomy) relates, "And it is not enough for them that they [the other nations of the world who refused the Torah] did not listen but even the seven religious duties that the children of Noah indeed accepted upon themselves they could not uphold before breaking them."

The biblical reader may feel outrage at the nations' behavior. After all, the text makes God's existence and creative role perfectly clear. But we approach the Bible with the entire story at our fingertips. We know how everything unfolds and why. The nations and individuals in the Bible obviously lack our wider, rather omniscient, perspective. As God slowly withdraws from intimate contact with humanity, the concept of One God without shape or form ultimately proves too difficult for the nations to comprehend. "The primitive mind finds it hard to realize an idea without the aid of imagination," Abraham Joshua Heschel writes, "and it is the realm of space where imagination wields its sway. Of the gods it must have a visible image; where there is no image, there is no god." (Heschel, 4)

Indeed, the early generations of humanity saw their relationship with God in more personal terms than we do. Witness Genesis' highly anthropomorphic portrait of God in Eden. Jeffrey Tigay comments that the concept of God having no visible form is post-biblical. (Etz Hayim on Deut. 4:12) But the role of visible images of gods may be more complex than we realize, Richard Friedman points out. Pagan religion was not simply idol worship. "Pagan religion was close to nature. People worshiped the most powerful forces in the universe: the sky, the storm wind, the sun, the sea, fertility, death. The statues that they erected were like the icons in a church. The statues depicted the god or goddess, reminded the worshiper of the deity's presence, showed the humans' respect for their gods, and perhaps made the humans feel closer to their gods. But, as a Babylonian text points out, the statue was not the god." (Friedman/ Who Wrote, 35) This accords with some scholars' belief that the golden calf made by Aaron in Exodus 32 was not intended to be a god but rather a footstool for the God of Israel—a visible symbol of His presence among the people in the wilderness.

Like a seed buried in the earth, monotheism appears to lie dormant. Yet in the post-Flood age—and given God's relationship with Noah—can all monotheistic knowledge have vanished? Maimonides, cited earlier in his *Mishneh Torah*, declares that monotheism *declined* rather than disappeared. We may conclude that here and there, pockets of monotheism—even in diluted form—

existed. Descendants of Adam and Eve, Seth, Enosh and Noah surely must have retained some remnants of the knowledge of the One God passed on by their forebears.

Such knowledge crops up now and then among non-Hebrews. Joseph, serving as Pharaoh's vice-regent in Egypt and unrecognized by his brothers who have come to buy grain, demands that the brothers leave a hostage until they bring the youngest, Benjamin, to him. Joseph reassures them of his honorable intentions: "Do this and you shall live, for I am a God-fearing man" (Gen. 42:18). The brothers demonstrate no sense of surprise at Joseph's self-description. While they may not share the same theology with their supposedly Egyptian host, the concept of God *in some form* bridges the cultural gap; it is a given.

Maimonides informs us that at the time God appeared to Moses within the burning bush, "all men, *with few exceptions* [italics mine], were ignorant of the existence of God: their highest thoughts did not extend beyond the heavenly sphere, its forms or its influences." (Maimonides, 1:63) Were those exceptions to be found only among the Hebrews in Egypt, which Moses had earlier fled?

But let us not get ahead of ourselves. When Genesis resumes after listing Noah's descendants through humanity's twentieth generation, we meet one individual strongly aware of the monotheistic concept and courageously willing to have it direct his life—Abraham.

Monotheism's Rebirth

The case for monotheism as humanity's natural religious state grows with the Israeli scholar Yehezkel Kaufmann. He points to Genesis demonstrating that primeval mankind from Adam on "appears to have been monotheistic." (Plaut, 89) Because God makes Himself known to humanity from the very creation of Adam and Eve, it is humanity's failings that result in God's being forgotten and the development of polytheism. Abraham, the first patriarch of Israel, no more discovers God than Columbus or the Chinese or the Vikings discovered North America, a continent known for thousands of years to its native inhabitants. Gunther Plaut concurs. He writes of

Abraham that, "The Torah does not depict him as the founder of a new religion." (Plaut, 21) Rather, Abraham helps humanity reclaim its monotheistic heritage.

Interestingly, when we first meet Abraham, he and God appear to have established a relationship. "The Lord said to Abram, 'Go forth from your native land and from your father's house to the land that I will show you'" (Gen. 12:1).

Imagine God suddenly appearing to any of us unbidden. Would we be startled? Frightened? Doubtful of our sanity? Even angered? Such a personal revelation in the modern world would be fraught not only with wonder but with fear and even danger, since reporting our encounter might subject us to mockery and hostility. Yet Abraham seems nonplussed. He offers no response of amazement or distress. Abraham seems quite familiar both with the *concept* of God and God Himself.

Just how did this relationship develop? The biblical narrative reveals nothing of the process by which Abraham arrives at a monotheistic point of view. We look to the Midrash for a number of back-stories concerning Abraham's conclusion that the world can have only one Creator, only one God. One midrash relates of Abraham smashing the idols in the shop of his father, Terach, who protests. Abraham reprimands Terach; the idols have proved defenseless and thus cannot be gods. It is worth repeating that many people believe this tale to be in Genesis. It is not.

Maimonides, ever the Aristotelian rationalist, picks up this theme in the section on Laws of Idolatry in his *Mishneh Torah.* Abraham, while still a child, wondered how the sun, moon, stars and planets began their motions, "till he arrived at the true path and perceived the line of righteousness from his own right reasoning. He perceived that that there was one God who governed the spheres and created all, and no other god existed save Him."[15]

It is possible that Abraham sought God out after determining His existence. At least, that is the approach of the Book of Jubilees, written in the second century BCE and not included in the Hebrew

15 Maimonides doubtless was aware of this line of reasoning—the stars fade at daybreak, the moon and sun both set—presented in the Quran (6:75-79).

Bible.[16] Jubilees 12 presents Abraham, who understands the foolishness of the worship of graven images, praying to God to establish his household forever so that humanity will never stray from God. In response, God sends His word to the patriarch to go forth.

While we must turn to the Midrash for the sources of Abraham's insight, the biblical narrative makes clear that Abraham's moral character is advanced. Six chapters after God commands Abraham to go forth from Haran to complete the journey to Canaan begun by his father, He contemplates informing Abraham about the impending destruction of Sodom and Gomorrah. Abraham merits service as God's confidant, God reveals, "For I have singled him out, that I may instruct his children and his posterity to keep the way of the Lord by doing what is just and right..." (Gen. 18:19).

Abraham confirms God's evaluation by confronting Him. "Far be it from You to do such a thing, to bring death upon the innocent as well as the guilty, so that innocent and guilty fare alike. Shall not the Judge of all the earth deal justly?" (Gen. 18:25). Abraham actually scolds God! The Creator must show justice to *all* His children even if they do not know Him as Abraham does—or do not know him at all. Abraham's accusing question makes a major statement. Actions are more important than beliefs. What is critical is how people conduct their lives. Moreover, Abraham assumes that at least *some* people—in Sodom and Gomorrah, and doubtless elsewhere—conduct their lives correctly.

Eight chapters later, God reveals more about Abraham's character. He promises his son, Isaac, that his heirs shall possess all of Canaan, "inasmuch as Abraham obeyed Me and kept My charge: My commandments, My laws, and My teachings" (Gen. 26:5). The reader may ask, "What charge, what commandments, what laws and what teachings?" Genesis contains no list of specific laws and teachings transmitted from God to Abraham other than the Noahide laws deduced by the Sages. These may suffice, but

16 Jubilees, also known by other names, including "Little Genesis," expands on Genesis and includes a great deal of material found in the Midrash, such as Abraham mocking his father's idols.

God does not give the Torah to Israel until centuries later at Sinai. Two possibilities present themselves. First, in Genesis 17:1, God again reveals Himself to Abraham and commands him to "Walk in My ways and be blameless." God then reaffirms his covenant with Abraham whom, we might imagine, accepts this command and will learn God's ways in order to keep his end of the bargain. Second, we can again look to the Midrash. Genesis Rabbah 1:1 informs us that the Torah was created before the world and even provided God with its "architectural plan."[17]

Even if Genesis makes no explicit statement, God clearly recognizes a very special quality in Abraham. The first patriarch obviously understands and adheres to the principles of justice and righteousness, which will become law to his descendants at Sinai. Abraham will serve God's purpose, and so God's command to journey westward includes a promise of greatness linked to a series of blessings:

> I will make of you a great nation,
> And I will bless you;
> I will make your name great,
> And you shall be a blessing.
> I will bless those who bless you
> And curse him that curses you;
> And all the families of the earth
> Shall bless themselves by you." (Gen. 12: 2-3)

The key to Abraham's personality is that he *acts*. He journeys to Canaan with neither question nor commentary—and this in spite of the fact that he and Sarah, at seventy-five and sixty-five, are childless and have no reasonable expectation of changing their status. Thomas Cahill calls the first two Hebrew words in Genesis 12:4, *vayelekh Avram*—"Avram went" [JPS: "Abram went forth"]—"two of the boldest words in all literature. They signal a complete departure from everything that has gone before in the long

17 Other midrash discuss God teaching Torah to Abraham and Abraham studying at the Torah academy run by Shem, son of Noah.

evolution of culture and sensibility." Abraham breaks with the past, and humanity will never be the same. "Out of mortal imagination comes a dream of something new, something better, something yet to happen, something—in the future." (Cahill, 63)

Nonetheless, Abraham, Isaac and Jacob, the Hebrew patriarchs, do not pioneer a new concept—that of a single God. From the perspective of the biblical narrative, they *reintroduce* God and monotheism to humanity, albeit on a limited scale. (Only following the Exodus does Moses relate a comprehensive set of monotheistic laws and a new tradition applicable to Israel as Abraham's descendants.) The patriarchs accept the task of *returning* humanity to its natural monotheistic state and the morality of the Noahide laws that preceded Abraham by ten generations.[18] The stories that follow of such non-Israelites as Melchizedek, Abimelech, Jethro, Balaam and Job reveal that Abraham is not the only person to know or have a concept of God, no matter how God may be defined. But it is Abraham who fathers the Israelite nation whose religion ultimately gives rise to Christianity and Islam. The last lines of God's blessing of Abraham—"And all the families of the earth / Shall bless themselves by you" (Gen. 12:3)—constitute what Nehama Leibowitz terms "a generous universalism." Abraham's monotheism will be a blessing both to Israel and all humanity, "illuminating the whole of mankind." (Leibowitz/Bereshit, 112) The One God is the God of all.

In fulfilling their destinies, the patriarchs demonstrate that "the God of Abraham" is different from other gods, which are inherently false. The gods of other nations are territorial. They reside only in those nations' lands.[19] Historically, many nations worshiped the same kinds of gods but under different names. Marduk, the Babylonian wind god, is Baal-Haddad in Canaan and Zeus in Greece. Geography,

18 So, too, the Quran states that it does not introduce a new religion but seeks to bring the Arab peoples into the original, unsullied Abrahamic monotheism revealed to all the prophets.

19 Rashi, on Genesis 28:12, points out an interesting territoriality regarding the angels Jacob encounters in a dream. Jacob sees a stairway or ladder ascending to heaven. Some angels go up; they may not leave Eretz Yisrael (The Land of Israel—Canaan) and can go no farther with Jacob. Other angels come down. They are restricted to lands outside Eretz Israel.

however, restricts their powers. The God of Israel, Who declares, "all the earth is Mine" (Ex.19:6), remains the universal God unfettered by boundaries. He appears to Abraham in Haran and travels west with Sarah and Abraham to Canaan, then south with the couple into Egypt. God accompanies Isaac and Rebekah to the land of Gerar where they encounter Abimelech, king of the Philistines, in a story that parallels that of Abraham and Sarah's encounter with Pharaoh (see *The Era of Abraham).*

God also promises to protect Jacob, fleeing the wrath of his brother, Esau, wherever he goes (Gen. 28:15) and appears to him in Paddan-aram where Jacob marries Leah and Rachel. Years later, upon setting off for Egypt to be reunited with Joseph, Jacob offers sacrifices "to the God of his father Isaac" at Beer-Sheba. He is obviously troubled by the journey that will take him from the land God has promised Abraham and his descendants. But God calls to Jacob in a night vision: "Fear not to go down to Egypt, for I will make you there into a great nation. I Myself will go down with you to Egypt, and I Myself will also bring you back…" (Gen. 46:3-4). Four centuries later, God appears to Moses at Horeb in the wilderness of Sinai, performs wonders in Egypt and then leads the Israelites through the wilderness to the east bank of the Jordan before going with them into Canaan.

From Exodus onward, the Bible reveals to the Israelites what the patriarchs have learned and the reader already knows: Other gods are not merely local in scope, they are non-existent—figments of human imagination. David's victory over the Philistines at Baal-perazim offers one example (2 Samuel 5). In defeat, the Philistines abandon their idols, leaving David and his men to carry them off. The world of the idol worshipper offers no steadfast direction, no enduring source of inspiration and right conduct, and no protection.

Indeed, the polytheistic concept of territoriality engenders great risk. Four centuries following the Exodus, Ben-hadad, King of Aram, lays siege to Samaria in the northern kingdom of Israel. The Israelites attack and rout the drunken Ben-hadad's troops at the town of Succoth. He escapes on horseback. However, his advisors encourage him to attack Israel again.

> Now the ministers of the king of Aram said to him, "Their God is a God of mountains; that is why they got the better of us. But if we fight them in the plain, we will surely get the better of them." (1 Kings 20:23)

At the turn of the year, Ben-hadad sets out with an army of vastly superior size to meet Israel at Aphek. The prophet Elijah tells the evil and undeserving Ahab, king of Israel,

> "Thus says the LORD: Because the Arameans have said, 'The LORD is a God of mountains, but He is not a God of lowlands,' I will deliver that great host into your hands; and you shall know that I am the LORD." (1 Kings 20:28)

The Israelites slay 100,000 Aramean foot soldiers in one day.

Isaiah affirms: "The Holy One of Israel will redeem you— / He is called 'God of all the Earth'" (Isaiah 54:5).[20] The One God knows no boundaries or limits. He also brooks no competitors.

Mosaic Monotheism: Opposition to Other Gods

Abraham, Isaac and Jacob, while monotheists, make no effort to argue the falseness of other gods. According to the theory of henotheism (also referred to as monolatry), they may even accept the existence of other gods while devoting themselves solely to the One God as supreme above all. But from Exodus onward, the Bible expresses great antagonism towards the gods of the nations. The strict monotheism of Moses and the Book of Deuteronomy emerges out of the two centuries through which Israel dwells in Egypt.

---

20 During the Babylonian exile in the sixth century BCE, Israel questions God's universal presence and power. The survivors of conquered Judah wonder if separation from the land of Israel means separation from God. Their captors want songs from the Israelites, who ask themselves, "How can we sing a song of the Lord / on alien soil?" (Ps. 137:4). The prophet Jeremiah responds with a letter to the exiles. He encourages them to flourish in Babylon—even seek the city's welfare—in preparation for their ultimate return to Jerusalem. The prophet Ezekiel also bolsters Israel's spirits with the promise of God's redemption and a rebuilt Temple.

The ten plagues leading to the Exodus stand as precursors to the Second Commandment and Israel's hostility to the very concept of other gods. The plagues and the drowning of Pharaoh's army in the Reed Sea provide Israel—and the nations—with proof of God's power. They also remind the emerging Israelite nation that it worships not merely a national God Who delivers them from bondage but the One God of all creation. Yet the biblical narrative poses challenging questions. Prior to the tenth plague, God instructs Moses on the ritual for the first Passover. The Israelites must eat hurriedly because He will strike down the first-born males of Egypt, both man and beast. "I will mete out punishments to all the gods of Egypt, I the LORD" (Ex. 12:12). Does God acknowledge the existence of other gods?

Rabbi Robert Gordis calls our attention to the difference between myth—a religious truth—and mythology—a literary allusion. (Gordis, xxix) The biblical narrative expresses the former while abounding with references to the latter. It acknowledges other peoples' beliefs in many gods while denying the *truth* of those beliefs. God disparages such beliefs. Nahum Sarna notes, "God's power to take Israel out of Egypt manifests His own exclusivity, mocks the professed divinity of the pharaoh, and exposes the deities of Egypt as nongods." (Sarna/Exodus, 56) The Book of Exodus replaces the live-and-let-live attitude of Abraham, who makes no pronouncements against the worship of other gods, with scorn and contempt.

The notion that no gods can be compared with the God of Israel gains reinforcement from the song Moses and Israel sing to the Lord after deliverance from Pharaoh's army at the Sea of Reeds. *"Mi chamocha ba'elim Adonai?"*—"Who is like You, O Lord, among the celestials?" (Ex. 15:11) Just who are these *ba'elim*? They are not gods at all, according to Sarna. Rather, they are "heavenly beings, the hosts of ministering angels that were imagined to surround the throne of God and to be at His service." (Sarna/Exodus, 80) Everett Fox and Richard Friedman, on the other hand, translate *ba'elim* as "gods." But no real conflict exists. Again, we understand mythology as literary allusion. Sarna writes, "The expression of God's uniqueness in comparative terms, and the mention of other celestial beings cannot be interpreted literally to imply recognition of the existence of divinities other then the one God." (Sarna/Exodus, 79) The triumphant tone of the song doesn't suggest that other gods are real but weaker than the God of Israel. Rather, it emphasizes that such gods are imaginary. *If* they existed, they would not compare to the God of Israel.

At Sinai, the Second Commandment makes God's intent explicit. "You shall have no other gods beside Me," means, according to Gunther Plaut, that "there is none else, and adoration of other gods will therefore be an idolatrous enterprise; useless for the nations and idolatrous for Israel." (Plaut, 245)

Thus Yehezkel Kaufmann cites the struggle with idolatry as beginning with the revelation at Sinai. "The Bible itself attests indirectly to the fact that Israel's monotheism is postpatriarchal." Genesis evidences no concern with combating polytheism. "The divine covenants with the patriarchs promise personal protection and future material blessings. But they never involve a fight with idolatry, nor do the patriarchs ever appear as reproaching their contemporaries for idolatry. Indeed, there is no religious contrast between the patriarchs and their surroundings." (Kaufmann, 222)

But even here disagreements abound. Some critical scholars, including Robert H. Pfeiffer, acknowledge Moses' historicity and genius but believe that it is the written prophets, including Amos and Isaiah, who introduce monotheism to Israel. Jack Finegan disagrees. He terms Moses "the initiator of a religious revolution, the creator of an original idea." (Finegan, 116)

The experience at Sinai, however, initiates Israel's active rejection of other gods. Deuteronomy 28 delivers a series of blessings and curses (a reiteration of Leviticus 26:3-45) resembling an overture before the curtain rises and Israel enters Canaan. Moses makes clear that polytheism and idolatry are forbidden. With the still-landless nation now large and powerful enough to defend itself and its uncompromising monotheism, the looser attitudes of the patriarchs must be abandoned.

But antagonism to other gods takes an interesting turn. Laying out the laws of war, Moses instructs the Israelites to offer terms of peace to any city lying *outside* its borders. What other peoples do in their own lands constitutes no business of Israel's even though polytheism is abhorrent. On the other hand, non-Israelite cities *within* Israel's borders must suffer *cherem*—proscription or total destruction.

> No, you must proscribe them—the Hittites and the Amorites, the Canaanites and the Perizzites, the Hivites and the Jebusites—as the LORD your God has commanded you, lest they lead you into doing all the abhorrent things that they have done for their gods and you stand guilty before the LORD your God. (Deut. 20:17-18)

This total separation—indeed, annihilation—of the Canaanites, Jeffrey Tigay emphasizes, is neither theologically nor racially motivated. "Proscription is prompted by the Canaanites' abhorrent rites, not their beliefs. Child sacrifice is singled out as their most barbarous rite, in addition to a number of other practices (see [Deut.] 12:31 and 18:9-14). These are regarded as the Canaanites' own abominations, not part of the worship of celestial beings ordained by the Lord for the other nations ([Deut.] 4:19)." (Etz Hayim, 1104)

Maintaining the purity of the land promised to Abraham's descendants remains a continuing obligation. Within that land, no quarter may be given to polytheism and false gods. Thus Moses, nearing the end of his long oration in Deuteronomy, places the responsibility for adhering to strict monotheism squarely on the shoulders of the Israelites:

> I call heaven and earth to witness against you this day: I have put before you life and death, blessing and curse. Choose life—if you and your offspring would live—by loving the LORD your God, heeding His commands, and holding fast to Him. (Deut. 30:19-20)

Moses' urging is bittersweet. Israel is free to cleave to God. Yet God knows *how* Israel will choose much as a parent may stand removed from a small child while knowing what the child will do. Prior to Moses' death and Joshua's leading the Israelite army across the Jordan, God predicts that Israel will fail Him.

> The LORD said to Moses: You are soon to lie with your fathers. This people will thereupon go astray after the alien gods in their midst, in the land that they are about to enter; they will forsake Me and break My covenant that I make with them. (Deut. 31:16)

God proves correct. The Israelites never completely rid the land of the Canaanite peoples. The prophets continue Moses' admonitions whenever Israel turns from God and renders the land impure, which occurs with alarming frequency. The prophets also extend hope that God will redeem His people if and when Israel repents. Thus the arc of the biblical narrative consists of cycles in which Israel follows God's commands and flourishes, then falls away, endures punishment, returns to God and falls away again. Only with the end of the Babylonian exile (although most Jews remain outside Eretz Israel) does Israel finally resist the lure of the Canaanite gods. The returnees build the Second Temple at the end of the sixth century BCE, and Ezra imposes new strictures to enforce the Torah in the fifth. Here the biblical narrative draws to an end. Two centuries later, however, Judaism faces the challenge of polytheistic Hellenism with its advanced and appealing philosophy.

Chosen for What?

Throughout the biblical narrative, the nations remain free to honor God in whatever monotheistic form is natural to them, bound only to the Noahide laws. The prophets rail not at them but against Israel's shortcomings since the nations' obligations to God are less complex. Israel's selection as God's Chosen People entails not privilege but responsibility.[21]

Nehama Leibowitz comments that, "the Almighty did not release Israel from the burden of persecution [in Egypt] in order to set them

21 Israel may not boast of its chosen status. The Sages of post-biblical Israel point out that while Israel is to be praised for accepting the Torah, God previously offered it to all the other nations. Moreover, the Talmud (Shabbat 88a) relates R. Avdimi bar Hama's view that God held the mountain (Horeb/Sinai) over the Israelites' heads and said, "'If ye accept the Torah, 'tis well; if not, there shall be your burial."

free from all burden or responsibility. He wished them to become free to accept another burden — that of the kingdom of Heaven — of Torah and Mitzvot." (Leibowitz/Shemot, 71-2)

As a nation of priests, Israel enjoys an elevated position among the nations. But as Rabbi Samson Rafael Hirsch, the father of modern German Orthodoxy, points out, if God grants the priest rights and privileges not available to ordinary people, God also places him under greater scrutiny. Hirsch imagines God saying, "The more a person stands out from among the people as a teacher and a leader, the less will I show him indulgence when that person does wrong." (Etz Hayim, 633-34)

The "yoke of the Torah" binds the Israelites to lives of righteousness and adherence to the highest standards of justice. Israel will impel, rather than compel, humanity to notice, admire and emulate its example. Israel will not rule. It will serve.

Like the priest, Israel, must accept its special status with a sizeable measure of humility. Amos reminds Israel that God also watches over *other* nations.

> True, I brought Israel up
> From the land of Egypt,
> But also the Philistines from Caphtor [Crete]
> And the Arameans from Kir. (Amos 9:7)

Underlying the prophet's words, according to Rabbi Joel Rembaum, "is the idea that *YHVH* maintains relations with all nations, with regard to whom God can act either as judge or as redeemer." (Etz Hayim, 1379) God's approval must be earned through conduct rather than bloodlines, and right conduct is available to all through adherence to the Noahide laws.

Honesty compels us to understand that the Bible evidences a great deal of hostility to the nations surrounding Israel. So, too, the Sages evidenced no little antagonism towards a larger world with an increasing Christian population that dominated and often brutalized the Jewish people. But even nations that fail to conduct themselves justly are not necessarily doomed. When they repent their abominable behavior, the Talmud (Sotah 35b) informs us, God will accept them. "So it is that amid all the Bible's anti-paganism," Rembaum writes, "seeds of tolerant attitudes toward idolaters can be found." (Etz Hayim, 1379). The righteous of all nations may find favor in God's eyes.

However much the Sages rail against the nations' improper behavior, they do not—indeed, they cannot—denigrate the basic human worth of non-Jews who, like Jews, have been created in God's image. Any society, no matter how wicked, may produce "God's others." God did not destroy Sodom and Gomorrah because no single righteous person lived there but because as many as *ten* righteous people could not be found.

Finally, if monotheism constitutes humanity's natural religious state, we must also recognize a corollary. All people contain the Divine spark. Within the biblical narrative, every person has been given the capacity to respond to the One God even if buffeted by competing—even dominant—polytheistic beliefs. Therefore, non-Israelites' encounters with God would be most exceptional if the Bible had *excluded* them. The favorite child may be loved more or placed under greater expectations. The Parent loves all His children.

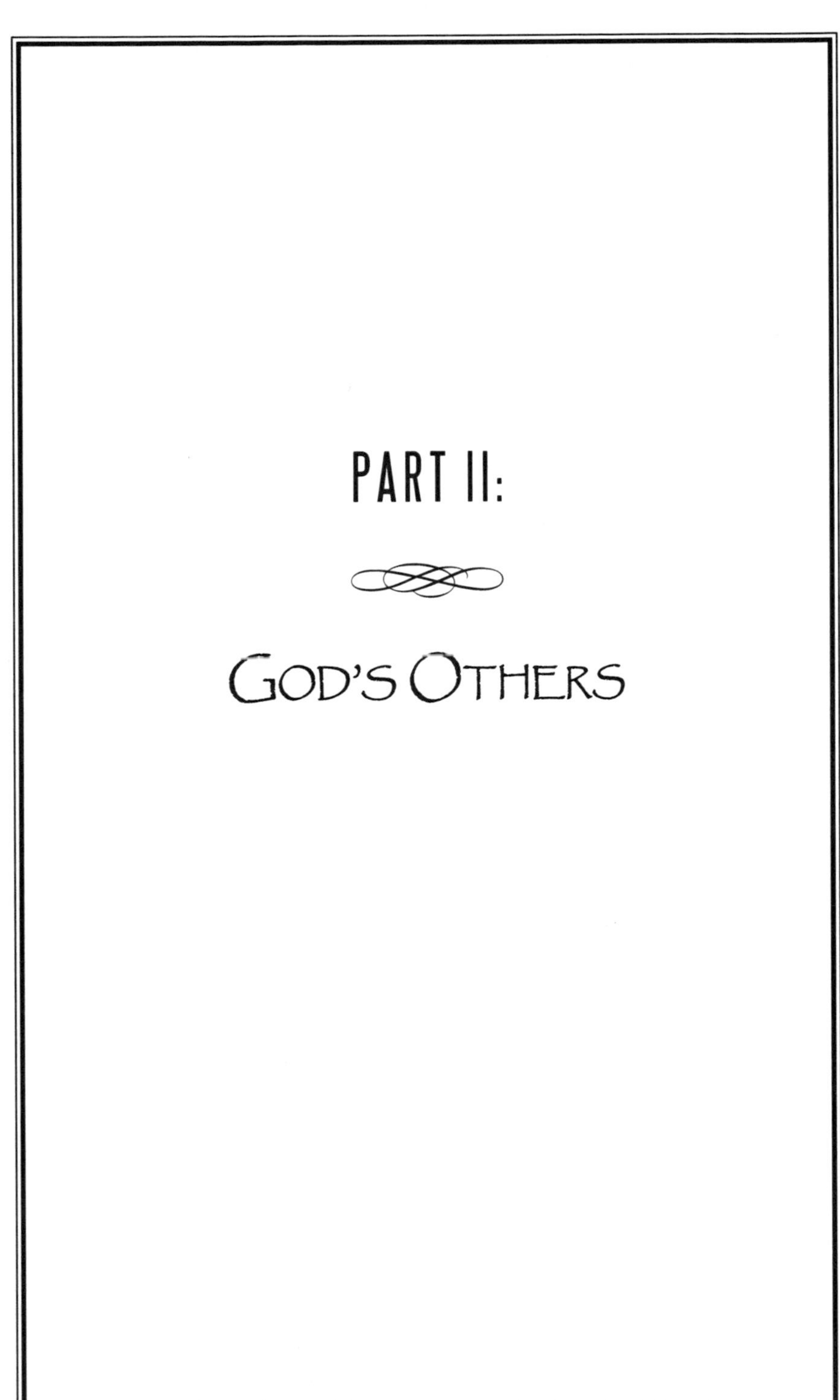

PART II:

GOD'S OTHERS

3

THE ERA OF ABRAHAM

The man bowed low in homage to the LORD and said, "Blessed be the LORD, the God of my master Abraham, who has not withheld His steadfastness from my master. For I have been guided on my errand by the LORD, to the house of my master's kinsmen."
Genesis 24:26-27

IF ABRAHAM IS NOT THE FIRST MONOTHEIST, he nonetheless embraces the critical task of fostering monotheism in a world that, for the most part, seems to have forgotten its Creator. The task will not be undertaken without rewards, although God does not reveal His seven-fold blessing for Abraham and Sarah until after they leave their home in Haran and journey to Canaan. And the blessing demands nothing other than great faith! Abraham at seventy-five and Sarah at sixty-five, an age at which childbearing no longer seems possible for a woman, will be the parents of a great nation.

Protests? Questions? Neither Abraham nor Sarah pose them. "Abram went forth as the Lord had commanded him..." (Gen. 12:4). Unlike Moses at the burning bush, Abraham expresses neither doubt nor fear when God speaks to him. We quickly learn that Abraham and Sarah exhibit the capacity to act based on obedience and faith—and to do so without hesitation.

Are Abraham and Sarah the only people of their generation to know God and make Him known?[22] The Midrash answers yes; in the ten generations from Noah to Abraham, God speaks only to Abraham. (Bialik, 31:2) Genesis, however, demonstrates that in the era of Abraham, God reveals Himself to others in a variety of ways. The biblical narrative also suggests that many, if not all, of these others know God in some manner *before* their paths cross Abraham's. They may not enjoy the same intimacy with God as Abraham does, but the concept of God is not foreign to them. True, God's concern lies with Abraham as the progenitor of a nation that will devote itself to Him and make His glory known throughout the world. But God is free to reveal Himself to any of His creatures when and as He sees fit. This is precisely what occurs during Abraham's lifetime.

---

22 The Midrash (Gen. Rabbah 39:14) relates Sarah's role in the reintroduction or reinforcement of monotheism. "Abraham made proselytes among the men and Sarah among the women." These activities most likely occurred within Abraham's acquired household, which was considerable in size. The biblical narrative offers no evidence of Abraham and Sarah attempting to convert the peoples around them.

THE PHARAOH WHO DESIRED SARAH

Witness to God's Power

When famine strikes Canaan, Abraham and Sarah go down to Egypt. Abraham fears that Pharaoh's officials will be impressed with Sarah's beauty—although she is at least sixty-five—kill him and take her to Pharaoh as a concubine. He urges Sarah to say that she is his sister to spare his life. She does so and indeed is taken to Pharaoh who gives Abraham, her "brother," much wealth. To protect Sarah, God sends unnamed plagues to strike Pharaoh's court. Pharaoh connects the plagues to Abraham's real status as Sarah's husband, although not to God, and dismisses the couple from Egypt.

One of the most pronounced strengths of the Bible lies in its portrayal of Israel's patriarchs, matriarchs, prophets and rulers as wholly human. Like us, they are capable of bad as well as good and must rise above their evil inclinations. Also like us, they must meet their physical needs, which include eating. After all, the patriarchs inhabit the natural world—an earthly environment that continually poses challenges to our comfort and survival. Eden and the effortless gathering of food are a distant memory. Canaan, the Promised Land, is fertile, but drought, storm and pestilence ravage it regularly. While the Bible refers to Canaan as a land of "milk and honey," this description appears first in Exodus rather than in Genesis.[23]

Reality hits home quickly. Soon after coming into Canaan, Abraham and Sarah encounter a severe famine. This presents a rigorous test of faith following God's promise that, "I will make of you a great nation" (Gen. 12:2). In search of food, they go down to Egypt, but Abraham is uneasy. He fears that the Egyptians will be captivated by Sarah's beauty—even at her advanced age; she is sixty-five and he seventy-five when they leave Haran for Canaan—and kill him so that Pharaoh will not commit the wrong of sleeping with

---

23 The Bible references "milk and honey" nineteen times to describe what will become the land of Israel. A twentieth, ironic reference appears in Numbers 16:13. The Israelites, wandering in the wilderness and lacking faith in God's providence, use it to describe Egypt, the land in which they had been enslaved.

another man's wife. Abraham tells her, "Please say that you are my sister, that it may go well with me because of you, and that I may remain alive thanks to you" (Gen. 12:13).

Some truth exists behind this smokescreen. In Genesis 20:12, which relates the second of three versions of this "beautiful wife in a strange land" tale, Abraham informs Abimelech that he and Sarah have the same father but not the same mother. In fact, Sarah is Abraham's niece, the daughter of his brother, Haran. The Rabbis, troubled with Abraham's less than candid approach, explain that a man often refers to a female relative as his "sister." And indeed, from an historical standpoint, the term "sister" references a Hurrian legal relationship between husbands and wives in the ancient Near East. (Plaut, 99) Whether or not Abraham is dissembling, Pharaoh's officials take Sarah to the palace. This constitutes a sin on Abraham's part, according to Nachmanides, because it exposes her to danger.

As to Abraham, all goes well. He acquires sheep oxen, asses and she-asses, male and female slaves, and camels. Isaac Abravanel (also known as Abarbanel), commenting in fifteenth-century Spain, finds no fault with Abraham's accepting lavish gifts from Pharaoh in return for Sarah being taken into Pharaoh's court. Had Abraham refused them, he notes, Pharaoh would have become suspicious.

Of course, God is not about to let the matriarch of Israel be abused. He afflicts Pharaoh with mighty plagues—according to Rashi, a terrible skin disease that would make sexual relations between Pharaoh and Sarah impossible and thus safeguard her chastity. Does Pharaoh acknowledge that God has intervened? The narrative offers no indication that he knows anything of Abraham's God. But Pharaoh understands cause and effect. Clearly recognizing that a greater power is at work, he sends for Abraham and asks:

> "What is this you have done to me! Why did you not tell me that she was your wife? Why did you say, 'She is my sister,' so that I took her as my wife? Now, here is your wife; take her and begone!" (Gen. 12:18-19)

Three times Pharaoh exclaims "wife" to emphasize the wrong Abraham has done him. The patriarch offers no explanation, as he will to King Abimelech in the tale that follows. Pharaoh, for his part, does not invite Abraham to settle in his country, as does Abimelech. This lack of hospitality, Rashi comments, reflects Pharaoh's knowledge that his country is essentially immoral, and that Abraham and Sarah will not be safe within his borders. Pharaoh does not understand the nature of God's intervention on behalf of the nation of Israel not yet created. The king of Egypt nonetheless has had a serious—if "anonymous"—encounter with God. Moreover, he has gotten off easily. The Pharaoh of the Exodus (see *Egypt: Slavery and Redemption*) will not be as fortunate.

MELCHIZEDEK, KING-PRIEST OF SALEM

Invoker of God's Blessing

A war of four kings against five draws Abraham into the conflict. When his nephew, Lot, is kidnapped, Abraham leads a small force of 318 men northward, rescues Lot and brings back a great number of possessions and people. Melchizedek, the king of Salem, greets Abraham with an offering of bread and wine then blesses him in the name of El Elyon—*God Most High. In return, Abraham gives Melchizedek a tenth of the spoils.*

Some individuals play a cameo role in the biblical narrative. Yet their brief appearance produces a considerable impact. Such is the case with Melchizedek of Salem, who validates Abraham's spiritual prominence at a time when polytheism represents the norm.

Melchizedek appears after Abraham rescues his nephew, Lot, from King Chedorlaomer and three other warring kings (Gen. 14:1ff). The king of Sodom comes to meet the victorious Abraham in the Valley of Shaveh, joined by Melchizedek, whose name means "righteous or rightful king."[24]

Melchizedek's city suggests his importance. The Midrash (Gen. Rabbah 43:6) considers the inhabitants of Salem as righteous individuals, identifying the city as Jerusalem, the future site of the Temple. The Sages further identify Melchizedek with Shem, one of Noah's three sons and the antecedent of the Semitic peoples, including the Israelites. Shem, while not the eldest son, is hailed as the wisest. The Midrash portrays Shem as being born circumcised and running a school of Torah, which boasted Jacob as one of its students. Thus Melchizedek is no ordinary holy man.

Although he enters the narrative without previous reference, Melchizedek's character makes a dramatic impression. He stands in marked contrast to the graceless and ungrateful King of Sodom who greets Abraham empty-handed.

---

24 Melchizedek is a not-uncommon name for monarchs in the ancient Near East, according to Nahum Sarna. (Sarna/Genesis, 380)

> And King Melchizedek of Salem brought out bread and wine; he was a priest of God Most High. He blessed him, saying,
> "Blessed be Abram of God Most High,
> Creator of heaven and earth.
> And blessed be God Most high,
> Who has delivered your foes into your hand." (Gen. 14:18-20)

Melchizedek's blessing invokes *El Elyon*—"God Most High"—one of God's many names, and one referred to in Jewish liturgy. But do he and Abraham worship the same God? The Sages think so. The Midrash (Gen. Rabbah 43:6) informs us that Melchizedek revealed Torah to Abraham. Rabbi Samuel b. Nachman adds that he instructed Abraham in the laws of the priesthood.

The seventeenth-century philosopher Baruch Spinoza—excommunicated by the Dutch Jewish community for his departure from traditional thought and behavior—comments on Melchizedek's blessing that, "All this shows well enough that before God founded the nation of Israel he had established kings and priests of Jerusalem and had appointed rites and laws for them." (Spinoza, 40) Spinoza also cites Genesis 26:4-5. God appears to Isaac after he has gone to Abimelech, King of the Philistines in Gerar, in a time of famine like that which Abraham experienced. God renews his vow to make the descendants of Abraham a great people:

> I will make your descendants as numerous as the stars, so that all the nations of the earth shall bless themselves by your offspring—inasmuch as Abraham obeyed Me and kept My charge: My commandments, My laws, and My teachings. (Gen. 26:4-5)

Spinoza points out that, "Abraham had not received from God any special rites, and yet it states in Gen. ch. 26 v. 5 that he observed the worship, precepts and statutes of God. This must undoubtedly refer to the worship, precepts, statutes and laws of King Melchizedek." (Spinoza, 40) The statutes and laws and laws of the Torah as we know them were not presented by God to Israel until after the Exodus from Egypt.

A critical perspective does not necessarily lead to clear-cut agreement with Rabbinic legends or Spinoza's rationale. To the Canaanites, El was the highest of many gods. "He sat at the head of the council of the gods and pronounced the council's decisions," Richard Friedman points out, and "was not identified with any particular force in nature." (Friedman/Commentary, 35)

We can consider, however, that all human beings need not know God in the same way. Abraham seems perfectly comfortable with Melchizedek and his blessing. The Rabbis understand why. According to Nahum Sarna, they regard Melchizedek as a man who "preserved the original monotheism of the human race in the face of otherwise universal degeneration into paganism." (Sarna/Genesis, 109) Sarna calls attention to the similarity of Melchizedek's invoking God's blessing with the blessing God bestows on Abraham in Genesis 12:2-3. He adds, "In rabbinic sources, [Talmud, *Sukkot* 52b], he is the righteous priest who takes his place with the Messiahs of David and Joseph and with Elijah." (Sarna/Genesis, 380)[25]

Richard Friedman concurs. "Abraham is not pictured as the only worshiper of this God on earth." (Friedman/Commentary, 56) Moreover, Melchizedek's status as a priest-king indicates that he does not worship God in isolation but rather as the head of a community. He combines spiritual and temporal power at the very site that is to become the spiritual-temporal focus of Israel and Judaism for millennia to come.

A strong case for a common God may be made. Abraham, following Melchizedek's blessing, gives him a tenth of the spoils he has captured. This tenth prefigures the tithe—one-tenth—Jacob later promises to God (Gen. 28:22), that of the flock or herd that are to be holy to the Lord (Lev. 27:32) and the tithe the Israelites are to provide the Levites (Num. 18:21). Rashi explains that Abraham provides the tenth because Melchizedek is a kohane—a priest.

---

25 The Christian tradition also hails Melchizedek. Hebrews 5:6-11 refers to Jesus as the "high priest after the order of Melchizedek." The ritual of communion through bread and wine recalls both Melchizedek's gifts to Abraham and the Jewish tradition of blessing bread and wine on the Sabbath.

Evidently, he is a priest of a god for whom Abraham the monotheist has great respect—God Himself.

Additionally, Abraham speaks to the king of Sodom in response to the latter's offer of booty following victory in the war: "I swear to the LORD, God Most High, Creator of heaven and earth, I will not take so much as a thread or a sandal strap of what is yours..." (Gen. 14:22-23). Abraham references the term *El Elyon* as Melchizedek had done. He also calls God "Creator of heaven and earth"—"Creator" being the JPS translation of *koneh*, literally "acquirer" or "possessor." Some scholars question whether Melchizedek's *El Elyon* is the same Creator as Abraham's. Nachmanides translates *koneh* as "owner"—a powerful position but lower than that of creator. Taking a different opinion, Rashi acknowledges that "Maker" indeed provides another translation for *koneh*. Among contemporary translators, Richard Friedman selects "creator" and Everett Fox another meaning, "Founder."

If the god of Melchizedek is not the God of Abraham—or not God understood in a different way—why does Abraham make a parallel reference to *El Elyon*? Abraham seems to do more than echo Melchizedek's worship of a god with a similar name. He appears to acknowledge that Melchizedek knows the One God Who revealed Himself first to Adam and Eve.

Such an opinion has its dissenters. Ibn Ezra suggests that Abraham refers to El Elyon only out of courtesy to Melchizedek. The contemporary scholar Baruch Levine comments, "In the ancient Near East, it was customary to pay respect to the deity of the host country." (Etz Hayim, 722) Abraham may well be content that he and Melchizedek share some beliefs; all their beliefs need not be identical. If a considerable gap exists in their concepts of *El Elyon*, Abraham can still play the gracious guest. Respect, after all, need not indicate belief. If Abraham must make his way in a different religious environment, it does not disturb him to do so as long as no one tries to turn him away from his own beliefs.

Or Hahayyim, an eighteenth-century commentator, has no difficulty praising Melchizedek. He notes that following the victory over Chedorlaomer, "The king of Sodom went forth to welcome

Abraham empty-handed, though he was under obligation to repay him generously. The wicked went empty-handed, whereas Melchizedek, the righteous, with no obligation, behaved generously and welcomed him with bread and wine." (Leibowitz/Bereshit, 131) Yet Or Hahayyim also sees Melchizedek's monotheism as limited since he was a priest to the highest of a number of gods worshipped by polytheists—a practice later to be termed henotheism. (See the previous chapter.)

Gunther Plaut, like Ibn Ezra, also rejects the thesis that Melchizedek's god is that of Abraham. Each uses the term *El Elyon,* Plaut comments, but Melchizedek invokes a pagan deity referred to in Phoenician records. "They worship together, each respecting the faith of the other," thus setting an example of "interfaith worship." (Plaut, 107) If Plaut is correct, such courtesy has much to teach us.

Whether Melchizedek is Abraham's equal—a priest of the One God as defined by Israel—we cannot know with certainty. Melchizedek/Shem, according to the Talmud (Nedarim 32b), forfeited his office for blessing Abraham before blessing God. But must Melchizedek and Abraham engage in a contest for status? Melchizedek need not be Abraham's equal to have encountered God and earned praise.

That other monotheists exist in the time of Abraham seems likely and, perhaps, a necessity if the world is to endure. When God cannot find even ten innocent men in Sodom and Gomorrah, He destroys these cities in their entirety. But the very concept of the world containing innocent or righteous people suggests that knowledge of God—in *some* fashion—continues to exist, even if believers constitute a small minority. If we assume that the world before Abraham and outside his family is strictly devoid of God-fearing people, how can Abraham possibly lift up a totally ignorant and corrupt humanity to prevent further, and seemingly inevitable, destruction? Without people sympathetic to his cause, no matter how few in number, Abraham's mission to be a blessing to humanity seems impossible to fulfill. His words must necessarily fall on deaf ears and his actions on blind eyes. He can guide himself and his family but who else?

Yet Abraham is *not* alone. In acknowledging Abraham and blessing him, Melchizedek affords the patriarch a status in Canaan that Abraham can never achieve through wealth and military might alone. Abraham now possesses impressive religious credentials meaningful only if at least scattered individuals—and perhaps even communities—already are attuned to the concept of monotheism or, at the very least, the prominence of God. Because he provides these credentials to Abraham, Melchizedek affirms himself as a righteous man. Thus the Talmud (Bava Batra 14b) cites Melchizedek as one of ten elders who collaborated with David to write the Psalms. This constitutes no small praise by any means.

Brief as it is, Melchizedek's cameo powerfully links God, Abraham and the spirit of generosity. It also suggests God's presence among a portion of humanity before Abraham carries his mission forward.

ABIMELECH, KING OF GERAR

Defender of Marital Integrity

Following the destruction of Sodom and Gomorrah, Abraham and Sarah journey to Gerar. There, King Abimelech falls prey to Sarah's beauty—even if she is now eighty-nine! Abraham states that Sarah is his sister, and Abimelech takes her into his household. Again, God protects Sarah, this time shutting up the wombs of the women of Abimelech's household. But Abimelech has an experience unlike Pharaoh's. God comes to him in a dream and reveals that Abraham is a prophet. Abimelech takes Abraham to task for exposing him to committing a sin, restores Sarah to him and gives the patriarch animals, slaves and silver. Abimelech also takes part in a similar story with Isaac and Rebekah. Although God does not appear to him in this story, Abimelech refers to YHVH *in making peace with Isaac.*

Abraham—foreshadowing the fate of Israel—wanders from one place to another before settling on the land promised him by God. After the destruction of Sodom and Gomorrah, the patriarch—formerly Abram and renamed by God—journeys south into the Negev and settles between Kadesh and Shur. From there, he travels to Gerar, located between Gaza and Beer-shebah. As on his earlier arrival in Egypt, Abraham fears that the beauty of Sarah—formerly Sarai—poses a threat to his life. Again he passes her off as his sister.

The beauty of such an elderly woman—Sarah is now eighty-nine—may startle the reader. But the Bible does not view age as we do.[26] That Sarah ultimately lives to 127, let alone retains her beauty, lies well within biblical parameters. The Talmud (Baba Metziah 87a) offers an explanation of her allure. Sarah's flesh has been rejuvenated, her wrinkles smoothed and her original beauty restored so that God can fulfill His promise to make Abraham a great nation through her. No earthly salon could do as much.

---

26 The generations prior to Abraham live into their six, seven, eight and even nine hundreds. Abraham lives to 175 and Jacob to 147. Moses, who dies at the end of Deuteronomy, lives to 120 with "his eyes undimmed and his vigor unabated" (Deut. 37:7). Job lives to 210.

As Pharaoh before him, Abimelech takes Sarah into his household. God, however, is not about to abandon her to dishonor. "But God came to Abimelech in a dream by night and said to him, 'You are to die because of the woman that you have taken, for she is a married woman'" (Gen. 20:3).

Think about it, and this event is at least as startling as Sarah's beauty. God has appeared to a non-Hebrew if "only" in a dream. That God grants Abimelech such a revelation attests to the latter's righteousness, according to the French medieval rabbi, David Kimhi. (Stone, 91-2) Maimonides dissents. He believes that we need not consider Abimelech as righteous since God's coming to a person in a dream "only informs us that the attention of the person was called by God to a certain thing, and at the same time that this happened at night." (Maimonides, 2:41) Righteousness, however, is not the issue. God *does* reveal Himself to Abimelech—a direct encounter to be sure. Just as important, Abimelech is moved to correct the situation. Why?

Sarah's status as a married woman precludes another man from having sexual relations with her. This provokes a strong reaction in Abimelech although the Israelite law prohibiting adultery is not given until Sinai. We have no idea what laws Abimelech lives by. We do know that he takes God to task for assuming him guilty of violating a moral injunction.

> Now Abimelech had not approached her. He said, "O Lord, will You slay people even though innocent? He himself said to me, 'She is my sister!' And she also said, 'He is my brother.' When I did this, my heart was blameless and my hands were clean." And God said to him in a dream, "I knew that you did this with a blameless heart, and so I kept you from sinning against Me. That was why I did not let you touch her." (Gen. 20:4-6)

Abimelech may not be a Hebrew, but his moral house seems in order even if taking beautiful, unmarried women into one's household does not fit our own sense of morality. In fact, Abimelech gets something of a free pass from Samson Raphael Hirsch, who comments that Abimelech sought to honor Sarah by making her his queen. (Stone, 93) Whether today's husbands would consider that an honor remains in doubt. But we do know that in Abimelech's era, maintaining concubines, along with slaves, was a normal practice. After all, Sarah herself gave her own handmaid, Hagar, to Abraham as a concubine—and at her own insistence. It is important to view events of the Bible in the context of their time and cultural imperatives as well as to acknowledge that even polytheists and henotheists may honor worthy moral codes.

More to the point, let us note Abimelech's reaction to his dream. Incredibly, he does not seem the least bit startled by his encounter with God. We could, of course, propose that Abimelech has had encounters with other gods; this is one more of several, or even many, experiences with the divine. But within the context of the biblical narrative, we know that other gods do not exist. Such encounters would be delusions. Yet Abimelech does not at all appear delusional. We can only conclude that he knows the One God in some way even if not in the manner of Abraham.

Furthermore, in seeking to establish the moral high ground, Abimelech echoes none other than Abraham. The latter challenged God's intended destruction of Sodom by asking, "Will You sweep away the innocent with the guilty?" (Gen. 18:23). Abimelech asks, "O Lord [*Adonai* as opposed to YHVH], will you slay people even though innocent?" (Gen. 20:4). There is, to be sure, a key difference between Abimelech and Abraham, and the Bible makes no effort to place the two on an equal footing. Whereas Abraham pleads for others, Abimelech pleads only for himself and his household. Indeed, the Rabbis take Abimelech to task for having Sarah brought to him in the first place. But even God acknowledges that Abimelech is innocent, although He tempers Abimelech's upstanding behavior by adding, "I kept you from sinning against me" (Gen. 20:6). Nonetheless, Abimelech maintains what Susan Niditch terms his "integrity of mind." (Niditch, 34) It is Abraham, not Abimelech, who has planned a deception that comes close to yielding unfortunate consequences.

Now, God makes Abimelech privy to special news: "Therefore, restore the man's wife—since he is a prophet…" (Gen. 20:7). This may lead to one or both of two conclusions. First, God has spoken with other prophets before or during the period in which He calls on Abraham. Second, God's mention of a prophet presupposes Abimelech's understanding of the term and its relationship to God's making Himself known through human beings. Abimelech has either inherited some form of post-Noahide monotheism and/or received prior revelations.

Reassured, Abimelech complains to Abraham. "What wrong have I done you that you should bring so great a guilt upon me and my kingdom? You have done to me things that ought not to be done" (Gen. 20:9). Abraham's answer is revealing. "'I thought,' said Abraham, 'surely there is no fear of God in this place, and they will kill me because of my wife'" (Gen. 20:11). Abraham makes the critical assumption that fear of God—which can only be based on knowledge of God—exists in other places among other peoples. True, Abraham uses the more general word *Elohim* rather than YHVH, God's name. But this does not presuppose that Abimelech has no sense of the universal God. In explaining himself, Abraham acknowledges that Abimelech *is* a God-fearing man.

In turn, Abimelech atones for the harm he may have caused—even if unintended. He gives Abraham sheep, oxen, slaves and silver along with the right to settle anywhere in his land. This act of generosity towards a prophet of God also represents a beseeching for forgiveness. Abimelech's plea is answered—but through Abraham:

> Abraham then prayed to God, and God healed Abimelech and his wife and his slave girls, so that they bore children; for the LORD had closed fast every womb of the household of Abimelech because of Sarah, the wife of Abraham. (Gen. 20:17-18)

The opening of the wombs of the women of Abimelech's household connects directly back to Abraham and Sarah. It is after this episode that God opens Sarah's barren womb, and she conceives Isaac. Of importance notes Rashi, the biblical narrative specifically mentions Abraham as fathering Isaac to avoid those who might mock that Sarah never conceived until she became Abimelech's prisoner.

Rashi adds midrashically that four years later, when Abraham and Sarah make a great feast to celebrate Isaac's weaning, Abimelech attends as a notable guest. The biblical narrative never mentions this. However, Abimelech and Abraham meet again following the celebration. Abraham reproaches Abimelech regarding a well that the king's servants have seized. Abimelech, accompanied by Phicol, his chief of troops, protests his innocence: "I do not know who did this; you did not tell me, nor have I heard of it until today" (Gen. 21:26). Again, Abimelech appears to be guiltless. In response, Abraham gives him sheep and oxen. The two then make a pact with Abraham providing Abimelech with seven ewes in return for undisputed title to the well.[27] Abraham remains in the land for many years.

Interestingly, Abimelech later figures in Genesis' third "she is my sister" story when Isaac and Rebekah flee famine in Canaan and come to Gerar. Critical scholars note that the two stories set in Gerar may reflect different biblical traditions. However, scholars are not necessarily in agreement. Gunther Plaut comments that Abimelech is, "Apparently the same king who figured in the similar incident in the Abraham story (chapter 20)." (Plaut, 179) Nahum Sarna disagrees. "This can hardly be the same king whom Abraham dealt with over seventy-five years earlier." He suggests that the name is a dynastic one akin to the Henry's, Edwards and Georges of England (Sarna/Genesis, 183)

A brief summary of the story nonetheless is in order. Like Abraham, Isaac fears that the men of Gerar will kill him for his wife. Also like Abraham, he passes off his wife—Rebekah—as his sister. This time, Abimelech is stirred not by a vision of God but by a vision of a man. He sees Isaac fondling his wife. In response, he sends for Isaac and exclaims, "What have you done to us! One of the people might have lain with your wife, and you would have brought guilt upon us" (Gen. 26:10). The aggrieved king then declares that anyone who molests Isaac or Rebekah will be put to death—perhaps justifying Isaac's initial fears.

---

27 The name *Beer-sheba*—"well of the seven" or "well of the oath" comes from this incident, *sheba* meaning either seven or oath.

Isaac becomes wealthy in Gerar, acquiring flocks, herds and a large household. However, his herdsmen clash with the Philistines, who stop up the wells Abraham dug earlier. Abimelech, ignoring Isaac's role as the son of a prophet, orders him to leave, "for you have become far too big for us" (Gen. 26:16). Isaac moves on to dig new wells. These lead to new disputes until a well, called Rehoboth (wide or broad spaces), yields water without quarreling. Abimelech then visits Isaac with his councilor, Ahuzzath, and Phicol, the general named in the Abraham story. The leaders of Gerar not only frame their comments in terms of God but also use His name.

> And they said, "We now see plainly that the LORD [YHVH] has been with you, and we thought: Let there be a sworn treaty between our two parties, between you and us. Let us make a pact with you that you will not do us harm, just as we have not molested you but have always dealt kindly with you and send you away in peace. From now on, be you blessed of the LORD! (Gen. 26:28-29)

While Abimelech receives no visitation from God in this third story, his knowledge of God—and God's blessing of Isaac—apparently gives direction to his moral response.

Whether Abimelech worships God as Isaac does we do not know. The rites of Abraham and Isaac are generally confined to building stone pillars and altars as well as sacrificing animals—common religious activities in the ancient Near East. Abimelech may have made such a sacrifice at this time since the narration continues, "Then he made them a feast, and they ate and drank" (Gen. 26:30). What is clear is that in the Isaac story, Abimelech—whether the same king who knew Abraham or a descendant—understands the nature and power of God.

* * *

THE DESCENDANTS OF ABRAHAM AND SARAH, who will comprise the people Israel, follow a lineage through Isaac, Jacob and Jacob's twelve sons. Abraham has other family, however. His nephew, Lot, becomes the father of the Moabites and Ammonites while his concubine, Hagar, an Egyptian, births his first son, Ishmael, progenitor of the Arabs. Laban, Abraham's great-nephew—the grandson of Abraham's brother, Nahor—becomes the grandfather of Jacob's children. None are Hebrews, but all encounter God as the first book of the Bible unfolds. There is also Abraham's senior servant, Eliezer. Not a relative, Eliezer is circumcised along with the rest of the household's males. Abraham designates him as his heir before the birth of Isaac. Eliezer, too, encounters God while playing a critical role in the Genesis narrative.

LOT, ABRAHAM'S NEPHEW

Survivor of God's Wrath

Lot accompanies Abraham to Canaan. When each man's flocks and herds grow too large, Lot leaves his uncle's household and settles in the region of Sodom and Gomorrah, eventually moving into Sodom. Messengers of God come to warn Lot of impending doom. The men of Sodom storm Lot's house and demand that he surrender the messengers, whom they believe to be mortals, for their sexual pleasure. Lot offers his virgin daughters instead. The men rebuff him. The messengers save Lot and his daughters. He flees with them and his wife to the small town of Zoar, where his wife looks back on the destruction and is turned into a pillar of salt. Lot and his daughters escape to a cave in the hill country. Fearing that no men are left on the earth, his daughters get Lot drunk and have relations with him to continue the human race.

We know from experience—sometimes painful—that members of the same family don't necessarily share similar views or demonstrate similar behavior. Cain and Abel attest to this in the earliest chapters of Genesis. The story of Lot, Abraham's nephew, does not reflect the violence that sometimes takes place within families, but it does remind us that family members are individuals who often move in profoundly different directions.

When Abraham leaves Haran for Canaan, he takes along his nephew, Lot. After accompanying Abraham and Sarah to Egypt, Lot goes up with them to the Negeb. But Lot's flock is sufficiently large so that the land cannot support both of them. Moreover, their herdsmen quarrel. The Midrash (Gen. Rabbah 42:5) identifies the cause of this family squabble: Lot's herdsmen leave his cattle unmuzzled while grazing on Abraham's land. Lot's herdsmen defend themselves, the Midrash relates, by saying that their cattle do no damage to Abraham. Besides, Lot will inherit the land promised by God to Abraham since Abraham has no heir.

The two determine to separate. Abraham offers Lot his choice of regions in which to settle.

> Lot looked about him and saw how well-watered was the whole plain of Jordan, all of it—this was before the LORD had destroyed Sodom and Gomorrah—all the way to Zoar, like the garden of the LORD, like the land of Egypt. (Gen. 13:10)

Lot chooses to journey eastward to Sodom. One of five cities in the vicinity of the Dead Sea, Sodom is, as even non-readers of the Bible know, a place whose wickedness will bring God's destructive fury. And the people of the area prove wicked indeed. To begin, four kings kidnap Lot in the process of sacking Sodom and Gomorrah. As the senior member of the family, Abraham journeys northward to the rescue. His smaller force of 318 men defeats the kidnappers and brings Lot home. Lot's trials, however, have only just begun.

Before destroying Sodom and Gomorrah, God sends two angels to Lot, who sits in Sodom's gate where the legal and commercial matters of cities were traditionally transacted.[28] He welcomes these *malachim*—Hebrew for messengers and translated as angels from the Greek *angelos*—although the narrative offers no hint that he recognizes them as other than human. Lot emulates the hospitality Abraham had previously displayed to three messengers of God in Genesis 18:2.

> When Lot saw them he rose to greet them and, bowing low with his face to the ground, he said, "Please, my lords, turn aside to your servant's house to spend the night and bathe your feet; then you may be on your way early." But they said, "No, we will spend the night in the square." But he urged them strongly, so they turned his way and entered his house. He prepared a feast for them and baked unleavened bread, and they ate. (Gen. 19:2-3)

Typical of the perversity of Lot's chosen city, "the men of Sodom, young and old—all the people to the last man," gather at Lot's house

---

28 My own cursory exploration of Tel Dan in Northern Israel indicates that the gate there provided both sufficient space and potential breezes outside the small, sweltering buildings and narrow lanes of the cramped city.

(Gen. 19:4). They demand that he yield the strangers to them for their own sexual purposes. Lot refuses. To protect his guests, he offers his virgin daughters in their place. The Sodomites show no interest and threaten Lot, reaching out for him. The two angels pull him inside then strike the Sodomites with blinding light so that they cannot find Lot's door (Gen. 19:10-11).

Now comprehending the nature of these "men," Lot pays attention when they tell him to gather his sons-in-law, sons, daughters and any of his people in the city, "For we are about to destroy this place; because the outcry against them before the LORD has become so great that the LORD has sent us to destroy it" (Gen. 19:13). Lot doubtless has learned of God from Abraham. Now he experiences a direct encounter. The message he receives clearly informs him that he cannot remain in Sodom. Unfortunately, neither the message nor the messengers prove sufficient for Lot's sons-in-law. They scoff, thinking that Lot only jests about Sodom's impending doom. Understanding the peril they face, Lot leaves with his wife and two unmarried daughters.

If, at first glance, Lot seems to compare well with Abraham, a second glance offers second thoughts. True, Lot has journeyed with Abraham to Canaan. But it is Abraham, not Lot, whom God commands to "Go forth from your native land…" (Gen. 12:1). Lot's good fortune, Rashi points out, comes about only because he accompanies his uncle. Lot reveals much more about himself in choosing to settle in corruption-filled Sodom.

Here we should note that while Sodom is associated with sexual immorality, the Bible and the Sages point to the Sodomites' selfishness as their most grievous sin. They have accumulated great wealth but refuse to share it. Ezekiel 16:49 says of Sodom, "Only this was the sin of your sister Sodom: arrogance! She and her daughters had plenty of bread and untroubled tranquility; yet she did not support the poor and the needy." The Midrash (Pirke D'Rabbi Eliezer 25) states that a proclamation was issued that anyone who strengthened the hand of the poor and the needy with a loaf of bread should be burned by fire.

Why then Lot's choice of Sodom? The city is wealthy and the land around it extremely fertile. Perhaps Abraham's God-centered morality is too constricting when it comes to doing business and building one's assets. Perhaps Lot would prefer to cut corners. Thus Rashi cites a Midrash in which Lot states, "I want neither Abraham nor his God!"

Let us now return to Lot's "hospitality." His offer of his daughters to the mob finds no acceptance. They desire only the "men." From a modern perspective, the offer remains subject to question. The seeming nobility of such a gesture by an ancient host duty-bound to protect his guests may well be undercut for moderns by the fact that daughters, as Nahum Sarna writes, were held in low esteem in the ancient Near East. (Sarna/Genesis, 137) Lot seems willing to give up only that which he does not treasure.

Further, unlike Abraham, who brings his entire household into his covenant with God, Lot fails to make God known to his sons-in-law. Why else would they scoff at his warning? The biblical narrative makes clear that the *malachim* do not save Lot for his own merits. Rather, "God was mindful of Abraham and removed Lot from the midst of the upheaval" (Gen. 19:29).

Finally, Lot fails to match Abraham's level of commitment. When God commands Abraham to journey to Canaan, he does so without hesitation. Lot's response to impending disaster is another matter.

> As dawn broke, the angels urged Lot on, saying, "Up, take your wife and your two remaining daughters, lest you be swept away because of the iniquity of the city." Still he delayed. So the men seized his hand, and the hands of his wife and his two daughters—in the LORD's mercy on him—and brought him out and left him outside the city. (Gen. 19:15-16)

Just before the destruction takes place, Lot again drags his feet. He tells the angels that he cannot live in the hills to which he is directed. They grant him permission to reside in the town of Zoar, the smallest of the five cities of the plain. But Lot's wife fails to heed an angel's warning not to look back on the sulfurous fire raining down on Sodom and turns into a pillar of salt. The willingness to move forward at God's direction does not appear to be a family trait.

Now, the story becomes more unsettling. Lot and his two unmarried daughters go up to the hill country and hide fearfully in a cave. Having no other frame of reference following the catastrophe, the unnamed daughters believe their father to be the last man on earth. In order to "maintain life through our father" (Gen. 19:32), they get Lot drunk with wine and sleep with him on successive nights. In a sense, what goes around comes around. Robert Alter points out that Lot is paid back for his willingness to give his virgin daughters to the mob. "The concluding episode of this chapter, in which the drunken Lot unwittingly takes the virginity of both his daughters, suggests measure-for-measure justice meted out for his rash offer." (Alter, 92) The modern reader understandably may gasp at this incestuous behavior. Yet the Torah does not condemn the daughters since they act out of genuine concern for humanity's future. Each bears a son. The older daughter produces Moab ("from father"), ancestor of the Moabites, and the younger, Ben-ammi, ("son of my people"), ancestor of the Ammonites.

Lot's encounters with God are less direct than are Abraham's, being undertaken through God's messengers. The loss of his wife and unwitting sexual activity with his daughters suggest a spiritual stature inferior to that of Abraham's. In fact, Rashi comments that Lot actually knows what is happening after his first daughter sleeps with him and allows the second daughter to get him drunk the next night. Moreover, Rashi writes, Lot's incestuous activity makes him notorious throughout the region, inducing Abraham to leave the area and journey south to Gerar and encounter Abimelech (see above).

Lot's daughters may actually display greater merit. They earnestly believe the world to have been destroyed—even though Lot knows that the destruction is limited since the angels earlier reveal, "For we are about to destroy *this* [italics mine] place (Gen. 19:13). From Lot's daughters descend what the Midrash terms "two precious treasures." Ruth—a Moabitess—becomes the ancestor of David. *(See Women of Valor.)* Naamah, an Ammonitess, marries Solomon. While Lot cannot be considered the equal of Abraham, his encounter with God is very real, and the fruit it bears ultimately—and profoundly—impacts the nation of Israel.

HAGAR, ABRAHAM'S CONCUBINE
Mother of the Arab Peoples

Seventy-five-year-old Sarah cannot conceive. Choosing an alternative, she gives her maidservant, Hagar, to Abraham so that he can at last father a child, which also will legally be Sarah's. The pregnant Hagar adopts a haughty attitude towards her mistress. In return, Sarah treats her harshly. Hagar runs away. An angel of the Lord instructs her to return. Hagar bears a son, Ishmael, but tensions run high between the women. Sixteen years later, when Sarah weans her three-year-old son, Isaac, she convinces Abraham to cast Hagar and Ishmael out. The concubine and her son wait to die in the wilderness but are rescued by an angel.

Islam, along with Judaism and Christianity, reveres Abraham, as "the first monotheist." The Arab peoples, among whom Islam developed, trace their descent to Abraham through the woman who bears Ishmael, his first son. The woman is not Sarah but Hagar, an Egyptian whose encounter with God is direct and powerful.

After rescuing Lot, Abraham hears the word of God in a vision. God promises a great reward. Abraham is skeptical. He and Sarah are old, and Abraham believes that he will die childless, leaving his steward, Eliezer, to inherit his household. God reassures Abraham that he will, indeed, have a son. Sarah, too, is concerned that Abraham have descendants. Ten years after their coming into Canaan, Sarah gives Abraham her Egyptian maidservant, Hagar, as a concubine/second wife. How has Hagar come to Abraham's household? The narrative does not say, although Abraham may have acquired her along with other male and female slaves during his journey in Egypt. Rashi believes Hagar to be a daughter of Pharaoh; she may have been included in Pharaoh's gifts to Abraham or assigned to Sarah in the palace.

Sarah makes clear both her instructions and intent. "Consort with my maid," she tells Abraham, "perhaps I shall have a son through her" (Gen. 16:2). While Hagar will birth the child, she will be akin to a surrogate mother. Sarah, as her mistress, will be the legal mother.

Abraham consents, and Hagar conceives. This, however, creates hostility in the household rather than joy. As the only expectant mother, succeeding where her mistress failed, Hagar no longer respects Sarah. Rashi relates Hagar saying of Sarah that, "she could not be so righteous since she has not conceived all these years, while I have become pregnant from my first union with Abram." Abravanel takes another approach, offering that Sarah's intent towards Hagar is not malicious. Sarah merely wants Hagar to correct her insolent behavior. This defense of Sarah may stem from the difficulty of accepting the matriarch's complex personality—the Bible depicts all of the patriarchs and matriarchs as fully human and thus capable of bad behavior as well as good.

If there is a case against polygamy, this may be it. At the age of eighty-five and ten years after first entering Canaan, Abraham finds himself caught between two feuding women. He defers to Sarah, who treats Hagar harshly. The concubine runs away.

With Hagar carrying the son of the first patriarch and headed towards potential danger, it is time to ask, what does she know of God? How will her son carry on Abraham's monotheistic tradition? The Bible portrays Egypt as a Godless nation dominated by perversity. Yet Hagar, in accompanying Abraham and Sarah on their journey through Canaan, must have learned something of their relationship with God and thus of God Himself. God is certainly aware of Hagar. She may flee into the wilderness, but she cannot flee the attention of her Creator.

> An angel of the LORD found her by a spring of water in the wilderness, the spring on the road to Shur, and said, "Hagar, slave of Sarai, where have you come from, and where are you going?" And she said, "I am running away from my mistress Sarai." (Gen. 16:7-8)

The angel—who may be God in a representational form—instructs Hagar to return to Sarah and submit.[29] The servant girl

29 God later appears as a messenger/angel, even, apparently, in human form. In Genesis 18, He slips "in and out of character" among the three "men" who appear to Abraham by the terebinths of Mamre (trees near Hebron) on the third day following the patriarch's circumcision.

will not be forgotten, however, because the angel also promises: "I will greatly increase your offspring, / And they shall be too many to count" (Gen. 16:9). The angel knows that Hagar is pregnant and tells her what the future will bring just as God revealed the future to Abraham.

> "Behold, you are with child
> And shall bear a son;
> You shall call him Ishmael,
> For the LORD has paid heed to your suffering." (Gen. 16:11)

Or *is* she pregnant? Here, translation influences how we view the biblical narrative. JPS translates *hara* as "you are with child." Rashi translates this word as "you will conceive," citing its use in the matter of the wife of Manoah in Judges 13:7, who tells her husband that an angel informed her, "You will conceive." (She does and bears Samson.) Thus, Rashi implies, Hagar had previously suffered a miscarriage and would again conceive when she returned to Sarah.

Either way, as Rabbi Michal Shekel points out, Hagar's experiences offer a parallel to those that Abraham will experience. (Goldstein, 58) In fleeing, Hagar leaves her home with Abraham as Abraham leaves the house of his father, Terach—although Abraham acts in response to God's command. God makes a covenant with Hagar assuring her of numerous offspring as he does with Abraham. And God commands her in the naming of Ishmael as God commands Abraham in the naming of Isaac. In turn, Hagar acknowledges her encounter with God. "And she called the LORD who spoke to her, 'You Are El-roi,' [God of Seeing] by which she meant, 'Have I not gone on seeing after He saw me!'" (Gen. 16:13)[30]

30 The spring at which Hagar receives her revelation is called Beer-lahai–roi in Genesis 16:13. Ironically, it is near this place that Sarah lives—apart from Abraham—after Abraham's aborted sacrifice of Isaac at Mount Moriah. And it is here that Isaac prays before returning to Sarah's tent, where he dwells after her death, when Eliezer brings Rebekah to him. Isaac and Rebekah continue to live near Beer-lahai-roi after Abraham's death.

Hagar may be an Egyptian servant caught in a difficult situation, but God sees her as a valued individual. And what has Hagar "gone on seeing after"? Perhaps she has continued to see the world around her—to remain alive, surviving a direct revelation from God. Moreover, Shekel writes, "She is the first person in the Torah who has the *chutzpah* [nerve—brackets mine] to endow the Divine with a name." (Goldstein, 58) A survivor indeed, Hagar later bears the eighty-six-year-old Abraham his son, Ishmael—"God heeds."[31] He will be "a wild ass of a man," the angel earlier relates to Hagar (Gen. 16:12). But, like Jacob, he will father twelve tribes.

Thirteen years later, Abraham, now ninety-nine, enters into another covenant with God. It is at this time that Abram becomes Abraham—"father of a great nation." Sarai, in turn, receives a new name, Sarah—"princess." The following year, after the destruction of Sodom and Gomorrah and a sojourn to Gerar and King Abimelech (see above), Sarah, age ninety, gives birth to Isaac.

Abraham's two sons apparently get along well. They play together at the feast celebrating Isaac's weaning, although some translations present a different story. These delineate the Hebrew word *metzachek* not as "playing" but as "mocking" or "making sport." The latter term, Rashi notes, can mean idol-worshipping, sexual immorality or murder. In Gen. 26:8, Isaac and Rebekah carry on together not realizing that Abimelech, king of Gerar, watches them. JPS translates *metzachek* in this verse as "fondling." The Stone Chumash offers "jesting," Everett Fox "laughing-and-loving," Richard Friedman "fooling around" and Robert Alter "playing."

All this does not sit well with Sarah. She fears that Ishmael, as the elder, will be the son through whom God's covenant and promise of nationhood will be fulfilled. Again the tensions of a polygamous relationship arise. Sarah tells Abraham, "Cast out that slave-woman and her son, for the son of that slave shall not share in the inheritance with my son Isaac." (Gen. 21:10).

31 This son of Abraham has a mother who is not a Canaanite. When Abraham later sends his servant, Eliezer, to find a wife for Isaac (see below), he specifically forbids finding a Canaanite match.

This distresses Abraham. He previously expressed his love for Ishmael when God revealed that Sarah would bear him a son: "O that Ishmael might live by Your favor!" (Gen. 17:18). Abraham longs for Ishmael to carry on his monotheistic mission, according to Samson Raphael Hirsch. (Stone 76) Moreover, Nachmanides comments, he now fears for Ishmael's death. God eases Abraham's fears by promising to bless Ishmael. No question exists, however, as to which son will succeed Abraham. "… Sarah your wife shall bear you a son, and you shall name him Isaac; and I will maintain My covenant with him as an everlasting covenant for his offspring to come" (Gen. 17:19).

Abraham repeats his fear and unease in response to the casting out of Hagar and Ishmael. Richard Elliott Friedman's translation of Genesis 21:11 takes a literal approach: "And the thing was very bad in Abraham's eyes in regard to his son." The Midrash (Shemot Rabbah 1), on the other hand, offers a negative view of Ishmael, presenting Abraham's distress as resulting from the boy's bad behavior. But this is not necessarily consistent with the plain meaning of the text.

Here we must again acknowledge the Bible's willingness to present a view of humanity—patriarchs and prophets included—that is totally rounded and believable. For propagandistic purposes, the narrative could have portrayed Abraham as indifferent to Ishmael, although this would not constitute a flattering glimpse of a father's relationship with his son, or cast Ishmael in a very negative light by detailing his wrongdoing. In the latter case, Abraham would have had all the justification he needed to banish his elder son. But as Friedman, working from the critical perspective, notes, "The Israelite who wrote this text—which favors his own ancestor, Isaac—still expressed sympathy for Ishmael. He wrote of Abraham's affection for him and God's promise for him." (Friedman/Commentary, 71) The Bible refuses to gloss over the weaknesses and failings of any of its protagonists. Its lens remains unfiltered.

God, of course, has His own plans. He advises Abraham:

> "Do not be distressed over the boy or your slave; whatever Sarah tells you, do as she says, for it is through Isaac that offspring shall

> be continued for you. As for the son of the slave-woman, I will make a nation of him, too, for he is your seed." (Gen. 21:12-13)

God's love of Abraham extends to *both* of Abraham's sons, although Ishmael's descendants will be neither Hebrews nor Israelites. In fact, they will not be monotheists until over two thousand years later when Muhammad restores the Arabs to their Abrahamic heritage.[32] Doubtless heavy-hearted but still trusting in God—he later dutifully obeys when God instructs him to sacrifice Isaac in Genesis 22—Abraham provides Hagar with bread and a skin of water for her journey. "He placed them over her shoulder, together with the child, and sent her away" (Gen. 21:14). But what have we here? Ishmael is sixteen, old enough to be married. His mother is carrying him? Have we a non-Jewish woman establishing the stereotype of the Jewish mother? Rashi proposes that Sarah has cast an evil eye on Ishmael who, stricken with feverish pains, cannot walk. Whatever the explanation, this puzzling portrait of a burdened mother and her helpless near-adult son either mocks the pair or serves to make the reader more responsive to their plight.

Mother and son set out, most probably to return to Egypt. But the road will not be straight or smooth. They lose their way and wander in the wilderness—a fate that plagues the post-Exodus Israelites. When their water runs out, Hagar cannot bear to see the death of her son. She leaves "the child" under a bush, walks off a distance and sits. This, according to Samson Raphael Hirsch constitutes a selfish act—Hagar should have comforted her son. (Stone, 97) Hagar may seem to give up, but God has other plans.

> God heard the cry of the boy, and an angel of God called to Hagar from heaven and said to her, "What troubles you, Hagar? Fear not, for God has heeded the cry of the boy where he is. Come, lift up

---

32 The direct link between Abraham and the Arabs through Ishmael may have come to Muhammad from friendly Arabian Jews, according to Karen Armstrong. (Armstrong/Muhammad, 161) Albert Hourani surmises that Muhammad's breach with the Jews of Medina placed a new emphasis on an existing line of spiritual descent binding Muhammad to Abraham. (Hourani, 18)

> the boy and hold him by the hand, for I will make a great nation of him." (Gen. 21:17-18)

God opens Hagar's eyes, an act consistent with the name Hagar has given Him—*El-Roi* or God of Seeing. Before her she sees a well, which Muslim tradition identifies as the well of Zamzam in Mecca where Abraham and Ishmael will build the Kaaba. Mother and son are saved. Such mercy may inspire us, but it troubles the Sages. The Midrash (Genesis Rabbah, 53:14) relates that the angels plead with God not to save Ishmael because of the future persecution by the Arabs of the Jews. But God refuses to abandon the boy based on future behavior when Ishmael's present behavior is righteous.

Ishmael flourishes. "God was with the boy and he grew up" (Gen. 21:20). Then, proving again that one needn't be Jewish to be a highly involved mother, Hagar obtains a wife for Ishmael from Egypt, her own land, rather than from Abraham's family in Haran. Her choice brings into focus both the connection and separation of Israel and the Arabs.

Ishmael's descendants play only a tangential role in the Bible with the exception of taking Joseph down to Egypt, an act instigated by Joseph's brothers. Yet God's intervention on behalf of Hagar and Ishmael clearly shows His love for them. Rashi takes this a step further, citing a midrash that the woman Abraham marries after Sarah's death, Keturah, is really Hagar. Hagar has been given a new name, which means incense, because of her beautiful deeds and chaste behavior after being sent away by Abraham. This midrash accords Hagar great respect.

Whether or not Hagar really is Keturah, her active role in the biblical narrative comes to an end. The Bible does not disclose how—or whether—Hagar and Ishmael pass on their knowledge of God. It does, however, cast an ironic tone on antipathy between Jews and Arabs. Upon Abraham's death, Isaac and Ishmael come together to bury their father in the cave of Machpelah. Whatever the differences between their mothers, the sons share sufficient love and respect for their father to reunite one last time.

ELIEZER

Servant of Abraham and God

After Sarah dies, Abraham seeks a wife for Isaac but will not permit his son to marry from among the surrounding Canaanite women. The patriarch sends his senior servant, Eliezer, northward to Haran and members of Abraham's own family. Eliezer, unsure as to how he will recognize Isaac's bride to be, asks God to fulfill a scenario in which the right woman will offer water both to him and his camels. He meets Rebekah at a well, experiences the scenario and thanks God for guiding his search. After relating his story to Rebekah's family, Eliezer receives Rebekah's permission to return immediately to Canaan with her, and they depart.

Every parent desires the right match for his or her child. Yet modern parents must stand aside as their children make their own choices of mates. Such was not the case in biblical times, particularly among nobles and clan leaders who weighed substantial political and economic considerations inherent in a marriage, which would join two families. Securing the right match poses an even greater challenge to the patriarchs and matriarchs. Where does one find a Hebrew woman—a woman prepared to uphold and propagate Abrahamic monotheism? Abraham and Sarah are not only the first Hebrews—they are the *only* Hebrews of their generation. Isaac, their son, is the only Hebrew offspring, and he must marry carefully to advance God's promise to make a great nation of Abraham's descendants. So after Sarah's death—she is deprived of the joy of a daughter-in-law and grandchildren—Abraham takes great care in seeking a wife for Isaac, now thirty-seven. Old, widowed and blessed by the Lord in all things, Abraham commands his senior servant, Eliezer ("My God is my help"), to journey northward in search of a suitable woman from among Abraham's relatives.[33]

33 Gen. 15:2 refers to Eliezer *ha-damashek*—the Damascan. Damascus, in Syria, lies on the route Abraham took with his father, Terach, from Ur of the Chaldees to Canaan. The Midrash (Genesis Rabbah) refers to Eliezer as a Canaanite.

Eliezer obviously holds Abraham's trust. He previously has been designated to inherit the estate of the childless patriarch and matriarch, but the births of Ishmael and Isaac change his status as beneficiary. Genesis presents no evidence of his being jealous or less than totally faithful. He understands his place and the role he is to play. The Midrash (Genesis Rabbah 59:8) reports that Eliezer—who is circumcised in keeping with God's covenant with Abraham—was a worthy man and a master over his passions as was Abraham. The Sages refer to Eliezer as the *rosh yeshivah*—the master teacher who taught Abraham's disciples. (Stone, 109) The Talmud (Nedarim 32a) offers that the 318 warriors Abraham led to rescue Lot (see above) were really only Eliezer; the numerical value of his name—each Hebrew letter has a number equivalent—totals 318.

Abraham leaves no doubt about his intentions. He instructs the trustworthy Eliezer with precision then makes him swear an oath.

> And Abraham said to the senior servant of his household, who had charge of all that he owned, "Put your hand under my thigh and I will make you swear by the LORD, the God of heaven and the God of Earth, that you will not take a wife for my son from the daughters of the Canaanites among whom I dwell..." (Gen. 24:2-3)

Why must Eliezer grasp or touch Abraham's thigh? Rashi comments that "thigh" is a euphemism for penis. Why then Abraham's penis? An oath must be taken on a sacred object, and Abraham had undergone much pain in being circumcised in old age to establish his covenant with God.

Why can Isaac not have a Canaanite wife? Samuel Luzzatto, a nineteenth-century Italian-Jewish scholar, suggests politics. If Isaac marries a woman from among the Canaanites, whose practices are evil, they cannot later be expelled from the land as God promised. (Leibowitz/Bereshit, 217) Samson Raphael Hirsch presents a different argument. A Canaanite wife will have her family and friends—and their specific religious practices—close at hand. Isaac and his children will be assimilated into the Canaanites' ways rather than his wife assimilating into Hebrew monotheism. (Leibowitz/

Bereshit, 219) Hirsch adds that other peoples of the region, including Abraham's family in Aram-naharaim to which Eliezer will journey, are also polytheists and idol worshippers. It is not the Canaanites' idol worship that worries Abraham, however, but their moral degeneracy. This follows Rashi that the deeds of the Egyptians and Canaanites were more corrupt than those of the other nations.

Eliezer's quest to find a fitting woman worthy of inheriting the mantle of matriarchy must take him far from home. That the bride will come from Abraham and Sarah's family to the north proves fitting for two reasons. First, Abraham knows these people. Better family than strangers. (Later prohibitions against marrying family members did not apply to cousins.) Second, the in-laws will remain physically distant. A wife brought to Isaac will leave not only her relatives behind but also her gods. Thus she will more easily be absorbed into her new Hebrew family.

Here, Abraham's instruction to Eliezer makes a critically important point. While Isaac's wife will leave her gods in Haran, the God of Abraham is no mere family or local god. He is the God Whose presence and power know no borders and can be found everywhere.

> "The Lord, the God of heaven, who took me from my father's house and from my native land, who promised me on oath, saying, 'I will assign this land to your offspring'—He will send His angel before you, and you will get a wife for my son from there." (Gen. 24:7-8)

Eliezer dutifully sets out although fulfilling the mission will be no easy task. Upon arriving at a well outside his destination and recognizing the limits of his own wisdom, he appeals to God: "O Lord, God of my master Abraham, grant me good fortune this day, and deal generously with my master Abraham." (Gen. 24:12) But even faith goes only so far. Eliezer pleads for a sign and determines one—that the right woman will respond to his request for water and offer to water his camels as well. Thus Eliezer becomes the first person in the Bible to appeal directly to God for guidance or good fortune. The sign does not, however, constitute an enchantment, something forbidden by Jewish law, Nehama Leibowitz emphasizes. Rather,

Eliezer's plea represents "a psychological test to probe the character of the woman worthy to be the wife of Isaac and the ancestress of the nation chosen for its moral calibre." (Leibowitz/Bereshit, 242)

Eliezer's prayer is answered. Rebekah appears, offers him water then draws water for his ten camels—no small physical task. Moreover, she does so without knowing that Eliezer is the servant of Abraham, her great-great uncle and a wealthy man. But her kindness doesn't stop there. Rebekah announces, "There is plenty of straw and feed at home, and also room to spend the night" (Gen. 24:25). Eliezer immediately acknowledges God's role in his discovery.

> The man bowed low in homage to the LORD and said, "Blessed be the LORD, the God of my master Abraham, who has not withheld His steadfastness from my master. For I have been guided on my errand by the LORD, to the house of my master's kinsmen." (Gen. 24:26-27)

After entering Rebekah's home, Eliezer relates his story—and tells of God's guidance—to Laban, Rebekah's brother (for more on Laban, *see Dissemblers and Provokers)* and her father, Bethuel. "I am Abraham's servant. The LORD has greatly blessed my master, and he has become rich…" (Gen. 24:34-35). In detail, he restates Abraham's instructions and Rebekah's response. Rashi casts a skeptical eye on Eliezer here. Reflecting on the difficulty of his charge, Eliezer reveals to Rebekah's family, "And I said to my master, 'What if the woman does not follow me?'" According to Rashi, Eliezer seeks a rationale for his own daughter to marry Isaac—an act Abraham forbids because Eliezer, according to the commentator, is a Canaanite.

From the perspective of the biblical narrative, however, Eliezer fulfills his oath to Abraham wholeheartedly. Whether or not he has secretly wished Isaac for his own daughter—and we know nothing of his family—Eliezer's experience at the well suggests the inevitability of Rebekah's marriage to Isaac, according to David Kimhi. (Leibowitz/Bereshit, 115) No wonder that Laban and Bethuel give Rebekah permission to go with Eliezer after they can observe an appropriate term of leave-taking—a year or perhaps ten months. Understanding the urgency of his task, Eliezer replies, "Do not delay me, now that the

Lord has made my errand successful" (Gen. 24:56). Rebekah assents to depart immediately. Accompanied by her nurse, she leaves with Eliezer to marry a man she does not know in a land she does not know.

And what of Eliezer? His return with Rebekah to Isaac marks the end of his role in the biblical narrative. Yet his position as one of "God's others" is not only secure but very much within the Hebrew framework. In the era of the patriarchs, Hebrew identity is defined by birth or marriage. But in the broader scope, Israelite or Jewish identity obtained through conversion remains an option to almost anyone—the exceptions being Ammonites and Moabites as instructed in Deuteronomy 23:4. Eliezer's circumcision and acceptance of God result in what may be termed a de-facto conversion. True, his descendants, assuming Eliezer has children, will play no role in the history of Israel. Only through Isaac, Jacob and Jacob's twelve sons will the Israelite nation emerge. It is not impossible, however, that Eliezer has granddaughters or great-granddaughters not specified in Genesis, who become the wives of some of Jacob's sons.[34] Genesis informs us that Judah marries a Canaanite woman named Shuah and also fathers twin sons through his daughter-in-law, Tamar. Joseph, made a viceroy by Pharaoh, is given an Egyptian—daughter of Potiphera, the high priest—as his wife. The Torah does not identify the wives of Jacob's other ten sons. Eliezer's granddaughters would make perfect matches, affixing the bloodline of this faithful servant to that of Israel. This, however, is purely midrashic speculation.

What we do know is that Eliezer encounters the God of Abraham and serves His will with distinction. Eliezer's faith and actions compare more than favorably with those of the generations of Israelites, who witness God's signs and wonders in Egypt, pass through the Reed Sea and stand in awe at Sinai to receive the Law only to dance around the golden calf and yearn for a return to the land that formerly enslaved them.

---

34 The Sages have mixed opinions about the identities of Jacob's sons' wives. Rashi points to R. Yehudah stating that each son had a twin sister whom he married. R. Nechemia believes the wives to be Canaanites. These could be Hivite women taken from the city of Shechem after the rape of Dinah and the murderous revenge instigated by Jacob's sons Simeon and Levi (Gen. 34).

4

Egypt: Slavery and Redemption

"It took a Jethro, a non-Israelite, to come and say, "Blessed be the Lord.""
Mechilta Amalek 3

If we ever wish to define a "love-hate" relationship, we can do no better than examine that of Israel and Egypt. Egypt is the land to which Abraham and Sarah flee during time of famine. It is the land in which Joseph becomes transformed from slave to master as Pharaoh's viceroy—a land that then welcomes Joseph's father, Jacob, along with his brothers and sister and their families. So honored is Jacob that when he dies, the Egyptians bewail him for seventy days. Pharaoh's senior officials and dignitaries even go up to Canaan with Joseph and his brothers for Jacob's burial in the cave of Machpelah, which Abraham purchased as a burial place for Sarah.

On the other hand, Egypt is the land in which Jacob insists he not be buried, and the kingdom that turns on the Israelites and enslaves them. The biblical narrative, which portrays Egypt as a generous host and benefactor, also holds it up as an example of all that is evil and godless. Sorcerers and magicians abound in Egypt. The nation, the Bible tell us, disgraces itself with abominations, including sexual depravity and worship of the dead—behaviors as objectionable as those of the Canaanites, whom God will dispossess for their immorality and wickedness. In the wilderness, following the Exodus, God makes clear the wrongs of both the Egyptians and the Canaanites when He instructs Moses to warn the Israelites, "You shall not copy the practices of the land of Egypt where you dwelt, or of the land of Canaan to which I am taking you; nor shall you follow their laws" (Lev. 18:3). Regardless, the Israelites, unused to freedom and the hardships it can impose, cry out against their sojourn in the wilderness. They plead to return to their familiar lives in Egypt. Moses tells them that they may never return, reminding them of the dreadful diseases to be found in Egypt and that should they turn from God, He can afflict Israel with them.

The affection for Egypt developed during the days of Joseph and the Hebrew clan's early years of pastoral life in Goshen near the Nile delta is real. It also belongs to the past. Yet God surprises us. Corrupt as the Egyptians may be, He will not turn his back on them. The prophet Isaiah declares that God will ultimately afflict the Egyptians then heal them.

> In that day, Israel shall be a third partner with Egypt and Assyria as a blessing on earth; for the LORD of hosts will bless them, saying, "Blessed be My people Egypt, My handiwork Assyria, and My very own Israel." (Isa. 19:24-25)

Egypt, too, is part of God's creation. But until Egypt merits God's blessing it is off-limits to Israel. Even though the prophet Jeremiah and fellow exiles from Judah paradoxically flee Nebuchadnezzar's conquering army southward into Egypt in the sixth century BCE, it is a symbol of all that Israel is to avoid.

God is everywhere, however. During the period leading to the Exodus He fills Egypt with His presence. "God's others" encounter Him when Joseph rises to power. They also witness God's wonders as the era of slavery concludes and He redeems His people through the final humbling of Pharaoh and his army at the Reed Sea. As we shall discover, Egypt's opportunity to encounter the reality of *El Shaddai*—God Almighty—is all part of God's plan.

POTIPHAR, PHARAOH'S CHIEF STEWARD

Joseph's Sympathetic Master

Joseph's ill fortune is matched only by his good fortune. Sold into slavery by his ten older brothers, he is acquired as a servant by Potiphar, Pharaoh's chief steward. Joseph makes a great impression on Potiphar. This high official recognizes that God is behind Joseph's successes and appoints him head of his household with almost unlimited responsibility. Alas for Joseph, Potiphar's wife becomes enamored of him. When Joseph refuses to sleep with her, she accuses him of attacking her, and Potiphar has him put in prison. But Potiphar may well understand who is in the right.

The challenging dynamics that play out in all families—particularly large ones—reveal themselves in the story of Joseph. In many families, one or both parents have a favorite. Jacob's is Joseph, the eleventh of his twelve sons. Joseph is the son of his old age and the image or reminder of the boy's beloved mother, Rachel, whom Jacob loved more than his other wives and who died bearing their youngest son, Benjamin. Onkelos, a first-century CE proselyte who translated the Torah into Aramaic, depicts Joseph as a wise son—an alternate translation of *ben-zekunim* or "son of his old age." Rashi comments that Joseph resembled his father, which created a special bond. Needless to say, Joseph's older brothers do not share their father's feelings. And how can we blame them? Joseph is, to put it bluntly, a spoiled brat.

Joseph alienates his brothers with both special privileges and tattling. He even has two related dreams of grandeur, which he insists on telling his brothers. In the first, his brothers' bound sheaves bow to him. In the second, the sun, moon and stars—representing the entire family—bow to him. Long story short: they hate him.

One day, Jacob sends the seventeen-year-old Joseph far from home to where the ten older brothers are pasturing their flocks. The father wants his favorite to report on their doings. After receiving directions from an unidentified man—perhaps an angel sent to assure that Joseph finds them—Joseph catches up with his brothers in Dothan. Obviously, Joseph has not been sent to work but to spy. Rather than shepherd's clothes, he wears his *k'tonet hapasim*—his ornamental tunic often referred to as a coat of many colors. The brothers' hatred passes the point of no return. They conspire to kill him. But Reuben, the eldest, persuades them to spare Joseph's life. In response, the brothers strip Joseph of his special tunic and throw him into an arid pit. Judah, fearful of committing or abetting murder, suggests that the brothers have more to gain by selling Joseph into slavery than letting him die in the pit. In what ultimately proves to be a complex series of transactions, they sell Joseph to passing Ishmaelite traders for twenty pieces of silver.[35]

Whatever the machinations that bring Joseph to Egypt, we may anticipate that slavery will end his story. Rather, good fortune follows: "The LORD was with Joseph, and he was a successful man; and he stayed in the house of his Egyptian master" (Gen. 39:2). Joseph makes a great impression on Potiphar, Pharaoh's chief steward. *Tanhuma*, an early medieval midrash, explains that wherever Joseph worked—in Potiphar's fields or in his house—that area prospered, while areas of Potiphar's affairs in which Joseph was absent did poorly. In this way, Potiphar understood that Joseph advanced his wellbeing. No fool, Potiphar recognizes that his success relates not only to Joseph but also to the God of the Hebrews.

> And when his master saw that the LORD was with him and that the LORD lent success to everything he undertook, he took a liking to Joseph. He made him his personal attendant and put him in charge of his household, placing in his hands all that he owned. And from the time that the Egyptian put him in charge of his household and of all that he owned, the LORD blessed his house for Joseph's sake, so that the blessing of the LORD was upon everything that he owned, in the house and outside. He left all that he had in Joseph's

35 In Genesis 37:28, the Ishmaelites bring Joseph to Egypt. Yet eight verses later, Midianites (offered as Medanites in the Hebrew) actually sell Joseph to Potiphar, chief steward to Pharaoh. Traditional scholars offer a variety of explanations that show Joseph being passed along among these groups. Critical scholars cite the combining of two different versions of the story.

> hands and, with him there, he paid attention to nothing save the food that he ate. (Gen. 39:3-6)

Has Potiphar had his own personal experience with God? More likely, according to Rashi, his encounter is real but at something of a remove, stemming from Joseph's discussions about the God of Abraham, Isaac and Jacob. The name of heaven was always on Joseph's lips, Rashi comments. If everything prospers under Joseph's hand, but Joseph insists on attributing all good fortune to God, how can Potiphar also not acknowledge God's power?

God's being with Joseph, however, does not set the story on a direct path to a happy ending. Joseph's tale—like the arc of the entire biblical narrative—is one of ups and downs. Joseph's good fortune presents a pivotal challenge. Potiphar's wife finds Joseph extremely attractive and desirable, since he "was well built and handsome" (Gen. 39:6). Perhaps Potiphar adds fuel to the fire by neglecting her. We don't know what he does with his time, since he leaves management of his entire household to Joseph. Or perhaps, because Joseph manages everything, Potiphar's wife has too much time on her hands. What we do know is that she attempts to seduce Joseph.

Is Joseph attracted to her? He is, after all, a single man at an age—within a wide range of years to be sure—when a man's thoughts focus on women. On the other hand, Joseph is grateful to Potiphar for his exalted position. Not all slaves receive such benign treatment. Moreover, the maturing Joseph no longer seems the spoiled favorite but a young man with new insights into how life is to be lived. The moral weight of Abraham guides him. And so Joseph protests, "How then could I do this most wicked thing, and sin before God?" (Gen. 39:9).

There is a Yiddish expression—to *noodge*. It means to keep whining and coaxing until the object of the noodging responds favorably. In the days that follow, Potiphar's wife noodges without end, but Joseph continues to spurn her. Then comes the confrontation—almost comic in some ways—that cannot be avoided. Alone with Joseph, Potiphar's wife catches hold of his garment and again pleads with him. Joseph not only flees, he leaves his garment in her hand.

Furious, she runs outside to tell the servants that the Hebrew has attacked her. When Potiphar returns home from wherever he spends his days, she repeats the accusation. She uses language designed to maximize his anger and the punishment he will mete out to Joseph: "The Hebrew slave whom you brought into our house came to me to dally with me; but when I screamed at the top of my voice, he left his garment with me and fled outside" (Gen. 39:17-18).

Is this woman pure evil? Not according to the Midrash (Gen. Rabbah 85:2). It relates that through astrology, Potiphar's wife learns that either she or her daughter will have a child by Joseph and provide continuity to his line. Joseph later marries Asenath, daughter of Poti-phera, priest of On, whom the Sages identify with Potiphar. Asenath gives birth to Ephraim and Manasseh, whom their grandfather, Jacob, later adopts as his own children and who become namesakes of two of Israel's tribes. Thus Potiphar's wife is only fulfilling her destiny.[36]

Whatever his real identity, Potiphar is on the spot. He has given Joseph his total trust. But how can he ignore his wife and show preference to a slave? The plain meaning of the text makes clear his reaction to the previous two verses: "When his master heard the story that his wife told him, namely, 'Thus and so your slave did to me,' he was furious" (Gen. 39:19).

But with whom is Potiphar *really* angry? Is this the first time his wife has had such an encounter with a handsome young man? Or does she have a history of seeking lovers? Does Potiphar even spur her on to seek lovers so that he can be left alone? As readers, *we* know that Joseph has done no wrong. The Midrash (Gen. Rabbah 87:9) suggests that Potiphar knows this as well. It relates that Potiphar tells Joseph, "I know that you are innocent," but takes him to prison to avoid a stigma falling on his children since his wife is a harlot. The Quran takes note of this event as well, stating that Potiphar, noticing that Joseph's shirt is torn from behind, says to his wife, "This is one of your tricks. Your cunning is great indeed!

36 Robert Alter disagrees, seeing no connection between the high chamberlain and the priest of On, which is not a deity but a city later called Heliopolis by the Greeks because it was a center of sun worship (Alter, 236).

Joseph, say no more about this. Woman, ask pardon for your sin. You have done wrong" (Sura 12:25ff).

Potiphar must save face. He cannot favor a slave over his wife. But he *can* mitigate the injustice that will be done to Joseph. According to Abravanel, Potiphar himself escorts Joseph to the prison out of respect. (Stone, 217) Doing prison time is no cakewalk, yet such punishment is much preferred to death. Moreover, Joseph's stay becomes a relatively comfortable one since he has friends in high places, human as well as Divine. A proven administrator, Joseph again lands on his feet when the chief jailer puts him in charge of all the prisoners. God certainly plays a role in this; He is the Providential Agent throughout Genesis. But the biblical narrative offers a strong hint that Joseph has a human benefactor in none other than Potiphar.

Some time after Joseph is imprisoned, Pharaoh's cupbearer and baker commit nameless offenses against the king.

> Pharaoh was angry with his two courtiers, the chief cupbearer and the chief baker, and put them in custody, in the house of the chief steward in the same prison house where Joseph was confined. The chief steward assigned Joseph to them, and he attended them. (Gen. 40:2-4)

The Hebrew term for chief steward, *sar hatabachim*, also describes Potiphar in verse 39:1. Potiphar may well place Joseph in his own prison so that he can offer his protection. In fact, Joseph receives the same high level of authority he had in Potiphar's house since, "The chief jailer did not supervise anything that was in Joseph's charge" (Gen. 39:23). Importantly, Joseph's assignment to Pharaoh's cupbearer and chief baker represents no menial task. "These two prisoners had occupied important places in the court," Robert Alter points out, "and Pharaoh may yet pardon them, so it makes perfect sense that they should be singled out for special treatment in prison, to be attended personally by the warden's right-hand man." (Alter, 226) Indeed, Joseph interprets the separate dreams of the cupbearer and the baker, correctly predicting that the cupbearer will be restored to his position while the chief baker will be executed. Later, he will be asked to interpret Pharaoh's puzzling dreams.

Potiphar's generosity towards Joseph may reflect something more than gratitude for a job well done. It appears that Potiphar has encountered God through Joseph. It is the young slave who, while receiving no direct revelation from God as do Abraham, Isaac and Jacob, attributes to God a providentially watchful eye over his family and a moral code that, when followed, makes the Hebrews worthy of God's attention. Joseph will later explain to his brothers that his sale into Egyptian slavery was all part of God's plan and not their responsibility. "God has sent me ahead of you to assure your survival on earth, and to save your lives in an extraordinary deliverance" (Gen. 45:7). It is quite likely that Potiphar understands that the source of his wellbeing is neither himself nor Joseph but the God of the Hebrews.

Of course, this portrait of Potiphar remains subject to question—and Rashi questions it. How he does so will be revealed in the very next story.

We can, however, ask this: While the Bible presents no evidence of Potiphar abandoning the gods of Egypt, wouldn't a polytheist welcome the protection of an additional god—particularly one who seems to have served him so well?

Potiphar's encounter with God emphasizes God's intent to fulfill His covenant with Abraham. He will watch over the Hebrews wherever their travels take them. God will also reveal Himself to others who need only recognize His presence and play their corresponding roles.

THE PHARAOH OF JOSEPH

Dreamer of Mysteries

Pharaoh dreams about seven thin, starved-looking cows devouring seven fat cows, and seven withered ears of corn swallowing up seven healthy ones. None of his magicians or courtiers can interpret these dreams. Pharaoh's cupbearer suggests summoning Joseph, who interpreted the cupbearer's dream while they were in prison. Joseph appears before Pharaoh and relates that it is not he but God who provides his skill at finding the solution to dreams. He then explains that seven years of plenty will be followed by seven years of famine. Pharaoh responds by making Joseph his second in command.

"It's good to be king!" The comedian Mel Brooks has Louis XIV say this in one of his movies. Most of us would agree. However, Shakespeare, in Henry IV, Part 2, puts the throne in perspective: "Uneasy lies the head that wears a crown."

The Bible offers plentiful proof that a royal scepter can weigh down the hand that holds it, and the Pharaoh of Joseph's time provides an excellent example. Pharaoh's position as god-king of Egypt mandates great responsibility. Great responsibility, in turn, brings restless nights. So it happens that Pharaoh becomes disturbed by two dreams. In the first, he stands by the Nile, which is not simply a river but a god to Egypt and the nation's lifeblood. Samson Raphael Hirsch points out that Pharaoh's position by the Nile emphasizes a key burden: his concern with the river's annual flooding. In a land without rain, this one river—which floods when snow melts in the mountains to the south—irrigates Egypt's canals and impacts virtually all of the kingdom's agricultural output (Stone, 222) As Pharaoh stands at the river's edge, seven fat cows graze in the reed grass. Seven gaunt cows then rise up out of the river and devour the seven fat ones—yet remain thin and ugly. In the second dream, seven ears of solid, healthy grain grow on a single stalk. Seven ears of thin grain, scorched by the east wind, devour the seven solid, healthy ears.

What does this all mean? Pharaoh's magicians have skills to be sure—skills they will display before Moses in the Book of Exodus. But those skills reach their limits. They and the wise men of Egypt cannot interpret Pharaoh's dreams.

Pharaoh's cupbearer comes to the rescue. He mentions Joseph, who interpreted the cupbearer's dream and also that of Pharaoh's chief baker when they all were imprisoned. The cupbearer explains that Joseph's explanations were validated—he was freed soon after while the baker was executed. Impressed, Pharaoh sends for Joseph, now a captive in Egypt for almost thirteen years and, approaching thirty, no longer a spoiled adolescent. Pharaoh relates that he has heard that Joseph can tell the meaning of dreams. Joseph responds with humility: "Not I! God will see to Pharaoh's welfare!" (Gen. 41:16). Pharaoh relates the dreams, and Joseph prepares to provide the solution to the puzzle. Before doing so, however, he again denies possessing any great wisdom, stating, "God has told Pharaoh what He is about to do" (Gen. 41:25).[37]

Joseph explains that Pharaoh has had a single dream in two parts. The fat cows and healthy ears of grain represent seven years of plenty. These will be followed by seven years of famine represented by the thin cows and parched ears. Then Joseph expresses his humility for the third time. "God has revealed to Pharaoh what He is about to do" (Gen. 41:28). Joseph repeats the warning of plenty followed by famine. Finally, for the fourth time, he attributes the dreams and the events that will follow to God. "As for Pharaoh having had the same dream twice, it means that the matter has been determined by God, and that God will soon carry it out" (Gen. 41:32).

Joseph's multiple references to God underscore God's providential role in history. All that happens in Egypt will serve only to fulfill His revelation to Abraham that the patriarch's descendants will become slaves in a foreign land (Gen. 15:13-14). As Rabbi Nosson Scherman points out from the traditional perspective, "When God wills something, nature and politics alike yield to make the impossible possible." (Stone, 226)

---

37 Daniel repeats such a statement of humility when summoned to interpret a dream for King Nebuchadnezzar (Dan. 2:28). See *Kings and Commoners.*

Now that Pharaoh understands the meaning of his dream(s), he must respond. But how? No shrinking violet, Joseph offers advice:

> Accordingly, let Pharaoh find a man of discernment and wisdom, and set him over the land of Egypt. And let Pharaoh take steps to appoint overseers over the land, and organize the land of Egypt in the seven years of plenty. (41:33-34)

Where is this man of "discernment and wisdom" to be found? Has Joseph cleverly positioned himself as that man in order to again arise from prison, this time to the very heights of Egyptian power? Opinions vary. Nachmanides suggests that Joseph indeed sees an opportunity to advance himself. Nehama Leibowitz takes exception, offering Abravanel's commentary that Joseph's advice "was prompted from beginning to end by the Holy Spirit. The prophet cannot keep back his prophecy and must unburden himself." (Leibowitz/Bereshit, 446-8)

Motives aside, Joseph clearly impresses Pharaoh and his courtiers. Pharaoh asks his advisors, "Could we find another like him, a man in whom is the spirit of God?" (Gen. 41:38). He then addresses the Hebrew prisoner.

> "Since God has made all this known to you, there is none so discerning and wise as you. You shall be in charge of my court, and by your command shall all my people be directed; only with respect to the throne shall I be superior to you." (Gen. 41:39-40)

The biblical text has made clear that Joseph recognizes a power greater than himself. Pharaoh appears to do the same, although his decision may be made with practical concerns in mind. The Talmud (*Sotah* 36b) tells of the royal astrologers protesting Joseph's appointment as viceroy. "Will you set over us a slave whose master bought him for twenty pieces of silver?" Pharaoh answers "Yes," obviously placing survival above their concerns. Nehama Leibowitz comments, "Pharaoh, king of Egypt defers for the first time to the supreme King of kings." (Leibowitz/Bereshit, 442)

It is no small thing for Pharaoh to appoint a stranger—and one from nothing more than a minor family of nomadic Semites—as his second in command. But Pharaoh seems willing to recognize the limitations of his godlike status. He understands his powerlessness to change the course of nature and will rely on the sagacity and insight of Joseph, whose ability to foretell the future comes from God—whoever God may be. Pharaoh then completes Joseph's ascendance, giving him an Egyptian name, Zaphenath-paneah ("God-speaks; he lives" or "creator of life"). He also gives Joseph an Egyptian wife, Asenath, daughter of Poti-phera, priest of On.

A question arises here: who *is* Poti-phera? Rashi considers him to be none other than Potiphar, whose wife's failed seduction led Joseph to prison and ultimately to Pharaoh. (See the story of Potiphar above.) Potiphar was renamed Poti-phera, Rashi relates, after being castrated in punishment for wanting to sodomize Joseph. Rashi, however, offers no textual basis for this.

Time passes and bears out the wisdom of Pharaoh's decision to elevate Joseph above Egypt. Seven years of plentiful harvests ensue followed by drought extending well beyond Egypt's borders to "spread over the whole world" (Gen. 41:56).

The shortage of food strikes Canaan with great severity. Facing disaster, Jacob sends his sons down to Egypt where Joseph's stewardship assures plentiful grain for sale. The Joseph story then plays itself out. Joseph tests his brothers' capacity for remorse over what they did to him. Finally, he reveals himself to them and invites Jacob and the family—with Pharaoh's express permission—to settle in the region of Goshen. There, in Egypt's eastern delta, they will tend their livestock and Pharaoh's before two centuries of slavery descend upon them.

Pharaoh's story also plays itself out, concluding with his role of welcomer to the Hebrews. Like so many non-Israelites, he encounters the God of Israel and is affected by Him without embracing Israelite monotheism. Pharaoh remains free to worship the Egyptian pantheon, and we have no reason to believe that he no longer does so. But his encounter with God plays a major role in advancing God's plan for Abraham's descendants. Ultimately, we know, the Hebrews' presence in Egypt transforms both Israel and their hosts. We may also consider that perhaps, in some subtle way, the Pharaoh who knew Joseph is himself transformed.

SHIPHRAH AND PUAH

God-fearing Midwives to the Hebrews

The generation of Joseph and his brothers dies in Egypt, and a new Pharaoh arises—one who did not know Joseph. Fearing that the growing number of Hebrews will betray Egypt if an enemy attacks, he orders the midwives to the Hebrews—Shiphrah and Puah—to kill newborn Hebrew boys at birth but spare the girls. The midwives fear God and refuse, and their explanation apparently satisfies Pharaoh. God rewards Shiphrah and Puah by establishing households for them. Pharaoh then changes strategy, telling the Egyptian people that they *must slay all Hebrew boys.*

In devoting considerable attention to non-Israelites, the Bible generally makes clear just who these individuals and groups are. One notable exception stands out. The tale of the two midwives called upon by Pharaoh to kill the male newborns of the Hebrews has puzzled the Sages, medieval commentators and modern scholars alike. Are these women Hebrews or are they Egyptians? Two millennia of study and debate have yielded only uncertainty. Because considerable support for the midwives being Egyptians exists, I include them among "God's others."

The midwives' story begins some time after the deaths of Joseph and his brothers. Egypt no longer serves as a haven to the Hebrews. Indeed, it cannot if God is to bring to fruition His plan to make Abraham's descendants into a great nation in the land of Canaan. From the perspective of the biblical narrative, God's will drives the history of the Jews and the nations with which they are involved. It must continue to do so. The small Hebrew family—seventy souls initially—grows significantly larger and evolves into what will become the multitudinous people Israel. This growth is so extensive that it reaches the critical mass at which the majority views a minority in its midst as threatening rather than quaint.

While time favors the Israelites, enabling the small clan to become a populous nation within a nation, it also serves as an adversary. The Pharaoh who embraced the Hebrews dies and royal protection disappears. "A new king arose over Egypt who did not know Joseph" (Ex. 1:8). While this Pharaoh is not to be confused with his successor—the hard-hearted pharaoh with whom Moses deals—he definitely fears the Hebrews.[38] As is typical of hatred of the "other," he bears no anger against anything they have done. The biblical narrative presents no hint that Jacob's descendants betray their host nation in any way. Rather, the new Pharaoh indulges his imagination regarding what the Hebrews *might* do. Because they are not ethnic Egyptians, he questions their loyalty—an accusation that continued to afflict Jewish communities around the world for millennia. Suspecting that a fifth column may arise, Pharaoh appeals to his people's worst xenophobic tendencies:

> "Look, the Israelite people are much too numerous for us. Let us deal shrewdly with them, so that they may not increase; otherwise in the event of war they may join our enemies in fighting against us and rise from the ground." (Ex. 1:9-10)

Pharaoh suggests neither expulsion nor a pogrom. Rather, he wants to contain the Hebrew population. The Hebrews can provide a huge pool of enforced labor, known today as a corvée. And they do. The Egyptians set taskmasters over them and force them to build the garrison cities of Pithom and Raamses.

Pharaoh's construction projects progress, but the strategy fails. Hard labor proves no barrier to the hyper-fertile Hebrews. Their growing numbers reflect, in Pharaoh's mind, a growing threat. Wary, he sets a more direct population-control plan in motion.

> The King of Egypt spoke to the Hebrew midwives, one of whom was named Shiphrah and the other Puah, saying, "When you deliver the Hebrew women, look at the birthstool: if it is a boy, kill him; if it is a girl, let her live." (Ex. 1:15-16)

38 Genesis 2:23 reports that the king of Egypt—the Pharaoh involved with Shiphrah and Puah—died a long time after Moses settled in Midian.

Pharaoh's intentions are diabolical, but his scheme seems rather illogical, revealing that he is neither an economist nor a demographer. Pharaoh fears the male babies, most probably because they can grow up to become men of war and produce a redeemer. But if they are all slain, the Hebrew work force ultimately will dwindle. Allowing the newborn girls to live provides no satisfactory solution, either. Every Hebrew male who escapes death theoretically can father children with many different women—the taking of multiple wives was permissible and not uncommon. Pharaoh's plan favors ideological fervor over practicality. Thus the Midrash (Exodus Rabbah 1:14) responds with cutting humor. God scoffs at Pharaoh: "O wicked one! He who gave you this advice is an idiot. You ought rather to slay the females, for if there be no females, how will the males be able to marry?" Playing devil's advocate, Robert Alter suggests that Pharaoh may have a different outcome in mind. Eliminating the males will leave the young females to "be raised for sexual exploitation and domestic service of the Egyptians, by whom they would of course be rapidly assimilated." (Alter, 311) One way or the other, Pharaoh's plan represents pure evil.

Potential outcomes aside, why does Pharaoh demand that the midwives slay the Hebrew males *during* birth and not after? The Midrash (Exodus Rabbah 1:14) responds that Pharaoh would not expect punishment from God for murder since the children would not be fully born. This suggests that as a human being—although a god to the Egyptians—Pharaoh must have some concept of right and wrong if one not totally aligned with our own.

A second question proves more perplexing and constitutes the focus of our story. It concerns the midwives' identity. The medieval commentators Rashi, Ibn Ezra, Rashbam and Nachmanides all believe them to be Hebrews. Indeed, the JPS translation upon which this book is based offers the phrase *lamyaldot haivriot* as "Hebrew midwives." The Talmud (Sotah 11b) supports this position. It states that Shiphrah and Puah are in reality either Jochebed, Moses' mother, and Miriam, his sister, or Miriam and Elishevah, Aaron's wife. This makes the midwives not only Hebrews but members of one of Israel's most celebrated families.

Not all ancient and medieval commentators share this opinion. Philo believes the midwives to be Egyptians. So does Josephus. The nineteenth-century scholar Samuel Luzzatto cites the Septuagint and Vulgate translations of the Bible as well as Josephus and Abravanel. All maintain that the midwives are Egyptians, as do several nineteenth-century Christian scholars.

From the contemporary perspective, Nahum Sarna points out that *lamyaldot haivriot* may mean "midwives *to* the Hebrews." (Sarna/Exodus, 7) Sarna believes it strange that the Hebrews, in spite of their vast numbers, have only two midwives and suggests that their names, Shiphrah and Puah, could have been the names of two guilds of midwives. This reflects Ibn Ezra who explains that Shiphrah and Puah are actually administrators in charge of at least five hundred other midwives (Leibowitz/Shemot, 37) Everett Fox translates *lamyaldot haivriot* as "the midwives *of* the Hebrews" and acknowledges the phrase's ambiguity. Moreover, while the midwives' names seem Semitic, Fox notes, their comments about the Hebrew women in Exodus 1:19—which we will review shortly—suggest they are Egyptian. Fox also cites a statement by Abravanel that Hebrew women would not be likely to kill Hebrew babies. (Schocken, 259) Were they Hebrews, why would Pharaoh have confidence that they would carry out his orders?

So do we identify Shiphrah and Puah as Hebrews or Egyptians? Gunther Plaut offers a third, intriguing alternative from a critical perspective. They are neither. Plaut agrees with Fox that the midwives' names are of a "northwest Semitic type." But some modern scholars theorize that the term "Hebrews" represents a wider group known as Habiru or 'Apiru. Plaut explains that they were "people who had lost their status in the community to which they had originally belonged. They were not necessarily related except by common fate, and such may in part have been the case of Egyptian slavery." (Plaut, 383) If they were, indeed, Hebrews, they were not necessarily descendants of Jacob. As the story unfolds, it offers more support to those who believe the midwives to be "God's others."

Pharaoh, alas, finds the wrong henchwomen. "The midwives, fearing God, did not do as the king of Egypt had told them; they let the boys live" (Ex. 1:17).[39] In fact, the Midrash (Exodus Rabbah 1:17) states that Shiphrah and Puah did even more, collecting food and water for the poor to keep their children alive.

This leads Nehama Leibowitz to support an Egyptian identity for the midwives. When the Bible uses the phrase "fear of God" elsewhere, she states, it relates not to Jews but to gentiles. In Rabbinic times, many gentiles, known as God-fearers, attached themselves to synagogues and Jewish study without converting to Judaism. Continuing her support for Egyptian identity, Leibowitz cites Nachmanides, who states that Pharaoh did not wish his murderous policy to be made public. Even a god-king knows his limits, and Pharaoh fears the potential consequences of his acts. Hebrew midwives could easily have betrayed him. He would have deemed Egyptian midwives far more worthy of his trust. (Leibowitz/Shemot, 35-6)

A major question raises its head here. If Shiphrah and Puah are *not* Israelites, why do they fear God? Has He appeared to them in a vision or a dream? The biblical narrative makes no mention of this. But a possible answer presents itself. The midwives would have spent a great deal of time working among the Hebrews who likely told them about the God of Abraham, Isaac and Jacob. Moreover, the midwives could have arrived at a fear or awe or reverence of God on their own. Leibowitz explains that, "in the Bible, the 'fear of God' is a demand made on every person created in His image." (Leibowitz/Shemot, 35) All human beings are capable of knowing God and taking responsibility for right behavior, which hearkens back to the seven Noahide laws (see *Monotheism: Humanity's Natural Religious State*).

What is Pharaoh's response to the midwives' piety? Displeased that they ignore a royal command, he summons Shiphrah and Puah for an explanation. The midwives defend themselves eloquently.

39 *Vatirenah*, translated as "and feared," also means "and held in awe." Alan Segal, professor of religion at Barnard College, Columbia University, explains, "Someone who 'fears' God is a religious person, not a frightened person, for the Hebrew Bible." (Segal, 449) Yet fear and awe need not be separated. If we hold God in awe then we must expect to do what God requires of us and, if we fail, fear the consequences.

They cannot kill the newborn males, "Because the Hebrew women are not like the Egyptian women: they are vigorous. Before the midwife can come to them, they have given birth" (Ex. 1:19). Their language—"before *the* midwife"—lends support to Ibn Ezra's view that Shiphrah and Puah are administrators; the midwives make no mention of "we" here. Pharaoh then surprises us. He offers no reprimand let alone a threat of punishment. Pharaoh accepts their excuse and moves on. Playing devil's advocate, we might believe that his lack of response indicates that the midwives are Hebrews after all. What else could Pharaoh have expected? His plan was a long shot ultimately doomed to failure.

Yet Pharaoh remains determined. Like a football coach whose game plan proves inadequate, he calls an unexpected play. Dropping interest in the midwives, he charges the entire Egyptian people, "Every boy that is born you shall throw into the Nile, but let every girl live." (Ex. 1:22) "Every boy" suggests to the Midrash (Exodus Rabbah 1:18) that Egyptian boys might be thrown into the Nile as well. Astrologers, the Midrash tells us, informed Pharaoh that a child would redeem Israel, but not whether the child would be Israelite or Egyptian. The biblical narrative indicates that such confusion is not unwarranted. Moses is an Israelite raised as an Egyptian prince. Pharaoh's new command forces the Egyptians to police the Hebrews, and they apparently receive sufficient latitude to murder Hebrew boys at virtually any age.

What of the midwives? While Pharaoh dismisses them, the Bible offers some closure. God rewards Shiphrah and Puah. Because they feared Him, "He established households for them" (Ex. 1:21). Exactly what this means we don't know. The word *batim*, translated as households, is unclear. The Sages offer a variety of theories ranging from Shiphrah and Puah having children of their own to the negative consequence of being imprisoned. The Midrash (Exodus Rabbah 1:17) proposes the former—the households are dynasties with Shiphrah (Jochebed) becoming an ancestor of the priests (*Kohanim*) and Levites, and Puah (Miriam) becoming an ancestor of David. Samuel Luzzatto offers that the midwives had been childless and then were blessed with families. (Sarna/Exodus, 8) Rashbam supports the position that the midwives were punished. Pharaoh, he comments, placed them under house arrest to keep them from further assisting with births. (Stone, 295)

Biblical scholarship may never reveal the identity of Shiphrah and Puah with any sense of certainty. Whether Egyptian or Hebrew, however, they set an example that has been followed by some and should inspire us all. Nehama Leibowitz comments, "Crimes of humanity are more likely to be perpetrated in the names of false gods. On the other hand, whoever resists temptation and risks his life for his principles may be regarded as a worshipper of God — the true God." (Leibowitz/Shemot, 35)

Hebrew or Egyptian, Shiphrah and Puah are women of God and deserve our praise. In foiling Pharaoh's murderous plan, they provide a shining example of moral courage made even more pertinent in a post-Holocaust world in which murderous hatred abounds. "The Torah indicates how the individual can resist evil," Leibowitz asserts. "He need not shirk his moral responsibility under cover of 'superior orders.'" (Leibowitz/Shemot, 36)

Good ultimately will triumph, the Bible assures us here, and in large part thanks to Shiphrah and Puah. In spite of the Egyptians' efforts, the Hebrews continue to increase in number. Moreover, Pharaoh's own daughter saves a very special Hebrew boy, Moses, who, eighty years after he is drawn out from the Nile, will lead the Exodus from Egypt.

JETHRO, PRIEST OF MIDIAN

Counselor to Moses

Jethro, priest of Midian, invites Moses into his home after Moses protects Jethro's seven daughters and their flocks at a well. He then gives his daughter, Zipporah, to Moses as his wife. Many years later, after encountering God in a burning bush, Moses leaves for Egypt to free the Israelites. Following the Exodus, Jethro brings Zipporah and Moses' two sons to the Israelite camp in the wilderness. Moses tells Jethro all that God has done for Israel. Jethro praises God. When he sees Moses overwhelmed by his duties as Israel's judge, Jethro advises the prophet to appoint outstanding men to judge lesser cases. Moses assents, creating the organizational structure of Israelite jurisprudence. Some time after, Moses asks Jethro to stay with the Israelites and guide them through the wilderness.

Only five individuals give their names to a weekly Torah portion. Jethro, the priest of Midian, is one of them (*Yitro*—Exodus 18:1-20:23). The others are Sarah (*Chaye Sarah,* The Life of Sarah), Korach, Balak and Pinchas. In truth, such naming does not represent an honor bestowed on the subject. Rather, Torah portions receive their names from the first key word(s) not used to name any previous portion. In fact, the Sages assail three of the above individuals—Korach, an Israelite rebel; Balak, a Midianite king who seeks to have Israel cursed (see *Dissemblers and Provokers*); and Pinchas (Phinehas), Aaron's grandson who, in his zealotry, slays an Israelite man and a Midianite woman engaging in sex at the entry to the Tent of Meeting.[40]

Of the two individuals meriting praise, only one, Sarah, is a Hebrew. Jethro, a Midianite, also earns high praise. It is Jethro, rather than Moses, who may be called the father of Jewish legal administration—no small matter for a people devoted to legal procedure. Moreover, Jethro, as Moses' father-in-law, offers us much positive guidance in the way parents should treat the spouses of their children.

40 God praises Pinchas (Num. 25:11-13), but the Rabbis do not hold him in such high regard. They oppose his bypassing judicial process to serve as judge, jury and executioner.

Jethro's story cannot be separated from that of Moses. The Sages sought an early connection between them. Thus a midrash (Exodus Rabbah 1:26) tells a story widely believed to be in the Bible. It refers to Jethro serving as Pharaoh's counselor when the infant Moses is offered a choice between a crown and coals of fire. The infant's decision will determine whether or not he will overthrow Pharaoh's rule. The angel Gabriel guides Moses' hand towards the coals, and the infant is spared. The connection in the biblical text begins with a display of righteous—and violent—anger by Moses, a young Hebrew-turned-Egyptian-prince but aware of his origins. Moses sees an Egyptian beating a Hebrew slave and recognizes the injustice of the act. Responding perhaps more with his heart than his head, he strikes and kills the Egyptian. To cover up the act, he buries the corpse in the sand. Regrettably for the young prince, someone has witnessed the deed. Word reaches the palace. "When Pharaoh learned of the matter, he sought to kill Moses, but Moses fled from Pharaoh" (Ex. 2:15).

Moses arrives in the land of Midian, traditionally located on the east side of the Gulf of Eilat (Aqaba) in northwest Saudi Arabia. This would force Moses to cross the entire Sinai Peninsula, although Robert Alter suggests a shorter journey: because the Midianites were seminomads who could have drifted westward, "Moses's country of refuge would appear to be a semidesert region bordering Egypt on the east, to the west by northwest of present-day Eilat." (Alter, 315)

Wherever Midian may be, Moses comes to a well—an important biblical symbol of new beginnings and relationships between men and women. It is at a well that Abraham's servant, Eliezer, discovers Rebekah (see *The Era of Abraham*) and Jacob encounters Rachel. Not surprisingly, Moses sees the seven daughters of the priest of Midian. The young women seek to water their flock, but shepherds drive them off. Moses, not a man to tolerate injustice and tough enough to confront wrongdoers, rises to the daughters' defense. Echoing the virtue of Rebekah, he draws water for them and tends to their flock.

At this point, we have not yet met Jethro but questions abound. To begin, how dare these shepherds drive off the daughters of such a powerful person? Rashi provides one answer: Jethro previously renounced polytheism and became something of an outcast.

Another interesting question also presents itself. Is Jethro more than one person? The biblical narrative first refers to the priest of Midian as Reuel—"Friend of God" (Ex. 2:18). But he bears other names in different biblical books—Jether (Ex. 4:18), "Hobab son of Reuel the Midianite, Moses' father-in-law" (Num. 10:29) and Hobab (Judges 4:11). Rashi attributes seven names to him (in Ashkenazi pronunciation)—Reuel, Yeser (Jether), Yisro (Jethro), Keini, Chovev (Hobab), Chever and Putiel.

This multiple naming may be confusing, but the Torah offers other examples. Abraham originally is Abram and Sarah is Sarai. An angel/God changes Jacob's name to Israel. The Midrash and medieval commentators supply a variety of reasons for the multiple naming.[41] Critical scholarship suggests that multiple names reflect strands of the biblical narrative written by different authors. Nahum Sarna even suggests that *Yitro* or *Yeter* is not a proper name but an honorific title—Excellency. (Sarna/Exodus, 12) All this being noted, it is to Jethro that we will refer.

Jethro indeed seems to be someone special. In his first appearance in Exodus, he reveals an open, hospitable character perhaps comparable to Abraham's. In Genesis 18:1ff, Abraham sits at the entrance of his tent in the heat of the day, sees three men/messengers/angels approaching, runs up to them, bows and offers them water and food. This takes place on the third and most painful day following Abraham's circumcision! Jethro also offers his hospitality to a stranger.

> When they returned to their father Reuel, he said, "How is it that you have come back so soon today?" They answered, "An Egyptian rescued us from the shepherds; he even drew water for us and watered the flock." He said to his daughters, "Where is he then? Why did you leave the man? Ask him to break bread." (Ex. 2:18-20)

41 According to Exodus Rabbah 27:8, Jethro's original name was Jether, but "when he became a proselyte, a letter was added to his name, as in the case of Abraham, and he was called *Jethro.*" Nachmanides explains that Jethro took the name Hobab when he converted. On the other hand, Rashi offers that Reuel was actually Jethro's father.

Moses may be a foreigner, but Jethro appreciates his chivalrous action. Moreover, Moses' character impresses Jethro sufficiently so that he considers him a proper match for his daughter, Zipporah, who bears Moses two sons, Gershom and Eliezer. (For the story of the crucial role Zipporah plays, see *Women of Valor.*) Far from the wealth of the Egyptian court, Moses settles down to the life of a shepherd. True to the Torah's often-spare nature, we know nothing else of Moses' life in Midian.

What we do find out, and quickly, is that Moses is not destined to complete his life in Midian. After encountering God at the burning bush on Mount Horeb and receiving instructions to return to Egypt, Moses asks Jethro for permission to leave but does not tell him why. Jethro makes no effort to restrain him. Nahum Sarna points out that Moses does not reveal his real reason for returning to Egypt—to lead the Israelites to freedom—because Jethro might think the mission impossible. (Sarna/Exodus, 22) "Go in peace," Jethro responds (Ex. 4:18). Unlike Jacob's uncle, Laban, who continually seeks to maximize the economic benefits of his nephew's labor (see *Dissemblers and Provokers*), Jethro is openhearted. He demands nothing more of his son-in-law.

The Exodus narrative unfolds with the ten plagues and the Exodus from Egypt, none of which involve Jethro. After the Israelites cross the Reed Sea, the Egyptians pursue and are drowned. The Israelites flee into the Sinai. Here Jethro reappears.

> Jethro, Moses' father-in-law, brought Moses' sons and wife to him in the wilderness, where he was encamped at the mountain of God. He sent word to Moses, "I, your father-in-law Jethro, am coming to you with your wife and her two sons." Moses went out to meet his father-in-law; he bowed low and kissed him; each asked for the other's welfare, and they went into the tent." (Ex. 18:5-7)

Clearly, the two men, although from very different backgrounds, enjoy a close relationship. Neither Jethro nor Moses displays a caricatured approach to the other, offering us a valuable lesson. In spite of clichéd attitudes about in-laws, a father- or mother-in-law may have as much love and wisdom to share with us as our own parents. In fact, Jethro's position as father-in-law receives considerable attention in the narrative. Thirteen times in this portion, Everett Fox notes, Jethro is described as or referred to as Moses' father-in-law, "perhaps playing up the importance of the relationship in Israelite society." (Schocken, 354) Such a relationship may be indicated by wordplay. The Hebrew word for father-in-law is *chotain*—similar to the Hebrew for bridegroom, *chatan*. Gunther Plaut notes that bridegrooms of biblical and pre-biblical times were frequently circumcised prior to their wedding. (Plaut, 412) This may suggest that Jethro wedded himself to the Israelites through the important advice he soon offers Moses.

Of greater certainty, Moses' going out to meet his father-in-law does Jethro great honor, recognizing both his previous kindness and his status. The Midrash (Exodus Rabbah 27:2) expands on this, reporting that Aaron, Aaron's sons Nadab and Abihu (who would soon perish), seventy elders and even the Ark of the Covenant (whose construction is not commanded until Exodus 25) all accompany Moses.

This honor must be earned, and it is. In fact, Jethro plays such an important role in the first stage of Israel's forty-year sojourn in the wilderness that his meeting with Moses excludes any further mention of Zipporah and the children. Richard Friedman offers an explanation: from the biblical perspective, Moses' key relationship is with God and Israel so "that his family situation is not permitted to impinge upon it." (Friedman/Commentary, 228-29)

What brings Jethro to the wilderness in the first place? His visit certainly reflects concern for his son-in-law. Jethro relates having "heard all that God had done for Moses and for Israel His people, how the LORD had brought Israel out from Egypt" (Ex. 18:1). The Talmud (Zevachim 116a) embellishes on Jethro's motivation: Jethro heard of Israel's victory over Amalek, the crossing of the Reed Sea and the giving of the Law at Sinai. As to the last event, we may object that the Israelites' arrival at Sinai does not take place until Exodus 19:1-2—in this very same portion. The Sages, however, did not feel bound by our modern sense of chronology. In interpreting the Torah, they adopted the principle of *ein mukdam o meuchar*—there is no early or late.

Following their greeting, Moses recounts all that God has done to free Israel from Egypt. Jethro responds enthusiastically.

> And Jethro rejoiced over all the kindness that the LORD had shown Israel when He delivered them from the Egyptians. "Blessed be the LORD," Jethro said, "who delivered you from the Egyptians and from Pharaoh, and who delivered the people from under the hand of the Egyptians." (Ex. 18:9-10)

Jethro's praise of God seems entirely in keeping with his priestly role, although his words do not explicitly identify him with Israel. As to the "you" who has been delivered—it may refer only to Moses. Or it may include all of Israel. What of Jethro's reference to "the Lord" (*Adonai*)—the Hebrew letters YHVH in the text? It leaves his precise religious inclinations in doubt. Use of the name of the God of Israel, Nahum Sarna explains, is common when non-Israelites address Israelites. (Sarna/Exodus, 99) Does Jethro indicate his recognition of Moses' God or his acceptance of Him? We just don't know.

Not surprisingly, another question follows. Is Jethro a monotheist as some of the Sages claim? Doubts arise with Jethro's statement, "Now I know that the LORD [YHVH] is greater than all gods..." (Ex. 18:11) The Midianite Jethro may well have inherited a knowledge or awareness of God, but it could be blended with the polytheism adopted by most of humanity. One midrash (Exodus Rabbah 2:26-27) opts for a polytheistic identity. "The Rabbis say: Jethro attributed reality to idols, as it is said, *Now I know that the Lord is greater than all gods.*"

If Jethro has never been a monotheist, however, he now is at least a henotheist—one who acknowledges God's supremacy even if believing, or accepting others' beliefs, in multiple gods. Such henotheism does not distance Jethro from the standards set by the patriarchs. While Abraham, Isaac and Jacob do not follow other gods, they certainly tolerate others' beliefs in their existence—an attitude that changes at Sinai (see *Monotheism: Humanity's*

Natural Religious State). The appeal of polytheism creates the arc of the biblical story until the return from captivity in Babylon seven centuries after the Exodus.

What seems beyond question is that Jethro experiences a powerful historic revelation, which he feels compelled to acknowledge. His response to God's deliverance of Israel is immediate and supportive.

> And Jethro, Moses' father-in-law, brought a burnt offering and sacrifices for God; and Aaron came with all the elders of Israel to partake of the meal before God with Moses' father-in-law. (Ex. 18:12)

Nachmanides expands on this. Jethro's offerings do more than serve to acknowledge the God of Israel; they celebrate his circumcision and conversion to Judaism. (Stone, 397) While the biblical narrative makes no mention of formal conversion—some non-Israelites simply attach themselves to Israel—Jethro does receive considerable honor. The presence of Aaron and the elders legitimizes Jethro's offerings to God. Gunther Plaut states that, "when he sacrificed to Him, he resembled Melchizedek in his doing obeisance to Abram's God (Gen. 14:19)." (Plaut, 512) (Read Melchizedek's story in *The Era of Abraham*.)

Whatever his experience of God in the wilderness, Jethro plays a major role in guiding Moses in his role as chief magistrate of Israel. This is no easy task. Each day, Moses informs his father-in-law, the Israelites stand before him from morning until evening to judge all matters of complaint. Jethro, an early model for today's management consultants, immediately recognizes that Moses' workload is crushingly impractical and responds directly:

> "The thing you are doing is not right; you will surely wear yourself out, and these people as well. For the task is too heavy for you; you cannot do it alone. Now listen to me. I will give you counsel, and God be with you! You represent the people before God; you bring the disputes before God, and enjoin upon them the laws and the teachings, and make known to them the way they are

> supposed to go and the practices they are to follow. You shall also seek out from among the people capable men who fear God, trustworthy men who spurn ill-gotten gain. Set these over them as chiefs of thousands, hundreds, fifties, and tens, and let them judge the people at all times. Have them bring every major dispute to you, but let them decide every minor dispute themselves. Make it easier for yourself, and let them share the burden with you. If you do this—and God so commands you—you will be able to bear up; and all these people too will go home unwearied." (Ex. 18:17-23)

Jethro's reference to "the laws and the teachings" may, indeed, prove that his appearance in the narrative is out of chronological order since the Law has apparently been given at Sinai. But what is most important is the wisdom he imparts. Jethro, the priest of Midian, is a man of character and experience; his voice must be heard. The phrase he uses in 18:19, "now listen to me," offers a clue to just how important and worthy he is. This is a broad translation of *shema b'koli*—"listen to, or hear, my voice." It closely resembles God's words to Moses in Exodus 19:5—"*im shamoah tishmeu b'koli.*" The key is the parallel use of the Hebrew *b'koli*—in or to my voice. This suggests that Jethro is doing more than providing Moses with good advice—he may be delivering a message inspired by, or relayed from, God. Jethro's comment, "and God be with you" may be as much a blessing as a wish.

Another phrase above also deserves our attention. Jethro says, "If you do this—and God so commands you." Here, as Rashi observes, Jethro may suggest that God must second his advice for it to be valid. But perhaps Jethro implies that God has previously communicated with him about the matter and will confirm the wisdom of Jethro's counsel. The difficulties posed by translation may affect our understanding of the relationship between Jethro and God. For example, Richard Friedman translates Exodus 18:23 as, "If you'll do this thing, and YHVH will command you…" which appears close to the intention of JPS. (Friedman/Commentary, 230) Everett Fox translates the verse as, "If you do (thus in) this matter / *when* [italics mine] God commands you (further)…" (Schocken, 358) Fox's translation has Jethro assume that God will affirm his advice. Thus Jethro may serve as God's messenger.

God *does* affirm Jethro's wisdom in the Book of Numbers. The Israelites, continuing their journey in the wilderness, complain of a lack of meat and fondly remember the foods of Egypt, the land that enslaved them. Exasperated, Moses tells God that he can no longer bear such a heavy burden. He would rather die than deal with these complainers and ingrates. God instructs Moses, reinforcing the need to delegate authority.

> Then the LORD said to Moses, "Gather for Me seventy of Israel's elders of whom you have experience as elders and officers of the people, and bring them to the Tent of Meeting and let them take their place there with you. I will come down and speak with you there, and I will draw upon the spirit that is on you and put it upon them; they shall share the burden of the people with you and you shall not bear it alone. (Num. 11:16-17)

As to Jethro's advice, Moses responds unequivocally, although he does not credit Jethro's suggestion when he recounts the episode in Deuteronomy 1:9ff. "Moses heeded his father-in-law and did just as he said" (Ex. 18:24). Jethro, the non-Israelite, plays a crucial role in shaping Israel's legal system and setting the standards for those who will judge the nation. Nahum Sarna marvels at this event. "This extraordinary fact testifies to the reliability of this tradition and to its antiquity." (Sarna/Exodus, 100) It certainly appears incredible that a people so dedicated to law would reference someone from another culture as playing a major role in its judicial life. Thus Jethro's relationship with Israel is elevated far above that of any other non-Israelite. Everett Fox comments that when Jethro joins Moses in the wilderness at Sinai, "Moshe himself has come full circle, returning to both the spot and the man in whose presence the mature adult phase of his life had begun." (Schocken, 354)

One critical approach goes further, presenting Jethro not only as an adviser to Moses but also as his spiritual mentor. Lawrence Stager proposes that in Midian, Moses learns of "Yahwism," the monotheism that is to become the Israelite religion and evolve into Rabbinic Judaism. It is also in Midian—on Horeb—that Moses encounters the burning bush. And finally, it is to Midian that the Israelites return to receive the Ten Words (Commandments) and make their covenant with God. (Oxford, 142-48)

The biblical scholar H.H. Rowley brings the Moses-Jethro connection even closer, suggesting that Moses' mother, Jochebed, may have been of Midianite descent. (Plaut, 1708) This takes just a bit of explaining. Exodus 2:1 states, "A certain man of the house of Levi went and married a Levite woman." This woman bears Moses and is later identified as Jochebed. Exodus 6:20 identifies Jochebed as the sister of Amram's father; she is his aunt! Amram's father is Kohat, whose father is Levi. So Jochebed is the daughter of Levi. But we do not know who Levi's wife or wives are—Jacob's sons would have had to marry non-Hebrews. We do know that Joseph married an Egyptian and Judah fathered sons by Tamar, a Canaanite. So the possibility of Jochebed's Midianite ancestry exists but cannot be known.[42]

Granting the importance of Jethro's role, his appearance in the Bible is nonetheless fleeting. Only three verses after Moses' accepts his father-in-law's advice, "Moses bade his father-in-law farewell, and he went on his way to his own land" (Ex. 18:27). Yet Jethro reappears briefly in the Book of Numbers:

> Moses said to Hobab son of Reuel the Midianite, Moses' father-in law, "We are setting out for the place which the LORD has said, 'I will give it to you.' Come with us and we will be generous with you; for the LORD has promised to be generous to Israel." (Num. 10:29)

---

42 Some critical scholars advance the Kenite hypothesis: Jethro's closeness with the Israelites reveals a special relationship between Israel and Midian, to which the Kenite people belongs. Genesis 25:2 states that Midian is one of six sons born to Abraham by Keturah, whom he marries after Sarah's death. Judges 1:16 relates that the descendants of the Kenite, the father-in-law of Moses, went up with the Judites from the City of Palms to the wilderness of Judah; and they went and settled among the people in the Negeb of Arad. King Saul protects the Kenites when he brings an army of 210,000 men to subdue the Amalekites, the eternal enemies of Israel who assaulted the Israelites in the wilderness after the Exodus. (1 Sam. 15:6)

Since the Hebrew of the biblical text contains no punctuation, we may well puzzle over the phrase, as translated by JPS, "Hobab son of Reuel the Midianite, Moses' father-in law." Is Hobab the son of Reuel/Jethro and thus Moses' brother-in-law? Or is Hobab really Jethro, Moses' father-in-law, whose own father is Reuel? Whatever the answer, Hobab replies that he will not accompany Moses, preferring to return to his native land. Moses responds with a plea and a promise:

> "Please do not leave us, inasmuch as you know where we should camp in the wilderness and can be our guide. So if you come with us, we will extend you the same bounty that the LORD grants us." (Num. 10:31-32)

The text does not make clear whether Hobab/Jethro/Jethro's son returns to Midian. The medieval commentators suggest that he converted his children to Judaism, and *they* joined the Jewish people. Rashi states that Jethro's descendants received a large, fertile area of land near Jericho. Nachmanides offers that Jethro did accompany the Israelites to Canaan. (Stone, 400) Sforno, a sixteenth-century commentator, disagrees, believing that Jethro's children stayed with Moses while he returned to Midian. (Stone, 786) Wherever Jethro may go in his concluding years, the above verses mark the last time we read of him in the Torah.

Reviewing Jethro's presence in the Torah, we may find it difficult to determine whether or not he has an intimate knowledge of God prior to meeting Moses. Nonetheless, Jethro experiences an historic encounter with the God of Israel, Who has freed His people and led them into the wilderness—an encounter that reverberates throughout history. Just as Jethro's hospitality to Moses shields Israel's eventual lawgiver from Egyptian vengeance, his advice shapes Israelite legal administration and plays a major role in establishing Israel as a people devoted to the Law.

THE PHARAOH OF THE EXODUS

Hard-hearted Icon of Evil

A new Pharaoh arises. He does not seek the death of Moses but continues to enslave the Israelites. Moses and Aaron return to Egypt to show Pharaoh a sign from God that Israel be released. Aaron casts down his staff, which turns into a serpent. Pharaoh's magicians do the same, and the haughty Pharaoh remains unimpressed. A series of ten plagues afflicts Egypt. Pharaoh refuses to relent. He hardens his heart after each of the first five plagues, even after his magicians acknowledge God's power as superior. Following the sixth plague, God hardens Pharaoh's heart. After the seventh, Pharaoh again hardens his own heart but fails to learn. Three more plagues follow, culminating in the death of the Egyptian first-born males—both humans and cattle. Pharaoh releases the Israelites only to pursue them with his army and reach his doomed end.

If there is a poster boy for the failure to recognize historic revelation, it is the Pharaoh who refuses God's repeated commands to let enslaved Israel go. This successor to the Egyptian ruler who ordered the deaths of the Hebrews' first-born males (see the story of the midwives, Shiphrah and Puah, above) would seem a caricature if the world had not continually suffered the horrific evil of conscienceless tyrants from ancient days to our own. As so often happens, the oppressor ultimately brings disaster upon his own head and those of his people.

The seeds of the Exodus and the wonders with which God punishes Pharaoh take root when Moses discovers the burning bush atop Mount Horeb (Sinai). God instructs Moses to go to Pharaoh and "free My people, the Israelites, from Egypt" (Ex. 3:10). Moses objects. He is not qualified, he responds; he has no way with words. God, not about to be dissuaded, lays out a simple plan. He will speak to Moses, Moses will speak to his brother, Aaron, and Aaron will serve as their communications link to Pharaoh. God then brings up a small complication. While Pharaoh will hear His words through Moses and Aaron, they will not prove sufficient.

> "Yet I know that the king of Egypt will let you go only because of a greater might. So I will stretch out My hand and smite Egypt with various wonders which I will work upon them; after that he shall let you go." (Ex. 3:19-20)

Unlike Abraham, who responds without hesitation to God's command to "Go forth from your native land" (Gen. 12:1), Moses continues to balk. He protests that the Israelites will not believe him; they will refuse to follow him. God remains adamant. Merely hinting at the power He will unleash against Egypt, He instructs Moses to cast his rod on the ground. Moses does so. The rod turns into a snake. God tells Moses to grasp the snake by the tail. Moses obeys, and the snake becomes a rod again. Nonetheless, God senses that Moses has not yet been convinced—a foreshadowing of Pharaoh's pessimism. So God encrusts Moses' hand with snowy scales then returns the flesh to normal. These, God instructs, will serve as powerful signs to the elders of Israel. However, if these wonders fail to sway the elders and then Pharaoh, Moses shall perform a third and turn water into blood.

God makes a powerful case. How can He not? Yet Moses' reaction is typical of that among prophets. He still begs off. But a person chosen for prophecy has no alternative. Moses finally assents. Then he turns to everyday matters, securing permission to leave from his father-in-law, Jethro. Taking his wife and sons along, Moses sets off to meet his brother, Aaron, who journeys towards him from Egypt. (For the intriguing story of God's threat to slay Moses on his journey and the heroism of his wife, Zipporah, see *Women of Valor*.)

Moses has his work cut out for him.

> And the LORD said to Moses, "When you return to Egypt, see that you perform before Pharaoh all the marvels that I have put within your power. I, however, will stiffen his heart so that he will not let the people go." (Ex. 4:21)

God has bigger things in mind than providing Pharaoh with a wake-up call. Accordingly, the first meeting goes badly. Moses and

Aaron dutifully relay God's instruction to "Let My people go that they may celebrate a festival for Me in the wilderness" (Ex. 5:1). But they withhold the signs and wonders given to them. Pharaoh responds with disdain: "Who is the LORD that I should heed Him and let Israel go? I do not know the LORD, nor will I let Israel go" (Ex. 5:2).

Pharaoh's statement that he does not know the Lord, according to Everett Fox, is another way of saying that "I care not a whit" for Him. (Schocken, 281) Pharaoh is a god to Egypt, and Egypt is a great civilization.[43] And who are the Hebrews but slaves? At best, their God is one of many and certainly no more powerful than Pharaoh. Moreover, the Hebrews' God is on Pharaoh's turf. Thus Nehama Leibowitz calls Pharaoh's denial of God "tantamount to a declaration of war." (Leibowitz/Shemot, 93) And "war" Pharaoh will get. Egypt and the rest of the world have long abandoned the One God. Now, God will make Himself known through drastic measures that will remove all doubts from among the nations.

His pride wounded, Pharaoh orders the taskmasters and foremen over the Hebrews to make their labor even harder. The Hebrews now must gather their own straw while maintaining their brick production levels. Facing an impossible task, the Israelite foremen castigate Moses and Aaron. Pharaoh seems to have gained the upper hand. Resolute, God again makes His intentions clear. "You shall see what I will do to Pharaoh: he shall let them go because of a greater might; indeed, because of a greater might he shall drive them from his land" (Ex. 6:1).

God will humble both Pharaoh and Egypt's false religion, He tells Moses. "See, I place you in the role of God to Pharaoh, with your brother Aaron as your prophet" (Ex. 7:1). The "god" of Egypt will yield to a human "god"—one who makes no claim to divinity but serves as the prophet of the God of Israel. God's concerns extend beyond Pharaoh, however. The people of Egypt themselves must see Pharaoh not only let Israel go but drive them out—and they must

43 The Midrash (Exodus Rabbah, 8:2) identifies Pharaoh as one of four men who claimed divinity and thereby brought evil on themselves. The others were Hiram, Prince of Tyre; Nebuchadnezzar, King of Babylon; and Joash, King of Judah.

understand why. God informs Moses that, "I will harden Pharaoh's heart, that I may multiply My signs and marvels in the land of Egypt" (Ex. 7:3).

Prepared, if somewhat pessimistic, Moses and Aaron return to Pharaoh. Following a well-planned script, Aaron casts his staff down. It turns into a serpent. Pharaoh's magicians, schooled in the occult arts, do the same. Nachmanides explains the power of such magic: God leaves earthly laws to the regulation of angels and other forces, which can be influenced by various incantations. Thus Pharaoh's magicians can perform astounding tricks although not compete with God. (Stone, 325) Not to be bested, God demonstrates His superiority. Aaron's serpent swallows the others, calling to mind the dream of Joseph's Pharaoh in which seven lean cows swallow seven fat ones and seven thin ears of corn swallow seven robust ones.

Moses and Aaron have presented an impressive sign. "Yet Pharaoh's heart stiffened and he did not heed them, as the Lord had said" (Ex. 7:13). To a morally corrupt leader, what message can a single wonder seemingly rooted in magic really communicate?

God raises the stakes with the first plague—the Nile's water turns to blood. Pharaoh remains unmoved. His magicians, as we know, possess considerable skills and perform the same feat. A second plague brings frogs out of the Nile to cover the land. Not to be outdone, Pharaoh's magicians duplicate this feat with their own spells—but with a telling weakness. The magicians cannot make the frogs go away. Pharaoh yields a bit and summons Moses and Aaron. "Plead with the Lord to remove the frogs from me and my people, and I will let the people go sacrifice to the Lord" (Ex. 8:4).

With liberation appearing to be at hand, Moses asks God to remove the frogs. And so He does. No longer under pressure, Pharaoh again becomes stubborn. As the Midrash (Exodus Rabbah 10:6) notes of the wicked, "When they are in trouble they cry, but when they have respite, they return to perversity." This necessitates a third plague. Aaron strikes the ground with his rod and the dust of the earth turns into lice all across Egypt. Eyes begin to open in Pharaoh's court.

> The magicians did the like with their spells to produce lice, but they could not. The vermin remained upon man and beast; and the magicians said to Pharaoh, "This is the finger of God!" But Pharaoh's heart stiffened and he would not heed them as the Lord had spoken." (Ex. 8:14)

The magicians recognize God's power, although they offer no evidence of turning away from their own gods towards Hebrew monotheism.

Some commentators, however, see the magicians minimizing the wonder of the plague of lice since they refer to the *finger* of God rather than to the *hand* of God, the usual reference in both Egyptian and Hebrew literature. Let us propose that this may be taken the other way. Such a feat may represent only a fraction of God's power. If God raises His whole hand, the results will be cataclysmic. Moreover, the finger of God is mentioned twice in connection with God's writing the Law on the tablets He presents to Moses (Exodus 31:18 and Deuteronomy 9:10). The Law is a powerful expression of God and not to be taken lightly. The Christian Bible (Luke 11:20) also supports the power of God's finger. Jesus states, "But if it is by the finger of God that (I) drive out demons, then the kingdom of God has come upon you." Surely God's finger contains more power than the hand of any supposed god. Pharaoh's heart is another matter. It again stiffens, continuing to reflect the shriveled nature of his soul.

A fourth plague, *arov*—translated by JPS as insects, by others as wild beasts and by Robert Alter as "the horde"—follows. And again Pharaoh's heart stiffens. He discovers, however, that in a contest of wills, God is not about to yield ground. Thus God tells Moses:

> "Go to Pharaoh and say to him, 'Thus says the Lord, the God of the Hebrews: Let My people go to worship me. For if you refuse to let them go, and continue to hold them, then the hand of the Lord will strike your livestock in the fields—the horses, the asses, the camels, the cattle, and the sheep—with a very severe pestilence.'" (Ex. 9:1-3)

God's word is true. The Egyptian livestock die from pestilence—the fifth plague. Yet "Pharaoh remained stubborn, and he would not let the people go" (Ex. 9:7). Pharaoh still cannot see past his own "godly" self. As a result, the Egyptians and the beasts of their fields suffer from a sixth plague—boils. Pharaoh's magicians, likewise afflicted, cannot find a cure. If this is merely the finger of God, woe unto them when God flexes his arm, which He soon will do.

The momentum of the story increases. Pharaoh and Egypt have reached the point of no return. God now stiffens Pharaoh's heart. Pharaoh and Egypt will have no choice but to recognize Him. Moses relates:

> "For this time I will send all My plagues upon your person, and your courtiers, and your people, in order that you may know there is none like Me in all the world." (Ex. 9:14)

Moses and Aaron warn of hail. This seventh plague threatens a major catastrophe such as the Egyptians have never seen. But the brothers also relay a life-affirming message from God:

> Therefore, order your livestock and everything you have in the open brought under shelter; every man and beast that is found outside, not having been brought indoors, shall perish when the hail comes down upon them!" (Ex. 9:19)

The warning yields mixed results.

> Those among Pharaoh's courtiers who feared the LORD's word brought their slaves and livestock indoors to safety; but those who paid no regard to the word of the LORD left their slaves and livestock in the open. (Ex. 9:20-21)

As foretold, the people and beasts left exposed die. All the Israelites and their cattle live.

Finally, Pharaoh appears to yield. He admits that, "I stand guilty this time. The LORD is in the right, and I and my people are in the wrong" (Ex. 9:27). He pleads with Moses to end "God's thunder" and hail—seemingly a direct acknowledgement of God's power. But Pharaoh's words are not heartfelt. His stubbornness resumes. He and his courtiers revert to their guilty ways. Yet again, Pharaoh refuses to let the Israelites go. Pharaoh will not acknowledge the multi-stage, historic revelation he has received in the form of seven plagues—blood, frogs, lice, insects, pestilence, boils and hail. He refuses to retreat. In turn, God will not relent. The matter must be played out to its logical and terrible conclusion.

Aaron now relays God's crucial question: "How long will you refuse to humble yourself before Me?" (Ex. 10:3). At this point, an issue troubling all readers and hearers of this story must be addressed. Does Pharaoh refuse to humble himself before God because he *will* not let Israel go? Or is it that he *cannot*? Why does God stiffen Pharaoh's heart and seemingly eradicate his free will when the exercise of free will—as complicated as this concept is—constitutes a major principle of Judaism?

Let us consider Pharaoh's responses to God's admonitions and wonders in the context of the story. Following each of the first five plagues, concluding with pestilence, *Pharaoh stiffens his own heart.* He indeed exercises free will by refusing to let the Hebrews go. Each time God responds by punishing him. Pharaoh simply doesn't get it! Only after the *sixth* plague—boils—does God stiffen Pharaoh's heart. Yet even after Moses stops the seventh plague—hail—God gives Pharaoh an opportunity to repent of his own free will. Pharaoh refuses.

> But when Pharaoh saw that the rain and the hail and the thunder had ceased, he became stubborn and reverted to his guilty ways, as did his courtiers. So Pharaoh's heart stiffened and he would not let the Israelites go, just as the Lord had foretold through Moses. (Ex. 9:34-35)

Pharaoh's own choices doom him. Each succeeding refusal to heed God pushes him further down the slippery slope until he is no longer capable of reversing his momentum. Commentators both ancient and modern observe that some individuals are so evil that they cannot repent and change their ways. In such cases, God may speed these individuals on their destructive paths in order to advance His designs. Thus the Midrash (Exodus Rabbah 13:3) quotes Shimon Resh Lakish: "When God warns someone once, twice and even a third time and that person does not repent, then and only then does God close his heart against repentance so that He should exact vengeance from him for his sins."

Numerous commentaries address the subject of free will, and while the subject is too broad to be considered here, it is worth spending a brief moment with several. Maimonides writes of Pharaoh in his introduction to *Avot* that, "He sinned, first of his own free will…until he forfeited the opportunity to repent." (Leibowitz/Shemot, 155) Sforno declares that if Pharaoh had repented sincerely any time after the first five plagues, his repentance would have been accepted, and he would have suffered no more. (Stone, 324) Nehama Leibowitz explains that once a person makes the first wrong choice, the balance between choosing good or evil is thrown off. "The more he sins, the more his sins act as a barrier between him and repentance." (Leibowitz/Shemot, 157)

Perhaps the most eloquent comment on the perils of taking that first and then subsequent steps down the "slippery slope" is found in Proverbs 2:12-15. Such a descent involves speaking of duplicity, leaving the paths of rectitude, rejoicing in doing evil and exulting in the duplicity of evil men, and finally, following evil men whose paths are crooked and devious. Each wrong step in the progression makes turning back more difficult until repentance becomes impossible.

As regards Pharaoh's choices, Richard Friedman takes compulsion out of the equation altogether. He translates the Hebrew as "God *strengthened* Pharaoh's heart" rather than hardened or, as in JPS, stiffened. Thus "God does not *change* the king's heart, but only gives the Pharaoh strength to follow his own resolve." (Friedman/Commentary, 585) God can impel but not compel. Thus Pharaoh has been free to choose wrongly all the time—and has done so. As Nahum Sarna writes, "his character has become his destiny." (Sarna/Exodus, 23)

Let us give dissenters their opportunity as well. Gunther Plaut comments that, "…all explanations attempting to 'absolve' God will remain forced." The main theme of Exodus is "to praise the absolute power and unsurpassable glory of God." Regardless of Pharaoh's intentions, this theme must be moved forward because, "all history stands ultimately under God's will and all men can move only within the framework of His design." (Plaut, 417) Robert Alter offers some agreement: Pharaoh hardening his own heart and God hardening it "may amount to the same thing" because "God is presumed to be the ultimate cause of human actions." (Alter, 360)

In this regard, it is worth noting that Pharaoh's is not the only heart God hardens or strengthens. Moses, at the beginning of his long speech that encompasses Deuteronomy, reminds the Israelites of their triumph against the Amorites on the east side of the Jordan. Two Amorite kings refused them safe passage into Canaan and paid the price.

> "But King Sihon of Heshbon refused to let us pass through, because the LORD had stiffened his will and hardened his heart in order to deliver him into your power as is now the case." (Deut. 2:30)

In the Book of Joshua, God again ensures the destruction of Israel's enemies. Following Moses' death and the Israelites' crossing the Jordan into Canaan, He stiffens the hearts of the Canaanite kings so that they do battle with Israel only to be defeated and utterly wiped out. The God of History has His purposes.

Now, as the narrative of Exodus approaches its climax, Pharaoh stands seemingly alone. When Moses and Aaron threaten Egypt with an eighth plague—locusts—Pharaoh's courtiers wave the white flag. They ask, "How long shall this one [Moses] be a snare to us? Let the men go to worship the LORD their God. Are you not yet aware that Egypt is lost?" (Ex. 10:7).

When Moses and Aaron return, Pharaoh yields—but only to a degree. He insists that only the Hebrew men may go into the wilderness. The women and children must stay behind. Here, what Pharaoh does *not* say delivers an important a message—the women and children will serve as perfect hostages. He then expels Moses and Aaron from his presence, a sure sign that the matter remains unsettled.

The locusts arrive according to God's word and strip Egypt of the little greenery left by the hail. Pharaoh hurriedly summons Moses and Aaron to make a second confession: "I stand guilty before the LORD your God and before you" (Ex. 10:16). These words come too late. God stiffens Pharaoh's heart again.

A ninth plague ensues, and God reveals his power on an entirely new level. For three days, a heavy, almost palpable, darkness falls over Egypt while the Israelites in Goshen continue to enjoy light. So fog-like was the darkness, Nachmanides comments, that it even extinguished the Egyptians' lamps. (Stone, 345) Rashi offers that a second three days followed during which the darkness was so thick that the Egyptians could not even move. That the darkness lasts for three days, Richard Friedman adds, dismisses any thought of Pharaoh's that a natural phenomenon, such as an eclipse, has taken place. (Friedman/Commentary, 203) Moreover, the darkness sends another powerful symbolic message to Egypt, according to Nahum Sarna. The sun, Egypt's supreme god, has been vanquished. (Sarna/Exodus, 51)

Faced with overwhelming disaster, Pharaoh relents. Again, however, he limits the terms of the Israelites' journey to the wilderness. This time, he says, all the people may go but not the cattle. Moses counters that the cattle are necessary and, moreover, Pharaoh is to supply animals for sacrifices and burnt offerings. Egypt must pay a penalty. Not surprisingly, the two leaders fail to reach an agreement. Also not surprisingly, God stiffens Pharaoh's heart. One more event must take place to free the Israelites, eliminate their doubts as their redemption takes place, and complete God's revelation to Egypt and the nations.

Before Moses' return to Egypt, God had told him to relate to Pharaoh that Israel was God's own "first-born." Pharaoh's refusal to free the Israelites would result in the slaying of Pharaoh's own first-born. (Ex. 4:22-3) The narrative moves to its ultimate conclusion. A tenth plague strikes. On the night of the first Passover, God slays the first-born males of the Egyptians—the very people who once sought to slay the Hebrews' male newborns. God also slays the firstborn males of Egypt's cattle. The results devastate Egypt.

> "And Pharaoh rose in the night, with all his courtiers and all the Egyptians—because there was a loud cry in Egypt; for there was no house where there was not someone dead." (Ex. 12:30)

Pharaoh's obstinate, stone-like heart has spurred ten plagues—an awesome historic revelation to which Psalms 78:49 aptly refers as "a band of deadly messengers."

Pharaoh can resist no longer. He summons Moses and decrees that all of the Israelites—and all their flocks and herds—are to go into the wilderness to worship the Lord. Then he cries out, having lost his oldest son and so much of the wealth and power of his kingdom, "And may you bring a blessing on me also!" (Ex. 12:32)

The Israelites leave Egypt the next day. True to God's earlier "prediction" to Moses (Ex. 3:21-2), the Egyptians not only urge the Israelites to leave, they press their valuables on them. Of course, Moses has more in mind than offering sacrifices to God for three days then returning the Israelites to bondage. Pharaoh picks up on this quite readily. So a final scene must be played out to conclude the tragedy. God tells Moses that He will stiffen Pharaoh's heart one last time, and so it happens. As the Talmud (Eruvin 19a) states, the wicked fail to repent even when standing on the threshold of Gehinnom—the netherworld.

Unrepentant to the last, Pharaoh leads his chariots, horsemen and soldiers in pursuit of the Israelites. At the Reed Sea, the angel of God blocks their way with a cloud of darkness, which casts a spell of night on the Egyptians. Three times the image of night and death has appeared—in the ninth plague of darkness, during the night when the tenth plague—the slaying of the Egyptian first-born—takes place, and again before the Egyptians face disaster at the Reed Sea. Moses holds his arm out over the sea, and the Israelites cross on dry land between walls of water. The Egyptians, committed to a course of reckless action, follow in the morning. The light of the new day witnesses their destruction. God slows the Egyptians to a crawl, throwing them into a panic and then locking the wheels of their chariots so that they are mired in the seabed.

Now God's purpose begins to be realized. The Egyptians acknowledge God's might, crying out, "Let us flee from the Israelites, for the LORD is fighting for them against Egypt." (Ex. 14:25) Too late! The waters of the sea rush down upon Egypt's army so that "not one of them remained" (Ex. 14:28). The Egyptian dead wash up on the shore. Here we find proof of the saying that what goes around comes around. The Egyptians, who sought to drown the Israelites' helpless first-born in the Nile, suffer the drowning of their powerful military men.

The tenth plague and the disaster at the Reed Sea may provide Egypt with its comeuppance, but these events trouble readers of the Bible. Why did matters have to come this far? The Egyptians' ultimate recognition of God's might is at stake here, but there is more. The great modern Orthodox rabbi Moshe Feinstein echoes Rashi that the Israelites themselves had to see that the Egyptians had been punished with death or the miracle of the parting of the sea would have been to no purpose. The righteous had to be saved and the wicked punished simultaneously. (Stone, 375)

God previously said He would send a message to the nations, and so He has. The parting of the sea makes His power known beyond Egypt and Israel. The biblical narrative informs us that Jethro, Moses' father-in-law, heard of the miraculous Exodus from Egypt. (See more on Jethro above.) In the Book of Joshua, Rahab, the harlot who hides Joshua's spies before the Israelites overrun Jericho, tells them that the entire city lies in dread having heard what God did to the Egyptians (see *Women of Valor*). Folk wisdom informs us that sometimes the only way to get the attention of a stubborn mule is to hit it over the head with a two-by-four. The destruction of Egypt's army at the Reed Sea cannot help but attract a doubting world's attention.

While Pharaoh appears to have met a violent and inevitable end, legends suggest other outcomes. One has it that Pharaoh learns his lesson and survives to become the king of Nineveh—the very king who repents when Jonah brings God's decree of destruction to the city. Upon his death, the legend relates, Pharaoh is stationed at the gates of the underworld to ask tyrants why they had not learned from his example. (Etz Hayim, 404) The Quran also presents a repentant Pharaoh: "But as he was drowning, Pharaoh cried: 'Now I believe that there is no God save the God in whom the Israelites believe. To Him I give up myself.'" (Sura 10:90ff)

What then can we make of Pharaoh's encounter with God? Perhaps we must first ask, why does the human heart act as perversely as it does? What blinds a human being to an obvious, observable truth? Pharaoh experiences a powerful and profound encounter, but his pride serves as a deadly counterweight. For Pharaoh, his court and all of the Egyptians whose practices—rather than persons—the Bible scorns, the failure to recognize the limits of human power can only be self-destructive.

Let us not, however, end this story without recognizing that while justice is served, it causes great pain not only to many readers ancient and modern but to God as well. The Talmud (Megillah 10b, Sanhedrin 39b) echoes Ezekiel 18:32 that God does not rejoice at the death of sinners. The angels, witnessing the Egyptians' destruction, want to sing. God silences them. "The work of My hands is drowning in the sea, and you desire to sing songs!" Truly, God displays love for all of His creatures no matter what the nature of their encounter with Him.

5

Dissemblers and Provokers

"The children gather sticks, the fathers build the fire,
and the mothers knead dough, to make cakes for the
Queen of Heaven, and they pour libations to other gods,
to vex Me. Is it Me they are vexing?—says the Lord.
It is rather themselves, to their own disgrace.
Jeremiah 7:22

Encountering God, whether directly or historically, constitutes a powerful experience that can change the course of a life—or of many lives. How can anyone, whatever his or her background or origin, see God or witness His power and fail to accept monotheism as well as live according to God's teachings? And yet the human heart is as capable of bad as of good, as prone to willful—and self-destructive—disobedience as to righteousness. Some human beings remain oblivious to reality even when it grabs them by the throat and shakes them violently. Others recognize what they have experienced, pause to catch their breath and then blithely ignore what has just happened to them. They continue down the same path, their eyes cast downwards, their souls shut off from the possibilities open to them.

Thus it hardly surprises us that some non-Israelites in the Bible encounter God and experience His power yet fail to embrace Him. Laban, brother of the matriarch Rebekah, and Balaam, an acknowledged prophet of the Gentiles, come into direct contact with God. (We examined a third dissembler and provoker, the Pharaoh of the Exodus, in *Egypt: Slavery and Redemption*.) However, they only pay lip service to God in order to ingratiate themselves with others from whom they may extract something of value. These two dissemblers and provokers may wish to placate God but only because they fear Him. To them, the God of Israel is no more than one of many powerful gods, all demanding human attention, and all threatening great harm if deprived of it. Laban and Balaam, who most certainly have Israelite counterparts, focus on their own selfish ends. They should know better—and perhaps they do—but the *yetzer hara*, the bad inclination, dominates them.

It is important to note that what separates these two dissemblers and provokers from other non-Israelites who encounter God is not their failure to accept the covenant God makes with Abraham or the one He makes with Moses and the Israelite nation at Sinai. As non-Israelites, they need only adhere to the seven Noahide laws easily within their grasp. (See *Monotheism: Humanity's Natural Religious State*.) Regrettably, their greedy or callous natures overwhelm their experience of God. As human beings free to choose, they cannot overcome their spiritual blindness to see what God ultimately demands of each of us: "Love your fellow as yourself" (Lev. 19:18).

LABAN, UNCLE OF JACOB

Portrait of Avarice

Eliezer, servant of Abraham, journeys to Aram-Naharaim (also known as Haran) to find a wife for Isaac from among Abraham's family. Recognizing Rebekah as the right woman, he gives her gifts of gold. Rebekah's brother, Laban, responds enthusiastically to the wealth Eliezer brings and represents. Laban even invokes God's name, although he is a polytheist with household gods. Rebekah goes with Eliezer to Canaan, but the initial portrait of Laban—particularly as interpreted by the Sages—is one of greed. We next meet Laban when Jacob flees the wrath of his brother, Esau, and journeys to Haran. Jacob falls in love with Rachel, the younger of his uncle Laban's two daughters. But Laban tricks Jacob into first marrying the elder, Leah. Laban keeps his nephew in his employ for twenty years to earn the daughters and build a household. Jacob, in turn, tricks Laban by using magical means to breed speckled and dark sheep and goats—unwanted by Laban and yet very hardy. Now wealthy and determined to return to Canaan and Isaac, Jacob leaves with his household. God comes to Laban in a dream and warns him to do nothing, either good or bad. Laban and his men catch up with Joseph. The incensed Laban searches for his household gods, removed and hidden by Rachel. Unable to find them or place blame on Jacob, who makes his own accusations, Laban makes a peace agreement with his son-in-law, then kisses his daughters and grandchildren goodbye.

The Christian Bible (1 Timothy 6:10) proposes that, "the love of money is the root of all evil." Many people misquote this verse, believing money itself to be evil. But it is greed—the *love* of money—that Timothy condemns. This excellent, if misunderstood, adage finds its antecedent in the Hebrew Bible. In Leviticus 19:35-36, God instructs the Israelites to measure and weigh goods for sale with complete accuracy—a command repeated in Deuteronomy and mentioned in Micah and Proverbs. The subtext is clear. We are free to engage in the business and commerce of this world and profit from our efforts—but we must do so honestly, even if that limits our profits. Yielding to greed violates God's Law because it leads to ignoring the sanctity of our fellow human beings. In harming others, we diminish ourselves.

To find such a portrait of greed, we need cast our gaze no further than Laban, the great-nephew of Abraham. The relationship may startle us. How can the first patriarch be part of a family containing such a conniving individual? But then, what family doesn't include a black sheep or two? That two relatives can be poles apart spiritually and morally reinforces our understanding that righteousness is not a genetic trait, and that the biblical text is very much rooted in the reality of the human condition.

Laban's story spans all three generations of the patriarchs and includes a direct encounter with God. We first meet him when Abraham sends his senior servant, Eliezer, to Abraham's family in Aram-Naharaim (known also as Haran) in search of a bride for Isaac. (See *The Era of Abraham.*) Eliezer stops at a well and sees Rebekah—"very beautiful, a virgin whom no man had known" (Gen. 24:16). After she provides water both to him and his ten camels, Eliezer returns her kindness with a gold nose ring and two gold bands for her arms. Impressed and excited by such largesse, Rebekah runs off to tell her household, which includes her brother, Laban. His response reveals much about his personality.

> Laban ran out to the man at the spring—when he saw the nose-ring and the bands on his sister's arms, and when he heard his sister Rebekah say, "Thus the man spoke to me." (Gen. 24:29-30)

This servant indeed brings wealth with him, and once Laban has seen it for himself, he is drawn to it like the proverbial moth to a flame. If Rebekah has been given such presents, what valuables will come to *him*? And how much more if he acts cunningly? Rashi comments that Laban understood at once that Eliezer's master was rich "and made plans to get at his money." His view reflects that of the Sages who note that Genesis 25:20 refers to Laban the Aramean. They transpose the Hebrew *aram* into *ramai* and label him Laban "the cheat." (Bialik, 43:52)

Laban demonstrates the cunning of a truly smooth operator. Unlike the courtesy shown by Abraham to the three men who suddenly appear following his circumcision (Genesis 18)—Abraham has no idea who they are—Laban fawns over Eliezer and urges him to stay in the family's home: "'Come in, O blessed of the LORD,' he said, 'why do you remain outside, when I have made ready the house and a place for the camels?'" (Gen 24:31).

Laban's words mislead, says Rashi, citing the Midrash (B'reishit Rabah 60:7). He has made the house ready or "cleaned" it meaning only that he has removed the idols from it. We may ask: how does Laban know the servant comes from Abraham, the monotheist? Rebekah may have overheard Eliezer when he blessed the God of his master, but this is conjecture. Eliezer does not yet reveal himself. The real question of the moment lies elsewhere.

Laban uses God's name, YHVH, acknowledging the God of Abraham. Is Laban in some way a fellow believer? We have no evidence that he has had a previous encounter with God. Most likely, he repeats what Rebekah has reported to him since she stands next to Eliezer when, having found the woman he has sought, he bows in homage and says, "Blessed be the LORD, the God of my master Abraham, who has not withheld His steadfast faithfulness from my master" (Gen. 24:27). Laban, we shall see, is a polytheist complete with household gods—but one quite willing to ingratiate himself with a guest. The German-Jewish scholar Benno Jacob (1862-1955) terms Laban, "A selfish, greedy, exploiting, suspicious man of wealth, who never fails to observe good manners." (Plaut, 207)

Eliezer then tells Laban and Bethuel—Laban and Rebekah's father—of his meeting Rebekah, not knowing that Rebekah has told them as well.[44] The servant concludes by asking whether they will permit him to bring Rebekah back to Isaac.

---

44 David Hoffman states that Laban must be the only or oldest son of the family in order to exercise such profound influence in Rebekah's life. (Stone, 114)

> Then Laban and Bethuel answered, "The matter was decreed by the LORD; we cannot speak to you bad or good. Here is Rebekah before you; take her and go, and let her be a wife to your master's son, as the LORD has spoken." (Gen. 24:50-51)

Again, Laban refers to YHVH, this time joined by his father. Does he genuinely respect the God of Abraham? The Sages are not inclined to think so. Everett Fox, from a modern viewpoint, offers a henotheistic dissent, noting that, "The family apparently worships the God of Avraham in addition to others." (Schocken, 105) It is possible that Laban and Bethuel have had some previous knowledge of God—perhaps but not necessarily through Abraham—but not accepted monotheism. More likely, Laban is bedazzled by Abraham's great wealth and desires to maintain ties with him. After all, Eliezer has arrived with ten camels and gifts for the family—jewelry for Rebekah and fruits for the rest.

When Eliezer asks his leave, however, Laban and his mother, who is never named, protest. "Let the maiden remain with us some ten days; then you may go" (Gen. 24:55). The ten days referred to by the family often is interpreted as ten months or a year, a period offered by the Talmud (Ketubot 57b) as sufficient for a young bride to prepare to leave her family. It would be natural to delay Rebekah's leave-taking since her family understands—long-distance travel being arduous and impractical in that era—that they are not likely to see her again. Rebekah, for her part, requires no delay. She assents to leave immediately. In response, Laban and their mother—Bethuel seems to have no role here—bless her.

> "O sister!
> May you grow
> Into thousands of myriads;
> May your offspring seize
> The gates of their foes. (Gen. 24:60)

Their blessing evokes God's blessing of Abraham on Mount Mariah after he desists from sacrificing Isaac.

> "I will bestow my blessing upon you and make your descendants as numerous as the stars of heaven and the sands of the seashore; and your descendants shall seize the gates of their foes." (Gen. 22:17)

Again, we are prompted to ask whether Rebekah's family worships the One God. Again, the Sages say no. In the Midrash (Gen. Rabbah 60:13), Rabbi Berekiah and Rabbi Levi offer the opinion that Rebekah remains barren for twenty years after marrying Isaac so that the heathens might not say that Laban and their mother's prayers were answered. Only when Isaac prays to God does Rebekah conceive.

Blessed and determined, Rebekah, accompanied by her nurse, mounts a camel and rides off with Eliezer. Like Abraham, she is ready to leave all that she knows to fulfill a special mission—one that ironically will bring her son, Jacob, back to Laban.

Genesis now focuses on Rebekah and Isaac. Although Abraham will live for another thirty-five years, he has passed the torch of monotheism to the next generation. Following decades of barrenness—echoing Sarah's inability to conceive—Rebekah gives birth to twins who are anything but identical. The elder, Esau, is hairy and ruddy. He becomes a hunter and man of the field—and Isaac's favorite. Jacob is smooth-skinned, a stay-at-home (and student of Torah, according to the Sages)—the favorite of his mother. Jacob, however, must bear his destiny to carry on his father and grandfather's monotheistic example. Yet Jacob is no angel. He tricks Esau—a seemingly good-hearted but spiritually limited man—into selling his birthright for a bowl of lentil stew. Then he steals Isaac's "innermost" patriarchal blessing from Esau through a plot devised by none other than Rebekah. Esau responds with pain and fury. (Esau may not "get it" regarding the patriarchal family's monotheistic mission, but the reader need not be unsympathetic to this simple, straightforward man.)

Justifiably fearing that Esau will murder his brother, Rebekah instructs Jacob to flee. Under the guise of seeking a non-Canaanite wife for him—as Abraham and Sarah did for Isaac—she sends Jacob in the footsteps of Eliezer to the only place where she can assure herself of his safety and a suitable bride—the home of her brother, Laban.

Following a long and spiritually challenging journey, Jacob meets Rachel by a well. Having duplicated Eliezer's journey, he repeats the senior servant's experience by finding Rebekah—and foreshadowing Moses' meeting Zipporah in Exodus 2.

Laban responds enthusiastically to Jacob's arrival.

> On hearing the news of his sister's son Jacob, Laban ran to greet him; he embraced him and kissed him, and took him into his home. He told Laban all that had happened, and Laban said, "You are truly my bone and flesh." (Gen. 29:13-14)

If the reader has suspicions, this is not uncommon. The Midrash (Genesis Rabbah 70:13) explains that Laban embraced and kissed Jacob to search his body for gold and precious stones.

Jacob accepts both Laban's welcome and his offer to work for his keep—and for Rachel. He will mind Laban's flocks for seven years in order to marry her. Importantly, Jacob is very precise about which of Laban's two daughters he loves. He states in no uncertain terms, "I will serve you seven years for your younger daughter Rachel" (Gen. 29:18).

Laban agrees. But here, he reveals his manipulative nature. "Better that I give her to you than that I should give her to an outsider" (Gen. 29:19). Rachel Havrelock notes that Laban is "asserting his power to 'give' Rachel to whomever he desires." (Eskenazi/Torah, 163) Jacob had better take the deal here and now or lose out forever. But an agreement is not always an agreement.

Jacob the trickster becomes subject to the adage—which can hardly be considered recent—that what goes around comes around. Laban tricks Jacob into marrying his elder daughter, Leah. Seeking to evade responsibility for the deception, he blames local custom, which decrees that the first-born daughter marry before the younger. Helpless, Jacob marries Rachel after the initial week's celebration of his marriage to Leah—and after consenting to work another seven years for Laban. Jacob then serves Laban for an additional six years to build up flocks of his own.

After twenty years in Haran, Jacob is ready to assert his independence. He asks Laban for permission to return to Isaac. Laban makes a startling revelation. "If you will indulge me, I have learned by divination that the LORD has blessed me on your account" (Gen. 30:27). Interestingly, the Bible does not prohibit divination as long as it is associated with God, such as through the Urim and Thummim carried by the High Priest. Is Laban's divination legitimate? That he has household gods, as we shall see, suggests that his source of divination is idolatrous.

Laban next asks Jacob to name his wages. Jacob requests only the small number of Laban's dark-colored sheep, and speckled and spotted goats—each an abnormality and of little value. Laban agrees but removes the animals that Jacob has asked for and sends them with his sons three days' journey away. Nonetheless, Jacob gets the better of him through a miraculous feat of genetic engineering. Jacob places poplar, almond and plane shoots, in which he peels white stripes, in front of the troughs where Laban's animals water. The animals mate there and produce offspring both discolored and extremely hardy. In a relatively short time, Jacob becomes very prosperous while Laban's flocks diminish.

Seeing their inheritance depleted, Laban's sons grow angry. Likewise, Jacob understands that Laban no longer acts as kindly towards him as in the past. God intervenes. He instructs Jacob to return to Canaan. Jacob does so, fleeing with his family and possessions. Rachel, incensed at her father, as is Leah, for not assuring his daughters a share in the family inheritance, takes Laban's household gods with her.

Laban pursues Jacob and experiences a direct encounter with God. "But God appeared to Laban the Aramean in a dream by night and said to him, 'Beware of attempting anything with Jacob, good or bad'" (Gen 31:24).

We have previously wondered how Laban and his family might be aware of God. Laban's blessings in the name of YHVH after meeting Eliezer may certainly have been a ploy. But now Laban comes "face to face" with God. It is striking that—as with Abimelech, king of Gerar in Genesis 20—Laban evidences no reaction to God's appearance. Quite possibly, he assumes that God is one of many gods who commonly speak to humans in dreams and is thus of no particular significance. But it is also possible that Laban *does* know something of God, which simply reflects the human experience as far back as the time of Adam and Eve.

Such knowledge, however, does not alter his personality. Playing the role of the victim to the hilt, Laban castigates Jacob for "carrying off my daughters like captives of the sword" (Gen. 31: 26). And true to the Bible's 360-degree portrait of human nature, Laban, the father and grandfather, also complains that, "You did not even let me kiss my sons and daughters good-by!" (Gen. 31:28). Then, setting aside his anger, Laban takes on the guise of peacemaker.

> "I have it in my power to do you harm; but the God of your father said to me last night, 'Beware of attempting anything with Jacob, good or bad.' Very well, you had to leave because you were longing for your father's house; but why did you steal my gods?" (Gen. 31:29-30)

Who then is God to Laban? He refers to "the God of *your* father"—of Isaac—not of his own father, Nahor. God has spoken to him directly, yet this seems to have had only a limited effect on him. Laban remains more concerned with his household gods—idols, which obviously cannot speak. Clearly, Laban's spiritual powers are limited. The God of Abraham, Isaac and Jacob is no more than one of many gods to him in spite of the revelation he has received.

Having suggested voluntary restraint on his part—he has no personal relationship with God but is in effect humoring Him—Laban proceeds to search all of Jacob's possessions.

Jacob protests his innocence. Ironically, he states that anyone found with Laban's gods will not remain alive. Jacob does not know that Rachel has stolen them and placed them under the camel cushion upon which she sits. She explains to her father that she cannot rise, "for the period of women is upon me" (Gen. 31:35). Sadly for Jacob, his threat does not lack power. On the march towards Isaac, Rachel dies giving birth to Jacob's twelfth and last son, Benjamin.

When Laban finds nothing, Jacob becomes the accuser. He points out all the hardships he has endured to serve Laban over two decades, emphasizing that his father-in-law, "changed my wages time and again" (Gen. 31:41)—a phrase translated by others as "ten times" and interpreted by the Sages (Genesis Rabbah 74:11) as one hundred times.

In response, Laban offers a pact of peace. Acceding to this request, Jacob takes a stone to build a pillar, which will mark the agreement and serve as a border separating the two camps. After sharing a ritual meal to complete the compact, Laban declares,

> "May the LORD watch between you and me, when we are out of sight of each other. If you ill-treat my daughters or take other wives besides my daughters—though no one else be about, remember, God Himself will be witness between you and me." (Gen. 31:49-50)

Laban appeals to God to serve as judge between them but only, so it seems, as a device for placating Jacob and forcing him to uphold his end of the bargain. He then concludes the agreement with another oath: "'May the God of Abraham and the god of Nahor'—their ancestral deities—'judge between us.' And Jacob swore by the Fear of his father Isaac" (Gen. 31:53). While Laban references multiple gods, Jacob swears only by "the Fear of his father Isaac" and makes no effort to recognize Laban's god or gods. The two are blood relatives but not members of the same religious family.

The next morning, Jacob's party prepares for its final departure. Laban kisses his sons and daughters—kisses and *blesses* them according to some commentators—and bids them goodbye. For all his faults, according to Sforno, Laban appears to be a loving father and grandfather—and totally sincere. (Stone, 169) On that note, Laban's role in the biblical narrative concludes.

A loving father and grandfather Laban may be. Men and women in the Bible reflect both positive and negative traits, which makes them entirely similar to us. Yet in spite of his direct and personal encounter with God, as well as with the patriarchal family, Laban remains a polytheist. His polytheism—his refusal to recognize the One God—the biblical narrative implies, provides the reason for Laban's greed and Maimonides' reference to him as "a perfectly wicked man, and an idolater." (Maimonides, 2:41)

Laban's fault is not that of worshipping God in a non-Israelite way. This poses no problem to the Bible or the Jewish tradition, which accepts the validity of the Noahide laws for others. Rather, Laban adheres to polytheism and idolatry—a violation of the first Noahide law. These bear within them the seeds of injustice and unkindness. The patriarchs may look the other way when they encounter such polytheists—save the Canaanites—but the covenant at Sinai will reject polytheism with an unflagging hostility. As to Laban, God has made Himself known directly, but Laban remains free to acknowledge or reject Him. Ultimately, his choice leads to rejection.

BALAAM, PROPHET OF MIDIAN

Proclaimer of Blessings and Curses

Balak, king of the Moabite-Midianite confederation, fears the Israelites poised on his borders after forty years' wandering in the wilderness. To forestall an invasion, he sends elders versed in divination to summon Balaam, a man known to have the power to curse as well as bless. Balaam asks the elders to spend the night so that he can await a revelation from the Lord (YHVH). God tells Balaam not to go, and he sends the elders away. A second delegation arrives and offers riches. That night, God tells Balaam he may go but do only what He commands. Balaam eagerly sets out. Incensed, God sends an angel to block his way. Balaam cannot see the angel but his ass can and balks. Balaam beats him, and the ass speaks to protest. The angel finally gives Balaam permission to go, again with the warning to say only what God wishes. Meeting with Balak, Balaam sets out to curse Israel but instead blesses Israel four times, crediting himself with the words of blessing rather than God. Angry, Balak sends him away. Unable to rely on a military victory, the Moabites send Midianite women to engage in sexual promiscuity with the Israelite men. After this, the Israelites defeat four Midianite kings and put Balaam to the sword as punishment for instigating the whoring episode.

The Bible's focus on the story of Israel may lead to the assumption that only Israelites can be prophets. Not so. The Talmud (Bava Batra 15b) informs us, "Seven prophets prophesied for the Gentiles: Balaam and his father, and Job and his four friends." So, too, the Midrash (Numbers Rabbah 20:1) advises, "You find that all the distinctions conferred upon Israel were conferred upon the nations. In like manner He raised up Moses for Israel and Balaam for the idolaters." In fact, the Sages of the Midrash (Numbers Rabbah 14:20) accord Balaam three qualities Moses did not have: Balaam always knew Who God was when He spoke to him, knew when God would speak to him and could speak with God whenever he wished.

The Sages and commentators nonetheless deliver mixed messages about non-Israelite prophets. While they acknowledge Balaam and Job (see *Job: God's Accuser*), they make a generalized distinction between the prophets of Israel and those of the nations. Israelite prophets, according to the Midrash (Numbers Rabbah 20:1), do not limit themselves to warning their own people against transgressions and drawing attention to God's commands. They take a broader view of humanity since, "all the prophets retained a compassionate attitude towards both Israel and the idolaters." Prophets from the nations, however, do receive God's word. Yet while Job is hailed, Balaam most often is reviled. The Mishnah (Avot 5:19) takes a harsh view: "But the disciples of Balaam the wicked inherit Gehenna [the somewhat nebulous Jewish concept of Hell] and go down to the pit of destruction…"

A key question arises. Is Balaam, son of Beor, a true prophet or merely a sorcerer? Numbers 22:5 expressly labels Beor the latter. This leads Rabbi Yohanan to acknowledge in the Talmud (Sanhedrin 106a) that Beor was originally a prophet but descended into a mere soothsayer. Whatever his status, Balaam definitely experiences intimate communication with God—direct encounters that neither the biblical narrative nor the commentators question. Balaam's worthiness, on the other hand, remains the subject of debate. The Sages recognize his prophetic powers but generally condemn him. The Torah itself justifies his violent death.

The majority of Balaam's story appears in the Book of Numbers within a Torah portion named for a non-Israelite, Balak—king of Moab, part of the Midian confederation. The events take place at the conclusion of the Israelites' forty years of wandering in the wilderness following the Exodus. Maintaining their great numbers and growing in strength, the Israelites defeat two powerful Amorite kings, Sihon and Og, then encamp on the steppes of Moab on the east side of the Jordan River. This positions them to cross into and conquer Canaan, the land promised to Abraham's descendants.

Balak's response seems very much in line with those of modern-day geopolitical leaders who pessimistically scrutinize the intentions not only of potential enemies but of friends as well. Balak greatly fears the Israelites, although Israel has no designs on Moab. From the reader's point of view, Balak's assumption is clearly mistaken. Moses soon will explicitly state to the Israelites (Deuteronomy 2:9) that they are not to harass or provoke the Moabites, whose land God has assigned to the descendants of Lot, Abraham's nephew. Thus it is possible that Israelite representatives have met quietly with their Moabite counterparts, engaging in under-the-radar diplomacy. The biblical narrative, however, does not hint at this.

Might there be other reasons why Balak fears Israel? In one midrash (Numbers Rabbah 22:2), Moses tells God that the Midianites persecute Israel because Israel has received the Torah and His precepts. Israel represents a *moral* threat to an immoral Midian. The Talmud (Zevachim 116a) depicts Balaam citing Psalms 29:11—an event out of historical sequence, since Psalms is a much later work of literature—to explain God's gift of the Torah to Israel.

Conjecture aside, we know that the sheer size of the new but still-landless Israelite nation unsettles Balak. He relates his fears to the elders of Midian (and presumably those of Moab): "Now this horde will lick clean all that is about us as an ox licks up the grass of the field" (Num. 22:4). Attempting to halt the Israelites on their march and end any potential threat without having to take the field of battle, he sends the elders of Midian and Moab, all versed in divination, to Balaam. The strategy seems reasonable in that Balaam is known to possess the power to communicate with God—at least, as God or a chief god is conceived of by Moab and Midian.

Balaam's ability to communicate with God should not surprise us, according to Richard Friedman. "It is surely significant that the Torah, a work that comes from Israel, pictures the creator as communicating with a non-Israelite prophet as well. It is a reminder that the Torah begins with the story of the connection between God and all the earth." (Friedman/Commentary, 503)

Arriving at Balaam's home in the north by the Euphrates River, the elders deliver Balak's message:

> "There is a people that came out of Egypt; it hides the earth from view, and it is settled next to me. Come then, put a curse upon this

> people for me, since they are too numerous for me; perhaps I can thus defeat them and drive them out of the land. For I know that he whom you bless is blessed indeed, and he whom you curse is cursed." (Num. 22:5-6)

Balak expects Balaam to curse—and doom—Israel. Here, the contemporary scholar Jacob Milgrom points out, he commits a grave error. Balaam is a diviner who predicts the future rather than a sorcerer who can actually alter the future. (Etz Hayim, 895) Divination and sorcery, we should note, stand in opposition to Israelite law. Deuteronomy 18:10-11 commands: "Let no one be found among you who consigns his son or daughter to the fire, or who is an augur, a soothsayer, a diviner, a sorcerer, one who casts spells, or one who consults ghosts or familiar spirits, or one who inquires of the dead." Joshua 13:22 refers to Balaam as an auger. Interestingly, Balaam himself later praises Israel's godly ways: "Lo, there is no augury in Jacob, / No divining in Israel" (Num. 23:23).

Will Balaam really curse God's people, Israel? Recognizing the limits of his own power—or perhaps engaging in false humility—he invites the elders to, "Spend the night here, and I shall reply to you as the LORD may instruct me" (Num. 22:8). It is particularly noteworthy that Balaam refers to YHVH, the specific name of the God of Israel, while speaking with non-Israelites. Moreover, Balaam's later reference to "the LORD [YHVH] my God" in Numbers 22:18 clearly demonstrates that the relationship is personal and devotional. How might Balaam have come to his knowledge of and reverence for God? The Christian scholar W.F. Albright presents an alternative reading of the Hebrew: Balaam is a convert who later abandons Israel's faith and joins with the Midianites against Israel. (Plaut, 1184-5)

We may now ask whether *Balak* truly knows who YHVH is? Does he believe that Balaam's powers flow from the God of Israel—the very God whom he, as king of Moab, opposes by seeking to curse the Israelites? Milgrom suggests that Balak might understand Balaam as having an allegiance to and intimacy with Israel's God—a position as an "insider" that could make the cursing of Israel successful. (Etz Hayim, 896) Clearly, however, Balak does not understand God's purpose in bringing Israel to his borders and through his land into Canaan. If he did, he would facilitate Israel's march, not oppose it.

Let us now return to Balaam's desire to summon God's counsel during the night. Apparently, he anticipates that God will come to him in a dream. Job 33:15 states that God visits people, "In a dream, a night vision, / When deep sleep falls on men, / While they slumber in their beds." Rashi comments, "The Holy Spirit rested on Balaam only at night. So too with all other prophets of Gentile nations." Maimonides reinforces this view that prophecy is given only in a vision or dream. (Maimonides, 2:44)

It is Balaam's *summoning* of God—his desire for and *expectation* of a night vision to resolve an important matter—that separates him from Israelite prophets such as Moses and Jeremiah. They only reluctantly accept the responsibility of prophecy. As Abraham Joshua Heschel points out, the prophet "is not moved by a will to experience prophecy. What he achieves comes against his will." (Heschel, 457) Nehama Leibowitz explains that unlike Israelite prophets, Balaam "hankers after prophecy, and strives, through magical means, to obtain such power, to force it down from Heaven, as it were, through the medium of seven altars, seven bullocks, enchantments and solitude." (Leibowitz/Bamidbar, 284)

Balaam's non-Israelite status certainly does not weaken his power. He seemingly *can* summon God, because God *does* come to him that night and asks, "What do these people want of you?" (Num. 22:9). The question surely is rhetorical. How can God *not* know? In Genesis, God asks Adam and Eve, following their eating of the fruit of the Tree of Knowledge, "Where are you?" and Cain, after his murdering Abel, "Where is your brother Abel?" God perfectly well knows but offers Adam and Eve, and Cain, the opportunity to open a conversation and take responsibility for their deeds. Regrettably, if not unexpectedly, they fail to do so. So, too, God gives Balaam an opening to explore what this invitation really means and why he should not accept it.

Balaam fails to engage truthfully. He answers by referring to Balak's request as if God has no idea of what is going on. In response, God issues a straightforward command: "Do not go with them. You must not curse that people, for they are blessed" (Num. 22:12). Balaam has sought God's counsel; now he knows precisely what behavior God expects of him and what God's intentions are towards Israel. We could easily say, "Period. End of story." But we would be wrong.

While Balaam appears to accept God's counsel, his words betray him. Arising in the morning, he sends the dignitaries off, telling them that, "the LORD will not let me go with you" (Num. 22:13). Balaam has relayed God's command to be sure. His statement, however, implies that he will not accompany the elders only because God has instructed him not to do so. He himself might willingly curse Israel. God, not Balaam's understanding of Israel's role in the world, prevents his undertaking the task Balak has requested.

What then should Balaam have told the dignitaries? Isaac Arama, a fifteenth-century Spanish commentator, points to Balaam's shortsightedness. He stresses that Balaam "should have striven with and upbraided the messengers of Balak." (Leibowitz/Bamidbar, 312) God may command, but human beings are obligated to understand to the best of their abilities.

On returning to Balak, the dignitaries erroneously report, "Balaam refused to come with us." (Num. 22:14) This leaves God out of their explanation. Perhaps their oversight reflects their disdain of the God of Israel, Who is not their God. On the other hand, the elders may accurately have read into Balaam's character. God has been forthright in His instruction, but Balaam may seem hesitant, unsure—perhaps devious. They *hear* Balaam's reason for sending them off, but they do not *believe* it. What, they may ask themselves, does Balaam *really* want? What will it take to win him over?

Not about to give up, Balak sends a second, even more impressive group of dignitaries. Well prepared to break down Balaam's resistance, they deliver an appealing message:

> "Thus says Balak son of Zippor: Please do not refuse to come to me. I will reward you richly and I will do anything you ask of me. Only come and damn this people for me." (Num. 22:16-17)

Balaam's reply seems straightforward.

> "Though Balak were to give me his house full of silver and gold, I could not do anything, big or little, contrary to the command of the LORD my God. So you, too, stay here overnight, and let me find out what else the LORD may say to me." (Num. 22:18-19)

Further review reveals a significant flaw in Balaam's character. He suggests not a refusal to accompany the emissaries but rather a negotiation of his fee. "A house full of silver and gold" serves as his opening position. This ploy's antecedent appears in Genesis. Ephron the Hittite apparently dismisses payment for land he is willing to give to Abraham as a burial place for Sarah. But Ephron's question, "A piece of land worth four hundred shekels of silver—what is that between you and me?" (Gen. 23:15) serves only to set a rather exorbitant purchase price that Abraham pays. Likewise, states the Midrash (Numbers Rabbah 20:10), Balaam's statement evidences a greedy soul.

Balaam's request that the emissaries spend the night also betrays his baser self. Surely he can be excused for inviting them to rest from their journey. But having heard the promise of a reward, he again seeks God's instruction in a dream, hoping that God's mind may change. Like a child who hears a parent's restriction but continues to ask for what is not allowed, Balaam fails to recognize "no" as meaning "no." God's response tests Balaam. "That night God came to Balaam and said to him, 'If those men have come to invite you, you may go with them. But whatever I command you, that you shall do.'" (Num. 22:20)

Why does God give Balaam permission to go? The Midrash (Numbers Rabbah 20:12), upholding the concept of free will, states that God lets a man go the way his heart desires. If Balaam is eager to go to Balak and perish, so be it.

What should Balaam have done? Nachmanides suggests that God desired that Balaam inform the emissaries that he would accompany them but not curse Israel. Balaam fails to do this, leaving the emissaries with some hope. Rashi relates that Balaam sees accompanying the emissaries as evil but still wants to go. And so he does.

The next morning, Balaam saddles his ass. This, according to the Sages and Nachmanides, betrays his apparent eagerness to depart and fulfill the emissaries' wishes. (Leibowitz/Bamidbar, 309) Why, we may ask, does a man as seemingly revered as Balaam saddle his own ass? Has he not a servant to do it for him? Rashi comments that in contrast with Abraham saddling his ass prior to setting out for Mount Mariah to sacrifice Isaac at God's request (Gen. 22:3), Balaam acts not out of zeal to obey God but out of hatred.

The journey's beginning clearly reveals God's response: "But God was incensed at his going; so an angel of the Lord placed himself in his way as an adversary." (Num. 22:22) Balaam cannot see the angel, but his ass can—and swerves away from the danger. Balaam beats the animal to turn her back to the road. Not easily deterred, the angel stations himself in a narrow lane between two vineyards with a fence on either side. Shying away, the ass presses against a wall, squeezing Balaam's foot in the process. Balaam again beats her. The angel then stations himself in a narrow spot in the road. The ass lies down. Balaam beats her once more. This scene reveals that Balaam is not a prophet in the Israelite mold for he is blind to a messenger of God recognized even by a common beast of burden. God, Rashi, comments, has endowed this humble ass with greater farsightedness than this man. Moreover, this is not a *dumb* animal in any sense of the word.

> Then the Lord opened the ass's mouth, and she said to Balaam, "What have I done to you that you have beaten me three times?" Balaam said to the ass, "You have made a mockery of me! If I had a sword with me, I'd kill you." The ass said to Balaam, "Look, I am the ass that you have been riding all along until this day! Have I been in the habit of doing thus to you?" And he answered, "No." (Num. 22:28-30)[45]

---

45 The only other non-human creature to speak in the Torah is the serpent in Genesis 3, who tempts Eve (and thus Adam) in the Garden of Eden.

The Midrash (Numbers Rabbah 20:14) states bitingly, "For here was this ass, the most foolish of beasts, and there was the wisest of all wise men, yet as soon as she opened her mouth he could not stand his ground against her!"

Incredibly, the ass's speech does not startle Balaam. His prophetic powers may have their limits, but he seems attuned to the world beyond our everyday senses. After all, he has spoken with God! Balaam's anger at the beast, however, is misdirected as he soon finds out. "The angel of the Lord said to him, 'Why have you beaten your ass these three times? It is I who came out as an adversary, for the errand is obnoxious to me'" (Num. 22:32).

Balaam concedes his error and offers to turn back, although this may be a ploy to appear repentant and avoid punishment. Here, the Midrash (Numbers Rabbah 20:15) makes an interesting observation. Balaam protests to the angel that he has begun his journey at God's request. God's desire that he now return home simply parallels the command given to Abraham, prepared to sacrifice Isaac on Mount Moriah. An angel instructs the patriarch to put his knife down. Balaam's midrashic reference to Abraham and Isaac evidences the Sages' opinion that he was versed in Torah and thus a quite serious, if imperfect, prophet.

The angel who has blocked Balaam's way responds with God's message: "Go with the men. But you must say nothing except what I tell you" (Num. 22:35). What *can* Balaam say on his own? Balaam serves only as a conduit for God's word. Balak and the Midianites do not understand this. They yield to Balaam a power he simply does not have.

Now the reward motif resurfaces. Balak, greeting Balaam at Ir-moab, wonders why Balaam did not come to him after his first invitation. "Am I really unable to reward you?" Balak asks (Num. 22:37). Here, let us give Balaam his due. He evidences some sense of his limits. He has been tempted by Balak's riches yet understands that he is powerless to win them without the granting of a very big Divine favor. Balaam responds, "I can utter only the word that God puts into my mouth" (Num. 22:38).

Balaam puts himself at Balak's disposal. But the word of God, Balaam believes, demands an impressive stage. The Law, after all, was given at Sinai amidst thunder and lightning. So he instructs Balak to build seven altars and prepare seven bulls and seven rams. Why seven of each? Numbers represent important symbols in the Bible, and seven is significant. It reflects the seven days of creation, the seven pairs of ritually pure animals brought on board Noah's ark, the seven good and seven lean years declared by Joseph as the meaning of Pharaoh's dream, and many other examples.[46]

Again, Balaam's legitimacy as a prophet—at least in the Israelite sense—comes into question. Abraham Joshua Heschel notes, "The prophet does not perform ceremonies in order to receive a revelation." (Heschel, 457) God cannot be summoned; it is God Who summons. Here, Balaam may be mocking Balak, who takes only a pagan perspective on prophecy. Balaam will go along with the king while fully knowing how fruitless his efforts will be. And so Balaam sets off alone to receive God's instruction. When he returns, he begins the first of four blessings, rhetorically asking Balak and the Moabite dignitaries: "How can I damn whom God has not damned, / How doom when the LORD has not doomed?" (Num. 23:8).

In spite of himself—or at least in spite of Balak's wishes—Balaam proceeds to bless Israel for its size and righteousness. "The sorcerer wishes to curse but he is forced to submit to the power of the Divine," writes Yehezkel Kaufmann. (Leibowitz/Bamidbar, 300) Moreover, Balaam's blessings carry extra weight, according to the Midrash (Deuteronomy Rabbah 1:4), since he hates Israel. Thus they cannot be misconstrued as anything but genuine.

In a battle of wills, God will always emerge the victor. Deuteronomy 23:6, which provides the last of the Balaam story, relates Moses telling Israel that, "the LORD your God refused to heed Balaam; instead the LORD your God turned the curse into a blessing for you, for the LORD your God loves you." Indeed, Balaam cannot control his words. As the Midrash (Numbers Rabbah 20:20) advises: just as a man puts a bit into the mouth of a beast and makes it go in

---

46 Job's three friends, accused by God of not having spoken the truth about Him, must sacrifice seven bulls and seven rams in expiation (Job 42:8).

any direction he pleases, so God controls a man's speech to achieve His own purposes.

Balak, frustrated by this initial failure, beckons Balaam to accompany him to another place, the summit of Mount Pisgah, which he believes will be more favorable to Balaam's cursing Israel. Balaam, still willing to satisfy the Moabite king, goes off to "seek a manifestation yonder" (Num. 23:15). Not surprisingly, God again puts words in Balaam's mouth. When he returns, Balak asks in anticipation, "What did the LORD say?" (Num. 23:17) Here, let us remember that Balak's question does not reflect a belief in or understanding of God. To Balak, Balaam's God—the God of Israel and, as the reader knows, the world—is one of many gods. Balak acknowledges Balaam's source of inspiration as personal, not universal.

Again, Balaam blesses Israel.

> No harm is in sight for Jacob,
> No woe in view for Israel.
> The LORD their God is with them,
> And their King's acclaim in their midst. (Num. 23:21)

Again disappointed, Balak leads Balaam to the peak of Peor. For a third time, the Moabites make ready seven altars, seven bulls and seven rams. But now, understanding that it pleases God to bless Israel, Balaam does not go off "in search of omens" (Num. 24:1). This phrase offers a strong statement by the biblical narrative that Balaam does not function like Israelite prophets. The latter refrain from omens other than those permitted by God—the Urim and Thummim consulted by the High Priest.

Balaam looks towards the wilderness where he sees Israel encamped tribe by tribe. Now he betrays his egoism. The spirit of God comes upon him, yet he begins his pronouncement with, "Word of Balaam son of Beor" (Num. 24:3), referencing himself, not God, as the source of his knowledge. Balaam then utters the famous blessing, "*Ma-tovu ohalecha Ya'acov, mishkenotecha Yisrael*—How fair are your tents, O Jacob, Your dwellings, O Israel!" (Num.

24:5). These words, uttered by a non-Israelite, hold a revered place in Jewish liturgy.[47]

The third blessing ends with: "Blessed are they who bless you, / Accursed they who curse you!" (Num. 24:9). Balaam's words echo God's promise to Abraham in Genesis 12:3 that, "I will bless those who bless you / And curse him that curses you." Nehama Leibowitz calls this "pure prophecy." (Leibowitz/Bamidbar, 292)

Not surprisingly, Balak is enraged. He still believes that Balaam has the power to alter God's words. And so he plays the "reward card" one step further: "Back with you at once to your own place! I was going to reward you richly, but the LORD has denied you the reward" (Num. 24:11).

Balaam, in turn, knows that God's will trumps his own. He protests:

> "But I even told the messengers you sent me, 'Though Balak were to give me his house full of silver and gold, I could not of my own accord do anything good or bad contrary to the LORD's command. What the LORD says, I must say.'" (Num. 24:12-13)[48]

Eventually, Balaam does deliver a curse. But here the law of unintended consequences strikes Balak: the curse targets Israel's enemies, including the Moabite confederation. Israel will smash them all. Even the Kenites, from whom Moses' father-in-law, Jethro, descends, will be taken captive by Assyria.

Having come to some sense of self-realization and avoided cursing Israel, Balaam now seems an honorable—if repentant—prophet. He leaves Balak and journeys home. But Balaam's story does not end peacefully. Although he has blessed Israel, Balaam

---

47 The Talmud (Bava Batra 60a) and Rashi cite this blessing as noting the arrangement of Israel's encampments, which promote modesty and control over sexual relations. Each Israelite's tent is aligned to block the views of other tents and assure privacy. The Sages also consider tents as a metaphor for synagogues. (Bialik, 96:112) Thus Israel is a pious nation that studies God's Law.

48 Balaam's insistence that he can say only what God commands finds a paralleled in 1 Kings 22:13ff. Messengers of King Jehoshaphat of Judah urge the prophet Micaiah to agree with four hundred prophets who see the king's success in battle. Micaiah replies, "I will speak only what the LORD tells me.

ultimately conspires to bring about its downfall. Why? The biblical narrative reveals no motive. Samuel Luzzatto suggests that on his way home, Balaam heard that the Israelites had committed harlotry with the daughters of Moab and understood that this was the one way to undermine Israel. "He therefore advised the Midianites to send their choicest maidens to seduce the Israelites into idolatry." (Leibowitz/Bamidbar, 376) Nehama Leibowitz adds that, "It was only after he had left Balak, when the Divine spirit had left him that he was once more overwhelmed by his baser thoughts." (Leibowitz/Bamidbar, 320)

If Balaam really is determined to undermine Israel, his advice bears fruit in the Torah portion that follows—Pinchas.

> While Israel was staying at Shittim, the people profaned themselves by whoring with the Moabite women, who invited the people to the sacrifices to their god. The people partook of them and worshipped that god." (Num. 25:1-2)

Because Israel's chastity and virtue seem to make it unassailable, says Samson Raphael Hirsch, what better way to attack it than through sexual temptation? (Leibowitz/Bamidbar, 317)

God responds angrily, sending forth a plague that kills 24,000 Israelites. The plague ends only when the zealous Pinchas (Phinehas) slays the Israelite man Zimri and the Moabite woman Cozbi. The Midianites become the target of even greater wrath from God, Who instructs Moses:

> "Assail the Midianites and defeat them—for they assailed you by the trickery they practiced against you—because of the affair of Peor and because of the affair of their kinswoman, Cozbi, daughter of the Midianite chieftain, who was killed at the time of the plague on account of Peor." (Num. 25:17-18)

Moses assembles an armed force of a thousand men from each tribe and avenges Israel.

> They took the field against Midian, as the LORD had commanded Moses, and slew every male. Along with their other victims, they slew the kings of Midian: Evi, Rekem, Zur, Hur, and Reba, the five kings of Midian. They also put Balaam son of Beor to the sword. (Num. 31:7-8)

Balaam's death seems to come out of nowhere since Numbers 24:25 reports him returning home, which would distance himself from the Israelites. Critical scholars view the episode of his death as originating in a separate biblical source fused into the established narrative. The traditional perspective maintains the unity of the text by acknowledging logical events simply not reported by the text. Ibn Ezra affirms that Balaam must have returned to Midian on some other occasion. (Plaut/Commentary, 1223) Whatever its source, the statement regarding Balaam's death is not unique to Numbers. Joshua 13:22 provides the same account.

But why is Balaam put to death after blessing rather than cursing Israel? Several verses later, the biblical text confirms what at first appears to be speculation regarding Balaam's innermost thoughts. Moses berates the Israelite warriors for sparing the Midianite women:

> "Yet they are the very ones who, at the bidding of Balaam, induced the Israelites to trespass against the LORD in the matter of Peor, so that the LORD's community was struck by the plague." (Num. 31:16)

Balaam stands behind the plot! Yet the text does not mention his complicity at the time of its occurrence. Here, Nehama Leibowitz advises, the Torah wishes to teach a special lesson. "Though it was Balaam who instigated the daughters of Midian to strike a blow at the purity of Jewish family life, though he was the evil genius who thought out the plan, the moral responsibility ultimately rested on the Israelites themselves." (Leibowitz/Bamidbar, 377) Today we might ask, "Who held a gun to your head? Couldn't you have ignored the Midianite women?" And so Balaam's "obvious" culpability is neglected until later in the narrative.

Richard Friedman takes another approach. He terms Balaam's death "a shock." Perhaps, he suggests, Balaam advises that the Moabites and Midianites employ their women against the Israelites although believing that this stratagem will not work. Or perhaps, in spite of his blessing them, Balaam has no affection for Israel. He has, indeed, pronounced only what God has instructed. From Friedman's contemporary perspective, "The text only lets us know that human motives are complex." (Friedman/Commentary, 350)

In spite of blessing Israel, and doubtless because of his execution, Balaam is most frequently assailed as a failed or false prophet—an example of duplicity. The Bible upholds this position beyond Numbers and Joshua. Through the prophet Micah, God warns Israel:

> "My people,
> Remember what Balak king of Moab
> Plotted against you,
> And how Balaam son of Beor
> Responded to him." (Micah 6:5)

Balaam is, in reality, a con man; prophecy and magic do not mix. Abravanel declares that, "Balaam's sorcery was world famous." (Leibowitz/Bamidbar, 305) Many modern commentators agree. Ultimately, says Nehama Leibowitz, Balaam's story focuses on "discrediting superstition and belief in magical practices." (Leibowitz/Bamidbar, 303) Gunther Plaut adds, "Despite the obviously intimate relationships which the text describes as existing between God and Balaam, traditional Jewish and Christian opinions almost unvaryingly see the man who blessed Israel and foresaw the doom of its enemies as a sorcerer, a man who loved money more than truth and who ended up in hell." (Plaut, 1184)

But what if Balaam had cursed Israel? Could his curses have undone God's own blessings? No, comments Abravanel, but they could have done considerable damage. "Had Balaam cursed Israel, the surrounding nations would have plucked up enough courage and gone to do battle with Israel on the strength of his curses." (Leibowitz/Bamidbar, 305)

Frequently vilified though he may be, Balaam has his defenders—if only to a degree. A midrash (Sifre Deuteronomy, 357) states that while no prophet the like of Moses arose in Israel, such a prophet arose among the nations, and that was Balaam. Ibn Ezra also gives Balaam his due, conceding that his prophecy had the stamp of truth.

Even Balak receives some praise. The Talmud (Sanhedrin 105b) comments that "as a reward for the forty-two sacrifices offered up by Balak, he was privileged that Ruth should be his descendant" (see *Women of Valor*).

All this leads us to ponder why God establishes a specific relationship with Balaam. Surely He knows whether a proposed prophet is worthy or not. Here, the theme of free will plays itself out. A prophet possesses a certain spiritual spark or insight. Nonetheless, he must choose to adhere to God's will and not bend the powers God gives him to his own uses.

But does God choose prophets from the nations at all? Doesn't Israel possess enough worthy souls? The Polish-Israeli scholar Ephraim Urbach answers that prophecy, as direct contact with God, "was bestowed, at the outset, on all human creatures." Regrettably—but not surprisingly—some prophets of the nations disappoint. "Balaam," Urbach comments, "represents the type of man who has been given the opportunity to scale the loftiest spiritual heights but fails to stand the test and forfeits his status." (Leibowitz/Bamidbar, 325-6)

Balaam's failure, it must be emphasized, is his own, not God's. Nehama Leibowitz reminds us that, "Man's own will is the sole factor determining whether he will use his qualities, talents and even the gift of prophecy bestowed on him for good, or, God forbid, misuse them for evil. It depends solely on his own freewill to aspire to the sainthood of a Moses or descend to the villainy of a Balaam." (Leibowitz/Bamidbar, 326)

Balaam makes his choices, but ultimately the story is not about him at all. Balaam is merely an agent of God. Gunther Plaut concludes that the three chapters in Numbers concerning Balaam, "focus not on him but on the God of Israel who loves and protects His people...."

The text, then, is less than the tale of a pagan, be he prophet or sorcerer, than a paean of God and His affection for the Children of Israel." (Plaut, 1185) Whatever Balaam's intentions, his encounters with God produce blessings for Israel and protection against armed struggle with Midian and Moab. Balaam's motives may be suspect, but the reality of his relationship with the Eternal is not.

* * *

While Laban and Balaam are well-known characters in the Bible, other dissemblers and provokers can be found in the narrative as well. We may consider them to be "minor" characters, but their stories also attest to non-Israelites' encounters with God and, in the following two cases of the colonists of Samaria and the Assyrian king, Sennacherib, the unfortunate inability to comprehend those experiences.

THE COLONISTS OF SAMARIA

Worshippers of Both God and Idols

The king of Assyria, having conquered the northern kingdom of Israel, deports the Israelites and replaces them in the region of Samaria with people from other nations. When the colonists fail to worship the God of Israel, God sends lions to punish them. The king responds by sending an Israelite priest to Samaria to provide instruction. The colonists, having encountered God through His fury, now worship God but continue to serve their own gods as well.

Why do human beings ignore the obvious? The *yetzer hara*—the evil inclination—overcomes our better judgment even after we have suffered dire consequences for our actions. Self-destructiveness seems a very human trait. And so it comes as no surprise that Israel turns from God time and again, in spite of the covenant at Sinai and God's clear instructions regarding reward for doing what is right and punishment for doing wrong. The more grave the wrongdoing, the more grave the punishment. Thus catastrophe strikes during the reign of King Hoshea (732-22 BCE) over the northern kingdom of Israel.

Hoshea rules as a vassal to the king of Assyria. Unfortunately, Hoshea's geopolitical skills betray him—and the nation. He sends envoys to Assyria's enemy, Egypt. He also fails to pay agreed-upon tribute—what the Bible itself terms "an act of treachery" (2 Kings 17:4). Disaster strikes. King Shalmaneser of Assyria—identified as Shalmaneser V by Josephus—arrests Hoshea and marches on the region of Samaria in which the capital city of Samaria is situated. Following a siege, Shalmaneser's successor, Sargon II, takes the capital (ca. 720—Biblical and secular history begin to intersect) and turns the northern kingdom into an Assyrian province.[49]

What had the Israelites done?

49 This story is detailed in 2 Kings 17 and repeated briefly in 2 Kings 18 in reference to Hezekiah, the God-fearing king of Judah.

> They worshipped other gods and followed the customs of the nations which the LORD had dispossessed before the Israelites and the customs which the kings of Israel had practiced. The Israelites committed against the LORD their God acts which were not right: (2 Kings 17:7-9)

The Israelites set up pillars and sacred posts, offered sacrifices to Canaanite gods and worshipped fetishes.

Such acts earn grave punishment indeed. The king of Assyria sends the Israelites into exile. Through this event the ten northern tribes become "lost"—absorbed into other peoples. To add insult to injury—God *is* making a point—the Assyrian king replaces the exiled population with non-Israelite colonists from Babylon and other nations.

The Israelites may surrender their holiness, but the land remains special to God. The people who reside in it—even colonists—find themselves bound to the Law given at Sinai. The new residents, however, are polytheists ignorant of the God of Israel. Their ignorance, however, does not excuse them. Because they fail to live according to the Torah, dire punishment strikes them.

> When they first settled there, they did not worship the LORD; so the LORD sent lions against them which killed some of them.[50] They said to the King of Assyria: "The nations which you deported and resettled in the towns of Samaria do not know the rules of the God of the land; therefore He has let lions loose against them which are killing them—for they do not know the rules of the God of the land." (2 Kings 17:25-26)

The colonists acknowledge the God of Israel only as a local god, "the God of the land" but one of a panoply of gods. This God, however, cannot be ignored. Although ignorant of His ways, the colonists understand that He is powerful—perhaps more so than most or all other deities. This presents the colonists with an important choice. They can respond to their historic encounter and change their ways

50 Hosea 13:6-8 uses lion imagery—as well as that of a leopard and a bear—to present God's anger at the Israelites who abandon Him in the wilderness.

or continue their various forms of polytheism. Should they choose the latter option, they must bear the consequences. The lions sent by God serve as a warning, something of a parallel to the plagues hurled at Egypt. The colonists surely face similar destruction.

The king of Assyria reaches an appropriate decision. He may not have a sharp theological bent, but he understands what today we call "the facts on the ground." Recognizing the overwhelming power of the God of Israel—if not necessarily His Oneness—the king acts a great deal more perceptively than did Pharaoh centuries earlier. After all, he has a new territory from which to extract wealth—one that also serves as a buffer against an attack from Egypt to the south. So the king sends an exiled Israelite—an unnamed priest—back to Israel to teach the colonists in Samaria "how to worship the LORD" (2 Kings 17:28).

The priest establishes residence in Bethel and provides instruction. The colonists don't quite get monotheism. As a result, "each nation continued to make its own gods and to set them up in the cult places which had been made by the people of Samaria; each nation [set them up] in the towns in which it lived" (2 Kings 17:29).

> They worshipped the LORD, but they also appointed from their own ranks priests of the shrines, who officiated for them in the cult places. They worshipped the LORD while serving their own gods according to the practices of the nations from which they had been deported. To this day, they follow their former practices. They do not worship the LORD [properly]. (2 Kings 17:32-34)

The word "worshipped" above represents the JPS translation of *yereim*. Others translate this word as "feared," which seems more accurate.[51] The Sages define fear in two ways: awe or reverence, and the state of being frightened. The colonists more likely feel the latter emotion, given their experience with the lions. Otherwise, they would have abandoned their polytheistic practices, which include

51 In Genesis 19:30, Lot leaves the town of Zoar following the destruction of Sodom and Gomorrah because he was afraid—*yare*. After God brings the Reed Sea down on the Egyptians, the Israelites "[and] feared" the Lord—*v'yare*.

the Sepharvites burning their children as offerings to their gods, Adrammelech and Anamelech. Rather, the colonists seem to adopt a policy that if one religion is good, two or more must be better.

Like Pharaoh and the Egyptians before the Exodus—and, as most readers will now have concluded, like the Israelites ensnared by local Canaanite religious practices—the colonists of Samaria fail to heed God's obvious warnings. Thus they serve as an object lesson to the Jews of the surviving southern kingdom of Judah whose responsibility the narrative now makes clear:

> You must worship only the LORD your God, who brought you out of the land of Egypt with great might and with an outstretched arm: to Him alone shall you bow down and to Him alone shall you sacrifice. (2 Kings 17:36)

The prophets also warn Israel by referring to the shortcomings of Samaria, whose colonists only repeat the sins of the Israelites who dwelled there. Micah writes that God will come down from the heavens to wreak vengeance:

> All this is for the transgression of Jacob,
> And for the sins of the House of Israel.
> What is the transgression of Jacob
> But Samaria,...(Micah 1:5)

God makes clear to Micah his vision for Samaria:

> I will turn Samaria
> Into a ruin in open country,
> Into ground for planting vineyards;
> For I will tumble her stones into the valley
> And lay her foundations bare. (Micah 1:6)

And what punishment do the colonists suffer? In the short term, none at all. "To this day, they follow their former practices" (2 Kings 17:34). Yet historical perspective affords us another take on the colonists of Samaria—a point of view the biblical author could not offer. The nations and cultures of Babylonia, Cuthah, Avva, Hamath and Sepharvaim all disappear.[52] Israel, however, in spite of its many violations of the covenant at Sinai, survives as a nation until its destruction by Rome then as a people dispersed across the globe. Jewish history is fraught with disaster, but Israel reemerges eighteen centuries later as an independent state in the modern world alongside active Jewish communities on every continent. Israel's faith in the face of extreme prejudice and violence maintains its existence while other peoples vanish.

---

52 The Midrash identifies the descendants of Cuthah, who become known as Samaritans, as opposing the building of the Second Temple under Ezra and Zerubbabel, and seeking to kill Nehemiah. (Bialik, 135:150)

SENNACHERIB, KING OF ASSYRIA

Mocker of God's Power

Hezekiah, king of Judah, allies with Egypt in a rebellion against Assyria. Sennacherib, the Assyrian king, seizes the fortified towns of Judah and sends forces to besiege Jerusalem. Three Assyrian officials approach the city's walls to declare that the God of Israel has sent Sennacherib against Judah; the Lord will not save the city. Moreover, Sennacherib mocks God's ability to defend Jerusalem. The prophet Isaiah tells Hezekiah's officials that Sennacherib will abandon the siege. After Hezekiah prays at the Temple, Isaiah sends the king a stronger message, mocking Sennacherib and prophesying the siege's end. That night, an angel of the Lord strikes down 185,000 Assyrian troops in their camp. Sennacherib returns home only to be assassinated by his sons.

That Judah was spared the destruction rent on the northern kingdom of Israel does not attest to the piety of its kings. Ahaz, who reigns from 743-727 BCE during the era of Assyrian power and just prior to the fall of Samaria, offers no model for proper behavior.

> "He did not do what was pleasing to the Lord his God, as his ancestor David had done, but followed the ways of the kings of Israel. He even consigned his son to the fire, in the abhorrent fashion of the nations which the Lord had dispossessed before the Israelites. (2 Kings 16:2-3)

Nonetheless, Ahaz dies seemingly naturally and at peace, a willing vassal of Assyria to the end. His son, Hezekiah (reigns 727-698 BCE), succeeds him and proves the old saying, "like father, like son," not always applicable. Hezekiah restores Israelite religion, renouncing other gods, abolishing their shrines, smashing their pillars and cutting down their sacred posts. He even destroys the bronze serpent called Nehushtan that Moses created at the instruction of God to cure Israelites bitten by serpents in the wilderness of Sinai. Hezekiah "trusted only in the Lord the God of Israel" and "clung to the LORD" so that "the LORD was always with him; he was successful wherever he turned." (2 Kings 18:7)

In the sixth year of Hezekiah's reign, the king of Assyria captures Samaria and deports the Israelites. But the Assyrian king is less powerful than he believes. He serves only as an agent of God since the Israelites, "did not obey the LORD their God; they transgressed his covenant—all that Moses the servant of the LORD had commanded" (2 Kings 18:12). Here, the ways of history and God's hand behind it prove difficult to fathom if not highly ironic. While the bad Ahaz avoids invasion, the good Hezekiah cannot. Eight years after Samaria falls, a new Assyrian king, Sennacherib (reigns 705-681), marches against Judah.

The biblical narrative only hints at the politics inflaming the region, the Israeli biblical historian Mordechai Cogan explains. Following the death of Sennacherib's predecessor and father, Sargon II, "rebellions erupted throughout the empire, from Babylonia as far as the Persian Gulf and along the Mediterranean coast down to the Egyptian border." (Oxford, 331) At first a willing vassal, Hezekiah leads the southern Syrian states in rebellion. Anticipating a violent Assyrian response, Judah's engineers reinforce Jerusalem's defenses, a matter reported by Isaiah 22.

Displeased, Sennacherib seizes all of Judah's fortified towns. Hezekiah protests that he has done nothing wrong and asks Assyria to withdraw. Sennacherib assents—providing that Hezekiah pays him 300 talents of silver and thirty of gold. Hezekiah goes to extraordinary lengths to meet Sennacherib's demands. He sends him all the silver in the Temple as well as the gold overlaid on the Temple's doors and doorposts. Unfortunately, these treasures fall short. In light of Hezekiah's disloyalty, which extends to Judah's joining forces with Egypt, Sennacherib wants more. While the matter may be only business and not personal, the king of Assyria will be avenged.

Sennacherib sends a large force to Jerusalem while he remains at Lachish, southwest of the Judean capital. Jerusalem comes under siege. Assyrian writings, according to Cogan, describe Hezekiah as locked up within Jerusalem "like a bird in a cage." (Oxford, p334)

Three high Assyrian officials—the Tartan, the Rabsarus and the Rabshakeh—approach and take up a position "near the conduit of the Upper Pool, by the road of the Fuller's Field" (2 Kings 18:17). In response, Hezekiah sends Eliakim, the man in charge of his palace, and two other court officials—Shebna and Joah—to meet them.[53]

The Rabshakeh informs Hezekiah's emissaries—in the full hearing of everyone present—that Judah has no reliable ally in Egypt. In fact, he dismisses that nation as, "that splintered reed of a staff" (2 Kings 18:21). Then the Rabshakeh gets nastier:

> And if you tell me that you are relying on the LORD your God, He is the very one whose shrines and altars Hezekiah did away with, telling Judah and Jerusalem, 'You must worship only at this altar in Jerusalem.' (2 Kings 18:22)

The Rabshakeh, Sennacherib or both seem to understand the great division of opinion in Judah as to whether sacrifices to God can be made only in Jerusalem. The northern kingdom of Israel—now destroyed—had established its own sites for offerings and suffered destruction.

What the Rabshakeh apparently does not understand is that Hezekiah's destruction of "holy sites" outside Jerusalem may anger some of his subjects but pleases God. Rabbi Abraham Cohen comments, "The Assyrian mind could not comprehend that the one altar in the central Sanctuary was more acceptable to God than the multitude of altars spread all over the country." (Soncino/Kings, 276)

God, however, does not accept Hezekiah's looking to Egypt for assistance. The prophet Isaiah calls for submission to Assyria. While the focus of our story is First Kings, the Book of Isaiah echoes the Rabshakeh's mocking of Judah's belief that it can defend itself against Assyria, if for other reasons. Judah mistakenly has turned to Egypt and its chariots; it has "not turned to the Holy One of Israel, / They have not sought the LORD" (Isaiah 31:1). Then again, Assyria also miscalculates, according to the prophet. It dominates the region not because of its own power or righteousness but because it serves as God's tool, "For the LORD is angry at all the nations" (Isaiah 33:2).

53 The tale of this encounter and what follows also is reported in Isaiah 36-37.

Hezekiah may see an agreement with Egypt to help save Judah and Jerusalem as keeping faith with God. But the king's attempt at Great Power politics, the biblical narrative tells us, represents resistance to God's will. Judah must yield to Assyria, God's chosen agent for administering punishment for the nation's wrongdoing.

The Rabshakeh smells blood. Moreover, he knows how powerful a weapon propaganda can be. Understanding the difficulty of Hezekiah's military situation and the religious opposition to Hezekiah's Egyptian card, he relays Sennacherib's mocking of Judah's pretension that it can defend itself. The Assyrians are on a mission from God. "And do you think I have marched against this land to destroy it without the LORD? The LORD Himself told me: Go up against that land and destroy it" (2 Kings 18:25).

Sennacherib and the Rabshakeh use Israelite beliefs to undercut Judah's resolve and induce Jerusalem's surrender. What defense can the city make when the God of Israel—the God of History Who raises and destroys nations—is determined to punish Judah for its wrongdoing?

Shaken and desperate, Eliakim asks the Assyrians to speak Aramaic, the diplomatic and commercial language of the region. He does not want the common people who overhear them to understand. The Rabshakeh refuses. Determined to bring matters to a close, he makes an end run around Hezekiah by addressing the prominent men atop Jerusalem's wall in "Judean":

> "Hear the words of the Great King, the King of Assyria. Thus said the king: Don't let Hezekiah deceive you, for he will not be able to deliver you from my hands. Don't let Hezekiah make you rely on the LORD, saying: The LORD will surely save us: this city will not fall into the hands of the king of Assyria. Don't listen to Hezekiah. For thus said the king of Assyria: Make your peace with me and come out to me, so that you may all eat from your vines and your fig trees and drink water from your cisterns, until I come and take you away to a land like your own, a land of grain [fields] and vineyards, of bread and wine, of olive oil and honey, so that you may live and not die. Don't listen to Hezekiah, who misleads you by saying, 'The LORD will save us.'" (2 Kings 18:28-32)

Without pausing for a response, the Rabshakeh continues. Sennacherib's ego now dominates his statement, as does the king's disparagement of the God of Israel.

> "Did any of the gods of other nations save his land from the king of Assyria? Where were the gods of Hamath and Arpad? Where were the gods of Sepharvaim, Hena, and Ivvah? [And] did they save Samaria from me? Which among all those gods of [those] countries saved their countries from me, that the LORD should save Jerusalem from me?" (2 Kings 18:33-35)

The Rabshakeh's speech, which first skillfully plays on the Israelite concept of God's role in history, ultimately reduces the God of Israel to the status of a local god less powerful than Sennacherib. And here, the Rabshakeh betrays the king's arrogance and ignorance. The Bible's omniscient point of view presents an understanding of the destruction of the northern kingdom of Israel and the later crushing of Judah by Babylon that extends beyond Sennacherib's worldview. The narrative knows that Assyria and Babylon serve only as God's agents and that these empires possess no power or merit of their own. They will be founded, flourish and then die as God wills.

Eliakim and the others, under orders from Hezekiah, make no reply. They are dumbstruck. Buying into Sennacherib's propaganda, they abandon hope and return to the king with their clothes rent—a symbol of grief and even mourning for the holy city about to be destroyed.

After hearing their report, Hezekiah likewise rents his clothes and covers himself with sackcloth. He then goes to the Temple while sending Eliakim, Shebna the scribe, and the senior priests to Isaiah. The prophet instructs:

> "Tell your master as follows: Thus said the LORD: Do not be frightened by the words of blasphemy against Me that you have heard from the minions of the king of Assyria. I will delude him; he will hear a rumor and return to his land, and I will make him fall by the sword in his land." (2 Kings 19:6-7)

At this point, Sennacherib seems either supremely confident or self-delusional. He leaves Lachish to attack Libnah. This presents Tirhakah, king of Nubia—in Hebrew, *Kush*, translated by others as Ethiopia—with the opportunity to attack Sennacherib. The Assyrian king must hurriedly transition from offense to defense. Furthermore, continuing the siege of Jerusalem will reduce his forces against Nubia.

Faced with a challenging situation, Sennacherib sends a letter via unnamed messengers—the Rabshakeh has gone to Libnah, although he could have returned again—to persuade Hezekiah to surrender on Assyrian terms. The letter pointedly calls into question God's ability to defend Jerusalem: "Do not let your God, on whom you are relying, mislead you into thinking that Jerusalem will not be delivered into the hands of the king of Assyria" (2 Kings 19:10). Sennacherib asserts that the Judean capital will fall not because God wishes it but in spite of God's will.

Hezekiah takes the letter to the Temple and prays.

> "True, O Lord, the kings of Assyria have annihilated the nations and their lands, and have committed their gods to the flames and have destroyed them; for they are not gods, but man's handiwork of wood and stone." (2 Kings 19:17-18)

Isaiah sends his own message to Hezekiah: God has heard his prayer and dismisses Sennacherib's threats with disdain. The prophet's words begin with scorn for Assyria:

> "Fair maiden Zion despises you,
> She mocks at you;
> Fair Jerusalem shakes
> Her head at you." (2 Kings 19:21)

These are strong words against an overwhelmingly superior foe, but Isaiah tells Hezekiah in no uncertain terms that he is to maintain his faith and defy Sennacherib. Assyria will retreat.

"I will place my hook in your nose
And My bit between your jaws;
And I will make you go back by the road
By which you came." (2 Kings 19:28)

Judah, threatened by annihilation, will survive; God wills it.

"For a remnant shall come forth from Jerusalem,
Survivors from Mount Zion.
The zeal of the LORD of Hosts
Shall bring this to pass." (2 Kings 19:31)

As to Sennacherib:

"He shall not enter this city:
He shall not shoot an arrow at it,
Or advance upon it with a shield,
Or pile up a siege mound against it.
He shall go back
By the way he came;
He shall not enter this city
—declares the LORD.
I will protect this city for My sake,
And for the sake of My servant David." (2 Kings 19:32-33)

What then of Sennacherib's encounter with God? It comes late in our story but very powerfully. The king of Assyria knows that the Israelites have a God. He has referred to Him by His name, YHVH. He also has used his knowledge of Israelite beliefs to undercut any hope of Hezekiah and Judah that they might defend themselves. All the while, however, Sennacherib fails to understand that God uses him—that he possesses no inherent power.

God brings the matter to an end, displaying His power to devastate Assyria as he devastated Egypt centuries before.

That night an angel of the LORD went out and struck down one hundred and eighty-five thousand in the Assyrian camp, and the

> following morning they were all dead corpses. So Sennacherib of Assyria broke camp and retreated, and stayed in Nineveh. (2 Kings 19:35-36)

Sennacherib receives an historic revelation of epic proportions—an event, according to tradition, that takes place on the first night of Passover, mirroring the deaths of the Egyptians' first-born males. (Bialik, 136:156ff) The historian Paul Johnson takes a critical stance. He suggests natural causes for the Assyrians' plight, citing the Greek historian, Herodotus, who attributes the Assyrian disaster to bubonic plague carried by mice. (Johnson, 73)

It's all downhill from there for Sennacherib. What God begins, the king's sons conclude.

> While he was worshipping in the temple of his god Nisroch, his sons Adrammelech and Sarezer struck him down with the sword. They fled to the land of Ararat, and his son, Esarhaddon succeeded him as king. (1 Kings 19:37)

The Bible does not provide a date or time frame for Sennacherib's assassination. Modern scholars, however, place it in 681 BCE, twenty years after the siege of Jerusalem. The two-decade interval, however, does not suggest that God fails to bring Sennacherib to justice. The biblical narrative directly links the three verses that tell of the Assyrian army's perishing and Sennacherib's withdrawal to Nineveh with his murder.

Call Sennacherib's death at the hands of his own flesh and blood big-time payback if you will. It is hardly undeserved. In seeking to exploit Judah's belief in the God of History, the king of Assyria mocks rather than honors Him. Even after seeing his army—or a major portion of it—perish overnight, Sennacherib remains blind to the cause of the disaster. Like so many other dissemblers and provokers, he ignores the obvious and fails to acknowledge his wrongdoing. Sennacherib, like the Pharaoh of the Exodus, serves as an object lesson: God moves history forward, offers mercy to those who revere Him and eventually brings to justice those who scorn Him.

6
Women of Valor

Grace is deceptive,
Beauty is illusory;
It is for her fear of the LORD
That a woman is to be praised.
Extol her for the fruit of her hand,
And let her works praise her in the gates.
Proverbs 31:30-31

MANY WOMEN—AND NOT WITHOUT CAUSE—express concern that women play only a limited role in the Bible. But a deeper reading of the biblical narrative reveals that it is women who make possible the development and survival of Israel. Without the emotional support and bold actions of the matriarchs—Sarah, Rebekah, Leah and Rachel—the patriarchs could not have fulfilled the covenant God makes with them and their families. The infant Moses would have perished without the protection of Miriam's watchful eye and clever playacting that gets Pharaoh's daughter to take him in and have a Hebrew wet nurse—Moses' own mother (and hers), Jochebed—care for him. Following settlement in the Promised Land, Israel's army, led by Barak, would have failed to gain a critical victory over the Canaanites under the command of Sisera if Deborah, the judge, had not accompanied him into battle.[54] These women are truly notable—and they are not alone.

Non-Israelite women also have encounters with God in the Bible. Zipporah, a Midianite, saves her husband, Moses, from God's wrath. Rahab, a harlot of Jericho, assists in the city's capture by Joshua. The Queen of Sheba helps Solomon put his wisdom in perspective. And Ruth, a Moabite—a woman from a nation whose male descendants are denied entry into the people Israel—undergoes a multi-stage process of conversion to Judaism that leads her to become the great-grandmother of none other than the fabled King David.

One way or another, God touches each of these non-Israelite women. They, in turn, impact Israel and its struggle to adhere to the monotheism of Abraham. Without them, the history of Israel would have been entirely different—if that history would be remembered at all.

54 Sisera was slain by a non-Israelite woman, Yael, wife of Heber the Kenite. While Yael plays an important role, she has neither a direct nor indirect encounter with God, and so her story does not appear in this volume.

ZIPPORAH, MOSES' WIFE

Redeemer Through Circumcision

After slaying an Egyptian, Moses flees Egypt and arrives in Midian. At a well, he meets Zipporah, one of seven daughters of Jethro, priest of Midian. Jethro gives Zipporah to Moses as his wife, and she bears him two sons. Tending his flocks at Horeb, Moses encounters a burning bush where God instructs him to return to Egypt and ask Pharaoh to release Israel from bondage. At a night encampment on the way, God threatens to slay either Moses or one of his sons—the brief episode of only three verses is unclear. Zipporah saves the intended victim by circumcising one of their sons.

No matter how much a biblical wife seems relegated to the background, her presence inevitably proves of great importance. No wonder that Proverbs advises:

> What a rare find is a capable wife!
> Her worth is far beyond that of rubies.
> Her husband puts his confidence in her,
> And lacks no good thing. (Proverbs 31:10-11)

Not infrequently, a woman must step forward to protect her family. When she does, she becomes a force to be reckoned with. So it is with Zipporah ("bird"), daughter of the Midianite priest Jethro. The story of her husband, Moses, is commonly known. Zipporah's is often overlooked and, when read, not understood. But without Zipporah's courage and determination, Moses cannot fulfill his mission; there can be no Exodus.

Zipporah's story begins with Moses, the Hebrew rescued from the Nile by Pharaoh's daughter and brought up in the royal court. As an adult, Moses slays an Egyptian who beats a Hebrew slave. Moses' lofty position cannot save him; he has overstepped his bounds. Fleeing Pharaoh's wrath, he escapes eastward to Midian. There he stops at a well where the seven daughters of Jethro, priest of Midian, have come early to draw water for their father's flock. (For more on this incident and Jethro, see *Egypt: Slavery and Redemption*.) The Zohar (2, 12b), the seminal book of Jewish mysticism, states that at this same well Rebekah met Eliezer, Abraham's servant, and Rachel met Jacob—even though Midian lies to the east of Israel and Haran, where Rachel lived, to the north. Shepherds drive Jethro's daughters off, but Moses—as does Jacob for Rachel—protects the girls and waters their flock.

Moses' courage and kindness impress Jethro. Incredulous that his daughters have not invited this "Egyptian" to break bread, he tells them to summon Moses for dinner. The Midrash (Exodus Rabbah 1:32) states that Zipporah "ran after him like a bird (*zippor*) and brought him home." But in fact, the Midrash relates, she was given the name Zipporah because she cleaned the house like a bird, picking up every crumb of dirt, or as others comment, cleansed the house of idolatry, making atonement with the blood of a bird.

Moses, facing a long period of exile, consents to stay with Jethro, who gives Zipporah to him as his wife. The idea of Israel's greatest prophet marrying a non-Israelite may seem shocking, but many of the great men of Israel—including David and Solomon—follow this practice up to the time of the building of the Second Temple. Pitron Torah, a medieval collection of Midrash, rationalizes that Moses was allowed to marry a non-Israelite because Zipporah converted to Judaism, and the marriage took place before the revelation of the Torah at Sinai, which forbade marriages to Canaanites, Moabites and Ammonites. (Cohen, 269) Moreover, Zipporah comes from a holy family. Jethro is a priest of Midian and perhaps no less the equal of Melchizedek, king-priest of Salem, whom the Rabbis hail. (See *The Era of Abraham*.) In fact, many commentators attribute Moses' monotheistic fervor to his father-in-law.

In time, Zipporah bears a son. Moses names him Gershom—"I have been a stranger in a foreign land" or more literally "a stranger or foreigner there." Then Zipporah fades into the background. Since Moses' arrival in Midian, she has not uttered a single word herself; the daughters speak as a group when they reveal to Jethro their story of the Egyptian at the well. We have no idea how Zipporah reacts when she finds out that Moses is the son of Hebrew slaves rather than an Egyptian noble. When she does speak later, her few words are shrouded in mystery, but her actions are resolute.

Moses, as we know, encounters God on a mountaintop, drawn to a bush that burns but is not consumed. Moses may be resigned to living out his life in Midian, but God has other plans. He instructs Moses to return to Egypt. Moses protests. God insists. After a discussion of some length, Moses agrees. How can he not? Being a good family man, he plans to bring his wife and *two* sons with him. The first-born is the aforementioned Gershom. The younger is Eliezer—"The God of my father was my help."[55]

How does Zipporah respond to this unexpected "corporate relocation" which promises only severe challenges? The text reveals nothing. The Midrash (Exodus Rabbah 5:5), however, relates that Moses brings his family along so that Zipporah and the boys can join the Israelites when God presents the Torah at Sinai.

As the journey to Egypt begins, Zipporah reemerges to play the crucial role in a brief and puzzling story. From the critical standpoint, this episode appears to be an insert—perhaps a snippet of some longer but forgotten tale. It contains only three verses:

> At a night encampment on the way, the LORD encountered him and sought to kill him. So Zipporah took a flint and cut off her son's foreskin, and touched his legs with it, saying, "You are truly a bridegroom of blood to me!" And when He let him alone, she added, "A bridegroom of blood because of the circumcision." (Ex. 4:24-26)

Three verses raise so many questions! Who is the "him" God seeks to kill? Which son is circumcised? And whose legs are touched?

Many commentators, including Rashi, believe it is Moses whom God seeks to kill. Others disagree. The Talmud (Nedarim 32a) offers R. Simeon ben Gamaliel's position that God, through Satan, intends to kill "the child." A midrash (Exodus Rabbah 7:9)

---

55 Unlike the matriarchs, Zipporah does not name her sons. Moses does so, following the practice of Joseph, an earlier Hebrew expatriate in Egypt.

points to the younger son, Eliezer, assuming that Gershom already would have been circumcised. This follows another Sage in the Talmud (Nedarim 31b-32a), Rabbi Yose. He suggests that Moses delayed circumcising his younger—and apparently newborn—son for three days due to the rigors of the journey to Egypt then busied himself with arrangements upon arriving at the inn—or night encampment—rather than circumcising the boy first. Nahum Sarna, from his modern perspective, presents a third opinion—God intends to slay the elder son, Gershom.

Questions continue. Why would Moses neglect the covenant of circumcision entered into by God and Abraham—one that remains critical to Jewish identity and practice today? We can only guess. S.R. Hirsch cites R. Eliezer Ha-Modai in the Mechilta: "…Jethro would only consent to give his daughter to Moses on the condition that her first son should be allowed to remain dedicated to idolatry." (Hirsch, 51) This, of course, undercuts Jethro's position as a monotheist and role model for his son-in-law.

Or, if Gershom is the uncircumcised son, perhaps Moses assumes that he, along with his family, will never return to Egypt and seeks to assimilate into Midianite culture. If circumcised, Gershom, and later Eliezer, may be shunned as outsiders in spite of their Midianite mother and the prestige of their grandfather, Jethro. Such a predicament reflects that faced by Joseph, who marries an Egyptian woman. Joseph raises his two sons as Egyptians, although they bear Hebrew names and undoubtedly understand their Hebrew background. The Bible makes no mention of his circumcising them. Yet circumcision was common among other Semites as well as the Egyptians. Zipporah, Nahum Sarna believes, would have been well aware of this practice. (Sarna/Exodus, 25)

Some modern scholars offer other rationales. Avivah Zornberg suggests that Moses' fault is his reluctance to return to Egypt as Israel's spokesman. God has had to exercise all His persuasive powers to obtain Moses' assent. (Zornberg, 96-7) Richard Friedman offers a related view. He translates Exodus 4:24 as, "And he was on the way, at a lodging place, and YHVH met him, and he asked to kill him." Moses, who admits to not being a public speaker, prefers that

God kill him, Friedman speculates, rather than be sent to Egypt. Friedman's idea is not without merit since public speaking commonly rates as one of people's biggest fears.

Likewise, while we may be disturbed by the idea that Moses would risk surrendering his life rather than obey God, Moses later expresses a suicidal form of frustration. In Numbers 11:15, he asks God to kill him so that he will no longer have to lead the ungrateful Israelites in the wilderness. Creating his own midrash, Friedman presents Zipporah as adamant that she will not be left widowed. He imagines her telling Moses, "You have a wife! You have a son, who should live to marry and be part of the covenant!" This woman's name may be "bird," but she is not fragile by any means. (Friedman/Commentary, 184)

William Propp offers another proposal. God seeks Moses' death to avenge the bloodguilt he bears for having killed an Egyptian. (Friedman/Commentary, 184)

Here we may ask: Why doesn't God kill Moses when he refuses to go to Egypt rather than after he sets out? And if Moses bears such great guilt for killing the Egyptian in the first place, why did God let him live and flee?

The puzzle now grows even more complex. If Moses is God's intended victim, how will this impact His plan to redeem Israel? If a better candidate than Moses exists, why doesn't God choose him—or her—in the first place?

But this is Zipporah's story, no matter how brief. And Zipporah proves herself to be a woman of action. Without hesitation, she circumcises her unnamed son, accepting a responsibility Judaism places on fathers, not mothers. After all, God commands Abraham, not Sarah, regarding circumcision in Genesis 17. Abraham dutifully circumcises Ishmael, considered to be thirteen at the time, and all the males of his household.

What's more, how does Zipporah know that Moses is in jeopardy and that circumcision is required to save him? One midrash (Exodus Rabbah 5:8) states that an angel makes Moses' predicament clear by swallowing Moses "from his head to his circumcised membrum." Zipporah takes the hint!

Then we have the matter of Zipporah touching someone's legs with the circumcised foreskin. But whose? According to Jonathan ben Uzziel, a pupil of Hillel, she thrusts the bloody foreskin at the feet of the attacking angel to propitiate him. (Plaut, 1710) Ibn Ezra offers that she casts the foreskin down at Moses' feet. Richard Friedman adds that, "this use of blood to avert death is a foreshadowing of the tenth plague in Egypt." (Friedman/ Commentary, 184) Indeed, God commands the Israelites to smear the blood of a lamb on their doorposts and lintels so that He will pass over their houses and they will avoid the death he metes out to the Egyptian first-born males.

What of Zipporah's reference to a "bridegroom of blood"? Rashi links the bridegroom to Moses. Zipporah believes that her bridegroom—Moses—would have been killed had the boy remained uncircumcised. Her son would have been her husband's killer.

Another approach examines the relationship between the Hebrew word *chatan* (bridegroom) and the Arab word *chatana* (circumciser). In the ancient Arab world, men often were circumcised prior to marriage as an act of atonement. Thus Ibn Ezra relates the term to the younger son, Eliezer. "It is the custom of women to refer to a child as a bridegroom when he is circumcised." An ancient practice may have made its way into the biblical narrative without historical or cultural reference.

Circumcising her sons to honor Moses' Hebrew tradition obviously confronts Zipporah with a weighty choice. Leaving for Egypt with her husband, she can remain a Midianite—and possibly a member of another monotheistic tradition, since the Sages view Jethro as one of three "righteous gentiles." Or she can leave her father's tradition to become a full member of Moses' extended family and people—a people whose fate she will share. Zipporah chooses the latter. Faced with a desperate situation, she unhesitatingly circumcises Gershom or Eliezer, clearly establishes her son's identity as a Hebrew and adopts a new identity for herself.

Now, one final question presents itself. What happens to Zipporah and the boys in Egypt? They never get there. According to Exodus 18:2, Moses sends them back to Midian. Their next, and final, appearance in the narrative presents them rejoining Moses in the wilderness—

but engaging in no action or dialogue—after word of the Exodus reaches Jethro. Rashi provides one explanation. Aaron, on meeting Zipporah and her sons, protests to Moses, "We grieve for the earlier [enslaved] ones… and now you come to add to their numbers!" Or perhaps Moses realizes that Zipporah and the children's presence in Egypt will only be a distraction. Moses, after all, must concentrate his energies on not one but two difficult challenges—being accepted by the Israelites as God's emissary then persuading Pharaoh to free them. It can little profit the prophet to come home at night after introducing yet another plague to Egypt only to hear, "Wait until I tell you what one of your sons did today!"

Zipporah returns to Midian after the circumcision episode—but as a different woman. "Like our ancestor Abraham," writes Rabbi Rebecca T. Alpert, "she teaches us about surrendering old beliefs for new ones, and about what it feels like to be compelled to take a knife to a child in pursuit of those beliefs." (Goldstein, 126)[56]

In three brief and difficult verses, Zipporah reaches into the depths of her soul to make a commitment to a future she never imagined as a girl. Thus Samson Raphael Hirsch states that on that pivotal journey to Egypt, "free from all influence of parents and relatives, alone, thrown back entirely on herself, Zipporah is to soar to the heights of Jewish womanhood." (Hirsch, 51)

56 In Genesis 22, Abraham prepares to sacrifice Isaac on Mount Moriah but is halted by an angel sent from God.

RAHAB, HARLOT OF JERICHO

Protector of Israelite Spies

Following Moses' death, Joshua prepares to lead the Israelite army into Canaan. He sends two spies to scout out Jericho. News of the spies reaches the city's king. He orders Rahab, a harlot whose house the spies were seen entering, to surrender the men. Rahab protects the spies, acknowledging the power with which God previously defeated Egypt and recognizing that God will give Jericho and the rest of Canaan to Israel. The spies guarantee the safety of Rahab and her family so long as all remain in the house, which is to be identified by a crimson cord tied around a window. Jericho is destroyed; Rahab and her family are saved.

What do we mean by "seeing" God? Judaism recognizes that God has no corporeal body, although the Torah does present an anthropomorphic God and affords Adam and Eve, as well as Abraham, Moses and Israel's elders, at least a glimpse—if not more—of Him. The prophets have visions of God as well. Moreover, God "appears" to Job out of a tempest. As the biblical narrative progresses, however, anthropomorphic images rapidly disappear. It is through God's *deeds* that He makes Himself known both to Israel and the nations. God becomes visible both to Israelites and non-Israelites through such historic revelations as the destruction of Sodom and Gomorrah, the plagues that strike Egypt, the parting of the Reed Sea and the victorious battles waged by Israel against the Amorites.

In light of these major events, it should not surprise us that the word of witnesses is likely to spread. While the grapevine of the ancient Near East lacked our technology, people were no less interested in news from near and distant places. Following the destruction of Pharaoh and his army in the Reed Sea, Moses and the Israelites sing a song praising what God has done, including the phrase, "The peoples hear, they tremble." (Ex. 15:14) As the Exodus concludes, the Canaanites not only hear of the size of the Israelite nation that has undergone a forty-year transformation in the wilderness, they observe this people poised on the east side of the Jordan River, across from Jericho. It might have been another of God's miracle had word—and fear—*not* traveled quickly.

Indeed, fear of Israel plays a major part in God's plan. In Egypt, prior to the onset of the seventh plague—hail—God instructs Moses to tell Pharaoh that He could easily destroy him and his people and be done with the matter. "Nevertheless I have spared you for this purpose: in order to show you My power, and in order that My fame may resound throughout the world" (Ex. 9:15-16). Likewise, following the giving of the law at Sinai, God assures Moses: "I will send forth My terror before you, and I will throw into panic all the people among whom you come, and I will make all your enemies turn tail before you" (Ex. 23:27).

The fear of God will aid Israel in other instances, as well. In Numbers 22, this huge people that "hides the earth from view" frightens Balak, King of the Midianite confederation. So filled is he with dread that he calls on the prophet Balaam to curse and destroy the huge multitude encamped on his doorstep. (See *Dissemblers and Provokers.*) Centuries later, the armies of the Ammonites and Moabites, along with some Ammonim (Meunites), confront King Jehoshaphat of Judah. God causes them to turn on the inhabitants of the hill country of Seir, to the east, then on each other. No one survives. As a result, "The terror of God seized all the kingdoms of the lands when they heard that the LORD had fought the enemies of Israel" (2 Chron. 20:29).

As to Rahab, the Book of Deuteronomy concludes with Moses' death and Israel, under the command of Joshua, ready to enter Canaan. The story continues in the Book of Joshua with D-Day at hand. God tells Joshua to prepare to cross the Jordan. In turn, Joshua orders to his officials:

> "Go through the camp and charge the people thus: Get provisions ready, for in three days time you are to cross the Jordan, in order to enter and possess the land that the LORD your God is giving you as a possession." (Joshua 1:11)

Fear envelops Jericho. But at least one enlightened individual experiences reverent awe. This person understands that Israel's flight from Egypt and journey to Canaan represents no earthly ambition for conquest but the unfolding of God's will. This sense of God is achieved neither by a sage nor a mystic but rather a by harlot. A woman named Rahab, as we shall shortly see, comprehends God's hand in history as well as His singular nature.

Of course, while God stands behind Israel, Israel in turn must accept responsibility for its destiny and carry out the attack against Jericho. As a capable general, Joshua seeks intelligence. However, he rejects the unfortunate precedent of Moses, who publicly sent twelve spies into Canaan only to have ten of them—Joshua and Caleb being the exceptions—fearfully warn the nation's leaders against going up into the land. Joshua cannot risk another humiliating report of this kind. Instead, he secretly sends just two spies, unnamed in the biblical narrative but identified by the Midrash (Genesis Rabbah 16:1) as Caleb and Phinehas.

The spies arrive at Rahab's house and lodge there. Why this house? We cannot be sure. But the biblical text situates it within the city's wall. Perhaps it offers minimal exposure to prying eyes, a quick escape route and a good view of the defenses to be breached. Why do they lodge with a harlot? Lust does not form part of the equation here. We find one possibility in the Hebrew word for harlot—*zonah*. Both the Targum—the translation and paraphrasing of the Bible into Aramaic—and commentators link *zonah* with *mazon*, Hebrew for food or meal. Rahab may be an innkeeper as well as a prostitute. Perhaps the spies believe that they will be taken for ordinary travelers and draw no notice.

As is typical, the biblical narrative discloses little else about Rahab. The Sages seek to fill in the meager outline of her portrait. The Talmud (Zevachim 116b) reports that Rahab was ten years old when the Israelites left Egypt forty years earlier; she is now fifty. During those forty years, she pursued harlotry with every prince and ruler in the region. Moreover, the Talmud (Megillah 14b) posits, Rahab was a dazzler. "There have been four women of surpassing beauty in the world—Sarah, Rahab, Abigail and Esther."[57] Rahab was so appealing, claims R. Isaac, the very mention of her name brought men to orgasm. (The Sages may have lifted their eyes heavenward, but their feet remained firmly on the ground.)

The spies' clandestine mission is compromised immediately. The king of Jericho learns that they have entered the city and lodged with Rahab. He orders her to produce them. Rahab has no intention of doing so and misleads the king's officials:

> "It is true," she said, "the men did come to me, but I didn't know where they were from. And at dark, when the gate was about to be closed, the men left; and I don't know where the men went. Quick, go after them, for you can overtake them." (Joshua 2:4-5)

Rahab compounds her treason by taking the Israelite spies up to the roof and hiding them under stalks of flax. The king's men, buying Rahab's story, head off towards the Jordan in pursuit. Only then does she reveal to the spies her reason for protecting them.

> "I know that the Lord has given the country to you, because dread of you has fallen upon us, and all the inhabitants of the land are quaking before you. For we have heard how the Lord dried up the waters of the Sea of Reeds for you when you left Egypt, and what you did to Sihon and Og, the two Amorite kings across the Jordan, whom you doomed. When we heard about it, we lost heart, and no man had any more spirit left because of you…" (Joshua 2:9-11)

How has news come to Jericho? Abravanel suggests that Rahab learned of Israel's power from the blessings issued by none other than the Midianite prophet Balaam. (Leibowitz/Bamidbar, 305)

Rahab's reaction takes her well beyond simple fear. The God of Israel appears to be no ordinary god, and her understanding of

57 Sarah's beauty draws the attention of Pharaoh and Abimelech, king of Gerar. (See *The Era of Abraham.*) Abigail provides food to David and his followers, and later becomes David's wife (1 Samuel 25). Esther is the well-known heroine of the Book of Esther who saves the Jews of Persia by foiling the wicked intentions of Haman.

this surpasses that of the people with whom she lives. Under no illusion that Jericho can mount a successful defense, she returns to the roof to explain herself, acknowledging that, "the LORD your God is the *only* [italics mine] God in heaven above and on earth below." (Josh. 2:11) Her statement echoes Abraham's instruction to his servant, Eliezer, to "swear by the LORD, the God of heaven and the God of the earth" (Gen. 24:3) as well as Moses' instruction to Israel: "Know therefore this day and keep in mind that the LORD alone is God in heaven above and on earth below; there is no other" (Deut. 4:39).

As readers, we may be a bit skeptical or even cynical. Does Rahab realize the truth of the One God? Or does she simply use her feminine wiles to ingratiate herself? This tactic would not be atypical of a woman who makes her living appealing to the vanity of men. Later statements from Rahab will reveal her sincerity. At the moment, Rahab focuses on survival. After rejecting all other gods and endorsing monotheism, she makes a very business-like plea:

> "Now, since I have shown loyalty to you, swear to me by the LORD that you in turn will show loyalty to my family. Provide me with a reliable sign that you will spare the lives of my father and mother, my brothers and sisters, and all who belong to them, and save us from death." (Joshua 4:12-13)

As a harlot, Rahab certainly understands the nature of trade between two parties. But credit must be given. She wants to do more than save her own skin. Rahab apparently has neither husband nor children, but she does have relatives and cares for them. In this regard, her request seems to bring her closer to Abraham than Noah. Abraham looks beyond himself, seeking mercy for Sodom and Gomorrah if only ten innocent people can be found there. Noah, when commanded to take his wife, sons and daughters-in-law on the ark, never asks God permission to bring others aboard.

The spies assent to Rahab's request but on the condition that she not disclose them. She responds by lowering a rope, enabling them to climb out her window and down the wall then hide for three days until they can return to Joshua. At this point, a practical dilemma arises. How are the invading Israelites to identify her house? The spies propose a solution, which doubles as a warning:

> "We will be released from this oath which you have made us take [unless,] when we invade the country, you tie this length of crimson cord to the window through which you let us down." (Joshua 2:17)

Whether the crimson cord refers to the rope by which the men are to escape or to a piece of their clothing or equipment we do not know. Nonetheless, they have chosen an interesting sign whose crimson color suggests two things: the lifeblood that God holds precious and the protective blood applied by the Israelites to the lintels and doorposts of their houses before God slays the Egyptians' first-born on the initial Passover evening.

The spies repeat their compact and warn that any member of Rahab's family venturing outside the doors of her house will have his blood on his own head. "But if a hand is laid on anyone who remains in the house with you, his blood shall be on our heads." (Josh. 2:19) The deal made, Rahab sends the spies off and ties the crimson cord to her window.

The conquest of Jericho unfolds. The Israelites cross the Jordan. Following God's instruction, they march around the city, making one complete circuit on each of six days. On the seventh, again as instructed, they circumnavigate the city seven times, after which the priests blow their horns. Joshua commands the people:

> "Shout! For the LORD has given you the city. The city and everything in it are to be proscribed for the LORD; only Rahab the harlot is to be spared, and all who are with her in the house, because she hid the messengers we sent." (Joshua 6:16-17)

The Israelites shout, and the walls of Jericho collapse. Slaughter follows. Men, women, children and animals fall to the sword. The Israelites then burn the city since proscription—*cherem*—demands total destruction. This proscription is so intense that Joshua curses anyone who will rebuild Jericho. Maimonides explains that, "the effect of the miracle was to remain for ever, so that any one who would see the wall sunk in the ground would understand that it was not in the condition of a building pulled down by human hands, but sunk through a miracle." (Maimonides, 2:50)

Only Rahab and her family survive. Her house also is spared, although David Kimhi, a twelfth-thirteenth-century commentator, offers that only the portions of the walls directly opposite the Israelite army fell; Rahab's house stood elsewhere on the wall. (Soncino/Joshua, 30)

The proscription of Jericho—or of any city for that matter—presents an issue both troubling and hopeful. Michael Fishbane notes that this total destruction was also imposed on every man, woman and child in every town ruled by King Sihon of Heshbon (Deut. 2:34) as well as in the seven Canaanite nations (Deut. 7:1-2). No one was spared. But events unfold differently in the Book of Joshua. "We must therefore assume," Fishbane writes, "that the text in Joshua rejects the harsh law of *cherem* and opts for mercy to those who display kindness. A silent protest (albeit hedged with signs and oaths and conditions) thus lies at the heart of the narrative. The human face of the enemy makes a compelling claim." (Etz Hayim, 856)

Rahab's is indeed a human face, and the biblical narrative presents her as a righteous woman worthy of heroine status. In this regard, she resembles Tamar in Genesis 38 who disguises herself as a harlot to seek justice from Judah and has twin sons by him, becoming an antecedent of King David. And why should Rahab not deserve great praise? It is the *human* spirit—not just the Israelite spirit—that seeks closeness with God. Rahab clearly recognizes God's signs and wonders. In this light, the narrative completes Rahab's story, reporting that, "she dwelt among the Israelites—as is still the case" (Josh. 6:25). Rahab becomes, at the very least, a *ger toshav*—a resident alien who lives by the laws of Israel. The Talmud (Megillah 14b), however, elevates her position, relating that she marries Joshua and bears him daughters. Eight prophets, including Jeremiah and the prophetess, Huldah, descend from her.[58]

While no formal conversion process exists in the Bible, a case can be made for Rahab as a true *ger tzedek,* accepting the God of Israel and the Torah as her own. This follows from a comparison of the statements of two of "God's others," who also acknowledge God. Following the Exodus, Jethro, Moses' father-in-law, declares, "Now I know that the Lord is greater than all gods…" (Ex. 18:11). The Sages laud Jethro, although he seems to leave open the possibility that other gods exist. (See *Egypt: Slavery and Redemption.*) Naaman, the general of Aram, takes a stronger monotheistic view. Cured of leprosy by the prophet Elisha, he states, "Now I know that there is no God in the whole world except in Israel!" (2 Kings 5:15). (See *Kings and Commoners.*) The word translated by JPS as "world"—*aretz*—usually means land or earth and thus appears to limit God's sovereignty. Rahab's statement goes beyond these, declaring, "for the Lord your God is the *only* [italics mine] God in heaven above and on earth below" (Josh. 2:11). She endorses the God of Israel as the God of all creation.

How does a non-Israelite in a polytheistic world arrive at monotheism? Rabbi Abraham Cohen writes eloquently: "The unity and omnipotence of God were one of the fundamental tenets impressed upon the children of Israel in the wilderness. Strange though it must have appeared in those days, it may well have percolated to other peoples and gained credence from some individuals among them." (Soncino/Joshua, 10)

We may marvel that a "lowly harlot" understands the power of God while kings and priests maintain their loyalty to idols. But Rahab demonstrates—as the Bible consistently informs us—that wisdom depends not on power or position but the openness of the soul to its Creator.

---

58 From the Christian perspective of the Book of Matthew, Rahab is the wife of Salmon (son of Nachshon) and mother of Boaz, ancestor of David (see the story of Ruth below) and thus of Jesus.

THE QUEEN OF SHEBA

SINGER OF GOD'S PRAISES

Hearing of King Solomon's wealth and wisdom, the queen of Sheba journeys to Jerusalem. There, she tests Solomon's wisdom and finds that it surpasses that about what she has heard. The king's court and the Temple impress her as well. In response, the queen blesses the God of Israel, stating that it is He Who has placed Solomon on the throne to administer justice and righteousness. She presents Solomon with great treasures before returning home with gifts of her own.

WE MAY WONDER HOW PEOPLE IN THE ANCIENT WORLD ever communicated across any distance, lacking the cell phones and email access we take for granted. Yet while word traveled far more slowly then, it still traveled. Merchants, sailors, soldiers, government functionaries and migrants carried information across vast distances. Thus news of the wisdom and wealth of King Solomon need not have been confined to the court in Jerusalem or within the borders of Israel.

As does Rahab in Jericho, the queen of Sheba—a nation probably located in Yemen on the southern tip of the Arabian Peninsula, although a case can be made for Ethiopia—learns of Israel and its God. The Bible makes brief work of her story in just the first thirteen verses of 1 Kings 10 (with a closely parallel telling in 2 Chronicles 9:1-12). Yet that story resonates to the queen's credit while making her one of the more recognized figures in biblical literature.

As with Rahab, the grapevine plays a major role. First Kings relates, "The queen of Sheba heard of Solomon's name, through the name of the LORD, and she came to test him with hard questions" (1 Kings 10:1). What is meant by "through the name of the LORD" remains uncertain. (The first verse in 2 Chronicles 9 omits this phrase.) Exact translations into English are often speculative since the hand-copied Masoretic texts on which they are based are only a thousand years old and appear to have been subject to continual scribal error. The Interpreter's Bible, for example, translates the Hebrew phrase, *l'shem Adonai* as "*concerning* the name of the LORD." What seems more certain is that 1 Kings links Solomon's reputation directly to God's blessing of him, a condition made explicit in the biblical text.

What is clear is that word has reached the queen of Sheba concerning the magnificent, twenty-year construction project—the Lord's House and the royal palace—undertaken by Solomon. Reports of the very powerful God of Israel, for whom the magnificent Temple has been built, likely have not escaped her, either. The queen, after all, is a woman of power, wealth and no doubt cunning, holding her throne in a world dominated by men.

Her curiosity piqued, the queen pays a state visit to Israel. A large retinue accompanies her, bearing impressive gifts—spices (frankincense and myrrh were in great demand in the ancient world), a great quantity of gold and precious stones.[59] But this sovereign undertakes an atypical royal mission. She desires neither a treaty nor gifts, although she will return home with the latter, such being the etiquette of statecraft.

What the queen of Sheba really seeks is wisdom. "When she came to Solomon, she asked him all that she had in mind" (1 Kings 10:2). Here, the queen distinguishes herself. Few monarchs possess the humility to declare or suggest that their knowledge or wisdom is limited. Certainly, traveling to Solomon's court brings her to the right person since, "there was nothing that the king did not know" (1 Kings 10:3). What questions did she ask? A legend from the Targum Sheni of Esther has her pose three difficult riddles, which Solomon solves.[60]

The splendor of Solomon's court—his palace, food, attendants and wine—and the burnt offerings he presents in the Temple so greatly impress the queen that, "she was left breathless" (1 Kings 10:5). She then reveals to Solomon that she was skeptical. Not content with the reports reaching her throne, she sought proof of what she had heard—hence her visit to Jerusalem. She has received it. As a result, she praises the God of Israel in Solomon's presence:

---

59 The wealth of Sheba is enumerated in Isaiah 60:6 and Ezekiel 27:22.

60 The Midrash enumerates a number of riddles, many found in *The Book of Legends*, edited by Bialik and Ravnitzky and in *Legends of the Bible*, assembled by Louis Ginzberg.

> "Praised be the LORD your God, who delighted in you and set you on the throne of Israel. It is because of the LORD's everlasting love for Israel that He made you king to administer justice and righteousness." (1 Kings 10:9)

The queen of Sheba both acknowledges the power of the God of Israel and provides Solomon with a critical reminder. It is God who has granted him wisdom and good fortune; Solomon has not acquired them on his own. Here, she displays keen insight as well as humility. The queen has intuited what we as readers already have learned. In passages beginning with 1 Kings 3:4—before the queen enters the biblical narrative—God appears to the young Solomon in a dream and says, "Ask, what shall I grant you?" Solomon replies, "Grant, then, Your servant an understanding mind to judge Your people, to distinguish between good and bad; for who can judge this vast people of Yours?" Since the king asks for wisdom rather than riches and glory, God grants him all three. Further, the queen's praise emphasizes God's eternal covenant with Israel—a people who must live justly and righteously in return for God's favor.

Like many of "God's others," the queen of Sheba acknowledges the God of Israel but does not necessarily consider Him to be the only god—or her own for that matter. "Praised be the LORD *your* God," she states initially. (The phrase "your God" is used twice in 2 Chronicles 9:8.) But God's power—all that He has done for Solomon and Israel—is not lost on her.

Returning to her duties as a monarch on state business, the queen presents Solomon with the treasures she has brought, including 120 talents of gold. Solomon, in turn, gives her "everything she wanted and asked for" in addition to unspecified treasure from his royal bounty (1 Kings 10:13). "Everything" is a rather broad term and may hint at the opportunity for a more intimate relationship, as we shall see next. The queen then returns home.

While the Bible's tale of the queen of Sheba is brief, it has made a lasting impact on other peoples. Ethiopian Christians cite the Kebra Negast, "The Book of the Glory of Kings," which states that the queen bears a son to Solomon—a son who becomes Ethiopia's King Menelik I.

The Quran also tells of the queen who reigns over Sheba (27:22ff). A bird reports of Sheba to Solomon, "She is possessed of every virtue and has a splendid throne. But she and her subjects worship the sun instead of Allah. Satan has seduced them and debarred them from the right path..." Solomon has the queen's throne brought to him and altered. He then tricks her into believing his glass-paved palace floor is a pool of water and baring her legs. Acknowledging her sin, she submits to Allah.

From the biblical perspective, an intriguing question arises that is applicable to so many of "God's others." If the queen of Sheba concedes the power and justice of the God of Israel, why does she not become a follower of the Israelite religion as do Rahab (preceding) and Ruth (following) and even convert all of Sheba? Ralph W. Sockman, a leading Christian commentator of the mid-twentieth century, notes, "There is no mention that the queen sought any further knowledge of Solomon's God or came to share the king's faith. The temple had aroused her wonder, but it had not won a new convert. She had been impressed with what the Lord had done for Israel, but she did not bring Him to herself." (Interpreter's, 96)

The biblical text most likely does not address itself to this matter because Judaism generally has not sought converts. God requires only Israel to fulfill the covenant at Sinai. The rest of humanity must adhere to the seven Noahide laws. (See *Monotheism: Humanity's Natural Religious State.*) Yet it remains likely that the justice and righteousness Solomon exercises through devotion to God are values that the queen shares. Doubtless, she worships some other god or gods. Upon returning to Sheba, she may even decide to incorporate the God of Israel into her pantheon. It is more than reasonable to assume, however, that God has affected her, and that her continuing reign reflects what she has seen and experienced in Jerusalem. The queen of Sheba has encountered God through the gifts He has bestowed on Solomon based on the just and righteous exercise of power. She cannot help but be wiser and more humble after the experience.

THE WIDOW OF ZAREPHATH

Witness to Resurrection

Elijah, the famed ninth-century BCE prophet, flees the wrath of King Ahab and goes to Wadi Cherith. There, thanks to God's protection, ravens bring him food. When the wadi dries up, God instructs him to go to Zarephath in Sidon to be fed by a certain widow. The widow recognizes Elijah as a man of God and tells him that she has only a handful of flour and a little oil. Elijah acts as the conduit for a miracle—the flour and oil never run out. When the widow's son becomes dangerously ill, Elijah brings him back to life.

God's punishments of evildoers often take the form of miracles. Many of these may be viewed as either suspensions or distortions of the laws of nature, or God-aided events within the scope of natural law. Whichever they may be, these events lie far apart from the ordinary, although critical scholars often seek to find logical explanations for them. It is sufficient for our purposes to acknowledge that the biblical narrative presents any number of God-caused calamities. The Flood annihilates all humanity except Noah and his family. Sulfurous fire falls from the sky to destroy Sodom and Gomorrah. Ten plagues impose great suffering on Egypt. The walls of Jericho collapse when the Israelites sound their horns, leaving the Canaanite city defenseless.

Miracles also protect the righteous. Thus a miracle saves the prophet Elijah from a king's wrath. Shortly after, a non-Israelite widow outside the land of Israel encounters God through not one but two life affirming miracles rendered by God through Elijah.

As a prophet, Elijah champions righteousness and justice. In modern terms, he "speaks truth to power." Because power does not like to be chastised, it comes as no surprise that Elijah antagonizes perhaps the most evil of all Israelite kings, Ahab, who ruled the northern kingdom of Israel from 873 to 852. The Bible condemns Ahab in no uncertain terms. "Ahab son of Omri did what was displeasing to the Lord, more than all who preceded him" (1 Kings 16:30). Just what did Ahab do? He married Jezebel, daughter of the Phoenician King, Ethbaal. He also built a temple for the god Baal in Samaria and made a sacred post, violating the injunction in Deuteronomy 16:21. So abhorrent is he that the biblical narrative is moved to repeat its condemnation: "Ahab did more to vex the Lord, the God of Israel, than all the kings of Israel who preceded him" (1 Kings 16:33).

In opposing the degradations of Ahab, Elijah hardly appears as a shrinking violet. "There is no biblical prophet more furious, impassioned, and uncompromising," notes Rabbi Joseph Telushkin. (Telushkin, 87) The outraged Elijah confronts Ahab directly. Flexing his prophetic power, he draws a line of righteousness in the sand: "As the Lord lives, the God of Israel whom I serve, there will be no dew or rain except at my bidding" (1 Kings 17:1).

Water, the lifeblood of any land and often a scarce commodity in the Near East, will be withheld, leading Israel to suffer famine because of the wrongdoings of the royal couple. Such a punishment can only come from God, of course. Ahab nonetheless directs his fury at Elijah, who serves simply as God's messenger and agent in this matter. If we require more proof of the king's evil shortsightedness, we have it here.

God knows the depths of Ahab's displeasure. Accordingly, he tells Elijah to flee to the Wadi Cherith, east of the Jordan River. How will Elijah survive? God instructs: "You will drink from the wadi, and I have commanded the ravens to feed you there" (1 Kings 17:4). Bringing to mind the quail and manna provided to the Israelites in the wilderness in Exodus 16, God performs a saving miracle. The ravens bring bread and meat to Elijah each morning and evening.

Acts of God may produce unforeseen consequences, however. When God withholds rain from Ahab, the wadi dries up. God then sends Elijah to the town of Zarephath, about ten miles south of today's Sidon in Lebanon and within Phoenician territory. There, God relates, a specific widow will feed him.

Elijah obeys and finds the widow. But surely he must be taken aback. The prophet discovers not someone of substance in a grand house but a poor woman gathering wood. Undismayed, he asks for water and a piece of bread. His request tests the widow much as

Eliezer, Abraham's servant, tests Rebekah in Genesis 24, when he asks for water for himself and his camels. The widow's response reveals the full extent of her poverty.

> "As the Lord your God lives," she replied, "I have nothing baked, nothing but a handful of flour in a jar and a little oil in a jug. I am just gathering a couple of sticks, so that I can go home and prepare it for me and my son; we shall eat it and then we shall die." (1 Kings: 17:12)

As with Shiphrah and Puah, the midwives to the Hebrews in the Book of Exodus (see *Egypt: Slavery and Redemption*), a question arises regarding religious/ethnic identity. Zarephath lies in Phoenician territory, between Sidon and Tyre, beyond Israel's northern border. The tribe of Asher appears to have settled on the Mediterranean south of Tyre, but at the time of Elijah, the territory was clearly Phoenician. Could the widow be an Israelite nonetheless? Obadiah 1:20 mentions exiled forces of Israelites possessing the coastal territory north of Israel—as far north as Zarephath—but this is in a future time. On the other hand, several sources, including the Jerusalem Talmud, offer that the widow's son, whom we shall soon meet, is the prophet Jonah, and that the widow belonged to the tribe of Asher, her husband to Zebulun. But the biblical text offers no proof that this woman living in Phoenicia is an Israelite, and other sources identify her as a non-Israelite.

Then we have the matter of the widow's reference to "the Lord *your* God," a common phrase in the Bible. This could suggest that widow is, indeed, a Phoenician. The British scholar I.W. Slotki offers a different viewpoint. He notes that such a phrase represented common usage and did not necessarily mean that the widow was a non-Israelite. (Soncino/Kings, 124) Yet Slotki refrains from stating that the phrase actually defines the widow of Zarephath as an Israelite. Leo L. Honor seems to support the non-Israelite view. "Her oath in the name of Elijah's God and in accordance with the formula used by Elijah himself (vs.1) does not imply that she was an Israelite or that she recognized the identity of Elijah. It was a customary courtesy in the pagan world to recognize the deity of another people in addressing oneself to a member of that people." (Honor, 251) Perhaps the widow of Zarephath is a God-fearer—a non-Israelite drawn in some way to the God of Israel but not a convert. Perhaps not.

Of critical importance, the widow acknowledges Elijah as a man of God, whether his reputation has preceded him or his speech gives away his Israelite identity and status. Again, the biblical narrative does not even hint at such details. But Elijah tests the woman's faith in "his God" by making a simple request. "Go and do as you have said; but first make me a small cake from what you have there, and bring it out to me; then make some for yourself and your son" (1 Kings 17:13).

Then the prophet promises a miracle. "For thus said the Lord the God of Israel: The jar of flour shall not give out and the jug of oil shall not fail until the day that the Lord sends rain upon the ground" (1 Kings 17:14).

The widow does as Elijah tells her, "and she and her household had food for a long time" (1 Kings 17:15). This renewal of flour and oil precedes two later events—one Jewish, one Christian. The first is the Chanukah story in which a single day's oil lasts for eight days during the rededication of the Second Temple following the Maccabees' victory over the Assyrians. The second reflects the Hebrew Bible's influence on the Christian Bible. Jesus, attending a wedding at Cana in the Galilee, turns water into wine (John 2) and feeds thousands with two fish and several loaves of bread (Matthew 14, Mark 6; Luke 9; and John 6).

The biblical text leaves the widow's reaction to our imaginations. If she harbors doubts about the God of Israel, however, an even greater miracle will convince her. Her son falls sick, "and his illness grew worse, until he had no breath left in him" (1 Kings 17:17). Distraught, she confronts Elijah: "What harm have I done you, O man of God, that you should come here to recall my sin and cause the death of my son?" (1 Kings 17:18).

What sin *has* the widow committed? Does she consider the illness and death of her son as punishment for some past offense against God? Might she have committed some sin unknowingly? We know of the strong connection between sin and punishment in the ancient Near East. It forms one of the Bible's major themes, although the Book of Job, which constitutes chapter eight of *God's Others*, offers a dissenting opinion. Is the widow contrite? Or does she simply compare herself unfavorably with the prophet? Here again, the text leaves our questions unanswered.

What we do know is that Elijah acts swiftly. He takes the boy upstairs—perhaps to the roof—lays the boy down on his own bed and cries out, "O LORD my God, will You bring calamity upon the widow whose guest I am, and let her son die?" (1 Kings 17:20). Then the prophet stretches out over the boy three times and cries, "O LORD my God, let this child's life return to his body!" (1 Kings 17:21). God hears Elijah's plea. The boy revives.

The Midrash (Num. Rabbah 14:1) cites this episode as proof of the resurrection of the dead at a future time. The Talmud (Sotah 49b) declares, "The Resurrection of the dead will come through Elijah." Many Jews do not realize that resurrection was a major theme of the Sages—one not found in the Torah. Yet two other resurrections occur in the Bible, both in 2 Kings. Elisha revives the son of a Shunamite woman, and a dead man thrown into Elisha's grave comes to life following contact with Elisha's bones. Elijah's bringing the boy back to life also serves as a precursor to Jesus raising Lazarus from the dead in the Christian Bible (John 11). Moreover, the Quran presents both the Day of Judgment and the resurrection of the dead as major components of Muslim belief.

The boy healed, Elijah carries him downstairs to his mother. The widow affirms the prophet's status: "Now I know that you are a man of God and that the word of the LORD is truly in your mouth" (1 Kings 17:24).

Let us bear in mind that the widow of Zarephath, in spite of the miracle that saves her son, makes no overt declaration that the God of Israel has become her God. But I.W. Slotki avers of her last statement: "This is a full and explicit avowal of faith in God in Whose name Elijah spoke and acted." (Soncino/King, 127) Certainly, the widow fully recognizes God's power. How can she not after witnessing the resurrection of her son? She also refers to Elijah as a "man of God" rather than "a man of *your* God" and to "the word of the LORD" rather than "the word of *your* LORD."

Whatever her former religious view and whatever relationship she may now assume with the God of Israel, the widow of Zarephath has encountered God directly through two very personal and life sustaining miracles.

RUTH THE MOABITE

FORERUNNER OF FORMAL CONVERSION

Famine strikes the kingdom of Judah, impelling the family of Elimelech—including his wife, Naomi, and their two sons—to leave Bethlehem for Moab. In their new homeland, the sons marry Moabite women, but all three men of the family die there. When the widowed Naomi hears that crops are again bountiful in Bethlehem, she plans to return and urges her daughters-in-law to seek new husbands from among their own people. One, Orpah, leaves her. The other, Ruth, vows to stay with Naomi and adopt her mother-in-law's people and her God. In Bethlehem, Ruth meets Boaz, a prosperous relative of Elimelech, during the barley harvest. Naomi sees an opportunity to have Boaz act as a redeemer by providing Ruth with a child in the name of her dead husband. Boaz first offers the role of redeemer to a closer relative, who turns it down. He then marries Ruth, who bears Obed, grandfather of King David.

ALTHOUGH WOMEN'S ROLES IN THE BIBLE are often muted, two women are the subjects of entire biblical books. These books, however, are quite different from each other. The Book of Esther concerns a Jewish woman of Persia, encompassing the Purim story and the Jews' escape from destruction—all without a single mention of God. The Book of Ruth relates the story of a non-Israelite from an earlier time following the Exodus from Egypt when judges, rather than kings, rule in Israel, and law and order are in short supply. Yet Esther and Ruth share much in common. Each must endure a vulnerable existence in a male-dominated society. And each, in responding to difficult challenges, reveals formidable strength of character and will.

The Book of Ruth also offers a striking parallel to a biblical text that tells the story of another well-known non-Israelite—The Book of Job (see *Job: God's Accuser*). The similarities between Ruth and Job entail far more than their non-Israelite status. Each book, while codified in the Hebrew Bible, challenges traditional Jewish thought. Job, who endures great suffering, rails against the commonly accepted view that God rewards people who do good and punishes those who do bad. Ruth poses no such challenge. She has no bone to pick with the God of Israel; she seeks to embrace God. Rather, the author—acknowledged as Samuel in the Rabbinic tradition and unidentified by critical scholars—puts forward Ruth's national origin alongside her gracious character to confront a legal prohibition that must later be explained away when David becomes king of Israel.

Ruth, you see, is a Moabite. Of course, the Bible presents many Israelite men taking non-Israelite wives. Moabite women, however, represent another matter. Deuteronomy 23:4 specifically prohibits Moabites (and Ammonites) from ever becoming Israelites. Nehemiah 13:1 references the prohibition in Deuteronomy, adding additional weight to it. What sin must Moab eternally bear? The Moabites' failure to meet Israel with bread and water on its journey to the promised land and its calling on Balaam to curse Israel (see *Dissemblers and Provokers)* bars them—even ten generations later—from inclusion in the Israelite nation.

The author of Ruth opposes the ban, supporting a more open, welcoming attitude. The text presents Ruth as such a good woman that we cannot imagine rejecting her. Indeed, the Talmud (Baba Kama 38a-b), which always includes dissenting and minority opinions, points out that God intentionally brings forth "two good doves" from these rejected nations—Ruth the Moabitess and Naamah the Ammonitess, Solomon's wife through whom the royal house of Judah and David descends.

Complex and often puzzling, the biblical narrative and its commentaries present both rejection and acceptance—God's command presented in plain language and then reinterpreted. No wonder that the contemporary biblical scholar Tamara Eskanazi terms the telling of Ruth's entry into Israel, "the most radical book in the Bible."[61]

---

61 All remarks credited to Tamara Eskenazi are the results of a personal conversation in December 2005.

That entry represents a step-by-step process told in four brief chapters—a process that foreshadows formal conversion while revealing a strong spiritual encounter with God.

From the outset, Ruth, whose fate intertwines with that of her mother-in-law, Naomi, faces difficult challenges. Hers is "a story of women struggling to survive in a man's world," Judith Kates explains from a contemporary woman's perspective. (Kates, 189) That story, which ends happily in fertility and new life, begins with a serious threat to life and unexplained deaths. Famine strikes Bethlehem, ironically so since *bet lechem* literally means house of bread.

Famine often proves a symbol of God's displeasure with Israel and a tool used by God to move forward a series of events. Abraham journeys to Egypt and Isaac to Gerar of the Philistines when famine strikes in Canaan. Famine forces Jacob's sons to journey to Egypt to buy food from Joseph, Viceroy to Pharaoh. Their reconciliation brings Jacob and his small Hebrew tribe to Egypt for a centuries-long sojourn that evolves into slavery and ends in the Exodus and the giving of the Law at Sinai. The Midrash (Ruth Rabbah 1:4) tells of ten famines in the world, nine of which had occurred, including the above, and one more yet to come.

When food becomes scarce in the southern kingdom of Judah, a man named Elimelech takes his wife, Naomi ("the sweet one"), and their two sons, named forebodingly Mahlon ("disease") and Chilion ("wasting"), from Bethlehem to Moab. Of Elimelech the biblical narrative provides no description. We can seek clues, however, in his rather puzzling name. It may mean, "My God is king," suggesting that he is a righteous man and that righteousness will follow as this story unfolds. The Midrash (Ruth Rabbah 2:5), no doubt attempting to explain his untimely death, offers another view. It interprets Elimelech as "To me, the king," suggesting that he is a prideful man who believes that he will become king of Israel. If so, he will make history since this story takes place in the time of the judges before Israel has a king.[62]

62 The priest/prophet Samuel chooses Saul as Israel's first king in 1 Samuel.

Whatever his ambitions may be, Elimelech leaves Israel for another land, an act that the Rabbis view quite negatively. Emigration may be unavoidable in certain circumstances, but the Midrash (Ruth Rabbah 1:4) suggests that he has deserted Israel unnecessarily. It castigates Elimelech, stating that the famine was not serious, and that he left to avoid providing his ample stores of grain to those who needed it. In doing so, writes the novelist and essayist Cynthia Ozick, Elimelech abandons the quality of mercy so prized by the Rabbis. "It is not merciful to forsake one's devastated countrymen; opportunism is despicable; desertion is despicable; derogation of responsibility is despicable; it is not merciful to think solely of one's own family: if I am only for myself, what am I?" (Rosenberg, 368) If this is so, Elimelech has acted like the Moabites condemned by Deuteronomy. Nonetheless, this is informed speculation. Ozick reminds us that the Rabbis, like us, seek answers not revealed by the biblical narrative. "There is not a grain of any of this in the text itself—not a word about Elimelech's character or motives or even his position in Bethlehem." (Rosenberg, 368)

The biblical narrative *does* inform us that the family lives in Moab for about ten years during which time Elimelech dies. His and Naomi's sons—whose names suggest their doom—marry Moabite women, Orpah and Ruth. Then the sons die, although the author presents no causes for their deaths. Whether all three men's deaths constitute God's punishing Elimelech for leaving Canaan and his two sons for marrying non-Israelites—and Moabites at that—we do not know. But such disaster falling on a single family strongly hints at wrongdoing. The Midrash sees the sons' deaths as a "silent protest" against intermarriage. (Soncino/Megilloth, 42)

Yet intermarriage is common long after the time of the Judges. What have Mahlon and Chilion actually done wrong? Perhaps their failure lies in not bringing their Moabite wives into the community of Israel. "They neither proselytized them, nor gave them ritual immersion," the Midrash (Ruth Rabbah 2:9) tells us.

It should be noted here that the Bible does not condemn intermarriage beyond that with Canaanites until the books of Ezra and Nehemiah. Thus Abraham instructs his servant, Eliezer not to find a bride for Isaac among the Canaanites but within his own, non-Hebrew extended family (see *The Era of Abraham*). Being part of a small family, the earliest Hebrew men had no choice but to take non-Hebrew wives. Moreover, Israelite men marry non-Israelite women throughout the arc of the biblical story. A strong tradition existed for patriarchal descent—Hebrew/Israelite/Jewish identity through the father. Thus Rabbi Abraham Geiger (1810-74), a German founder of Judaism's Reform movement and early scientific biblical scholar, suggests that the Book of Ruth was composed following the return from Babylon as a protest against Ezra's command that Israelite men cast aside their foreign wives. (Bettan, 51)

Whatever the cause of the men's deaths, Naomi and her Moabite daughters-in-law survive—all three of them childless. Without the protection of husband or sons, Naomi has no future in Moab. However, as Ozick asserts, Naomi refuses to abandon her future. She is transformed overnight. "Under the crush of mourning and defenseless, she becomes, without warning or preparation, a woman of valor." (Rosenberg, 371)

Naomi has some reason to be optimistic "…for in the country of Moab she had heard that the Lord had taken note of His people and given them food" (Ruth 1:6). In response, she prepares to return to Bethlehem.

The revival of the agrarian economy offers no promises but does raise Naomi's chances to survive. She begins the homeward journey accompanied by Orpah and Ruth. The three women are, after all, family. Then second thoughts strike Naomi. How can we blame her? If one widow faces great difficulties—an unmarried woman with no family may no more be able to survive in Judah than in Moab—what opportunities lie ahead for *three* widows? Moreover, Naomi is obviously long past marriageable age. And what chances do Orpah and Ruth have to find husbands? They are no longer virgins and apparently have no wealth with which to attract men. Also, they are Moabites whom Israel is commanded to shun. So after traveling some distance, Naomi instructs her daughters-in-law: "Turn back, each of you to her mother's house. May the Lord deal kindly with you, as you have dealt with the dead and with me!" (Ruth 1:8).

Naomi's blessing reveals that her daughters-in-law's status as Moabites has not impeded their relationship. They are worthy women. But God—not Naomi—will have to look after them if they are to find the security of a husband and the opportunity to build families even among their own people.

At this point we may wonder whether Orpah and Ruth have converted to the Israelite religion. Wouldn't that have been the natural thing to do? Ibn Ezra believes so. Yet the biblical text provides no evidence that two Moabite women, while expected to meet the religious and cultural norms of their husbands' family, have become worshippers of the God of Israel. No formal religious conversion process existed at the time. Then again, none was needed.

Shaye Cohen remains dubious that any form of conversion was undertaken in the Book of Ruth. He explains that before "rabbinic innovations of the second century of our era, conversion to Judaism was entirely a private and personal affair. The conversion was not supervised or sponsored by anyone, and there were no established standards that had to be met (except for the act itself—circumcision)." (Cohen/Beginnings, 51) Of considerable importance, conversion applied only to men. A non-Israelite woman simply was absorbed into Israelite society when she married an Israelite man—until the time following the return of Babylonian exiles to Jerusalem when Ezra prohibited such marriages. A woman proselyte would still be regarded as a gentile, and in the case of divorce would return to her father's house. Cohen does not see Ruth as a "religious convert" but rather as "a foreigner whose foreignness remains even after she has attempted to adopt the ways of her surroundings." (Cohen/Beginnings, 122-23) Prior to the Mishnaic era, he writes, becoming a Judahite, Judean or Israelite involved a change in cultural or historical—not religious—identity.

What if an attempt at conversion actually had been made? Since Elimelech and Naomi had taken up residence in Moab, any form of public conversion or acknowledgement of private conversion might have been met with hostility by the local people. Likely, it would have been kept quiet. Then again, had Orpah and Ruth become true

Israelites, Naomi surely would not have wished them to abandon God by returning to their mothers' homes—idolatrous by definition (Ruth 1:15). Naomi clearly understands that as non-Israelite residents of Judah, the younger women will be strangers in a strange land with little hope of protection let alone finding husbands or even acceptance.

It is also worth noting that Naomi defines her daughters-in-law's family affiliations by their mothers rather than by their fathers.[63] In the Bible, the father determines Israelite lineage, including tribal affiliation. It is the Rabbis who post-biblically define a Jew as the child of a Jewish mother. Perhaps this suggests that Orpah and Ruth will find more emotional comfort with their mothers than with their fathers. Perhaps matrilineal descent is the Moabite custom. Or as the contemporary scholar Gail Twersky Reimer suggests, Naomi faces destitution as a childless widow and can only send the women back to "the culture of conventional expectations." (Kates, 97)

Orpah and Ruth, with so many doors closed to them, must follow in the footsteps of their mothers and encounter all the risks of dependence and helplessness that Naomi herself faces. There is nothing, Naomi tells them, that she can do.

> "Turn back, my daughters! Why should you go with me? Have I any more sons in my body who might be husbands for you? Turn back, my daughters, for I am too old to be married. Even if I thought there was hope for me, even if I were married tonight and I also bore sons, should you wait for them to grow up?" (Ruth 1: 11-13)

It is generous of Naomi to suggest that if she could bear sons, she would offer them as husbands to Orpah and Ruth. But Naomi, if she could bear children for her daughters-in-law—whom she actually refers to as "my daughters" (*b'notai*)—is under no obligation to do so. This would approximate the levirate obligation by which the brother-in-law of a widow must marry her to provide a son who will

---

63 The Talmud (Sanhedrin 105a) declares Ruth to be the daughter of King Eglon, grandson of Balak, king of Moab in the Balaam story (see *Dissemblers and Provokers*).

carry on the dead brother's name.[64] There is no doubting Naomi's concern for the young women. It is not that she doesn't want to help them. She simply can't because, "the hand of the LORD," as she reminds them with a Job-like complaint, "has gone out against me" (Ruth 1:13).

Her dire outlook aside, Naomi's pushing away her daughters-in-law may actually represent her desire to bring them closer. For the past two thousand years—following Ruth's time to be sure—the dominant Jewish position on conversion has been to rebuff a potential convert three times. Doing so constitutes a measure of self-defense, since a Jew-by-choice faces no small measure of hostility from a dominantly non-Jewish world and may ultimately prove disloyal. Proselytes to Judaism are nonetheless both welcome and respected. The Midrash (Ruth Rabbah 2:16) states, "A man should rebuff with his left [weaker—DP] hand, but bring near with the right" and "Come and see how precious in the eyes of the Omnipotent are converts" (Ruth Rabbah 3: 5). A non-Jew must *really* want to convert. Three times Naomi rebuffs the younger women—perhaps not to reject them but to test them.

If this *is* a test, Orpah fails. She kisses Naomi farewell and disappears from the story. We can only imagine her fate. "But Ruth clung to her" (Ruth 1:14). Naomi urges Ruth to follow Orpah who "has returned to her people and her gods" (Ruth 1:15). Life in Judah under Israelite law will not be easy for Ruth. The Midrash (Ruth Rabbah 2:22) suggests a variety of limitations, including no longer being allowed to attend theaters and circuses.

Ruth passes this first test. She cannot cling to any assurances that life in Bethlehem will be better, but Naomi's protestations do not diminish her loyalty—and her faith. In a classic passage of world literature, she pledges herself to Israel and its God.

---

64 Edward F. Campbell, Jr. cites the Christian scholars, Thomas and Dorothy Thompson, who comment that the levirate practice "is not simply concerned with producing a male child, nor even with producing an heir to the dead man's property; it is concerned every bit as much with the care of the widow." (Campbell, 136) Jewish commentators focus on the production of an heir.

> "Do not urge me to leave you, to turn back and not follow you. For wherever you go, I will go; wherever you lodge, I will lodge; your people shall be my people, and your God my God." (Ruth 1:16)

Ruth's statement represents the first step in her informal and yet-unrecognized conversion process. It also stands as an act of great courage. To the rest of the biblical world, Judah may fancifully be termed in today's language a "rogue" nation. The Israelites cling to monotheism—in principle if frequently not in fact—foregoing and opposing the polytheistic norm. Ruth, by rejecting a "culture of conventional expectations," as Gail Twersky puts it, aggressively seeks to change rather than resign herself to returning home a childless, and defeated, widow. In doing so, she more resembles a twenty-first century woman who insists on defining her own life rather than have others—particularly men—define it for her.

Ruth certainly is no gold digger. The Midrash (Ruth Rabbah 2:22) views her as spiritually motivated rather than inspired by finances or social status—although survival logically poses a major concern to Ruth as well as to Naomi. Ruth eagerly seeks conversion, according to the Midrash, telling Naomi, "I am fully resolved to become converted under any circumstances, but it is better that it should be at your hands than at those of another." This, of course, presents another question. Why does Ruth wish to cleave to the God who has so afflicted Naomi? Surely her mother-in-law has every right to expect more from life—and God—than widowhood and poverty. Perhaps the answer lies in Ruth's developing a spiritual maturity surpassing that of Naomi. Ruth may realize, as Job eventually does, that God's ways are too complex for humans to understand, and that while she must devote herself to God, she must rely on her own actions to build a better life. Avivah Zornberg suggests an additional motivation for Ruth's clinging to Naomi, "that Ruth loves her husband Mahlon with a fever in her bones… She has that fire of Mahlon, who will find his life in the world through her." (Kates/Ruth, 75-6)

Here we can draw a parallel between Ruth and Abraham. To come closer to God, Ruth, like the first Hebrew patriarch, must leave the land of her birth and family to build a new life in a new land. Of course, this parallel extends only so far. God commands Abraham to go to Canaan but offers no such direct revelation to Ruth. This may make her faith even stronger than the patriarch's. Yet surely she cannot avoid being wary at the same time. As the playwright and poet Merle Feld writes, "She doesn't know what's in store for her if she returns to her mother's house, what's in store for her if she veers from that course to walk with Naomi. What she does know is that she cannot ignore the strength of her instinct." (Kates, 167)

Ruth may feel butterflies flitting about in her stomach, but she remains determined. She plunges ahead with a conversion process that is internal and personal rather than communal and legal. Ruth makes no appearance before a religious court or levitical priest. Rather, she pledges her loyalty in an ascending order of qualifications. Like the matriarch Rebekah going off to become Isaac's wife, she declares her willingness to leave all that she knows behind to live with Naomi in a strange land. She will initially become a *ger nochri*—an alien residing within Israel on what at first may be termed a temporary basis. Then Ruth will accept the Israelites as her own people, expanding her loyalty beyond Naomi and her relatives in Bethlehem. Ruth's residence amidst Israel will become permanent, raising her status to that of a *ger toshav*—a permanent alien living according to the laws of Torah. Finally she will become a *ger tzedek*, accepting the God of Abraham, Isaac and Jacob as her own and embracing both the rewards and responsibilities of an Israelite.

Is such a conversion genuine? According to the Midrash (Ruth Rabbah 2:14), "R. [Rabbi—DP] Ze'eera said, the scroll of Ruth tells us nothing of the laws of cleanness or uncleanness, of what is prohibited or permitted. Why then was it written? To teach you how great is the reward of those who do deeds of kindness." Edward F. Campbell, Jr. expands on this: "What makes Ruth a true Israelite is that she, like others in the story who are generically Israelites, behaves like one." (Campbell, 82) It is her *chesed* (kindness) towards Naomi, Campbell stresses, that binds her not only to her mother-in-law but also to Israel and God. The importance of kindness—of living the *spirit* of the law—must be acknowledged.

Ruth makes it clear that there should be no misunderstanding about the sincerity of her conversion. "Where you die, I will die, and there will I be buried. Thus and more may the Lord do to me if anything but death parts me from you" (Ruth 1:17). Even in death, Ruth will remain true to Naomi and Israel, whose holy ground she assumes will be her final resting place. Ruth's is no opportunistic conversion. Without any promise of benefit or even the basic comforts of life, she vows to accompany Naomi and join her fate to Israel's unto death. Her oath ("Thus and more...") is definitive. It is also typical of the ancient Near East where pacts concluded with slaughtering an animal and dividing its parts, indicating that such should be the fate of the party who breaks the agreement. God and Abraham make the Bible's first such pact in Genesis 15.

Faced with Ruth's relentless determination, Naomi takes her daughter-in-law to Bethlehem. If the reader expects a triumphant return, however, those hopes are quickly dashed. The dejected Naomi asks the people of the city to now call her Mara—bitter—because "I went away full, and the LORD has brought me back empty" (Ruth 1:21). Clearly, it is Ruth, the budding convert, rather than Naomi, who has placed her full trust in God. Fortunately, the women's situation is not without hope. They arrive in Bethlehem at the beginning of the barley harvest when God has restored His favor to the land.[65]

Ruth has *chutzpah*—guts. Without it, she and Naomi will never eat. She goes out to the fields to glean what the reapers leave behind—perhaps informed by Naomi of the commandment given in Leviticus 19:9 that farmers may not reap the corners of their fields so that the poor may glean from the residue. (The commandment not to go back for a forgotten sheaf is provided in Deuteronomy 24:19.) Moreover, the field in which she gleans offers special promise. "She came and gleaned in a field, behind the reapers; and, as luck would have it, it was the piece of land belonging to Boaz, who was of Elimelech's family" (Ruth 2:3).

---

65 The barley harvest takes place in spring. It is associated with the fifty-day period following Passover that culminates in the festival of first fruits known as Shavuot, which, at a later period, marked the giving of the Torah at Sinai. The book of Ruth traditionally is read on Shavuot.

Naomi has quietly guided Ruth to a kinsman, a standout in the community. Boaz means "with him is strength" and Ruth 2:1 refers to the man as a *gibbur chayil*—"a man of substance" as translated by JPS (which translates *anshei* [men] *chayil* in Exodus 18:21 as "capable men"). Malbim considers this to mean a man possessing all the finest human qualities.

Because Ruth may be seen as fair game for any man who wishes to force himself upon her, Boaz acts protectively. He orders his men not to molest Ruth. After all, she is still identified as a Moabite—the narrative continues to refer to "Ruth the Moabite." Thus the men may believe it their right or even duty to subject her to the indignities of a condemned stranger. Or perhaps Ruth is still attractive and may draw unwanted and improper attention regardless of her national status. Ruth is not necessarily a child, but she is still a relatively young woman. We don't know how long she had been married to Mahlon, so she may be as old as her mid-twenties (quite mature for that era) or as young as her mid-teens. Boaz is considerably older. He refers to her indirectly as a "girl" and directly as "daughter." Whatever her age, Ruth has vowed her attachment to the God and people of Israel but has not yet been integrated into Bethlehem society and so requires a protector.

Strong-willed though she may be, Ruth is not ignorant of her situation. She understands that her acceptance by the people of Bethlehem is anything but guaranteed no matter how great her loyalty to Naomi. No doubt Boaz intrigues her as well. And so—in a very Jewish way—she responds to his kindness with a question: "Why are you so kind as to single me out, when I am a foreigner?" (Ruth 2:10)

Boaz responds that he has heard of all that Ruth has done for Naomi. Then he states, "May the Lord reward your deeds. May you have a full recompense from the Lord, the God of Israel, under whose wings you have sought refuge!" (Ruth 2:12)

But Tamara Eskenazi asks, just how kind has Boaz really been? Surely he can do more than let this widow of a kinsman—and seemingly a paragon of virtue—glean in his fields with the rest of Bethlehem's poor. Why should Ruth have to depend solely on God when Boaz can serve as God's agent? Nonetheless, Boaz's "blessing" brings Ruth further into Israelite society. A Moabite has been welcomed, not shunned.

Ruth responds humbly that she is "not so much as one of your maidservants" (Ruth 2:13). The Midrash (Ruth Rabbah 5:5) tells of Boaz responding, "Heaven forefend! Thou art not as one of the handmaidens (amahoth) but as one of the matriarchs (imahoth)." Boaz obviously sees Ruth as possessing a very special character. Moreover, the recompense from God of which Boaz speaks will come from Ruth's relationship with him, whom Naomi refers to as "one of our redeeming kinsman" (Ruth 2:20). As we shall soon see, it is Boaz who will keep Mahlon's name alive and maintain Elimelech's line by fathering a son with Ruth. But before this happens, humans must play their role in a plan seemingly conceived by the Divine.

Naomi, reconciled to struggling for survival without a husband, certainly understands the opportunity that lies before them. She tells Ruth to bathe, anoint herself, dress up and go to the threshing floor. There, after Boaz has fallen asleep sated with food and drink, she is to uncover his feet—a sexually charged but not necessarily promiscuous invitation—and lie down. Ruth follows Naomi's instructions. Boaz startles, and Ruth reveals herself. Then she asks Boaz, "Spread your robe over your handmaid, for you are a redeeming kinsmen" (Ruth 3:9). In effect, Ruth asks Boaz to claim her as his wife. Boaz is greatly impressed. Given their difference in age, he looks upon Ruth as an attractive woman who, despite his material success, would not ordinarily be interested in him. He declares, "Be blessed of the Lord, daughter! Your latest deed of loyalty is greater than the first, in that you have not turned to younger men, whether poor or rich" (Ruth 3:10).

To be sure, Boaz is no fool suddenly enthused by the delights of a May–December—or perhaps May-September—romance. He recognizes Ruth's worthiness—her compassion for Naomi and her acceptance of levirate marriage—and defines her by her very positive qualities rather than by her status as a hated Moabite.

Ruth surely understands that Boaz is a very desirable catch. He possesses good character. And he can provide amply not only for Ruth but for Naomi, as well.

Yet Boaz may represent something more to Ruth than a good provider, according to the literary scholar Nehama Aschkenasy. "Ruth is looking to find a niche for herself within the Israelites' religious and ethical structure and therefore wishes to enter the Israelite family through the institution of the levirate marriage." (Kates, 122-23) Ruth seeks as complete a conversion and integration into Israel's religious life as possible. Boaz can provide it. Just as Boaz's blessing asks for Ruth's protection under God's wings, Ruth seeks fulfillment of that blessing through Boaz when she tells him on the threshing floor to spread his robe over her as a redeeming kinsman. As Tamara Eskenazi points out, Boaz has a critical role to play in seeing that justice is done, and Ruth will not let him sit by passively.

We may sense the approach of a happy ending, but the matter cannot be solved so easily. Boaz informs Ruth that another family member is closer to Mahlon than he is and must be given the right of redemption first. Then, seeking to bring the matter to a quick close, Boaz approaches the kinsman in the city's gate. There, in front of witnesses—ten elders of the town—he offers the unnamed kinsman Mahlon's inheritance. Naomi owns the land because her husband had no other living heirs. Of course, it will take some effort to make the holding fruitful; no doubt it has not been cultivated in years. But he, Boaz, will serve as redeemer if the kinsman won't.

The kinsman is willing to purchase the property but demurs when he learns that to do so, he must also acquire Ruth as a wife. Estate planning is nothing new. The kinsman evidently has children and fears that the son he provides for Ruth in Mahlon's name may claim not only Elimelech's land but also other portions of the kinsman's estate. In a formal ceremony, one of the men takes off his sandal—the text is unclear as to which. Either Boaz does so to symbolize payment for the role of redemption (the Midrash—Ruth

Rabbah 7:12—prefers this scenario) or the kinsman removes his sandal to lawfully refuse to act as redeemer.[66]

With the relative eliminated, Boaz announces his intention to marry Ruth. He has cleared any legal hurdle regarding levirate marriage in the presence of Bethlehem's elders so that his "claim" on Ruth cannot be derided.

What really is Boaz's intention? Tamara Eskenazi asserts that the proposed marriage serves to right a wrong—to change the law that perpetually prevents Moabites and people of any other nation from becoming Israelites. Whether this is Boaz's intention or the author's we cannot know. What the biblical text does reveal is that Boaz has fallen in love with a younger woman whom he finds as morally appealing as physically attractive regardless of her ethnicity.

Ruth's structured, if not formal, conversion then comes to completion. The elders—backed into a corner by a prominent and respected man, according to my good friend, Dan Weiss—accept her into the nation of Israel. They address Boaz:

> "May the LORD make the woman who is coming into your house like Rachel and Leah, both of whom built up the House of Israel! Prosper in Ephrathah [Bethlehem–DP] and perpetuate your name in Bethlehem! And may your house be like the house of Perez whom Tamar bore to Judah—through the offspring which the LORD will give you by this young woman." (Ruth 4:11 12)

What does the reference to the house of Perez mean? Genesis 38 relates that Judah's son, Er, dies leaving his wife, Tamar, childless. Judah's next son, Onan, refuses to fulfill the levirate obligation to

---

66 A shoe or sandal plays a major role when the brother of a widow's husband, who is obligated to marry his sister-in-law and provide a son for his late brother according to the law of *Yibbum*, refuses to do so. He must undergo the ritual of *chalitzah*, according to Deuteronomy 25:5ff. If the elders of the town cannot convince the man to marry her, the spurned woman must pull the sandal off her brother-in-law's foot and spit in his face, freeing him from his obligation while shaming him. Levirate marriages were performed until after the destruction of the Second Temple but lost favor as a social institution in light of the commandment, "Do not uncover the nakedness of your brother's wife; it is the nakedness of your brother" (Lev. 18:16). Orthodox rabbis, however, maintained the *chalitzah* ritual.

provide a son to carry on Er's name. After Judah fails to provide his third son, Shelach, for this purpose, Tamar tricks him. She masquerades as a harlot. Judah sleeps with her, and she gets pregnant. Then she reveals Judah's wrongdoing, which Judah freely acknowledges. Tamar bears twins. One, Perez, becomes ancestor to Boaz.

As to Ruth, she is welcomed into the fold. Ruth not only becomes a true *ger tzedek* but also fulfills the blessing she receives. She conceives a son, Obed ("one who serves"), who fathers Jesse who in turn fathers David. Ruth's position as great-grandmother to the celebrated king of Israel is especially meaningful considering Deuteronomy's prohibition against bringing Moabites into the community of Israel.

But how can this contradiction be resolved? The Mishnah (Yevamot 8:3) arrives at a simple answer. It declares the prohibition against Moabites to be only against males. Tamara Eskenazi calls their rationale "just an excuse to find a way to justify the marriage." The Sages, she comments, sought a loophole to deal with the book of Ruth and perhaps with David as the great-grandson of a Moabite.

After giving birth, Ruth gains further acceptance from the women of Bethlehem. Speaking to Naomi, they refer to little Obed as "…born of your daughter-in-law, who loves you and is better to you than seven sons" (Ruth 4:15).

With Ruth having fulfilled her destiny, the conclusion of the story veers away from her. Following the birth of Obed, all attention focuses on Naomi. The women of Bethlehem celebrate the birth by declaring, "A son is born to Naomi!" (Ruth 4:17). Like the matriarchs Sarah, Rebekah and Rachel, Naomi's "barrenness" ends, although Naomi does not physically bear a child. Nonetheless, Obed replaces Naomi's dead sons and will renew and sustain her in her old age. Moreover, Naomi, not Ruth, will rear the boy according to the Talmud (Sanhedrin 19b).

It should be noted that the Bible presents the motif of barrenness several times, but Naomi's case offers a twist. The matriarchs and Hannah, mother of Samuel, all remain barren before having their first child. Naomi loses her children, is too old to conceive, and remains childless until the birth of her grandson. The matriarchs and Hannah pray for children. Ruth's resolute action replaces prayer.

As the tale comes to its end, Ruth the Moabite has transformed into Ruth the Judahite—a critical link between the tribe's heritage and Israel's future. This transformation, says Eskenazi, is radical, changing the law of Deuteronomy 23 that excludes Moabites by 180 degrees. Ruth's allegiance to the God of Israel reverberates throughout the generations as the theme of redemption played out by Boaz is repeated in the story of David, who redeems Israel from the Philistines and creates the united monarchy expanded by his son, Solomon. Of course, to be the great-grandmother of Israel's greatest king might be reward enough. But Ruth enjoys even greater honor. The Midrash (Ruth Rabbah 2:2) states that she remains alive to witness the glory of David and her great-great-grandson Solomon's wisely judging the famed case of the two harlots (1 Kings 3:16 ff)—women who claim the same child whom Solomon is willing to cut in half. [67]

Ruth's step-by-step conversion concludes most satisfactorily. Interestingly, however, the Book of Ruth makes no mention of God's laws or the ways in which God is to be worshipped. Ruth's path to Israelite identity involves no credo and no rituals. Rather, she embraces Israel in its totality—its culture, traditions, people and allegiance to God.

It is the relationship between Naomi and Ruth that speaks volumes about the Law and what God expects of Israel. Judith Kates and Gail Twersky Reimer note that, "If we understand Torah, the gift of God 'who brought you out of the land of Egypt,' as directed centrally to the sustenance and liberation from suffering of the *ger, yatom vealmana*—'the stranger, the orphan, and the widow'—then the Book of Ruth, the protagonists of which embody all those vulnerable figures, speaks to the essence of Torah. Its women characters challenge the Jewish world to live up to Torah ideals and, in so doing, make manifest to us what sort of society—what sort of people—Torah is supposed to create." (Kates, xix)

---

67 The real mother pleads with Solomon to spare the child and give it to the other woman, earning the king's favorable judgment and winning the child.

In this light, Tamara Eskenazi writes, "Ruth the Moabite stands as the exemplar of what it means to love, including loving the stranger... Ruth's behavior and commitment become a model for others..." (Eskenazi/Torah, 716)

Ruth's story cannot end, however, without one last question. Was Ruth an historical figure or a literary one? We cannot say with any assurance. The scholar Judah Slotki sees an historical basis. "There would surely be little point in inventing a foreign ancestry for the greatest and most dearly loved king of Israel, even as little as inventing, for the origin of the nation itself, the bondage in Egypt." (Soncino/Megilloth, 37) Like Jethro, the Moabite father-in-law of Moses who gives Israel its concept of magistrates to judge disputes (see *Egypt: Slavery and Redemption*), Ruth comes from outside Israel to help forge a new Israelite tradition.

Tamar Frankiel, a scholar of Jewish mysticism, offers a spiritual point of view that perhaps opts for a literary approach. David, king of Israel from whom the Messiah will come, descends from incest (Lot with his daughters, Tamar with her father-in-law, Judah), cruelty (the Moabites who refused to provide food and water to Israel) and desertion of the land of Israel (Elimelech and his family). All this serves a purpose. "The rabbinic and mystical traditions assert that God can turn evil to good—indeed, that God intends good to be born from evil in order to 'raise the sparks,' to redeem the good that is hidden in every evil. This is the *tikkun* or correction that will bring the world to perfection." (Kates, 325) David's greatness extends from the very evils of his ancestry.

Rabbi Joseph Telushkin puts Ruth's conversion and role as ancestor of David into thoughtful perspective. "The Book of Ruth has long served as an important antidote for any Jew prone to exaggeratedly nationalistic feelings. How chauvinist can one become in a religion that traces its Messiah to a non-Jewish convert to Judaism?" (Telushkin, 105)

7

Kings and Commoners

He brings potentates to naught,
Makes rulers of the earth as nothing.
Isaiah 40:23

That Israel as a "kingdom of priests" (Ex. 19:6) continually falters represents one of the Bible's most fascinating themes. Just as the Bible presents individual human beings—including the patriarchs, Moses and David—as possessing the capacity for both good and bad, it offers a warts-and-all portrait of Israel as a people. Moreover, the Sages who canonized the texts and retained the option to extend a heavy editorial hand understood that Israel's written legacy should not—indeed *could not*—be whitewashed. We may be frustrated by Israel's fits-and-starts journey towards acceptance of monotheism, but the text refuses to indulge us. We witness Israel's constant failure to cast aside polytheistic influences until the end of the narrative at which the books of Ezra and Nehemiah mark the return of the Jews to Israel from Babylonian and Persian exile. These books mark a progression in identity from Israelites to Jews—a people widely scattered beyond the borders of their homeland even after the return to build the Second Temple. Religious texts and prayer underwent necessary and continual development in Babylon, far from Jerusalem and the destroyed First Temple, planting the seeds of Rabbinic Judaism that flowered following the Second Temple's destruction by Rome in 70 CE.

It comes as no surprise that God continually chastises Israel for failing to heed His commandments and hold up its end of the covenant. God, after all, repeatedly pledges His faithfulness to Israel. Early on, as Israel wanders in the wilderness, God makes clear what is at stake. In Leviticus, He offers the first of two lengthy warnings, which Moses recapitulates in Deuteronomy: If Israel follows God's laws, the people will prosper. Nature will be generous and the land will know peace. Should Israel neglect the covenant, nature will withdraw its bounty with terrible consequences. Peace will yield to violence, destruction and bondage. "I will set My face against you: you shall be routed by your enemies, and your foes shall dominate you" (Lev. 26:17).

Even in the best of times, Israel, as all nations, will have enemies. This is the condition of the world, and the geopolitics of the ancient Near East played out in no less tumultuous a fashion than those of our era. Yet Israel can resist physical and moral assaults; righteousness will earn God's protection. Maintaining that righteousness, however, poses an ongoing challenge. The nations that still occupy much of the land promised to the descendants of Abraham, Isaac and Jacob represent constant temptation to embrace other gods. But temptation can be overcome. If Israel upholds the Torah, God announces not long after the Exodus, He will drive the Canaanite peoples from the land. He will do it slowly "lest the land become desolate and the wild beasts multiply to your hurt" (Ex. 23:29). However, should Israel act as a faithless partner, the Canaanites will remain and become a snare that causes the nation to sin and weaken. The warning having been issued and human nature being imperfect, the outcome seems inevitable. And so it is.

In the time of the Judges, Israel as a loose tribal confederation fails to dispossess the Canaanites in its midst. An angel of the Lord relays God's displeasure: "Therefore, I have resolved not to drive them out before you; they shall be a snare to you" (Judges 2:3). Battles with the peoples of Canaan and with the Philistines who live along the Mediterranean coast continually occupy Israel and bring it misery.

The Israelites turn further from God when the people demand that the prophet Samuel appoint a king over them. Samuel protests. God does not favor such a ruler. Moreover, Deuteronomy 17:14ff anticipates such a request and places kingship under numerous restrictions. Unlike all other nations, Israel is to be a kingdom of priests. The Torah, rather than a monarch, should provide its legal infrastructure. Nonetheless, God permits the reluctant Samuel to anoint Saul while expressing His disappointment: "For it is not you they have rejected; it is Me they have rejected as their king" (1 Sam. 8:7) In turn, Samuel warns the Israelites, "But if you do not obey the LORD and you flout the LORD's command, the hand of the LORD will strike you as it did your fathers" (I Sam. 12:15).

The growth of Israelite power under the next two kings, David and Solomon, suppresses old hostilities, but new and greater threats arise. Following Solomon's death, the monarchy splits into rival northern (Israel) and southern (Judah) kingdoms. Both continually turn from the covenant to follow the practices of the Canaanite peoples who remain among them.

Over the span of five hundred years, the prophets call to account the people and kings of Israel and Judah who flout God's commandments and yield to idol worship and immorality.

Ultimately, God loses His patience. Seeking to correct His wayward children, God turns violence upon both north and south with threats originating outside the land. Assyria and Babylonia extort and ultimately wreak havoc on Israel and Judah respectively. Their power, however, is limited. The biblical narrative makes clear that foreign kings, generals and even common foot soldiers, who vex or humble Israel, serve God's will rather than their own. In the process, non-Israelites encounter God. Some of these discover that God's power, rather than their own, guides their victories and the broader course of history. Others, such as Naaman, the general of Aram, and Nebuchadnezzar, king of Babylon, arrive at a special relationship with God. All recognize God's power and are humbled by it.

THE PHILISTINES AND THE ARK OF THE COVENANT

Captors of God

In the days of the Judges, constant warfare takes place between Israel and the Philistines. Following a costly defeat, the Israelites call for the Ark of the Covenant to be brought from Shiloh to assure God's presence with Israel's armies in the next battle. Yet the Philistines again defeat Israel. Moreover, they seize the Ark, believing that they now hold Israel's national god in their power. They cannot grasp the concept of God's universality and the powerlessness of their idols—but not for long. Plagues of hemorrhoids and mice strike the Philistines. They send the Ark from one city to the next to halt their suffering but to no avail. Finally, the Philistines send the Ark back to the Israelite city of Beth-Shemesh. The Philistine priests and diviners announce their willingness to acknowledge God's power—if the Ark's driverless wagon reaches its destination instead of turning back. But establishing such a condition only exemplifies their limited vision.

The God of Israel may not commonly be worshipped in Canaan and the lands surrounding it, but He is surely known. Forty years after the Exodus, the destruction wreaked upon Egypt at the Reed Sea causes the people of Jericho—including the harlot, Rahab (see *Women of Valor*), to tremble before the Israelite army led by Joshua. Some two centuries after, the Philistines, whom the Israelites avoided on their journey to Canaan, still remember the strong hand and outstretched arm with which God crushed Pharaoh.

The Israelite tribes, ruled by elders and judges, have settled in Canaan but do not possess the land in its entirety. As a result, they face a challenge no different from the one that confronts Diaspora Jewry today. They must retain their religious integrity in an environment that poses great challenges to it. The Book of Judges relates a continuing ebb and flow of faithfulness to the covenant at Sinai. The emergence of such leaders as Deborah and

Gideon, however, enables the loosely confederated tribes to remain sufficiently strong, keep from being overwhelmed by Canaanite practices and resist military forays by the Philistines who live along Canaan's southern Mediterranean coast.[68]

Just as in the wilderness, periods of strength and resolve give way to weakness and doubt. When Israel lacks strong leadership, the people turn their backs on the covenant and worship local gods. Disaster befalls them. Fortunately, new leaders arise. Gideon frees Israel from seven years' subservience to Midian—a punishment for offending God. However, he refuses kingship, stating that, "the LORD alone shall rule over you" (Judges 8:23). Forty years of tranquility follow, but faithfulness to the covenant proves fragile.

> After Gideon died, the Israelites again went astray after the Baalim, and they adopted Baal-berith as a god. The Israelites gave no thought to the LORD their God, who saved them from all the enemies around them. (Judges 8:33-34)

A long period of warfare follows, including Samson's battles against the Philistines and a civil war that pits Benjamin against the other tribes. Periods of uncertainty and violence continue to alternate with those of peace and prosperity.

The Temple in Jerusalem has not yet been built. It is a task David will leave to his son, Solomon. However, the Israelites maintain a powerful symbol of God's presence among them—the Ark of the Covenant, the design and construction of which are detailed in Exodus 25ff. The Ark contains the second set of tablets on which Moses wrote the Ten Commandments and perhaps, as is speculated, the fragments of the original set inscribed by God and broken by Moses after learning of the golden calf. Serving as a physical reminder of Sinai, the Ark resides in Shiloh, some twenty miles north of Jerusalem, in the territory of the tribe of Ephraim.

---

68 The Philistines, termed *Caphtorim*—people of Crete—by Amos and Jeremiah, were an Aegean sea people. They settled in Canaan from Gaza to as far north as Jaffa in the twelfth century BCE and occupied five principal city-states—Gath, Gaza, Ashdod, Ashkelon and Ekron. A lord (*seren* in Hebrew) ruled each.

Following a military defeat and the deaths of four thousand men at the hands of the Philistines, the elders of Israel suggest, "Let us fetch the Ark of the Covenant of the LORD from Shiloh; thus He will be present among us and will deliver us from the hands of our enemies" (1 Sam. 4:3). The idea has a strong precedent. The Israelites carried the Ark around Jericho prior to the city's conquest (Josh. 6). Later it accompanies Israel to war against the Ammonites (2 Sam. 11).

The Israelites burst into a great shout when the Ark arrives—a shout that affects the Philistines.

> And when they learned that the Ark of the LORD had come to the camp, the Philistines were frightened; for they said, "God has come to the camp." And they cried, "Woe to us! Who will save us from the power of this mighty God? He is the same God who struck the Egyptians with every kind of plague in the wilderness!" (1 Sam. 4:6-8)

Like Rahab the harlot, the Philistines have no personal experience of God. Theirs is an historic revelation. And while they have heard of God's wonders to be sure, they remain polytheists. The panicked Philistines refer to "*this* mighty God." The God of Israel is just one of many gods, although perhaps more powerful than even their own gods. Their polytheistic attitude represents a fatal mistake. Because the Philistines cannot conceive of the oneness and thus universality of God, they fail to comprehend the source of Israel's strength. The Israelites' power on the battlefield, they believe, emanates from possession of the Ark of the Covenant—a physical item that can be seen (touching is forbidden)—rather than from the presence of an unseen God among the righteous. However, let us make no mistake here. The Ark for Israel is a potent physical symbol. Thus, it represents, beyond hope, a potential danger. A symbol can be transmuted into the reality it represents—the God for whom no physical image is permitted because such an image remains at odds with God's unknowable actuality. The Ark can become an idol!

Fearful of being enslaved as they have enslaved the Israelites, the Philistines muster their courage. God withholds victory, and the Philistines win in a rout, slaying thirty thousand Israelite foot soldiers and capturing the Ark of the Covenant. So powerful is this event that when the old priest, Eli, hears of the Ark's capture, he falls backward off his seat, breaks his neck and dies—after surviving news of the deaths of his two sons, Hophni and Phinehas (1 Sam. 4:17-18).

The Philistines glory in their unusual booty. "They were convinced that by doing so they had taken captive the God of Israel Himself Who was now their vassal," notes Nehama Leibowitz. (Leibowitz/ Bereshit, 240)

Here, an old adage must be honored: "Be careful what you wish for; you may get it." The Ark places in the Philistines' hands more power than they can grasp—a concept exploited by the movie director Steven Spielberg in Raiders of the Lost Ark. The Philistines perceive the Ark to be another man-made object of idolatry similar to their own god, Dagon. They will discover their mistake.

The Philistines remove the Ark to the temple of Dagon in Ashdod and set it beside Dagon's statue. This sets the stage for a critical one-on-one confrontation:

> Early the next day, the Ashdodites found Dagon lying face down on the ground in front of the Ark of the Lord. They picked Dagon up and put him back in his place; but early the next morning, Dagon was again lying prone on the ground in front of the Ark of the Lord. The head and both hands of Dagon were cut off, lying on the threshold; only Dagon's trunk was left intact. (1 Sam. 5:3-4)

The Philistines don't get it. They remain unable or unwilling to comprehend the power of God and His nature. God, obviously, is not pleased. He punishes them with a plague. The Philistines of Ashdod come down with hemorrhoids—identified by some modern scholars as tumors or boils, the latter a symptom of bubonic plague.

Then the truth begins to dawn on the Ashdodites—at least in part. Understanding that their suffering is caused by the Ark's presence, they send it to Gath—later the home of Goliath. The inhabitants of Gath also suffer hemorrhoids and send the Ark on to Ekron. Needless to say, the Ekronites do not want it! Many die. They determine to send the Ark back to the Israelites but leave it in Philistine territory for seven months. Finally, Philistine priests and diviners determine to return the Ark to its place in Shiloh accompanied by an indemnity. Only then can the God of Israel be appeased and the Philistines healed. And what is this indemnity to be? The Philistine priests and diviners choose five golden hemorrhoids and five golden mice—one each for the Philistines' five major cities.

Mice? These, according to the Philistine priests and diviners, are ravaging the land (1 Sam. 6:5). A midrash (Bialik, 115:66) presents the Philistines as being skeptical, suspecting that God's power had been exhausted after the ten plagues that afflicted Egypt. "The Holy One replied, 'Do you suppose I have no other plague left? I will bring a plague upon you, the like of which has not been in the world—mice that will pull your innards [when you sit down to ease yourselves].'"

The Philistines suffer but remain unconvinced. How can they be certain that the God of Israel has struck them for holding the Ark prisoner? Has not some other power brought these hemorrhoids and mice upon them? The priests and diviners suggest an answer: Place the Ark on a cart to be pulled by two milch cows and send it on its way.

> "Then watch: If it goes up the road to Beth-Shemesh, to His own territory, it was He who has inflicted this great harm on us. But if not, we shall know that it was not His hand that struck us; it just happened to us by chance." (1 Sam. 6:9)

Off goes the Ark only to stop in the field of Joshua of Beth-shemesh. The people of Beth-shemesh rejoice, split up the cart and burn the cows as an offering to God. The Levites among them place the Ark and a chest with the gold hemorrhoids and mice on a large stone. But the Ark proves as dangerous to the Israelites of Beth-shemesh as to the Philistines.

> [The LORD] struck at the men of Beth-shemesh because they looked into the Ark of the LORD; He struck down seventy men among the people [and] fifty thousand men. (1 Sam. 6:19)

Why do the men of Beth-shemesh perish? The Ark is a holy object off limits to ordinary Israelites. Deuteronomy 10:8 relates that God set apart the Levites to carry the Ark. Ordinary Israelites, even with the best of intentions, lack the ritual purity necessary to handle and transport it. We find an example of this in 2 Samuel 6. David sets out to bring the Ark to Jerusalem. The oxen pulling the cart on which it rests stumble. Uzzah, one of the drivers, grasps it. Even though Uzzah attempts to protect the Ark, God strikes him down on the spot.[69]

Following their disaster with the Ark, the people of Beth-shemesh send a message to the town of Kiriath-jearim whose men come and take possession of it.

The Philistines, having ridden themselves of the Ark, believe they also have eliminated God's power to hurt them. The God of Israel remains a local god to them—one whose influence extends no further than a limited radius from the Ark. In spite of their knowledge of Egypt's humbling at the Reed Sea and of their own downfall in the presence of the Ark, the Philistines cannot rise above their limited polytheistic views.

The Israelites, on the other hand, yearn after the Lord. Promised deliverance by the prophet Samuel, they remove alien gods from their midst. They receive their reward. Twenty years after the Ark arrives in Kiriath-jearim, the Philistines march out to meet the Israelites at Mizpah. As Samuel presents a burnt offering, the Philistines advance but, "...the LORD thundered mightily against the Philistines that day. He threw them into confusion and they were routed by Israel" (1 Sam. 7:10).

---

69 The Talmud (Sotah 35a) explains God's anger: If the Ark could divert the waters of the Jordan so that the priests carrying it and all of Israel could cross the river on dry ground on their way to conquering Canaan [in the Book of Joshua], it certainly could right itself without human assistance.

Like the Egyptians, the Philistines witness God's intervention on behalf of Israel. God's power makes a deep impression but obviously not a complete one. The Philistines fail to comprehend God's oneness—the universal God who is Creator of all humanity. For this, they ultimately pay a heavy price and disappear from history.

NAAMAN, GENERAL OF ARAM

Ironic Convert

What human beings view as miraculous in the Bible really represents God's power to influence nature when and as He wishes. Naaman, commander of the army of Aram, discovers that power when he suffers leprosy. Unable to find a cure, he turns to the Israelite prophet Elisha. Dubious at first regarding Elisha's simple instructions to immerse himself in the Jordan River, Naaman ultimately complies. Cured, he vows to worship only the God of Israel. Naaman then asks Elisha for two mule-loads of Israelite earth to build an altar to God on his return home and slaughter offerings upon it. The God of Israel will be his only God.

Most non-Israelites who encounter the God of Israel acknowledge His power. Some already recognize God as Creator and Ruler of the world but continue to worship Him in their own way. A few—Ruth being the foremost example—become part of Israel. One non-Israelite, however, adopts a unique position. He dedicates his worship solely to the God of Israel yet retains his citizenship and distinctive role in a non-Israelite society.

Naaman, commander of the army of the king of Aram, presents a host of ironic contradictions. Naaman means "pleasantness," yet he is a successful man of war. In fact, Naaman leads the forces of the king of Damascus (Ben-Haddad II) to victory against Israel, "for through him the Lord had granted victory to Aram" (2 Kings 5:1). Tradition even has it that Naaman was the bowman who slew Ahab, king of Israel, whom God punished for his evil ways (1 Kings 22:34). Like Nebuchadnezzar and Cyrus, whose tales follow, Naaman has risen to the heights of power to serve as a tool of God. He will then be humbled only to be elevated spiritually.

The irony of Naaman's life becomes more sharply defined when the conquering general suffers from a terrible affliction since "the man, though a great warrior, was a leper" (2 Kings 5:1). The disease receives much attention from the Torah in two weekly portions—

Tazria (Lev. 12:1-13:39) and Metzora (Lev. 14:1-15:33). The Talmud (Aruchin 16a) states that "leprosy" reveals one or more of seven sins—slander, bloodshed, vain oath, incest and adultery, arrogance, robbery and greed. However, the Hebrew term, *tzara'at* does not necessarily refer to what today is known as Hansen's Disease.

Why has Naaman been stricken? The biblical narrative offers no answer, but the Midrash (Numbers Rabbah 7:5) suggests that he exhibits vanity and haughtiness. Naaman is, after all, a conqueror—and a conqueror of Israel at that. Perhaps God has afflicted Naaman with some form of skin condition to display His power, as with Moses at the burning bush (Ex. 4:6), or to rebuke him, as with Miriam (Num. 12:10). Moses and Miriam, however, came to terms with God and quickly recovered. Naaman continues to suffer.

Hope arises for Naaman through another irony. A captive Israelite girl, who serves Naaman's wife, informs her mistress about Elisha. This prophet, residing in Samaria and a disciple of Elijah, can serve as a conduit for God's miracles to cure the general.

Naaman relates this news to his king who, apparently misjudging the situation, believes that Jehoram, king of Israel, possesses an impressive mastery of magic. The king of Aram values his general, so he sends Jehoram a letter, along with much silver and gold plus ten changes of clothing.

Jehoram, whose peace with Damascus is less than stable, responds with both disbelief and perturbation. He rends his clothes and asks, "Am I God, to deal death or give life, that this fellow writes to me to cure a man of leprosy? Just see for yourselves that he is seeking a pretext against me!" (2 Kings 5:7). Jehoram understands that he has no magical powers, which would represent violations of Israelite law. Miracles happen, but only as God wills them.

When news of Jehoram's distress regarding Naaman reaches Elisha, he sends a message to his king: "Why have you rent your clothes? Let him come to me, and he will learn that there is a prophet in Israel" (2 Kings 5:8).

Naaman, replete with a splendid show of horses and chariots, journeys to Elisha's house. Elisha does not bother to see him. Instead, he sends messengers offering a simple remedy: Naaman is to bathe in the Jordan River seven times. If only all our medical challenges could be dealt with so easily!

Ironically, Naaman is discomfited by Elisha's remedy. The general takes such a simple task as an insult. He responds angrily: "Are not the Amanah and the Pharpar, the rivers of Damascus, better than all the waters of Israel? I could bathe in them and be clean!" (2 Kings 5:12). The Jordan makes no great impression on Naaman. Its curative powers cannot possibly be effective.

Another irony now comes into play. Naaman receives a wise response not from men of rank and power but from his own servants. The general would perform a truly difficult act if Elisha so instructed, they tell him. Why not perform a simple one?

Here, the biblical narrative reminds us that God need not be perceived solely in terms of overwhelming phenomena, such as the parting of the Reed Sea or the thunder and lightning at Sinai. The prophet Elijah tells of finding God in the small things:

> And lo, the LORD passed by. There was a great and mighty wind, splitting mountains and shattering rocks by the power of the LORD; but the LORD was not in the wind. After the wind—an earthquake; but the LORD was not in the earthquake. After the earthquake—fire; but the LORD was not in the fire. And after the fire—a soft murmuring sound [also translated, a still small voice—DP]. When Elijah heard it, he wrapped his mantle about his face and went out and stood at the entrance of the cave. (1 Kings 19:11-13)

Naaman relents, immerses himself in the Jordan the requisite seven times and is cured.[70] This presents us with still another irony. The general who has brought so much death to Israel finds new life for himself in Israel.

Anger yields to gratitude. Naaman appears before Elisha and confesses, "Now I know that there is no God in the whole world except in Israel!" (2 Kings 5:15). We can find significance in this

70 The New Testament points out that not all who suffer are healed. In Luke 4:27, Jesus reminds the Jews of Nazareth that, "there were many lepers in Israel during the time of Elisha the prophet; yet not one of them was cleansed, but only Naaman the Syrian."

remark. Michael Fishbane points to a similar statement made by Jethro, Moses' father-in-law, in Exodus 18:11: "Now I know that the LORD [YHVH] is greater than all gods..." (see *Egypt: Slavery and Redemption*). According to Fishbane, "The formal correspondence between the two passages is striking. Apparently, some pagan conversions in Israelite antiquity required merely a credal statement along with a commitment to sacrifice to the Lord. These avowals typically include reference to a new knowledge of the supremacy of the God of Israel, based on experience." (Etz Hayim, 672) Also like Jethro, Naaman will not remain with the Israelites. Rather, he will become their kinsman through God rather than residence and citizenship.

It must be said that Naaman's statement, like Jethro's, leaves some room for doubt regarding the Israelite concept of monotheism. When Jethro states, "Now I know that the LORD is greater than all gods," he leaves us to wonder whether he acknowledges the existence of other gods or mocks such a notion. So with Naaman who recognizes there is no other God in the whole world except in Israel. From what might doubt spring? The Hebrew word translated as "world" by JPS, *aretz*, generally means "earth" or "land." Does Naaman believe that the God of Israel is the only God of earth but not of the heavens? Or is His sovereignty even more limited to Israel and perhaps the surrounding lands in the region? We cannot be sure, although Abraham Cohen takes the latter view. "In Naaman's primitive belief, the God of Israel was associated only with the land of Israel... The concept of God ruling over all the earth was beyond him." (Soncino/Kings, 193-94)

Naaman nonetheless recognizes the power of the God of Israel and offers Elisha a gift. The prophet refuses it to demonstrate that the general's cure comes not from a human being but from God. Naaman then turns the tables and asks for a gift for himself—one that will formalize his new relationship with the God of Israel: "Then at least let your servant be given two mule-loads of earth; for your servant will never again offer up burnt offering or sacrifice to any god, except the LORD" (2 Kings 5:17).

Naaman's request reflects the commandment in Exodus:

> "Make for Me an altar of earth and sacrifice on it your burnt offering and your sacrifices of well-being, your sheep and your oxen; in every place where I cause My name to be mentioned I will come to you and bless you." (Ex. 21:21)

However, Naaman will not bring offerings to the Temple in Jerusalem. Following the practice of the northern kingdom of Israel, he will sacrifice at an alternate site—in this case, one outside Israel but still holy, he believes, because the soil of Israel will make it so. Naaman will sustain his connection to God in his own land—even if his country remains in conflict with Israel!

The narrative does not reveal the prophet's response. Perhaps Elisha raises an eyebrow. Or perhaps his silence speaks to the general. Naaman certainly feels compelled to explain himself. He is about to return to Aram a different man. Along with privileges, he states, his rank imposes great responsibilities which, when carried out, may be misinterpreted.

> "But may the LORD pardon your servant for this: When my master enters the temple of Rimmon to bow low in worship there, and he is leaning on my arm so that I must bow low in the temple of Rimmon—when I bow low in the temple of Rimmon, may the LORD pardon your servant in this." (2 Kings 5:18)

Naaman suffers no confusion about the source of his cure and turns his back on all other gods. Three times he mentions the temple of Rimmon—Aram's god and the Assyrian god of thunder—as if to reassure all about him that he has worshipped a false god previously but will do so no more, even if it appears so as part of his official duties.

What else must Naaman do to keep his leprosy at bay? Nothing. Elisha requires neither gifts nor vows from him. Moreover, Naaman need not enter into the covenant at Sinai since he will return to his own land. The lesson is simple. God's grace is available to everyone and requires only recognizing Him as the God of all. Adherence to the seven basic Noahide laws—of which monotheism constitutes the first—is sufficient for any non-Israelite.

In effect, Naaman has adopted a new and unique role as an early "Diaspora Jew," although the term is used loosely. Joseph represents the first, and no doubt more legitimate, Diaspora Jew. Born an Israelite and Jacob's favorite son at that, he is sold into Egyptian slavery by his brothers. After rising to power as viceroy to Pharaoh, he becomes an assimilated, acculturated Egyptian complete with Egyptian name and Egyptian wife. The sojourn of the Israelite nation in Egypt that follows brings full meaning to the notion of Diaspora.

Naaman, however, has at least some claim to Diaspora status. While he will reside outside Israel as a non-Israelite, he will worship the God of Israel—and *only* Him. Naaman thus redefines his religious status in an age when religion, culture and citizenship remain inseparable. No formal conversion process is required—indeed, none exists at this time. Moreover, Elisha's silence makes clear that Naaman, by returning to Aram, need not accept the covenant at Sinai and thus all the *mitzvot*—the 613 commandments—incumbent on Israelites. Naaman receives no welcome into the people of Israel but neither is his request rejected nor his intent denigrated.

Naaman's new religious loyalty is so focused and clear that the Talmud (Sanhedrin 96b and Gittin 57b) regards him as a *ger toshav*—a resident alien who lives among Israelites and within their laws. This represents the middle of three rungs upon which a non-Israelite resides. On the lowest is the *ger nochri*, the sojourner traveling through Israelite territory on business. On the highest is the *ger tzedek*, the righteous sojourner who accepts the God of Israel and His commandments, and settles permanently among the Israelite people—the de facto status Ruth achieves (see *Women of Valor*).

A postscript must be added to this story. After Naaman leaves for home, Elisha's servant, Gehazi, runs after him to obtain some of the gifts Elisha declined. Responding to the pretext that the gifts are for two sons of prophets from the hill country of Ephraim, Naaman gives Gehazi not the one talent of silver requested but two. When Gehazi returns, Elisha inquires as to where he has gone. "Your servant has not gone anywhere," Gehazi replies (2 Kings 5:25). Knowing what

Gehazi has done, Elisha curses him. Naaman's leprosy shall cling to Gehazi and his descendants forever. Gehazi leaves "snow-white with leprosy" (2 Kings 5:27).

Gehazi's moral failure offers an ironic contrast with the *t'shuvah*, or turning, made by Naaman. The former, an attendant to a prophet, succumbs to greed. The latter, commander of a pagan army, becomes a worshipper of the One God. Belief alone, it seems, is not sufficient. One's actions, the Bible informs us, determine how others see us—and on what basis God will judge us.

Let us here consider one last irony. It is now possible that the Aramean man of war who continues to serve his king personally may never again consent to lead his army against Israel. His king and countrymen may not know God's power, but Naaman surely does.

NEBUCHADNEZZAR, KING OF BABYLON
God's Sword

God chooses Nebuchadnezzar, king of Babylon, to serve as His "sword" and punish Judah, whose kings flaunt His commandments. Nebuchadnezzar's story spans several books of the biblical narrative—from 2 Kings (repeated in 2 Chronicles) through Daniel. Not knowing that God's hand guides him, Nebuchadnezzar removes Egyptian influence from Judah and imposes his own choice of kings on the nation. Two of them rebel. Sieges of Jerusalem follow, the second of which results in the destruction of the city and the Temple. The prophet Jeremiah tells the Judeans to submit to God's will and accept Nebuchadnezzar and their captivity in Babylon. Nebuchadnezzar himself does not recognize God's power at work—or realize that he is merely a pawn of history—until the Book of Daniel. This text reveals another dimension of Nebuchadnezzar who, anticipating Shakespeare's Lear, goes mad only to achieve wisdom. Ultimately, Nebuchadnezzar blesses God as "Most High" and "the Ever-Living One."

God's role as Redeemer of Israel is central to the Bible and one Israel continually requires Him to play. Israel may be a nation of priests aspiring to the Divine, but its failures reflect its rootedness in the human condition. Frustrated as the reader may be, Israel must—and does—reveal serious flaws. The story of Adam and Eve in the Garden of Eden informs us that humanity cannot know the good without knowing bad. The question is not whether we will stumble and miss the mark but whether we will rise after doing so. Thus Israel's many redemptions stem from its failures and the punishments they generate—often destruction at the hands of other nations. Such destruction, from the biblical view, originates not in geopolitics, of which an abundant historical record exists, but with the God of History, Who uses powerful rulers to chastise his chosen-but-errant people.

Nebuchadnezzar, king of Babylon (ruled 604–562 BCE), represents one of two warrior-kings who exemplify historical service to God.[71] (Cyrus, King of Persia, serves as the second agent through whom Israel is later redeemed from its Babylonian captivity, and his story follows.) Nebuchadnezzar's impact reaches across many books of the Bible—2 Kings (and 2 Chronicles), Isaiah, Jeremiah, Ezekiel, Micah, Habakkuk, Lamentations and Daniel. But only in Daniel—placed not with the books of the Prophets (*Nevi'im*) but with the Writings (*Kethuvim*)—does Nebuchadnezzar come to know God and praise Him.

The Bible sets Nebuchadnezzar's tale against the backdrops of the long-shattered northern kingdom of Israel, crushed by Assyria, and the religiously rebellious southern kingdom of Judah. As the story unfolds, I will provide some historical dates, which the Bible never mentions—biblical writers were unaware of our secular calendar and dated events according to the reigns of the kings of Israel and Judah. Yet biblical events involving Nebuchadnezzar and Babylon begin to emerge from mythos into history, so these dates provide meaningful reference points. Nonetheless, we will focus on the biblical narrative—drawn on historical events but interpreted and embellished to form scripture.

The seeds of Judah's catastrophe are planted in 605 BCE when Nebuchadnezzar defeats Neco of Egypt at Carchemish on the Euphrates River. From there, the Babylonians move southward. History confirms these activities; archaeological discoveries and documents tell us much about politics and warfare in the ancient Near East. But the biblical narrative of Nebuchadnezzar—and that of Cyrus as well—serves a religious objective rather than an historical one. It portrays the God of History as causing Israel's crushing defeats. In so doing, the Bible again raises the question—why does God's own people suffer so terribly?

The answer is "simple." The exile of the ten northern tribes (722 BCE) fails to prompt many of southern Judah's kings to turn from their evil ways. Foreign political intervention also fails to set Judah on the right path. In 609, Neco, from his base in Egypt, removes

71 JPS also spells the king's name Nebuchadrezzar, with an "r," which is closer to the original. This Hebrew spelling appears with great frequency in the text.

Jehoahaz from the throne in Jerusalem and replaces him with Jehoiakim (nee Eliakim). But Jehoiakim "did what was displeasing to the Lord, just as his ancestors had done" (2 Kings 23:37). The stage is set for another disaster.

Attempting to play one great power against another—and demonstrating that, as Ecclesiastes states, there really is nothing new under the sun—Jehoiakim turns from Neco and becomes Nebuchadnezzar's vassal. Three years later, with the strategy failing to prove satisfactory, Jehoiakim rebels. This constitutes an offense not merely against Babylon but against God. It is God who has placed Nebuchadnezzar over Judah, and God does not suffer insubordination lightly. The Midrash (Leviticus Rabbah 19:6) tells of the Great Sanhedrin—Israel's religious leadership—acknowledging Nebuchadnezzar's role in carrying out God's historic plan. They call on the king and ask if the time of the Temple's destruction has come. At the moment, however, it is only Jehoiakim whom Nebuchadnezzar seeks. Disaster will wait for another day.

And disaster does come. The attack begins under God's hand:

> The Lord let loose against him the raiding bands of the Chaldeans, Arameans, Moabites, and Ammonites; He let them loose against Judah to destroy it, in accordance with the word that the Lord had spoken through His servants the prophets. (2 Kings 24:2)

Judah is ravaged and Jehoiakim is taken. Still, the lesson remains unlearned. His son, Jehoiachin, succeeds to Judah's throne. Jehoiachin continues to debase the Law, doing "what was displeasing to the Lord, just as his father had done" (2 Kings 24:9).

In response, God guides Nebuchadnezzar in laying siege to Jerusalem. In doing so, Nebuchadnezzar fulfills his destiny. A midrash (Tanchuma Balak 1) points out that God rose up both Solomon and Nebuchadnezzar over the earth—Solomon to build the Temple and Nebuchadnezzar to destroy it.[72]

---

72 A legend draws an even closer parallel between this Babylonian king and Solomon. It states that Nebuchadnezzar is the very son of Solomon and the Queen of Sheba (Ginzburg, IV, 300).

Jehoiachin surrenders (597 BCE) and is taken into captivity. The imperial temper aroused, Nebuchadnezzar punishes Judah by stripping the Temple and royal palace of its treasures. He also exiles "all the commanders and all the warriors—ten thousand exiles—as well as all the craftsmen and smiths; only the poorest people in the land were left" (2 Kings 24:14).

The Book of Jeremiah picks up the story—backtracking before it advances—and also emphasizes God's role in history. Cautioning against a false prophecy of hope, Jeremiah reveals that the nations Nebuchadnezzar conquers under God's unseen direction will continue to serve him.

> Thus said the LORD of Hosts, the God of Israel: I have put an iron yoke upon the necks of all those nations, that they may serve King Nebuchadnezzar of Babylon—and serve him they shall! I have even given the wild beasts to him." (Jer. 28:14)

God later tells Jeremiah to deliver one of many messages to Jehoiachin's uncle/successor, Zedekiah (nee Mattaniah). Judah will be conquered. Jeremiah instructs the king: "Thus said the LORD: I am going to deliver this city into the hands of the king of Babylon, and he will destroy it by fire" (Jer. 34:2). But God will not abandon His people. While Israel will go into exile, it need not suffer. In a letter to the exile leaders, Jeremiah reveals God's command that Israel is to establish itself in Babylon—build houses, plant gardens, take wives and have children. Israel is also to "seek the welfare of the city to which I have exiled you and pray to the LORD in its behalf; for in its prosperity you shall prosper" (Jer. 29:5-7).

God's word proves true. Zedekiah, as his predecessors, learns nothing from Israel's history of violating God's commandments and historical imperatives. Nine years after ascending the throne, he rebels against Babylonian suzerainty. Why does he take such a chance? Is he merely young and reckless? Mordechai Cogan offers that to suggest youth and inexperience as the keys to Zedekiah's behavior would be to indulge in modern psychohistory. Zedekiah may be a more astute player of geopolitics since, "observers in the west might have thought that Babylonia was going into decline. After his victory in Jerusalem, Nebuchadrezzar faced several serious threats to his rule." (Oxford, 351)

Nebuchadnezzar again lays siege to Jerusalem. After two years, the Babylonians breach the city's walls. As 2 Chronicles reports, the Judeans suffer terrible destruction unleashed by a conqueror…

> "…who killed their youths by the sword in their sanctuary; He did not spare youth, maiden, elder, or graybeard, but delivered all into his hands. All the vessels of the House of God, large and small, and the treasures of the House of the LORD and the treasures of the king and his officers were all brought to Babylon. They burned the House of God and tore down the wall of Jerusalem, burned down all its mansions, and consigned all its precious objects to destruction. Those who survived the sword he exiled to Babylon…" (2 Chron. 36:17-20)

Zedekiah flees but cannot escape Nebuchadnezzar's long reach. Captured, the king of Judah endures great suffering, according to 2 Kings. Nebuchadnezzar has Zedekiah's children slaughtered before his own eyes. Then he has the king's eyes put out.

The Book of Jeremiah repeats much of the fall of Zedekiah and Jerusalem. It is 586 BCE, and the Temple lies in ruins, as does much of Jerusalem. The Babylonians have also depleted the kingdom of much of its population. Only "some of the poorest people who owned nothing were left in the land of Judah" (Jer. 39:10).

The biblical portrait of conquered Judah is bleak, but is it accurate? From Mordechai Cogan's critical perspective, Jeremiah's account is overstated. "Judah was neither totally devastated nor depopulated, as some biblical writers would have us believe. The rural population held on, eking out a living for several generations until their fortunes took another turn." (Oxford, 356) Even Jeremiah contradicts the figure of 10,000 exiles offered by 2 Kings. He tallies 3,023 in the seventh year of Nebuchadnezzar's reign, 832 in the eighteenth year and 745 in the twenty-third. "The total amounted to 4,600 persons" (Jer. 52:30). But the Bible concerns itself with a greater truth than statistics reveal. The blow to Judah, numbers aside, represents catastrophe. Thus the Book of Lamentations mourns, "The princess among states / Is become like a widow" (Lam. 1:1).

Jeremiah falls under the protection of Nebuchadnezzar. The king's chief of the guards, Nebuzaradan, releases the prophet from among the Jerusalemites and other Judeans being exiled to Babylon. This high official of Babylon offers an interesting back-story. The Talmud (Sanhedrin 96b) relates that Nebuzaradan, evidently a military man, first feared to attack Jerusalem but was prodded by God. He pressed forward, slaying many, and tried to set the Sanctuary of the Temple on fire, at which point a divine voice halted him. Filled with remorse for the slaughter, he converted to Judaism and was "a righteous proselyte."

Whether recognizing God's power or making a clever political statement to staunch potential opposition, Nebuzaradan makes an official announcement to keep the remaining population of Judah from growing restive:

> "The LORD your God threatened this place with this disaster; and now the LORD has brought it about. He has acted as He threatened, because you sinned against the LORD and did not obey Him. That is why this has happened to you." (Jer. 40:2-3)

Turmoil and strife afflict the remaining leaders of Judah. The remnant of the people, fearful of their Babylonian conquerors, sets out for Egypt, the nation that once enslaved them. But God tells Jeremiah they have nothing to fear and must remain subject to Nebuchadnezzar's rule.

> "Do not be afraid of the king of Babylon, whom you fear; do not be afraid of him—declares the LORD—for I am with you to save you and to rescue you from his hands. I will dispose him to be merciful to you: he shall show you mercy and bring you back to your own land. (Jer. 42:11-12)

Nebuchadnezzar orders many Judeans to be taken to Babylon. The prophet Micah, however, assures them of God's ultimate mercy. The same king who destroys Jerusalem will protect "Fair Zion" in exile.

> And you will reach Babylon.
> There you shall be saved,
> There the LORD will redeem you
> From the hands of your foes. (Micah 4:10)

The Judeans will not listen. They refuse to accept Babylonian exile and journey to Tahpanhes in Egypt. God expresses His displeasure, instructing Jeremiah to tell them:

> "Thus said the LORD of Hosts, the God of Israel: I am sending for My servant King Nebuchadrezzar of Babylon, and will set his throne over these stones which I have embedded. He will spread out his pavilion over them. He will come and attack the land of Egypt, delivering
> Those destined for the plague, to the plague,
> Those destined for captivity, to captivity,
> And those destined for the sword, to the sword. (Jer. 43:10-11)

The Book of Ezekiel also reveals that God will "strengthen the arms of the king of Babylon and will put My sword in his hand" to break the arms of Pharaoh (Ezek. 30: 24).

Of course, if God can grant power to Nebuchadnezzar, He can also withdraw it. And so God later tells Jeremiah that, "Babylon is captured... For a nation from the north has attacked her..." (Jer. 50:2-3). Babylon now engages in a life-or-death struggle with Persia for regional dominance. The determining factor of history, God makes His intent clear. Nebuchadnezzar will be humbled.

> I set a snare for you, O Babylon,
> And you were trapped unawares;
> You were found and caught,
> Because you challenged the LORD. (Jer. 50:24)

Babylon has served God's purpose. It also has "acted insolently against the LORD" (Jer. 50:29), although the biblical text does not reveal the specifics. Thus Babylon will be despoiled, as were Sodom and Gomorrah. God has used Nebuchadnezzar and Babylon as his "war club" (Jer. 51:20). Now they "shall become rubble" (Jer. 51:37).

At this point we cannot help but ask: Has Nebuchadnezzar no idea that he serves as God's agent and that his own power is limited? Does he recognize the God of Israel at all? The answers depend on which book of the Bible we read.

In all but Daniel, Nebuchadnezzar's encounters with God are one-sided. The king seems ignorant that he is manipulated by a power far greater than his own. The Book of Ezekiel offers an excellent example. God informs Ezekiel that Nebuchadnezzar is planning military strategy by consulting pagan omens.

> For the king of Babylon has stood at the fork of the road, where two roads branch off, to perform divination: He has shaken arrows, consulted teraphim, and inspected the liver [of a sacrificed animal—JPS footnote]. In his right hand came up the omen against Jerusalem—to set battering rams, to proclaim murder, to raise battle shouts, to set battering rams against the gates, to cast up mounds, to erect towers. (Ezek. 21:26-27)

Nebuchadnezzar seems clueless that the God of Israel, not the false Babylonian gods, sets his course. The destruction of Jerusalem constitutes part of a greater plan to cleanse Israel of idolatry and secure devotion to the Law. Abraham Joshua Heschel aptly notes: "The Jerusalem man is destroying, God is erecting." (Heschel, 177)

But the Bible's arc is long. As regards Nebuchadnezzar, the Book of Daniel changes everything.

Critical scholars place Daniel's origins in the reign of the Assyrian tyrant, Antiochus IV Epiphanes (176-164 BCE), overthrown by the Maccabees. This period comes well after those in which previous books involving Nebuchadnezzar were written. The persecutions of the Antiochus era generated much apocalyptic discussion related in the name of Daniel, an earlier writer. Given its evidently late date of composition, Daniel seems to draw freely on earlier biblical traditions.

The narrative presents Daniel as one of four Israelites of royal descent brought to Babylon to be educated for service in the royal palace. He proves to be an exceptional student. When Nebuchadnezzar has a puzzling dream, none of his magicians, exorcists, sorcerers, and Chaldeans (Chaldea lies in the south of Babylon)—the learned class of Babylonians—can explain it. Readers of Genesis understand what will happen next.

Reflecting Joseph's service to Pharaoh, Daniel makes known that he can interpret dreams. A night vision, he exclaims, has revealed the answer. Daniel first tells Nebuchadnezzar *what* he has dreamed—of a great statue with a head of gold, breast and arms of silver, belly and thigh of bronze, legs of iron, and feet part iron and part clay. A stone has struck the statue's feet—its weak spot—and all its parts have been crushed. Daniel then reveals the dream's meaning. God has given power to Nebuchadnezzar, but now the king's realm—the head of gold—will be destroyed. A series of successor kingdoms will rise and fall until "the God of Heaven will establish a kingdom that shall never be destroyed…" (Dan. 2:44). Also like Joseph, Daniel reveals that God, not he, "has made known to the king what will happen in the future" (Dan. 2:45).

Nebuchadnezzar responds dramatically, prostrating himself and ordering offerings made to Daniel. Then he quite unexpectedly replies, bearing in mind his attitude in previous books: "Truly your God must be the God of gods and Lord of kings and the revealer of mysteries to have enabled you to reveal this mystery" (Dan. 2:47).

Just as Pharaoh places Joseph above all Egypt save himself, Nebuchadnezzar makes Daniel governor of the province of Babylon. Then in a flashback to the Purim story in the Book of Esther, Nebuchadnezzar commissions a statue of gold some sixty cubits (ninety feet) high to which all the peoples in his empire must bow. The fiery furnace awaits all who fail to comply. The Jews refuse, just as Mordecai refuses to bow to Haman. "Certain Chaldeans" inform the king. Nebuchadnezzar, filled with rage, consigns Daniel's three companions—Shadrach, Meshach and Abed-nego—to the flames.[73] Yet the king later sees them unharmed, walking with a fourth figure who "looks like a divine being" (Dan. 3:25).

The astonished Nebuchadnezzar exclaims:

> "Blessed be the God of Shadrach, Meshach, and Abed-nego, who sent His angel to save His servants who, trusting in Him, flouted the king's decree at the risk of their lives rather than serve or worship any god but their own God. I hereby give an order that [anyone of] any people or nation of whatever language who blasphemes the God of Shadrach, Meshach, and Abed-nego shall be torn limb from limb, and his house confiscated, for there is no other God who is able to save in this way." (Dan. 3:28-29)

If Nebuchadnezzar is still a polytheist, the God of Israel tops his list. He sends a message to all the peoples of the earth:

> "The signs and wonders that the Most High God has worked for me I am pleased to relate. How great are His signs; how mighty His wonders! His kingdom is an everlasting kingdom, and His dominion endures throughout the generations." (Dan. 3:32-33)

Now, understanding that he has served God's purposes and recognizing his haughtiness, the mightiest of earthly rulers falls. Prefiguring Shakespeare's Lear, Nebuchadnezzar loses his wits and is driven away from human beings. He eats grass like cattle and is drenched by the dew of heaven. Sufficiently chastised, his reason is restored. He lifts his eyes to heaven and relates:

> "I blessed the Most High, and praised and glorified the Ever-Living One,
> Whose dominion is an everlasting dominion
> And whose kingdom endures throughout the generations.
> All the inhabitants of the earth are of no account,
> He does as He wishes with the host of heaven,

73 Rashi, in a comment on Leviticus 22:32, notes that the three Jews do not expect a miracle to save them but willingly submit themselves to a fiery death out of love of God.

And with the inhabitants of the earth.
There is none to stay his hand
Or say to Him, 'What have You done?'" (Dan. 4:31-32)

Nebuchadnezzar, possessing radically new insights, can only "praise, exalt, and glorify the King of Heaven, all of whose works are just and whose ways are right, and who is able to humble those who behave arrogantly" (Dan. 4:34). Certainly, the Book of Daniel's portrait of the Babylonian king appears to be painted with a very different brush. Nebuchadnezzar speaks like an Israelite prophet, supporting the theory that Daniel was written during the rebellion against Antiochus IV. The successful trials of Daniel, Shadrach, Meshach and Abed-nego undoubtedly served to encourage the Jews to take heart and resist as did the words of such a powerful, newly aware conqueror as Nebuchadnezzar, who finally grasps the truth about the God of Israel.

What do the Sages think of the Babylonian conqueror? For the most part, they hurl vitriol at him. Nebuchadnezzar may be God's instrument, but the Judeans' suffering makes him a lightning rod for their anger and frustration. Such emotions, aroused by destruction and exile, cannot be directed at God Whose justice—Job aside (see the following chapter)—cannot be questioned.

The Talmud devotes much attention to the matter. Rabbi Yohanan (Shabbat 149b) says, "As long as that wicked man lived, the sound of mirth was never heard in the mouth of any living creature." Rabbi Hamnunah (Berachot 57b) declares that on seeing the ruins of Nebuchadnezzar's palace, one should say, "Blessed be He who destroyed the palace of wicked Nebuchadnezzar." Why such wrath? The Talmud emphasizes that Nebuchadnezzar was also merciless to the Judean exiles. He massacred thousands of handsome young men to whom Babylonian women would have been attracted and had their corpses mutilated. (Sanhedrin 92b) Moreover, he was a pederast. (Shabbat 149b) The Midrash (Leviticus Rabbah 19:6) also excoriates Nebuchadnezzar: When he put Jehoiakim to death, he had him cut into olive-size pieces.

In light of the Book of Daniel, however, some Sages propose Nebuchadnezzar as a righteous man who serves God, if unknowingly. The Talmud (Taanith 18b) tells of two Jews sentenced to death by the Roman emperor Trajan. Trajan challenges God to rescue them the way God rescued Shadrach, Meshach and Abed-nego. The Jews reply that the Hebrews of Babylon were righteous and worthy men. Moreover Nebuchadnezzar was an honorable king and worthy of a miracle.

Given the multiple sources for Nebuchadnezzar's encounters with God, a single view of the king of Babylon cannot be achieved. We know from the biblical text, however, that God seeks out Nebuchadnezzar for His own purposes. In turn—at least in the Book of Daniel—Nebuchadnezzar finds God.

CYRUS, KING OF PERSIA

God's Anointed One

After punishing Israel with Nebuchadnezzar, God redeems His people through Cyrus, King of Persia. Following Persia's victory over the Babylonians, Cyrus acknowledges God's role in delivering the nations to him. He releases the treasures looted from the Temple, encourages tens of thousands of Jews to return to Jerusalem and authorizes payment for the Temple's reconstruction. The project is completed during the reign of Darius I, who also acknowledges the God of Israel.

For every action, Isaac Newton posits in his third law of thermodynamics, there is an equal and opposite reaction. In many ways, this truth presents itself in the biblical narrative. Good and bad, purity and impurity, wrongdoing and punishment, destruction and redemption all highlight both humanity's and Israel's development. It should come as no surprise that if God wields His sword against Israel through the (mostly) unwitting Babylonian king, Nebuchadnezzar, He also devises a mechanism for restoring Israel. That mechanism is Cyrus II, known historically as Cyrus the Great, king of Persia (reigned 559–530 BCE).

The prophet Isaiah foretells Cyrus' role in freeing Israel. While Israel will weep over the loss of Jerusalem and the Temple to Babylon, it will experience redemption. He relays the word of God:

> It is I who say of Jerusalem, "It shall be inhabited,"
> And of the towns of Judah, "They shall be rebuilt;
> And I will restore their ruined places." (Isaiah 44:26)

Jerusalem will not arise from the ashes in a miraculous act of creation similar to that of the first chapters of Genesis. Rather, the city's rebirth will follow the natural order of human history. To ensure that this takes place, God raises up Cyrus. "He is My shepherd; / He shall fulfill my purposes!" (Isaiah 44:28). While conquerors such as Assyria's Shalmaneser and Senecharib, and

Babylon's Nebuchadnezzar, act as unwitting agents of God, the biblical narrative makes clear not only that God chooses Cyrus for a special purpose but that He informs him as well.

> Thus said the LORD to Cyrus, His anointed one—
> Whose right hand He has grasped,
> Treading down nations before him,
> Ungirding the loins of kings,
> Opening doors before him
> And letting no gate stay shut:
> I will march before you
> And level the hills that loom up;
> I will shatter doors of bronze
> And cut down iron bars.
> I will give you treasures concealed in the dark
> And secret hoards—
> So that you may know that it is I the LORD,
> The God of Israel, who call you by name.
> For the sake of My servant Jacob,
> Israel My chosen one,
> I call you by name,
> I hail you by title, though you have not known Me.
> I am the LORD, and there is none else;
> Beside Me, there is no god. (Isaiah 45:1-5)

Cyrus may not previously know God, but God knows Cyrus, and the Persian king will play a pivotal role in Israel's history. God calls him, after all, His "anointed one." The title is important albeit sometimes confusing. The Hebrew *moshiach*, literally "anointed one," is commonly translated as "messiah"—a term denoting "savior" to Christians but having a very different meaning to Jews. Anointing the head with oil represents a not-uncommon practice for the great—Israel's high priests and kings—as well as for the future descendant of David who will restore Israel to peace and security rather than cleanse the souls of humanity.

Alan Segal notes that Cyrus is the first non-Jew designated as messiah, but "the term was not nearly as well fixed as some today think; indeed, 'messiah' could describe not just Judean kings, prophets, and priests but Saul's shield and a number of other objects set up for an official purpose by the rite of anointing." (Segal, 199) The Talmud (Megillah 12a) points out that Cyrus serves only as a tool of God; he is *not* the Messiah who will restore Israel.

It is only natural that we wonder how God actually speaks to Cyrus. Does God appear when Cyrus is waking or dreaming? As a human or as an angel? From within a pillar of fire or cloud, or as just a voice? We do not know. But God's message echoes His promise to Moses to free the Israelites—"I will send forth My terror before you…" (Ex. 23:27)—when He tells Cyrus:

> I will march before you
> And level the hills that loom up;
> I will shatter doors of bronze
> And cut down iron bars. (Isaiah 45:2)

God makes it equally clear to Isaiah—and thus to Judah and all Israel—that Cyrus advances His cause. No mistake should be made that Cyrus' power is his own.

> It was I who roused him for victory
> And who level all the roads for him.
> He shall rebuild My city
> And let My exiled people go
> Without price and without payment
> —said the LORD of Hosts. (Isaiah 45:13)

Here the biblical narrative and history dovetail. According to the archeologist Israel Finkelstein and the biblical historian Neil Asher Silberman, "both Cyrus and his son Cambyses (who ruled from 530-522 BCE) supported the building of temples and encouraged the return of displaced populations elsewhere in their vast empire. Their policy was to grant autonomy to loyal local elites." (Finkelstein, 308) Earthly rulers may arrive at practical strategies for preventing rebellion among conquered subjects, but such strategies as they relate to Israel, according to the biblical perspective, reflect the will of God.

The Babylon of Nebuchadnezzar therefore suffers defeat because God wills it. Having served his purpose, Nebuchadnezzar is cast aside. Thus Isaiah warns Babylon of doom:

> Sit silent, retire into darkness,
> O Fair Chaldea;
> Nevermore shall they call you
> Mistress of Kingdoms. (Isaiah 47:5)

As to Cyrus, the Persian king is no rank amateur. He brings an historical record of successes to the table—victories not lost on the biblical authors. In 550, he rebels against the Median king Astyages and defeats him. Four years later, Cyrus brings the Greek cities of Asia Minor's Ionian coast under his control. Then in 539, he defeats Nebuchadnezzar's successor, Nabonidus (ruled 556-539), to create an empire stretching from the Aegean Sea to the Caspian.

From the Bible's perspective, Cyrus' redemption of the Jews fulfills God's promises relayed both by Isaiah and Jeremiah (29:10). The king's story then unfolds in the Book of Ezra with 2 Chronicles repeating the highlights. God rouses Cyrus to issue an inspired proclamation to Jews throughout his realm.

> "Thus said King Cyrus of Persia: The LORD God of Heaven has given me all the kingdoms of the earth and has charged me with building Him a house in Jerusalem, which is in Judah. Anyone of you of all His people—may his God be with Him, and let him go up to Jerusalem that is in Judah and build the House of the LORD God of Israel, the God that is in Jerusalem..." (Ezra 1:2-3)

As with Nebuchadnezzar in the Book of Daniel, a question arises. Cyrus has publicly recognized the power of God. Has he then become a monotheist and follower of the God of Israel? Once again, we do not know. Cyrus first refers to "The LORD God of Heaven." But he then speaks of "the God that is in Jerusalem," suggesting that the God of Israel may be only a local god if nonetheless a very powerful one. Is Cyrus a respecter of all gods? Historically speaking, the "Cyrus Cylinder," a pro-Cyrus document produced by the Babylonian priesthood, represents Cyrus as the Babylonian god Marduk's "friend and companion." (Oxford, 375, 377) The conquered Babylonians seem to take the same position as the Jews—"Our god/God loves Cyrus"—even though the Persians were Zoroastrians.

Whatever Cyrus' religious beliefs, they seem to indicate a fairly expansive view towards others. Paul Johnson suggests that Cyrus' release of Jewish exiles from Babylonia may have reflected his beliefs. "Indeed Cyrus seems to have regarded it as a religious duty to reverse the wicked deportations and temple-destructions of his predecessors." (Johnson, 85)

Again peering through the lens of history provided by Finkelstein and Silberman, Cyrus may have had more practical motives to encourage the Jews to rebuild the Temple. In allowing subject peoples to follow their own religions, the Persian king may have been more a savvy politician than a religious libertarian. Respecting subject peoples—Jews and Babylonians included—likely made them more comfortable with Persian rule and less inclined to rebel, which would entail a costly military response. Moreover, a relatively autonomous, prosperous Judah with Jerusalem as its renewed capital would both pay considerable taxes and serve as a buffer between Persia and Egypt. The religious historian Mary Joan Winn Leith notes, "Cyrus was following the lead of earlier Mesopotamian rulers by strategically granting privileged status to some cities, often in sensitive areas, whose support and cooperation could benefit the empire." (Oxford, 378)

Thus the historical Cyrus did not necessarily share the Bible's view of the God of History. According to Josephus, however, he may well have been aware of Isaiah's prophecies and willing to acknowledge them to achieve his objectives. (Soncino/Daniel, 111) Leith turns this view on its head, suggesting that Isaiah's prophecies reflect the knowledge of Cyrus' practice of recognizing conquered nations' religions. (Oxford, 376) This makes history rather than God the basis of Isaiah's prophecies.

But let us return to the biblical text. Fully supportive of the Jews, Cyrus releases all of the Temple's treasures looted by Nebuchadnezzar.

> So the chiefs of the clans of Judah and Benjamin, and the priests and Levites, all whose spirit had been roused by God, got ready to go up to build the House of the LORD that is in Jerusalem. (Ezra 1:5)

A new chapter begins in Israelite history. More than forty-two thousand men, along with their families, return to Jerusalem. Cyrus authorizes them to make payments to craftsmen and suppliers for the rebuilding the Temple. The Temple's foundation is laid. Then the building stops, thwarted by those who earlier had been brought into the land by Assyria and seek to take part in the project—and capture a share of the funds provided for it.

Construction remains in limbo through the reigns of Cyrus and his son, Cambyses (ruled 529-22). Then Darius I (ruled 522-486) ascends the throne. Here, the biblical record becomes confusing. A movement to rebuild the Temple begins in 520 sparked by the prophets Haggai and Zechariah—perhaps, as Mary Joan Winn Leith suggests, because of upheavals in the Persian empire brought about by Darius' ascent. (Oxford, 392) The project moves forward with the Temple completed in 516 or 515. Yet Ezra relates that Artaxerxes, at the behest of Rehum the commissioner and Shimshai the scribe, orders a halt to the construction. However, Artaxerxes I rules from 465–424 BCE, the period in which Nehemiah, who returns from Persian exile, serves as governor of Judah. Leith notes that Ezra may not have arrived in Judah in 458—prior to Nehemiah—as the Bible implies, but as far afterward as 428 or even 398. (Oxford, 373)

Nonetheless, Darius grants permission for construction to continue after the discovery in Media of a memorandum from Cyrus. It orders the imperial government to pay all expenses. "Allow the work of this House of God to go on," Darius instructs Tattenai, governor of the province of Beyond the River [Euphrates] (Ezra 6:7). "And may the God who established His name there cause the downfall of any king or nation that undertakes to damage that House of God in Jerusalem" (Ezra 6:12).

Darius, like Cyrus, knows the power of the God of Israel. In the book of Daniel, he comforts Daniel before the Israelite is about to be thrust into the lion's den for defying a ban on petitioning any god or man besides the king. “Your God, whom you serve so regularly, will deliver you” (Dan. 6:17). The next morning, Darius discovers Daniel unharmed. The king throws the plotters and their families to the lions, then sends a message to all the inhabitants of the earth:

> “I have hereby given an order that throughout my royal domain men must tremble in fear before the God of Daniel, for He is the living God who endures forever; His kingdom is indestructible, and His dominion is to the end of time; He delivers and saves, and performs signs and wonders in heaven and on earth, for He delivered Daniel from the power of the lions.” (Dan. 6:26-28)

When Ezra goes to Jerusalem to rebuild the Temple, Darius echoes Cyrus, instructing the treasurers of the province of Beyond the River to fund all of Ezra’s requests.

> Whatever is by order of the God of Heaven must be carried out diligently for the House of the God of Heaven, else wrath will come upon the king and his sons. (Ezra 7:23)

The Cyrus of the Bible and the Cyrus of history may well represent two different interpretations of a single conquering king. Cyrus’ attitude towards the God of Israel within the historical record remains unknown. The biblical narrative, on the other hand, leaves no doubt that Cyrus encounters God, recognizes His power and serves as His agent for Israel’s redemption.

THE GENTILES OF JONAH

Exemplars of Repentance

God calls on Jonah, an Israelite, to go to the evil city of Nineveh and warn of its impending destruction. Jonah refuses and flees on a ship bound for far-off Tarshish. In response, God creates a great storm. The ship's sailors—all gentiles—fear for their lives. Jonah goes down to the hold but is aroused from his sleep by the captain, who asks him to cry out to his god. The sailors cast lots to determine who has brought about the storm. The guilt falls on Jonah. He asks to be cast into the sea. The sailors first refuse then do so reluctantly, fearing the power of the Hebrew God. A great fish swallows Jonah. He remains in the fish's belly for three days. After reciting a psalm blessing God, he is spewed out on dry land. God again calls on Jonah to go to Nineveh. Jonah obeys and issues his warning to the city. The king leads the populace in immediately repenting. Expecting that God's justice will trump His mercy, Jonah journeys to the east side of the city and awaits Nineveh's destruction. But God accepts the Ninevites' repentance. When God provides a plant to shade Jonah then lets it whither overnight, Jonah mourns for the plant. God upbraids him for thinking so much of the plant and so little of the Ninevites.

What does God want from people who transgress? The stories of Sodom and Gomorrah in the Book of Genesis and of Egypt in the Book of Exodus suggest that human beings can be so evil as to exclude the possibility of redemption and thus merit destruction by God's hand. Yet this is hardly the Bible's sole—or even dominant—view of wrongdoing and punishment.

The Book of Jonah, from its later position in the biblical narrative, presents an entirely different point of view. God *does* forgive. Indeed, God *wants* to forgive. As we shall see, the king and people of Nineveh—the capital of ancient Assyria located on the Tigris River across from modern-day Mosul, Iraq—prove sufficiently evil to prompt God's anger. But their story takes a far different turn from that of the Sodomites and Egyptians. The

Ninevites' encounter with God sets an example of *t'shuvah*—turning or repentance—for Israel and all humanity. Moreover, the reaction of Jonah, the prophet chosen by God to warn Nineveh of impending doom, serves as an object lesson regarding God's ultimate intentions relating to wrongdoers outside Israel—and within it.

Like the Book of Ruth (see *Women of Valor*), the Book of Jonah tells a very rich story in only four short chapters. However, the differences between these two books prove more revealing than their similarities. Ruth is a Moabite whereas Jonah is an Israelite. Ruth displays boundless kindness; she truly loves her mother-in-law, Naomi. Jonah, as will be evident, displays nothing but contempt for the Ninevites in spite of God's opposite stance.

Who *is* Jonah? The Jerusalem Talmud identifies him as the unnamed son of the Widow of Zarephath—the boy revived from death by Elijah (see *Women of Valor*).

Jonah does make one appearance in the Bible prior to that in his own book, however. Second Kings 14:25 identifies him as the son of Amittai from Gath-hepher, who relayed God's promise to restore the territory of Israel from Lebo-hamath to the sea of the Arabah. King Jeroboam, son of Joash, accomplishes this task when he becomes king in Samaria. Thus the story in 2 Kings places the biblically "historic" Jonah in the eighth century BCE.

Many scholars believe that the use of Aramaic—the region's *lingua franca*—and specific grammatical constructs demonstrate that the Book of Jonah was written as much as three hundred years later, during the Second Temple period.

Does it matter when the Book of Jonah was written? The Israeli scholar Uriel Simon finds such dating ultimately to be immaterial because Jonah occupies a place outside the course of history, as does Job. (Simon, xviii) Jonah's tale, like Job's, intrigues us because it presents a universal question as important today as in the distant past: Can we accept others' genuine repentance after the wrongs they have done us and thus forego justice in terms of vengeance?

Jonah's story begins with a clear call to prophecy.[74] From the outset, God makes no secret of his mission. "The word of the LORD came to Jonah son of Amittai: Go at once to Nineveh, that great city, and proclaim judgment upon it; for their wickedness has come before Me" (Jonah 1:1-2). How wicked is Nineveh? Wicked enough for the Book of Nahum to pronounce:

> Ah, city of crime,
> Utterly treacherous,
> Full of violence,
> Where killing never stops! (Nahum 3:1)

Wicked enough for the Book of Zephaniah to prophesy:

> And He will stretch out his arm against the north
> And destroy Assyria;
> He will make Nineveh a desolation,
> Arid as the desert. (Zeph. 2:13)

What has Nineveh done? The Jonah narrative doesn't say. In fact, it offers no detail about the city other than its large size. On the other hand, both the Bible and history attest to the fact that Nineveh served as the capital of the Assyrian empire that destroyed the northern kingdom of Israel in 722 BCE and exiled its Ten Tribes to oblivion. If the Book of Jonah was indeed written during the Second Temple period, the author was no doubt familiar with—and hostile to—Nineveh's past. Yet Nineveh, destroyed in 612 BCE, no longer stood as a threat to Judah.

What importance then does the story of this city of gentiles play in the Bible? If God focuses His attention on the history and spiritual purity of Israel, a book—no matter how brief—detailing Jonah's mission to wicked Nineveh seems out of character. But as the story unfolds, the opposite proves true. We find a parallel of

74 For Christians, Jonah prefigures Jesus. In Luke 11:29-30, Jesus says, "This generation is an evil generation; it seeks a sign, but no sign will be given it, except the sign of Jonah. Just as Jonah became a sign to the Ninevites, so will the Son of Man be to this generation."

sorts in the Book of Genesis. Abraham pleads that God spare the terribly wicked citizens of Sodom, thus teaching us a great lesson about compassion and mercy. When ten just men cannot be found in Sodom, we also discover how corrupt human beings can be. However, Genesis focuses less on Sodom than on Abraham and his championing justice rather than revenge. So, too, the Ninevites, and the gentile sailors we meet prior to encountering them, serve to reveal Jonah's attitude towards compassion and mercy, and what these values should mean to us. So let us now see how this plays out in the narrative.

Jonah, commanded to go to Nineveh and issue his warning, responds to God in a most unusual way. He offers not one word of protest or argument. Neither does he demur, as does Moses, who asks God at the burning bush, "Who am I that I should go to Pharaoh and free the Israelites from Egypt?" (Ex. 3:11). Rather, Jonah runs "away from the service of the LORD" and boards a ship sailing westward to Tarshish (Jonah 1:3). In doing so, he ignores the wisdom of David: "Where can I escape from Your spirit? / Where can I flee from Your presence?" (Psalms 139:7). The adage, "You can run, but you can't hide," has biblical roots.

What prompts Jonah's behavior? Does he fear that the Ninevites will laugh at him? Or is he concerned that they will take his message to heart and repent? Whatever his reasoning, Jonah seems not to consider that refusing a request from God risks grave punishment. Yes, Abraham argues with God. So does Moses. But Jonah offers us no evidence that he has attained the status of a patriarch or lawgiver.

And why does Jonah seek to flee to Tarshish? Here an answer readily presents itself. Tarshish lies far, far away. Many scholars identify it with Tartessus on the southwest coast of Spain past the Straits of Gibraltar. Tartessus was a Phoenician colony engaged in mining silver and tin, which were shipped to Tyre in what is now Lebanon. Doubtless, the city served as a powerful symbol of remoteness—as far west from Judah as one could go and in the opposite direction from Nineveh.

Jonah not only wants to go far, he wants to do it quickly. The Talmud (Nedarim 38a) relates that he paid the fare of the entire ship so that it would leave immediately. Why such haste? The voyage will remove him from the land of Israel so he cannot receive a second, *specific* instruction from God. According to the sixteenth-century commentator Moshe Alshich, only the Land of Israel is conducive to the revelation of prophecy. (Alshich, 35) The more distance Jonah puts between himself and the land, the more distance he puts between himself and God—or so he believes.

Jonah's flight proves not only ill considered but perilous. A tempest threatens the ship. The crew's members—all gentiles—pray each to his own god for deliverance. Then, in an effort to lighten their load, they fling cargo overboard while Jonah, separating himself from them, sleeps peacefully below decks. He seemingly resigns himself to dying rather than going to Nineveh.

As the storm continues, the captain wakens Jonah. "How can you be sleeping so soundly! Up, call upon your god! Perhaps the god will be kind to us and we will not perish" (Jonah 1:6).

Here, two divergent translations are of interest. JPS translates *elohecha* in the above verse as "your god" and *ha-elohim* as "the god," both non-specific terms. But the Soncino translation offers the Israelite "your God" and "God." Thus Soncino's commentator, S. Goldman, writes, "The use of *God* as a generic term is remarkable in the mouth of a heathen, who had just prayed to his own national deity. It suggests that, with their worship of idols, some at least of the heathens had a vague apprehension of one supreme God; and in a moment of great danger, such apprehension would come to the forefront of their consciousness." (Soncino/Prophets, 140)

Fearing for their lives, the sailors cast lots to determine who has brought them to the brink of disaster. Not surprisingly, the guilt falls on Jonah, whose identity they seek. Jonah speaks freely. "'I am a Hebrew," he replied. "I worship the Lord, the God of Heaven, who made both sea and land'" (Jonah 1:9). Jonah may worship, but he does not necessarily obey.

Learning that Jonah is fleeing from this powerful God, the sailors ask what they must do to save themselves. In contrast with Jonah, these gentiles, whose particular religions are never revealed, move *towards* the God of Israel. Jonah instructs them to heave him overboard—an apparently noble response indicating that he understands his error and the wrath it has produced. The sailors, who hold the life of an alien Hebrew in their hands, refuse. Instead, they row harder to reach the safety of the shore where they may also return Jonah to God's power and escape his destructive presence.

When the sea grows even more violent, the sailors raise their voices in anguish.

> Then they cried out to the LORD: "Oh, please, LORD, do not let us perish on account of this man's life. Do not hold us guilty for killing an innocent person! For You, O LORD, by Your will, have brought this about." (Jonah 1:14)

Seeing no alternative, they toss Jonah into the sea. The sea stops raging. In thanks, they offer a sacrifice and make vows to appease God with further sacrifices upon reaching their destination.

Have the sailors stopped being pagans? Some commentators believe so. Rashi states that the sailors vow to convert to Judaism. The earlier *Perkei d'Rabbi Eliezer*, an eighth-century midrashic narrative, offers that they vow to bring their wives and households to the worship of the Hebrew God. (Zlotowitz, 104)

Jonah, as even most non-readers of the Bible know, does not drown. Instead, he spends three days and three nights in the belly of a huge fish—*dag gadol* meaning great or large fish, not whale. This fish is not random. Midrash Jonah declares that it was created during the six days of creation (Bialik, 133:142).

Suspended between life and death, Jonah prays what Uriel Simon terms "a hymn of thanksgiving" rather than "a psalm of entreaty." (Simon, 15) It begins:

> In my trouble I called to the LORD,
> And he answered me;
> From the belly of Sheol I cried out,
> And You heard my voice. (Jonah 2:3)

In this challenging poem, which encompasses eight of the chapter's eleven verses and may have been appended to the original story (Simon deals with this in his commentary), Jonah thanks God for his deliverance as if he was already on dry land. Jonah seems to recognize that in distancing himself from Nineveh, he has distanced himself from God. Thus he says:

> I thought I was driven away
> Out of Your sight:
> Would I ever gaze again
> Upon Your holy Temple? (Jonah 2:5)

Now, Jonah apparently draws near to God. God responds favorably, commanding the fish to spew Jonah out on dry land.

The Quran likewise points out Jonah's error in fleeing God, "how he went away in anger, thinking We had no power over him. But in the darkness he cried: 'There is no god but You. Glory be to You! I have done wrong'" (21:87-88). Had Jonah not praised God, "he would have stayed in its belly till the day of Resurrection" (37:139ff).

But Jonah's second chance at life earns him no reprieve from the task God has set for him.

> "Then the word of the LORD came to Jonah a second time. Go at once to Nineveh, that great city, and proclaim to it what I tell you." Jonah went at once to Nineveh in accordance with the LORD's command. (Jonah 3:1-2)

At last, Jonah reaches Nineveh. The JPS translation describes it as "an enormously large city" (Jonah 3:3). However the literal translation of the Hebrew—*ir-g'dolah l'elohim*—offers another approach: "a large city of God" or, possibly "gods," since *elohim* can denote either the singular or the plural. Nineveh may be a major religious center as well as a political one.

Now dedicated to obeying God, Jonah heads towards the city center. After one day's walk—the city is three days' walk across—he declares his prophecy: "Forty days more, and Nineveh shall be overthrown!" (Jonah 3:4). This is the sum total of his warning. Jonah offers neither a reason for impending disaster nor a means to avert it. Nineveh's fate apparently is sealed, its time waning.

The Talmud (Sanhedrin 89b) suggests the possibility of a second outcome. The literal translation of the Hebrew word *nehepachet* is "overturned," rather than "overthrown." Jonah does not know whether Nineveh will be overturned for good or for evil—whether the city will be destroyed or will turn to God and be saved. This Talmudic view may have emerged from hindsight. Uriel Simon presents a different view, pointing to the three-letter root of *nehepachet*—h-f-k—as connoting complete destruction. He finds no basis for believing that Jonah prophesies Nineveh's repentance. Yet this is exactly what happens!

We know that the godless people of Sodom and Gomorrah cannot produce even ten innocent men. Israel, in spite of its redemption from Egyptian slavery and the gift of the covenant at Sinai, continues to turn from God and arouse the chastisement of the prophets. But Nineveh needs not another word to understand that change is in order.

> The people of Nineveh believed God. They proclaimed a fast, and great and small alike put on sackcloth. When the news reached the king of Nineveh, he rose from his throne, took off his robe, put on sackcloth and sat in ashes. (Jonah 3:5-6)

Miraculously, Jonah performs no signs or wonders to convince the Ninevites of God's power, unlike Moses and Aaron when they seek Israel's freedom from Pharaoh. The biblical text offers no reason at all that the Ninevites should respond. Yet they seem to understand the power of God and acknowledge the gravity of their sins. Although given forty days to reflect on their situation, they respond immediately.

Moshe Alshich offers an interesting explanation. The Ninevites' immediate repentance represents a message to intransigent Israel. Regarding Nineveh, "...God knew that its inhabitants would repent. Once this had been accomplished, God could turn to Israel and rebuke them by saying, 'See, even the uncircumcised gentiles have repented though I have only just begun to call to them. You, on the other hand, have been repeatedly warned by My prophets, but you have persisted in your stubbornness and have not repented.'" (Alshich, 33-34) Thus Jonah initially flees to Tarshish because he wants no part in publicizing Israel's guilt.

The king, bringing to mind Job in his mourning period (see *Job: God's Accuser*, which follows), physically removes himself from his throne and sits on ashes—a requirement he makes of no one else. Then he orders that the people *and their flocks and herds* neither eat nor drink. The Ninevites and their animals also are to don sackcloth and "cry mightily to God" (Jonah 3:8). That the animals of Nineveh are included in the city's repentance may seem odd, but there is something of a parallel in Exodus. The tenth plague in Egypt involves the deaths not only of the first-borns of the Egyptians but of their cattle as well. And as we shall see shortly, God declares His love and mercy not only for the people of Nineveh but also for their beasts.

Critically important, the king orders his subjects to do *more*. "Let everyone turn back from his evil ways and from the injustice of which he is guilty" (Jonah 3:8). Finally, the king proclaims, "Who knows but that God may turn and relent?" (Jonah 3:9). The king cannot guaranty that Nineveh will be saved, but he recognizes both God's power to punish and to grant mercy, no matter how foul Nineveh's sins.

Who is this responsive, God-fearing king? The Mekhilta—a commentary on Exodus compiled about 400 CE—offers an intriguing identity. It asserts that the King of Nineveh is none other than the Pharaoh of the Exodus who survived his defeat at the Reed Sea.

Of one thing we are certain: God responds positively.

> God saw what they did, how they were turning back from their evil ways. And God renounced the punishment He had planned to bring upon them, and did not carry it out. (Jonah 3:10)

The Ninevites' repentance is genuine, according to the Mishnah (Taanith 2a), not because the populace dons sackcloth and ashes but because "God saw their works." Repentance can only be achieved through right action. One legend even has it that some Ninevites, in pursuit of justice long denied, destroyed their own palaces to give back even a single brick to its rightful owner. (Ginzberg, 606)

The Ninevites' repentance comes with qualifications, according to some commentators. Abraham bar Chiyyah, a twelfth-century Spanish commentator, offers that the Ninevites feared the power of God but did not recognize Him as the Supreme Being. (Zlotowitz, 123) Abravanel writes that the Ninevites repented of robbery and injustice but did not change their pagan beliefs. (Zlotowitz, 129) Another legend claims that the Ninevites' repentance was short-lived; they departed from the path of piety after forty days and were then destroyed. (Ginzberg, 607)

Nonetheless, the Ninevites' actions within the biblical narrative reflect what Judaism views as three stages of repentance: recognizing wrongdoing, determining not to repeat wrong actions and, finally and critically, acting properly. Asking for forgiveness and promising to change one's behavior are not in themselves sufficient for either an individual or a community.

As to Jonah's role in all this, the reader may say, "Mission accomplished." Uriel Simon proposes that, "No prophet has ever had such spectacular success." (Simon, 27) But the story does not end here. God may be pleased, and we may be pleased, but Jonah is not. For the Ninevites and their king—non-Israelites all—the word of God is sufficient. Jonah, who originally sought to flee from God, proves less faithful. Drawn more to the warning he has delivered than to its purpose, Jonah reveals his great disappointment:

> "O LORD! Isn't this just what I said when I was still in my own country? That is why I fled beforehand to Tarshish. For I know that you are a compassionate and gracious God, slow to anger, abounding in kindness, renouncing punishment." (Jonah 4:2)

Just what *did* Jonah say to God following God's first command to go to Nineveh? Most probably something like, "The destruction of Nineveh is non-negotiable." And most probably God responded, "Everything is on the table." Jonah would have expected as much, no doubt aware of God's words to Moses:

> The LORD passed before him and proclaimed: "The LORD! The LORD! A God compassionate and gracious, slow to anger, abounding in kindness to the thousandth generation, forgiving iniquity, transgression, and sin..." (Ex. 34:6-7)

Of course, God brought Egypt to its knees for Pharaoh's refusal to release the Israelites. But even a wicked nation may be spared as God tells Jeremiah:

> At one moment I may decree that a nation or a kingdom shall be uprooted and pulled down and destroyed; but if that nation against which I made the decree turns back from its wickedness, I change My mind concerning the punishment I planned to bring on it. (Jer. 18:7-8)

The Book of Ezekiel reinforces God's compassion. "Is it my desire that a wicked person shall die?—says the LORD God. It is rather that he shall turn back from his ways and live" (Ezek. 18:23).

Were God as vengeful as Jonah, his new prophet gladly would have taken His word to Nineveh. The prospect of mercy sent him towards Tarshish instead. Now, having proclaimed God's word and seen the Ninevites spared, Jonah feels pushed beyond his limits. Rather than praise God, Jonah confronts Him. "He reproves heaven by stating that he does not consider the divine attribute of mercy to be praiseworthy," Uriel Simon writes. (Simon, xxxvii) However, Simon does give Jonah credit, pointing out that, "Both Jonah and Abraham are courageous enough to appeal against the decisions of the Judge of the earth—one championing greater leniency, the other holding out for greater stringency." (Simon, 40)

From this point on, the narrative takes no further note of the Ninevites and turns the focus back on Jonah, who expresses his disappointment in the gravest terms. "Please, LORD, take my life, for I would rather die than live" (Jonah 4:3). This statement is audacious to say the least. Seeking death from the Creator of life represents a terrible offense. Yet God responds not with an angry outburst but with a compassionate question: "Are you that deeply grieved?" (Jonah 4:4). Jonah makes no reply, and God drops the matter.

We now find Jonah again traveling in his own direction—east of the city rather than heading westward towards home. He sits in the shade of a booth (*sukkah*) waiting to see what will happen. Perhaps God will yield to Jonah and destroy Nineveh after all—or the Ninevites will quickly fall back into their evil ways, vindicate him and meet their doom. Jonah does not lack sympathizers among the commentators. Maimonides offers some support to Jonah's contention that the Ninevites should perish rather than be forgiven. In his commentary on repentance and the pharaoh of the Exodus (Hilkiah Teshuvah 6:3), he writes, "It is possible for a person to commit such a great sin, or so many sins, that justice before the Judge of Truth provides…that repentance be foreclosed from him and that he not be permitted the right to repent from his wickedness…"[75] Should God bring His wrath down on Nineveh, Jonah will have the best seat in the house.

Jonah's wait proves difficult. The city remains undisturbed. What's more, the booth that Jonah has made fails to offer sufficient protection from the sun. God comes to the rescue, providing a plant—a ricinus (castor plant) in JPS, a gourd according to other translations—that grows up over him. In doing so, God delivers an important message: Jonah's safekeeping lies in His hands and not Jonah's. To prove it, God demonstrates that what He gives He can take.

> Jonah was very happy about the plant. But the next day at dawn God provided a worm, which attacked the plant so that it withered.

---

75 Pharaoh hardens his own heart after each of the first five plagues. Only after the sixth—boils—does God harden Pharaoh's heart so that he loses all possibility of repentance. See *Egypt: Slavery and Redemption*.

> And when the sun rose, God provided a sultry east wind; the sun beat down on Jonah's head, and he became faint. (Jonah 4:6-8)

Jonah remains adamant. Again he tells God that he would rather die. And again God responds seemingly without anger but with more than a hint of sarcasm: "Are you so deeply grieved about the plant?" (Jonah 4:9) Then God drives home His point. Jonah did not work for and grow the plant, which appeared overnight and perished overnight. It is God Who creates and gives life.

> And should not I care about Nineveh, that great city, in which there are more than a hundred and twenty thousand persons who do not yet know their right hand from their left, and many beasts as well!" (Jonah 4:11)

The Book of Jonah concludes on this question rather than on a response from Jonah—what we might consider to be a very Jewish ending. The answer is clear to the reader because the question is so obviously rhetorical. Whether Jonah understands we do not know. Uriel Simon takes a positive view of Jonah. He believes that unlike Job, who clearly states his submission to God, Jonah is "not a man of words" and presents his submission through silence. (Simon, 48)

That silence, however, may really be mystification. Abraham Joshua Heschel offers that, "God's answer to Jonah, stressing the supremacy of compassion, upsets the possibility of looking for a rational coherence of God's ways with the world. History would be more intelligible if God's word were the last word, final and unambiguous like a dogma or an unconditional decree." Jonah's speechlessness may reflect only confusion since, "beyond justice and anger lives the mystery of compassion." (Heschel, 287)

What seems clear is that the Ninevites—as child- or cattle-like as they may be in their initial ignorance of good and evil—are God's living creations. And God cares deeply about them. Many are innocents, not yet knowing their right hand from their left—children too young to be corrupted or fully responsible for their actions.

The people and king of Nineveh may have drifted away from God, but they have not lost their capacity for good. Their encounter through Jonah returns them to God, and this lesson is not lost on the Sages. The Mishnah (Ta'anit 2:1) points out that the Ninevites actually changed and abandoned their evil ways rather than merely go through the motions. "The power of Nineveh's repentance so impressed the rabbis," notes Joseph Telushkin. "that they chose this short book to be a central reading in the synagogue on Yom Kippur, the Day of Repentance." (Telushkin, 99)

What then may we take from Jonah's story? Two things. First, words of repentance are good but insufficient. God demands not lip service but action. Second—and of equal importance—God is pleased by the proper repentance of *all* human beings. "This is one clear case in which God is willing to forgive not only individuals but nations, and not only Israel but others," Elliot Dorff comments. "The Rabbis probably chose this book for reading on the Day of Atonement (Yom Kippur) for its assurance that repentance can procure God's mercy, but it is striking that the example of repentance is specifically a nation, and a non-Jewish one at that." (Dorff/Right, 192-93) The scholar Rabbi David Lieber points out that, "Jonah does not rail against the gentiles, but only against the evildoers among them. In fact, the pagan sailors in chapter 1 are described in very sympathetic terms." (Etz Hayim, 1246) This provides our focus, according to S. Goldman. "The essential teaching is that Gentiles s*hould not be grudged* God's love, care and forgiveness." (Soncino/Prophets, 137)

Let us note that neither the Ninevites nor any other people need become part of Israel. Living a Godly life does not require conversion to Israelite practice or Judaism. "The Hebrew Bible," Joseph Telushkin notes, "makes a considerably more restrained appeal to the non-Jewish world: just that people refrain from evil behavior, and do good." (Telushkin, 99)

The God of Israel, the Book of Jonah emphasizes, is the God of all nations. "Neither justice nor repentance, sin nor restitution, has ethnic or religious boundaries," Jonathan Sacks points out. "The people of Nineveh are God's creatures no less than others. That is what the book of Jonah is about." (Sacks/Heal, 118)

The lesson of Jonah seems abundantly clear. If we seek mercy for ourselves, we must allow it for others. The mercy God shows towards the Ninevites proves an ample illustration of Israel's—and all humanity's—duty to follow the commandment, "Love your fellow as yourself" (Lev. 19:18).

8

Job: God's Accuser

"Sow righteousness for yourselves;
Reap the fruits of goodness..."
Hosea 10:12

Why does the way of the wicked prosper?
Why are the workers of treachery at ease?
Jeremiah 12:1

For My plans are not your plans,
Nor are My ways your ways
—declares the Lord.
Isaiah 55:8

Job is a wealthy and powerful man of the east. Moreover he is tam*—blameless or wholehearted. When the celestial beings gather, one of them—ha-Satan (Satan, the Adversary)—challenges God to let Job suffer and see if Job maintains his righteousness. God gives ha-Satan power over Job, and suffer Job does. He loses his wealth and all his seven children. Yet he remains faithful to God. Ha-Satan still scorns Job. Let us see what happens, he tells God, when Job himself suffers physical pain. God strikes a new deal—ha-Satan may do anything to Job but must spare his life. Painful physical ailments strike Job. Three friends come to comfort him in his grief. A series of dialogues takes place, which quickly become heated. Job maintains that he has done no wrong to deserve such punishment. If he could confront God in a court of law, he* *would win his case—God Himself would rule in Job's favor. The friends insist that only the wicked are punished; Job must confess his guilt. Neither side convinces the other. A young man, Elihu, steps forward to replace the failed friends. Job is not necessarily guilty, he states. Rather, God brings misfortune on proud people to warn them against taking the wrong path. Job remains adamant. Finally, God appears and informs Job that the world He has created is so vast and complex that no human being can understand God's justice. God also recognizes Job's innocence and declares the friends' accusations to be mistaken. Job acknowledges his limitations and is rewarded with double the riches he previously had, along with ten new children and long years.*

In 1421, lightning started a fire that destroyed Beijing's Forbidden City, the palace of the Chinese Emperor Zhu Di. A Persian ambassador, Hafiz Abru, wrote of the stunned emperor: "In his anguish he repaired to the temple and prayed with great importunity, saying, 'The God of Heaven is angry with me, and, therefore, has burnt my palace; although I have done no evil act. I have neither offended my father, nor mother, nor have I acted tyrannically.'" (Menzies, 75-76) Because Chinese emperors ruled with the mandate of heaven, Zhu Di confronted an unnerving dilemma. He believed that God had punished him for transgressions he had not committed. Why, he undoubtedly wondered, do innocent people suffer? And why, conversely, do the wicked so often go unpunished? Justice—and hence the stability of the world—had been thrown off kilter.

Zhu Di's puzzlement and anguish span both time and geography. They resonate today, and they were anything but new in his era. Some two millennia earlier, the Book of Job asked the same questions. One of the most enigmatic yet revealing stories in the Bible, Job has been studied by Jews, Christians and Muslims alike—and has made a deep and lasting impression. Following the reward-and-punishment theme that spans the Hebrew Bible, the Christian Bible (Galatians 6:7-8) warns, "Make no mistake: God is not mocked, for a person will reap only what he sows, because the one who sows for his flesh will reap corruption from the flesh, but the one who sows for the spirit will reap eternal life from the spirit." The Quran (6:120) admonishes, "Sin neither openly nor in secret. Those that commit sin shall be punished for their sins."

Job puts all this to question in what Rabbi Victor Reichert hails as "a unique spiritual epic, a supreme drama of the human soul." (Soncino/Job, x) Indeed, so powerful and disturbing are the questions Job raises that this challenging book also has engrossed those with no religious faith, who read it solely as one of the world's great literary accomplishments. So timeless is the Book of Job, writes the political columnist William Safire, that it even serves as "the blueprint for modern dissidence." (Safire, xv)

While it is the story of Job in the biblical narrative that is critical to us in these pages, a brief introduction is in order. To begin, the Bible devotes an entire book to Job's plight. Thus the character Job is often assumed to be an Israelite. He is not. The narrative clearly identifies Job as an Uzzite from a land east of Canaan. But make no mistake. Job is central to a challenging discussion seeking to explain God's relationship with justice—and from an Israelite perspective.

That non-Israelites in the Bible can be truly righteous, as Job proves to be, hardly represents an upstart idea. The Rabbis recognize many such individuals whose tales appear in these pages. Melchizedek, king-priest of Salem (see *The Era of Abraham*) and Jethro, priest of Midian and Moses' father-in-law (see *Egypt: Slavery and Redemption*) join Job in a righteous triumvirate hailed by the Sages. Yet Melchizedek, who appears in only three verses of Genesis 14, and Jethro play only brief, supporting roles in the Bible.

Job, on the other hand, is a star! He stands apart from all the other non-Israelites among God's others, perhaps excepting Ruth (see *Women of Valor*). Considering length—a reasonable if not totally accurate measure of importance—Job far outdistances Ruth. The Book of Ruth consists of only four chapters. Job is the subject—the hero if you will—of *forty-two* chapters. Moreover, the Book of Job is marked by a very unusual distinction. It makes no mention of Israel, Israelites or Jews.[76]

---

76 In an interesting semi-parallel, The Book of Esther, read on the holiday of Purim, marks the Jews' delivery from the evil Persian minister Haman but makes no mention of God.

How incredible this is! Why would the Sages who canonized the Bible include a book without Israelite characters or even a single reference to Israel? Maimonides offers one possibility. He sees compelling universal value in the Book of Job, which he views as fiction "conceived for the purpose of explaining the different opinions which people hold on Divine Providence" while serving as "a source of perplexity to all thinkers." (Maimonides, 3:22) Eight centuries later, and from an entirely different perspective, William Safire proposes that Job's status as a non-Israelite serves as a ruse. The questions Job raises do indeed spring from a very Israelite point of view. The character of Job— and hence the author(s)—is "less likely to be accused of blasphemy or of undermining the Hebrew religion" when he questions God's justice. (Safire, 34)

That the author would disguise or universalize Job and the characters appearing with him makes sense when we consider that he (or she) has written a truly revolutionary book. Job's argument that good people often suffer while the wicked often are rewarded poses a considerable challenge to traditional Israelite faith. In more blunt terms, it stands orthodoxy on its ear by confronting head-on the reward-and-punishment themes of both the Torah and the Prophets—a stance not intended or expected to make friends within the establishment. The writer must have met with great hostility in his day, the scholar Moses Buttenwieser surmises, because, "Without a doubt the book was considered sacrilegious." (Buttenwieser, xi)

How does one reconcile Job's stark look at reality with other biblical texts that insist that the good prosper while the wicked pay for their misdeeds? Job's canonization undoubtedly reflects the Sages' realistic approach—life does not necessarily yield to us what we might wish or expect let alone think we have earned. In the language of the nineteen-sixties and seventies, Job "tells it like it is." Thus in the Mishnah (Avot 4:15), Rabbi Yannai, with the plight of Job doubtless well in mind, advises, "It is not given us to understand the well-being of the wicked or the suffering of the righteous." Like Job, however, we *want* to understand. What's more, we *insist* upon it.

To put this issue in context, the Book of Job does not present the biblical reader's only challenge to understanding the misfortunes of those who seem entirely innocent. In Genesis, Abraham banishes his concubine/wife, Hagar, and their son, Ishmael, to die in the wilderness. It takes a messenger of God to save them (see *The Era of Abraham*). The Book of Exodus relates God Himself slaying all the first-born males of Egypt—a matter I will refer to at the end of this chapter—while 1 Samuel 18:7 salutes David, a brigand as well as a king, for having slain "his tens of thousands." The ancient reader may have taken all this in stride. The Sages and medieval commentators understood that these stories were problematic and felt compelled to explain the circumstances. The modern reader tends to feel a high a degree of discomfort.

It is not the mystery of God's justice, however, that makes the Book of Job unique. Rather, it is the refusal of a suffering human being to accept a much later bit of traditional wisdom offered by Robert Browning in his poem, "Pippa Passes": "God's in His heaven—All's right with the world." As such, Job's story does far more than demonstrate the obvious—that good or innocent people suffer. It pointedly asks *why*. And this, according to the writer Elie Wiesel, makes Job timelessly relevant. "Whenever the Midrash runs short of examples," Wiesel offers, "it quotes Job, no matter the topic—and it is always pertinent." (Wiesel, 227)

Who Wrote Job?

A discussion of Job's authorship and background is better suited to academic books than to *God's Others*, but a few points are worth noting before we focus on the story itself. The traditional position taken by the Talmud (Baba Batra 14b) considers Moses to be the author. But two Sages—R. Yohanan and R. Eleazar (Baba Batra 15a)—suggest that Job was among those who returned from the exile in Babylonia. This occurred some seven centuries after Moses' death.

Critical scholars offer a variety of opinions as to whether one or more men and/or women authored Job and who they were. Opinions also vary about when Job was written and over what length of time. Rabbi Robert Gordis believes Job to have been written in the last quarter of the fifth century BCE or later. Consistent with this, Karen

Armstrong views the author as a survivor of the Babylonian exile who uses an old legend to inquire about God's responsibility for human suffering. Nahum Glatzer posits a broader period of creation from between the fifth to the first century. On the other hand, Glatzer points out, the eighteenth-century scholar Johann Gottfried Herder believes Job to be the oldest of biblical writings, a position in keeping with the Talmud's view of Moses as the book's author. (Glatzer, 141)

Moses Buttenwieser goes so far as to reorder almost all of the chapters and verses in his translation and complete the book with verse 42:11. He drops the remainder of the concluding epilogue, considering it an appendage. We will review that ending in due time.

How then is the reader to approach Job if traditional Judaism offers differing views and critical scholars add their own hypotheses? A guiding hand may be found with the British writer G.K. Chesterton, a Catholic, who dismisses these concerns altogether. Chesterton terms Job a "tribal work" and praises what he determines to be "unity in the sense that all great creations have unity; in the sense that Canterbury Cathedral has unity." (Glatzer, 229-30) Chesterton's comment focuses not on any superiority of Christian art but on the power of Job as measured against *any* great work of art. The whole, in effect, is greater than the sum of its parts. Rabbi Solomon Freehof adds sage advice: "Some parts are older than others, but all are ancient and genuine, and if, as is evident, the mood of one section does not quite fit the mood of another, that did not bother those who admitted the book as it stands into the canon of the Sacred Scripture." (Freehof, 14)

Approaching a Complex Structure

The unity Chesterton praises binds three basic components. The story begins with a prose prologue that encompasses chapters 1 and 2. The prologue may represent an older legend that ends with Job's passive acceptance of his fate, although Moses Buttenwieser believes the prologue and dialogues that follow to be the work of the same author. (Buttenwieser, 7) These two chapters, when set aside from the rest of the book, delineate "the patience of Job" as interpreted by the Christian tradition—a position I will discuss shortly. The prologue, however, serves only to begin a long, energetic debate about reward and punishment that takes place in chapters 3 through the beginning of 42. These thirty-nine chapters are written in poetry of some length and consist of a number of discrete units. These present dialogues pitting Job against three friends then a younger onlooker, Elihu—introduced in a brief prose passage—and finally God. The poem also offers what is referred to as the Hymn to Wisdom, which may or may not have been written by the same poet originally or at a later date. The prose epilogue—most of chapter 42—seeks to tie everything up in a neat package by restoring Job following his suffering. Yet as we will see, the epilogue actually produces a number of loose ends leading to significant questions that may leave many readers uncomfortable and agitated.

Why poetry? To begin, poetry is quite common in the Bible. It gives form to many of the text's oldest components, such as the Song at the Sea following the Israelites' escape from the pursuing Egyptians (Ex. 15:1-18) and the Song of Deborah, which celebrates the Israelites' victory over the Canaanites (Judg. 5:1-31). Poetry was a dominant technique of ancient Near Eastern literature in an era when most people could not read. Wisdom, as well as entertainment in the form of storytelling, was passed on orally. Meter and rhyme make poetry far easier to memorize and recite, as well as to follow. Songs tend to remain with us—often for years—while great prose illuminates us in a flash of brilliance but generally fails to attach itself to memory.

According to Herder, poetry brings nature to life, as well. Herder creates a character named Euthyphron, who engages in a dialogue about Job with Alciphron and declares that poetry "makes the objects of nature to become things of life, and exhibits them in a state of living action… The soul is hurried forward, and feels itself in the midst of the objects described, while it is a witness of their agencies." (Glatzer, 152) Poetry, in short, takes us out of ourselves and into another place.

The poetry of the Book of Job also serves as the vehicle for detailed arguments about whether or not God freely punishes the innocent while leaving the wicked to enjoy their ill-gotten gains. The modern reader might insist that these arguments would better be made as more brief prose statements. But poetry establishes a more emotional tenor while possibly serving two additional purposes. First, it powerfully expresses the issues of God's strength, creativity and justice through a language elevated above that of prose. These are no ordinary dialogues, and so they must be approached through extraordinary language. Second, the use of poetry suggests that the story of Job offers us not a glimpse of history—history and law typically are delineated by prose in the Bible—but rather of a more philosophical and impassioned discussion of a common human dilemma. We are not to take Job literally and get sidetracked by historical investigations. The poetry of Job elevates the debates between Job and his friends—and God—to a higher, more universal and timeless plane. Thus the Israeli scholar N.H. Tur-Sinai (Torczyner) offers: "By virtue of the strong emotion attending it, speech within a narrative context assumed a fixed, elevated form—the form of poetry." (Tur-Sinai, LVI)

The poet and translator Stephen Mitchell calls the shift to poetry a "change in reality" to a more multi-dimensional point of view than the one the seemingly simplistic prose prologue offers. (Mitchell, xi) Charles Freeman offers a parallel, pointing to the Greeks' use of *muthos* (myth) in writing about their gods rather than *logos*, reserved for such rational enterprises as science, mathematics, history and geography. "The Greeks realized that telling a story has its own uses far beyond entertainment and fulfills important emotional needs." (Freeman, 23) *Muthos* provides the proper form for such an undertaking. Thus poetry seems quite appropriate, since the Book of Job serves as both a philosophical debate—a theodicy explaining the ways of God to man—and a hymn to God in what the nineteenth-century poet, Alfred, Lord Tennyson, called "the greatest poem of ancient and modern times." (Glatzer, ix)

True, the Book of Job is endlessly challenging. We encounter questions that neither traditional nor critical analysis can answer, and competing translations lead as much to confusion as to clarity. As a result, we must take a different approach to this book that

Maimonides describes as “strange and wonderful.” (Maimonides, 3:22) Solomon Freehof offers helpful guidance. He suggests that the Book of Job is more akin to a modern painting, “a succession of moods and colors,” rather than a logical chain of arguments. “It is a series of reactions and the relation of speech to speech reflects the relation of personality to personality, and is artistic more than syllogistic. The relevance is deeper than logical. It is existential.” (Freehof, 237) So let us accept that looking at Job may leave us with more questions than answers—and that it is the posing of these soul-wrenching questions that is of greatest importance.

Who Was Job?

A few last words before beginning the story. Let us consider the identity of Job a bit further. He is probably not an historical individual—at least in the sense of the Bible's presentation of Israelite history—although Ezekiel 14:14 mentions Job as one of three righteous men, along with Noah and Daniel. The Sages of the Talmud could not come to agreement on this issue. Most likely, Job is a dramatic construct—a parable according to the Talmud (Bava Batra 15a). Of course, in true Talmudic spirit, Rabbi Samuel b. Nachman dissents. But Maimonides agrees, terming Job “poetic fiction.” (Maimonides, 3:22)

As to Job's nationality, the very first verse of the narrative establishes him as a non-Israelite: “There was a man in the land of Uz named Job. That man was blameless and upright; he feared God and shunned evil” (Job 1:1).

The author nonetheless hints at some connection with Israel, no doubt to draw in the reader—or hearer—for whom the book is intended. According to Genesis 10:23, the nation of Uz was founded by Uz, grandson of Shem, son of Noah. Shem is the ancestor of the Semitic nations. Uz also is the son of Abraham's brother, Nahor, born to him by his wife, Milcah, and the brother of Bethuel, father of Rebekah (Gen. 22:20-22).

Critical theories regarding the location of Uz abound. Nahum Glatzer offers that Uz is the land of Edom—descendants of Esau, Jacob's brother—on the eastern side of the Jordan River. (Glatzer,

4) Stephen Mitchell suggests that Genesis 10:23 places Uz in northern Mesopotamia, while another tradition locates it in Edom southeast of Canaan. (Mitchell, xxxi) In this regard, Lamentations 4:21 mentions Edom—an attacker of defenseless Jerusalem when Babylon conquered the city and destroyed the Temple—as dwelling in the land of Uz. Eschewing reality, the British classical scholar Gilbert Murray considers the setting simply as mythological, while the American philosopher Leon Roth finds the geographical setting of Uz to be irrelevant. (Glatzer, 73)

This same first verse also establishes Job's elevated character. The text tells us that Job is *tam*—blameless in the JPS translation. The word relates to *tamim*, which appears in Deuteronomy 18:13 and means "wholehearted" (JPS, Everett Fox), "unblemished" (Richard Friedman) or "perfect" (others). *Tamim* also describes Noah (Gen. 6:9), a specific quality God expects from Abraham (Gen. 17:1) and the Israelites about to enter Canaan (Deut. 18:13), and God's own deeds in the poem that concludes Deuteronomy (32:4). Job may not be a sage, according to Yehezkel Kauffman, but he is very much a righteous man. (Glatzer, 66) By providing such a strong character reference,the author impresses us with an individual who must be respected. As Arthur Miller writes in his play *Death of a Salesman*, "Attention must be paid." When Job suffers and protests his suffering when he makes his case against accepted orthodoxy—we cannot easily dismiss him.

The Story Begins

Job seems the righteous man par excellence. In fact, his righteousness is expressed through not one but four characteristics. He is *tam* (blameless internally) and *yashar* (upright externally). He also fears God and shuns evil. This brings cause and effect sharply into play, because the first two chapters also establish righteous Job as a man who has everything:

> Seven sons and three daughters were born to him; his possessions were seven thousand sheep, three thousand camels, five hundred

> yoke of oxen and five hundred she-asses, and a very large household. That man was wealthier than anyone in the East. (Job 1:2-3)

The New English Bible interprets the word for "wealthier"—*gadol*—as "greatest," making Job "the greatest man in all the East." This ascribes to Job enormous power as well as riches. Yet Job is the picture of modesty. He dutifully acknowledges God as the source of his wealth. Moreover, he fears some misdeed will jeopardize it. So each time his sons conclude a round of feasts—to which they magnanimously invite their sisters—Job sends word that they should sanctify themselves. A parent who today might be viewed as having trouble letting go, he also rises early in the morning to present burnt offerings on their behalf. "Perhaps," he thinks, "my children have sinned and blasphemed God in their thoughts" (Job 1:5). As readers, we see what is coming. The clues are obvious. How can a wealthy, powerful, righteous man not be set up for a fall?

It is not, of course, uncommon to fear that good fortune may not last—that the evil eye may cast its gaze upon us. In the Mishnah (Sotah 5:5), Joshua b. Chananiah comments that this fear increases Job's devotion to God—while Joshua b. Hyrcanus dissents that Job served God out of love, not fear.

Job's fears become realized when divine beings present themselves before the Lord—the name revealed to Israel, YHVH, is used. This occurs on Rosh Hashanah, the Day of Judgment, according to Rashi and Ibn Ezra. One of these beings or angels, *ha-Satan*—the Adversary— rendered by Stephen Mitchell as Accusing Angel, reports that he has been roaming all the earth.

Let us note here that Satan makes few appearances in the Hebrew Bible. Zechariah (ch. 3) sees him in a vision. Psalms 109 mentions him once as a tormenter who stands by the wicked. And 1 Chronicles 21:1 reports that Satan caused King David to take a census, which displeased God. Satan is mentioned in the Talmud (Berachot 46a), very possibly influenced by Christian thought, which offers a prayer to defend against him. Centuries later, Maimonides, the Aristotelian rationalist, writes that Satan is not a being at all but the *yetzer hara* (evil inclination) who "turns us away from the way of truth, and leads us astray in the way of error." (Maimonides, 3:22)

However, the word *satan* as a noun rather than a name appears in the Book of Numbers. God places an angel in the way of Balaam, mounted on his ass (see *Dissemblers and Provokers*), *l'satan lo*—"as an adversary." (Num. 22:22) The Satan of the Job story, Moses Buttenwieser comments, "is essentially different from the Satan met with in the later Jewish and Christian literature." (Buttenwieser, 31)

Satan, however, plays a major player in the Book of Job, setting our story in motion. In a remarkable instance of seemingly casual conversation, God asks the Adversary where he has been. The Adversary answers, "I have been roaming all over the earth" (Job 1:7). God's question is bound to startle us. If God is omniscient, does He really *not* know where the Adversary has been? *Can* he not know? God's question, however, is rhetorical, a device hardly unknown in the Bible. When God asks Adam and Eve where they are in the Garden of Eden and questions Cain regarding the whereabouts of his brother, Abel, *we* know that *He* knows.

Then it appears that the conversation is not quite as casual as we may have thought, that God has something in mind. He asks, "Have you noticed My servant Job? There is no one like him on earth, a blameless [*tam*] and upright man who fears God and shuns evil!" (Job 1:8). God's use of the term "my servant" bestows more than ordinary honor on Job. The same term describes Abraham (Gen. 26:24), Moses (Num. 12:7), Caleb (Num. 14:24), David (2 Sam. 3:18), Jacob (Is. 41:8) and one other non-Israelite—Nebuchadrezzar (Nebuchadnezzar), king of Babylon (Jer. 25:9), who plays a major role in God's chastising of Judah (see *Kings and Commoners*). Job, we learn again, is an exemplary man.

But, as they say in countless TV commercials selling the latest gadgets every home should have, "Hold everything!" Not only has the evil eye been opened, it has been opened by God! God's praise brings forth the Adversary's malicious spirit. Does God intend this? Is He Himself malicious? Or does He, in reality, doubt Job's faithfulness and His own powers? About this we can only conjecture. And why does God single out Job? Is he the only blameless human being on earth? Again, the narrative does not inform us, although with his great wealth, as Stephen Mitchell so aptly notes, Job certainly has much to lose if put to a test. (Mitchell, ix) Job's being singled out so puzzled the Sages that they created their own apocryphal stories linking him to Abraham, Pharaoh, Moses, Jacob, Samson, Solomon and others. A legend has it that Job remained neutral to Pharaoh's proposal to the Egyptian midwives in Exodus 1:15-16 that they slay the Hebrews' male newborns. Job would thus have to experience bad in addition to good.

Of one thing we can be sure. Job's life will never be the same. The Adversary responds pointedly and provocatively. Job fears You, he tells God, because You have blessed him so greatly. Given all his wealth, why shouldn't he? "But lay your hands upon all that he has and he will surely blaspheme You to Your face" (Job 1:11). It must be noted that the Hebrew of the text, *yevarachecha,* means "bless You" but is used euphemistically; the writer simply could not write "blaspheme" or "curse" in regards to God. The Adversary then lays out a challenge. God accepts it but with one caveat—the Adversary may not lay a hand on Job. This appears to offer the Adversary more than enough opportunity to prove himself right.

In quick succession, a series of messengers report to Job—messengers reminiscent of the stream of servants who bring Jacob's gifts to Esau in Genesis 32. They speak of one disaster after another. Sabeans carried off Job's oxen and she-asses and also murdered his herders. Fire from heaven burned his sheep and their shepherds. Three columns of Chaldeans carried off the camels and slew their young herders. And finally, a mighty wind from the wilderness brought down his eldest son's house and killed all his children.

Given these catastrophes, what are we to think of God even before reading Job's response? Let us be aware, Robert Gordis notes, that shock and even anger may not reflect the response of the ancients. "Neither the writer nor his earliest readers (or hearers) felt in the slightest that the Lord is guilty here of cruelty or injustice, particularly since He is pictured as a king who has unlimited power over His creatures." (Gordis, 2)

Job's reactions combines pain with stoicism.[77]

> Then Job arose, tore his robe, cut off his hair, and threw himself on the ground and worshipped. He said, "Naked came I out of my mother's womb, and naked I shall return there; the LORD [YHVH] has given, and the LORD has taken away; blessed be the name of the LORD." (Job 1:20-21)

Here, Job echoes the wisdom literature of the Bible—a common occurrence given the high familiarity the author likely had with existing biblical texts or, considering a very early time period for the story's creation, that other authors had with Job. Ecclesiastes 6:14 remarks about every person's ultimate death: "As he came out of his mother's womb, so must he depart at last, naked as he came. He can take nothing of his wealth to carry with him." Moreover, when Job refers to YHVH, he refers to the name of God known to the Israelites. There is little doubt, from the perspectives of both the biblical narrative and Job, that Job worships the God of Israel.

The first chapter ends with the author's approval of Job. "For all that, Job did not sin nor did he cast reproach on God" (Job 1:22). The reader may be satisfied. The Adversary is not.

Yet again the Adversary presents himself to God. Again he has roamed the earth, and again God asks if the Adversary has noticed His servant, Job, who remains blameless and upright. God seems not to be pleased, however. "He still keeps his integrity; so you have incited Me against him to destroy him for no good reason" (Job 2:3). The Adversary holds firm.

> "Skin for skin [a proverb of uncertain meaning—JPS]—all that a man has he will give up for his life. But lay a hand on his bones and his flesh, and he will surely blaspheme You to Your face." (Job 2:4-5)

77 The Mishnah (Berachot 9:5) comments that a person must bless God for evil as well as for good. Everything is part of God's creation even if some things are beyond our comprehension. Thus when someone dies, the traditional response of a Jew is not anger at God but, *"Baruch Dayan ha-Emet"*—"Blessed be the Judge of truth."

God accepts the challenge but again insists on a proviso. The Adversary may do anything he wishes except take Job's life. Maimonides believes that this prohibition refers not to taking Job's life but his soul, "that element in a man that survives him." (Maimonides, 3:22)

Limited but hardly powerless, the Adversary afflicts Job with a severe inflammation (boils) from head to toe. So great is Job's discomfort that his wife—unnamed in the standard text but identified as Dinah (Jacob's daughter) in the Targum or Aramaic translation—suggests, before disappearing from the text, "Blaspheme God and die!" (Job 2:9). However, the poet once again offers a Hebrew euphemism—*bareich* (bless)—to avoid even hinting that anyone could actually curse God.

Job replies: "You talk as any shameless woman might talk! Should we accept only good from God and not accept evil?" (Job 2:10). Job, the text comments, says nothing sinful.

The prologue continues with the introduction of three friends who have heard of all that has befallen Job and come to console him. The oldest is Eliphaz the Temanite. He bears the same name as the first-born of Esau (son of Isaac) who fathers Teman, possibly an ancestor of the people of Tema in Northern Arabia. Temanite caravans are mentioned in Job 6:19. Also come are Bildad the Shuhite and Zophar the Naamathite. All may be chiefs or notables of Northern Arabia, but whether their designations refer to clans or locations we do not know.

The friends sit silently on the ground with Job for seven days and nights—a period corresponding to the traditional Jewish mourning period of *shiva* (seven). The Book of Lamentations describes a similar scene of mourning.

> Silent sit on the ground
> The elders of Fair Zion;
> They have strewn dust on their heads
> And girded themselves with sackcloth; (Lam. 2:10)

The friends say nothing until Job speaks.[78] When Job does utter his first words, one of humanity's most challenging religious and literary puzzles begins. Job and his friends enter into a dialogue consisting of three rounds of accusations and rebuttals—eight prosecutions and defenses in all—with Eliphaz and Bildad each offering three replies to Job's speeches and Zophar two.

Job's First Complaint: Why Was I Born?

In breaking the silence, Job curses the day of his birth. Here he echoes Moses, who asks God to kill him when he can no longer tolerate the burden of caring for the Israelites. Jobs asks, "Why did I not die at birth, / Expire as I came forth from the womb?" (Job 3:11). Death brings rest and peace even to the prisoner and the slave, Job says. Continued life constitutes an injustice.

> Why does He give light to the sufferer
> And life to the bitter in spirit;
> To those who wait for death but it does not come… (Job 3:20-21)

If Job ever comes close to cursing God, this may be it. How can the righteous Job wish to have ended the life given to him by God—a prerogative that only God may exercise?

Job's plight is excruciating not only because he suffers but also because he does not know why. No logic or justice explains his physical and emotional pain. Maimonides comments that this is precisely the point. Job may be a good man, but he lacks sufficient knowledge, wisdom and intelligence—the philosophical virtues that raise human beings above even the moral plane. Otherwise, he would understand his suffering. But what knowledge, wisdom and intelligence can offer a satisfactory explanation? (Maimonides, 3:22)

Rabbi A.J. Rosenberg takes a vastly different approach. God did not cause Job to suffer at all. Rather, He left the workings of the

78 Accordingly, Jewish tradition requires visitors to a bereaved person to refrain from speaking first and let the mourner guide any conversation. Blu Greenberg believes that this practice cautions the visitor "against offering a rationale for the decree of death." (Eskenazi/Torah, 633)

world to the stars. Job "cursed the day he was born and the night he was conceived because his future would be controlled by the constellations ruling at that time." (Rosenberg, A.J., 19)

Eliphaz's First Response and the Logic of Job's Guilt

Eliphaz is the first to answer. And here it should be noted that the Book of Job offers a full exploration of the questions raised by the suffering of the innocent. The friends disagree not only with Job but with the author as well, yet they receive a full hearing. Each engages in a meaningful dialogue with Job, and each is given free rein to present his arguments, which may offer varying shades of meaning. Solomon Freehof, citing Maimonides and Gersonides, suggests three different personalities for the friends: Eliphaz speaks as a man of religious conviction, Bildad as a more secular man of experience and Zophar as a zealot. (Freehof, 122)

Unfortunately for Job, neither he nor his friends know what we know—that Job is being tested. In this respect, the reader enjoys the unlimited perspective offered by an omniscient narrator. When disaster strikes *us*, however, we, like Job, prove to be only human. Because our perspective narrows as our suffering broadens, we must each provide our own comforting narration.

As to Eliphaz—he begins his indictment with considerable sensitivity. Yes, he admits, Job has been a good man. But now, Job must heed the counsel Job has given to others and realize that he must have done something wrong to be in such a state. Let reason prevail. Thus Eliphaz, from his limited and author-controlled perspective, states ironically, "Think now, what innocent man ever perished? / Where have the upright been destroyed?" (Job 4:7).

How does Eliphaz know what he knows? He reveals that he had a secret—and frightening—night vision and learned that man, by his nature, cannot be pure in the eyes of God. Even the angelic beings cannot achieve such purity. It therefore follows that Job must be guilty of some considerable misdeed.

Not surprisingly, Eliphaz's words fail to comfort Job and thereby impact Jewish tradition. The Talmud (Baba Metziah 58b) counsels a visitor to one who is suffering or afflicted, or has buried a child, not to speak to him or her as Job's companions spoke to him.

Eliphaz proceeds: "For man is born to [do] mischief, / Just as sparks fly upward…" (Job 5:7). His comment suggests Adam and Eve, and Cain and Abel, whose stories illustrate the struggle between the good inclination (*yetzer hatov*) and bad inclination (*yetzer hara*). We cannot take this comment of Eliphaz lightly. After the Flood, God Himself proclaims, "…the devisings of man's mind are evil from his youth" (Gen. 8:21). Only a fool, Eliphaz intimates, fails to admit he has done wrong when suffering comes upon him.

Job may find hope, however, if he admits his guilt and submits. "See how happy is the man whom God reproves; / Do not reject the discipline of the Almighty" (Job 5:17).

God will then undo Job's suffering and healing since, "He injures, but he binds up; / He wounds, but His hands heal" (Job 5:18).

What of the role of the Adversary? This troublemaker has maneuvered God into subjecting Job to great suffering for apparently no good reason. Yet none of the friends suggests the Adversary as the cause of Job's torment. Perhaps, as the philosopher Walter Kaufmann posits, they fear "…denying either God's justice or His omnipotence." (Glatzer, 239)

Job's Second Complaint: I am Right; There is No Justice

Death offers one consolation, Job tells the friends. Even though he writhed in pain, "I did not suppress my words against the Holy One" (Job 6:10). But what does this mean? The JPS translation suggests that Job has not withheld condemnation of God's injustice. He has refused to cave in. Robert Gordis, on the other hand, translates this verse as, "I never have denied the words of the Holy One." (Gordis, 64) Others offer similar translations. These would appear to have Job saying, "I have protested God's justice and yet remained faithful to Him." Job therefore has rejected God's justice but not God or, by extension, His laws. It may well be that both translations are accurate, leaving both Job and readers, ancient and modern alike, to bear a point of tension that makes the book so challenging.

This matter will be addressed later. But let us now turn to Job's death wish.

To Job, death represents not a transition but an end—or perhaps more closely, what Robert Gordis terms the Bible's classic view of "a shadowy type of semi-existence." (Gordis, 152) Death is final, and Job has no expectation of an afterlife as a reward.

> There is hope for a tree;
> If it is cut down it will renew itself;
> Its shoots will not cease.
> If its roots are old in the earth,
> And its stump dies in the ground,
> At the scent of water it will bud
> And produce branches like a sapling. (Job 14:9)

A tree may look to renewed life, but God makes human life finite. "You overpower him forever and he perishes; / You alter his visage and dispatch him." (Job 14:20)

What then of the hereafter? "Consider that my happiness is but wind; I shall never see happiness again," Job says (7:7). Rashi points to this statement as Job's denial of the resurrection of the dead. Maimonides, who includes resurrection of the dead among his thirteen principles of Judaism, disagrees. He comments that Job merely acknowledges that he cannot bring himself back to life. (Soncino/Job, 31) Indeed, the traditional Amidah (standing) prayer praises God Who brings the dead to life.[79]

Sages and commentators have struggled with the concept of life after death, because the Bible's only unequivocal passage regarding reward and punishment after death is found in Daniel 12:2: "Many of those that sleep in the dust of the earth will awake, some to eternal life, others to reproaches, to everlasting abhorrence." This question is not, however, central to the Book of Job, according to the biblical scholar H.H. Rowley, since "…no faith in an afterlife can touch the problem with which the Book of Job is concerned." (Glatzer/Job,

---

79 The Reform prayer book, *Mishkan T'filah*, offers an optional phrase, "Who gives life to all."

127) The philosopher Horace Kallen takes a different view. Job's rejection of life after death—of a heavenly or similar reward—may be significant. It is the very reason Job earned God's praise as *tamim* in the first place. "If, therefore, man seeks righteousness, he seeks it not because of any extrinsic advantage, but because being what he is, righteousness is proper virtue, the security and fulfillment of his inward excellence." (Glatzer, 179) No wonder Job is so angry. As a righteous man focused on *this* life, it is in *this* life that he must have justice from God.

Alas, Job's calls for justice fall on deaf ears. The three friends dogmatically assume him to be guilty of wrongdoing. Job dissents. "Teach me; I shall be silent;" he urges. "Tell me where I am wrong" (Job 6:24). But this is merely a rhetorical device. The friends cannot prove him wrong. And so he urges them, "Relent! Let there not be injustice; / Relent! I am still in the right" (Job 6:29).

Job's insistence calls to mind Abraham's beseeching God, Who is about to destroy Sodom and Gomorrah. The patriarch does more than speak directly to God. He upbraids Him.

> "Far be it from You to do such a thing, to bring death upon the innocent as well as the guilty, so that innocent and guilty fare alike. Far be it from You! Shall not the Judge of all the earth deal justly?" (Gen. 18:25)

Yet a key difference exists between Abraham and Job, according to Elie Wiesel. "Abraham challenged God while defending someone else's interests, Job spoke out against injustice only when it affected him personally." (Wiesel, 234) Nonetheless, Job *does* challenge God's justice, dissenting from the traditional view that God rewards the righteous and punishes the wicked. This is no small thing. Victor Reichert points out the challenging nature of the problem: "Prophetic Judaism had achieved the faith in an Almighty God Who ruled His universe with absolute justice." (Soncino/Job, xiv)

Job's going against the grain provides exactly the reason for Yehezkel Kaufmann to praise him. "Job's successful resistance is put forward as a model for all." (Glatzer/Job, 66) While the Christian tradition, citing the Epistle of James 5:10-11, focuses on the saintly, patient Job enduring his afflictions, the Jewish tradition sees Job demanding redress from God—and demanding it *now*. As the narrative will reveal, Job asks, "How long have I to live, that I should be patient?" (Job 6:11) and "Why should I not lose my patience?" (Job 21:4). Having assumed a contrarian's position, Job will not be silenced.

> On my part, I will not speak with restraint;
> I will give voice to the anguish of my spirit;
> I will complain in the bitterness of my soul. (Job 7:11)

Job then shifts his point of view. He addresses not Eliphaz, Bildad and Zophar but God Himself: "What is man, that You make much of him, / That you fix Your attentions upon him?" (Job 7:17).

As the prologue demonstrated, God bears responsibility for Job's plight by giving the Adversary free rein. Why, Job asks, has God absorbed Himself so much with a single human being?

> If I have sinned, what have I done to You,
> Watcher of men?
> Why make of me your target,
> And a burden to myself?
> Why do You not pardon my transgression
> And forgive my iniquity? (Job 7:20-21)

If Job has done something wrong, he is unaware, and the limbo within which he lives proves unbearable. He is tormented by not knowing what he could have done to receive so terrible a punishment. Doesn't justice demand that God confront him with the charges?

Bildad's First Response: People Suffer for a Reason

Bildad presents the second of the friends' responses. Unlike Eliphaz, he is blunt from the first. He admonishes Job that God does not pervert justice. Job may not know why terrible things have happened to him but assuredly there is a reason. "If your sons sinned against Him, / He dispatched them for their transgression" (Job 8:4).

As to Job's own afflictions, recourse is possible.

But if you seek God
And supplicate the Almighty,
If you are blameless and upright,
He will protect you,
And grant well-being to your righteous home. (Job 8:5-6)

God, Bildad asserts, "does not despise the blameless" (Job 8:20). If Job is truly innocent, his travails will not last because God will look after him. "He will yet fill your mouth with laughter, / And your lips with shouts of joy" (Job 8-20).

Job's Third Complaint: God is Not Just

Job continues to maintain his innocence while expressing his frustration at not being able to make his case because, "Man cannot win a suit against God" (Job 9:1). Moreover, God is something of a bully, according to Job. "God does not restrain His anger" and no one can call Him to account (Job 9:13). Job insists that he is in the right, yet he can do nothing. Further, Job's blamelessness seems of no importance to God—at least in any way that can be understood by a human being. "He destroys the blameless and the guilty" (Job 9:22). Perhaps most troubling to Job, God has not only withdrawn from acting justly, he has actively encouraged injustice.

The earth is handed over to the wicked one;
He covers the eyes of its judges.
If it is not He, then who? (Job 9:24)

How can we fail to empathize? And how do we reconcile the God of Job with the God of the prophets who hails the just man while promising woe to the wicked, and with the God of Psalms 146:8 Who "loves the righteous" but "makes the path of the wicked tortuous"?

Job sees no hope for redress. Since nothing he can say or do will change his condition, he turns his words to God with resignation.

> I know that You will not acquit me.
> It will be I who am in the wrong;
> Why then should I waste effort? (Job 9:28-29)

The very crux of his predicament—a one-sided dispute—is clear. "He is not a man, like me, that I can answer Him, / That we can go to law together…" (Job 9:32).

Divine *in*justice leaves humans without recourse. Job would speak out if his words made a difference, but they do not. Moreover, God's terror frightens him. If he has done nothing and yet has been so afflicted, how much worse might his suffering be if he protests? Job directs these words to Bildad, Eliphaz and Zophar as well as to God. His punishment makes no rational sense, yet his friends cannot acknowledge that the innocent may suffer.

Job points to the common values he shares with his friends. He is not as distant from them as they might think. He would like to believe as they do that only the guilty are punished, but he cannot. Then as if presenting his case in court—which he has acknowledged is impossible—Job aggressively questions God, seeking to put Him on the defensive. "You know that I am not guilty, / And that there is none to deliver from Your hand" (Job 10:7).

Job's plea falls on seemingly deaf ears. God has stacked the deck against him. In the court to which Job would appeal, God serves as judge, jury and executioner. God creates and destroys as He wills. This, Job emphasizes, is a shameful abuse of power. "Is it something to be proud of to hunt me like a lion, / To show yourself wondrous through me time and again?" (Job 10:16).

Pick on someone your own size, Job says in effect. But of course, God has no equal. Job's accusation is clear. God flexes His muscles at Job's expense. God does what He does simply because He *can*, perhaps akin to a child squashing bugs or spiders solely for the perverse fun of it. This constitutes both injustice and a failure of God to meet His responsibilities. Having expressed his frustration at ever being born at all—a rejection of the sanctity and importance of human life emphasized throughout the Torah—Job can only ask to be left alone without further vexation before he dies "never to return" (Job 10:21).

Zophar's First Response: God Knows Iniquity When He Sees It

Job's third friend, Zophar, speaks next. He comments briefly and offers no comfort. Job's words, Zophar insists, consist merely of voluminous "prattle." No human being can unravel the mystery of God. This thought resides well within Jewish tradition. The Torah defines God by His Thirteen Attributes—none of them physical—when God Himself exclaims:

> "The Lord! the Lord! a God compassionate and gracious, slow to anger, abounding in kindness and faithfulness, extending kindness to the thousandth generation, forgiving iniquity, transgression, and sin; yet He does not remit all punishment, but visits the iniquity of parents upon children and children's children, upon the third and fourth generations." (Ex. 34:6-7)

Maimonides, eschewing anthropomorphism, defines God by His *negative* attributes. God has no body, God is not male or female, and so on. We know God only by what God is *not*.

Yet God surely knows iniquity when He sees it, Zophar states, so Job *must* be guilty. Then like the other friends, Zophar, holds out hope. Repeating Bildad's advice, he urges Job to "spread forth your hands toward Him," confess iniquity and appeal for forgiveness (Job 11:13-14). Job then will "be like the morning" with a fresh beginning (Job 11:17). Continued protestations only condemn him to further misery.

Job's Fourth Complaint: Righteousness is Easy to Claim When There is No Suffering

Job responds by mocking his friends. In seeing themselves as the last bastion of wisdom, they delude themselves. He, however, cannot be fooled and must be taken seriously. "But I, like you, have a mind, / And am not less than you" (Job 12:3). Eliphaz, Bildad and Zophar may consider themselves a body of religious authority, but they possess no greater authority than Job's, even if they outnumber him.

Job then ratchets up his offensive. "In the thought of the complacent there is contempt for calamity" (Job 12:5).

The friends, suffering no affliction, consider themselves righteous, rather than lucky, while insisting on Job's guilt. They indulge themselves in false logic. Job, after all, has observed the ways of the world. "Robbers live untroubled in their tents, / And those who provoke God are secure…" (Job 12:6).

How then can they assume him to be guilty? Job suffers not through any fault of his own but at God's whim. "In His hand is every living soul / And the breath of all mankind" (Job 12:10). He has observed that God destroys the mighty as he chooses.

Now, Job throws down the gauntlet of litigation. "I insist on arguing with God," he announces (Job 13:3). Only God could possibly understand his plight—were He willing to do so. Job dismisses Eliphaz, Bildad and Zophar as quacks, who invent lies to cover over what God has done. They certainly are not fit to serve as his judges since they lack any sense of objectivity. "Will you be partial toward Him?" Job asks (Job 13:8).[80] Rashi shares Job's low opinion of the friends, commenting that they seek only to flatter God. (Soncino/Job, 61)

The friends' lack of integrity, Job warns them, will come down on their own heads.

> He will surely reprove you
> If in your heart you are partial toward Him.
> His threat will terrify you,
> And his fear will seize you. (Job 13:10-11)

Job does understand that he runs the risk that God may impose retribution against him for seeking his day in court. But he will not be cowed and pushes any fears aside. He will maintain his position regardless of the consequences. "He may well slay me; I may have no hope; / Yet I will argue my case before him." (Job 13:15)

---

80 Job's concern with receiving a fair hearing reflects Exodus 23:2-3: "You shall neither side with the mighty to do wrong—you shall not give perverse testimony in a dispute so as to pervert it in favor of the mighty—nor shall you show deference to a poor man in his dispute." Likewise, Deuteronomy 16:19 states, "You shall not judge unfairly; you shall show no partiality…"

Here, translation and interpretation again vary. The Mishnah (Sotah 5:5) translates this verse as, "Yea, though He slay me, yet will I trust in Him." In this regard, Job lives with an unbearable tension, assailing God and yet retaining his faith. Robert Gordis, however, suggests that this is not the case with Job. Modern commentators, he points out, find Job's affirmation of unshakable faith out of context with his arguments. (Gordis, 144)

But let us play devil's advocate here. (Further discussion will follow shortly.) If Job holds two contradictory positions, his doing so reflects an all-too-common human predicament—the clinging to a love-hate relationship, which seems to mock all objectivity and common sense.

Job nonetheless remains encouraged. He knows that he is neither an impious man nor a hypocrite. He possesses a clear conscience. He asks only that God not restrain or frighten him, which would pervert the proceedings. God can summon Job, or Job will speak out and await God's response. The burden of proof, he insists, is on God to advise him of his transgressions and sin. Moreover, Job is engaged with the big picture. He calls God to task not merely for his own sufferings but for those of all humanity. "Man born of woman is short-lived and sated with troubles," he observes (Job 14:1). Lower forms of life enjoy remarkable resilience, while humans come to a final, crushing end. Cut a tree down and a new shoot will rise, Job remarks, "But mortals languish and die" (Job 14:10). Day after day, little by little, just as water wears stones smooth and reshapes the earth, so God destroys hope.

Eliphaz's Second Reply: The Battle is Joined

Job's assertions of righteousness fall on deaf ears. Abandoning his previous sensitivity, Eliphaz counters that he, too, can claim wisdom. Job has only offered "windy opinions" and "words that are of no worth" (Job 15:2-3). Why does Eliphaz so oppose Job? Perhaps Eliphaz sees a grave threat to the establishment—to the orthodoxy of the day. We can imagine him wagging his finger in Job's face as he condemns his friend: "You subvert piety / And restrain prayer to God" (Job 15:4).

But let us give Eliphaz his due. He speaks the truth—from the traditional point of view. Job refuses to endorse the scheme of reward and punishment proposed by the Torah and the written prophets. Job's innocence reveals to him that punishment of the wicked and reward for the guiltless is a myth, a principle that may have been acceptable in the distant past but no longer retains its validity. Of course, Job makes no reference to the Torah or other biblical sources, which, along with Israel, are never mentioned in this book. But the context is hardly lost. It must also be noted that the Torah's concept of reward and punishment focuses on the community and the nation; the individual plays a secondary, although not unimportant, role. In this sense, Job's suffering may be looked upon as inconsequential. Yet Job maintains his rebellious position.

As far as Eliphaz is concerned, such a protest against orthodoxy must be squashed. When contention arises between God and man, he asks—repeating his argument in 4:17-21—how can man overthrow accepted norms and beliefs? "What is man that he can be cleared of guilt, / One born of woman, that he can be in the right?" (Job 15:14). The orthodox view of justice remains unassailable. The wicked suffer all their days. The lives of the ruthless are short. Punishment reveals evidence of guilt.

Then Eliphaz gets personal: "He will not be rich: / His wealth will not endure" (Job 15:29). Job may have been the richest man in the east, but his wealth offered him no protection.

Rubbing salt into Job's wounds, Eliphaz declares that the ultimate misery awaits him:

> He will wither before his time,
> His bough never having flourished.
> He will drop his unripe grapes like a vine;
> He will shed his blossoms like an olive tree. (Job 15:32)

Even the guilty man's descendants—those who would prolong his life through memory—will be cut off just as Job's ten children have died. Job, insists Eliphaz, bears responsibility for the death of his offspring and the end of his line. All of Job's afflictions represent nothing less than proof of his guilt.

Job's Fifth Complaint: Innocence Must be Revealed

No shrinking violet in spite of his pain, Job gives as good as he gets, accusing the friends of being "mischievous comforters" (Job 16:2). He concedes that were Eliphaz in his place, he, Job, would speak the same way. This concession, however, only suggests that what has happened to Job lies beyond Eliphaz's understanding. In spite of his suffering and the world's condemnation, Job will—indeed must—maintain his innocence. "Earth, do not cover my blood; / Let there be no resting place for my outcry!" (Job 16:18).

Job's remark about leaving his blood uncovered clearly recalls God's confronting Cain with the evidence of his murder of Abel: "Hark, your brother's blood [literally in Hebrew the plural, bloods—DP] cries out to Me from the ground!" (Gen. 4:10). Job believes his reputation to have been murdered—a matter taken very seriously by the Sages of the Talmud. Such a crime cannot go unnoticed let alone unpunished.

Job continues in three challenging verses.

> Surely now my witness is in heaven;
> He who can testify for me is on high.
> O my advocates, my fellows,
> Before God my eyes shed tears;
> Let Him arbitrate between a man and God
> As between a man and his fellow. (Job 16:19-21)

Who is Job's witness? Rashi believes it to be God. Who else can arbitrate such a dispute? Or will some other celestial being—perhaps the Adversary himself—clear Job's name? If it *is* God, can He be a fair judge and witness when He Himself is one of the parties to the dispute? If any other being—vastly inferior to God by definition—can understand that Job has been wronged, how can God not know it?

Regardless of this dilemma, Job maintains what Victor Reichert terms, "…one of the amazing peaks of spiritual faith and human paradox that make this Book immortal. Job here appeals from the God Who had cruelly smitten him to the God of his faith, the God of justice and loving mercy."[81] (Soncino/Job, 84-5)

Job is desperate, his spirit crushed. His suffering reduces him to an object lesson, a symbol of the punishment wrongdoers may expect from the traditional perspective. But he rallies himself and tosses a satiric, if sad, jibe at his accusers: "The pure are aroused against the impious" (Job 17:8). The friends foolishly—and perhaps more to the point, ignorantly—assume themselves to be pure because good fortune smiles upon them.

Then, in a verse dripping with irony, Job declares, "The righteous man holds to his way; / He whose hands are clean grows stronger" (Job 17:9).

The righteous men who have come to comfort him reveal themselves to be no more than self-righteous. They refuse to listen to reason and heed Job. Rather, every day that Job suffers makes them more secure in their convictions. Yet Job knows that it is he who is truly righteous. Therefore he will maintain his convictions, which strengthen his resolve even as his suffering increases. And so Job continues to question God's specific implementation of justice while adhering to the *principle* of justice. God, like man, has obligations but refuses to live up to them. As to his friends' words, he finds no consolation. "I shall not find a wise man among you" (Job 17:10).

Bildad's Second Response: Punishment Always Falls on the Wicked

Bildad finds no validity in Job's argument, believing that Job's ego blinds him to his friends' counsel. Bildad argues not that they are

---

81 The eleventh-century poet Solomon Ibn Gabirol writes in *The Royal Crown:*
Therefore though You Slay me, I will trust in You.
For if You pursue my iniquity,
I will flee from You to Yourself
And I will shelter myself from Your wrath in Your Shadow…

wiser than Job but rather that they are no *less* wise. "Why are we thought of as brutes, / Regarded by you as stupid?" (Job 18:3).

Ultimately, Bildad insists, justice *is* served. "Indeed, the light of the wicked fails" (Job 18:5). The guilty party's iniquitous strides are hobbled, the noose tightens, his progeny hunger, his home is covered with sulfur and, perhaps worst of all, "All mention of him vanishes from the earth; / He has no name abroad" (Job 18:17).

From the perspective of the ancient Near East—and perhaps no less than that of the twenty-first century West—this may be the most terrible consequence of all. A person's name intertwines with his existence. To be forgotten is truly to die. Having descendants assures that an individual's name will continue to be mentioned and that he or she will live on in memory. In this regard, obliterating someone's name represents stern judgment in the Bible. Thus in Deuteronomy, Moses instructs the Israelites regarding the revenge they are to take on Amalek before they enter Canaan. The Amalekites refused to let the Israelites cross their land. Instead, they attacked and murdered the weak and aged at the rear of the Israelites' march. "Therefore, when the LORD your God grants you safety from all your enemies around you, in the land the LORD your God is giving you as a hereditary portion, you shall blot out the memory of Amalek from under heaven. Do not forget!" (Deut. 25:19). The Amalekites do disappear as a people yet ironically their memory lingers in the Torah.

JOB'S SIXTH COMPLAINT: HE RECEIVES NO COMPASSION

Shifting his focus from legal arguments, Job laments the lack of compassion shown to him. The friends humiliate him. Their words crush him. God has chosen to make Job suffer for His own reasons, and they fail to understand that justice has nothing to do with it. Job's fall from wealth and power is total; even the lowest of the low treat him as an outcast. And now his friends have turned on him as well. Surely they can do better.

> Pity me, pity me! You are my friends;
> For the hand of God has struck me!

> Why do you pursue me like God
> Maligning me insatiably? (Job 19:21-22)

Of course, Eliphaz, Bildad and Zophar do not know what God and the reader know: Job *is* innocent. He remains *tamim*. Neither has Job any suspicion that the Adversary stands behind his suffering. So Job insists that God's reasons for afflicting him are beyond the friends' understanding. God alone can clear Job's name. Job is confident that He will. "But I know that my Vindicator lives; / In the end He will testify on earth—" (Job 19:25).

The Hebrew for "my Vindicator," *goali*, is more commonly translated as "my Redeemer." Christians believe the latter translation to foreshadow Christ and his resurrection. Jewish interpretation sees the Vindicator as God, Who knows that Job is innocent and must ultimately make things right. In a dissenting opinion, Ibn Ezra believes the Redeemer not to be God but rather a person who, whether alive during Job's time or to be born later, will accept Job's innocence. (Soncino/Job, 99)

Job's vindication, unfortunately, must take place in the future. At the moment, a conflict rages between his anger and his faith that God *will* make amends. How can it be in God's nature to allow injustice to stand? It is the friends, in condemning the innocent, who commit injustice, and they will pay the penalty. "Know there is a judgment!" Job warns (Job 19:29). This assertion seems to contradict Job's previous arguments regarding the lack of justice in the world, but as Robert Gordis suggests from the critical perspective, Near Eastern poetry does not adhere to Western rules of logic. Job "is incapable of abandoning his conviction that right must triumph in the world." (Gordis, 208)

Zophar's Second Reply: The Guilty Cannot Flee

Zophar remains unmoved. In fact, he relates, Job's reproof insults him. Completing the second round of the friends' accusation-laden responses, Zophar reiterates their position, asking,

Do you not know this, that from time immemorial,
Since man was set on earth,
The joy of the wicked has been brief,
The happiness of the impious, fleeting? (Job 20:4-5)

No matter how rich or powerful, the wicked "perishes forever, like his dung" (Job 20:7). As Bildad before him, Zophar describes the inevitable downfall of the guilty, banished from public view, vomiting out his riches and seeing his children die to leave him with no descendants to carry on his name. "This is the wicked man's portion from God, / The lot God has ordained from him" (Job 20:29).

Job's Seventh Complaint: Sinners Prosper

Job wants no part of Zophar's belief that God punishes the wicked. The truth, Job insists, is that the wicked escape punishment to prosper and grow wealthy. They also enjoy their children and grandchildren—perhaps life's greatest gift and one denied to Job. Impending death means nothing to them. "They spend their days in happiness, / And go down to Sheol in peace" (Job 21:13). Job's observation is not unique in the Bible. Psalms 73:12 bemoans, "Such are the wicked; ever tranquil, they amass wealth." The prophet Jeremiah also asks, "Why does the way of the wicked prosper?" (Jer. 12:1) although he does so in the context of the Babylonian exile during which Israel as a nation and a people suffers at the hands of an oppressive empire.

Blessings and curses, reward and punishment—Job will have none of it. The Book of Lamentations advises:

The Lord is good to those who trust in Him,
To the one who seeks Him;
It is good to wait patiently
Till rescue comes from the Lord. (Lam. 3:25)

Job rejects patience. He has trusted God only to be betrayed, while the wicked knowingly reject God and prosper. The friends believe that wealth proclaims righteousness. They are fools. Job knows better.

Maimonides agrees, writing that, "…it cannot be said of every one who is assisted in a certain undertaking, as in the acquisition of property, or of some other personal advantage, that the spirit of the Lord came upon him, or that the Lord was with him, or that he performed his actions by the holy spirit." (Maimonides, 2:44) Ultimately, one man dies, tranquil and untroubled. Another dies embittered. Determining which one lived righteously lies beyond our understanding. What we *do* know, Job insists, is that in his case earthly justice has not been served. Job's desire for justice consumes him in direct proportion to his belief that God *ought* to be unquestionably just.

The biblical narrative now threatens to pull us, as readers, apart. We know that Job is innocent. From our own experience, we must accord Job's argument great merit. Who has not observed that the guilty often really do go unpunished—at least in this world, which is our only experiential frame of reference? At best, we may content ourselves with the idea that those who do wrong suffer great psychological and spiritual harm even as they enjoy material gain. But Job's response to Zophar does not lead to this conclusion. Rather, Job presents justice as beyond God's concern, suggesting that justice falls only within the human realm. Further, we may be quite rankled by the arbitrariness of God's decision to let the Adversary have his way with Job. We can come to grips with accidents, illnesses, the caprices of nature and even the deliberate acts of other human beings causing us harm. That God knowingly causes or enables suffering for no reason that we can discern lies beyond our understanding and acceptance. We want to believe that Zophar is right—that the wicked *are* punished because God judges each of us. Unfortunately, the arguments of Zophar and his friends fail to support that position.

Job is not finished with Zophar, however. Zophar suggests that the wicked man has no hope of escape from God's wrath. "He will not see his children tranquil" (Job 20:20). Perhaps Zophar hedges his bet here. If the guilty person doesn't suffer direct punishment, his children will be punished in his stead. Job will have none of it. He goes on the attack: "[You say], 'God is reserving his punishment for his sons,'" (Job 21:19). This will not do. He who commits the crime must pay the price himself.

Let it be paid back to him that he may feel it,
Let his eyes see his ruin,
And let him drink the wrath of Shaddai ! (Job 21:19-20)

Here Job speaks out against another traditional teaching. The Book of Exodus instructs that God "visits the iniquity of parents upon children and children's children, upon the third and fourth generations" (Ex. 34:7). This may lead us to conclude that the innocent suffer. However, another interpretation offers itself: the wicked man creates an environment leading his children, grandchildren and even great-grandchildren to emulate him and live improperly. Thus the wicked man, not God, punishes his descendants.

Would this realization—that the wicked man bears responsibility for his children and grandchildren's downfall—deter him? Zophar might concede so, but Job cannot. As long as he escapes direct punishment in this life, the wicked man is content. Job, we know, displays no belief in a conscious afterlife. Moreover, it is the very nature of the wicked man that he cares only for himself. Job asks: "For what does he care about the fate of his family, / When his number of months runs out?" (Job 21:21).

Death defines the statute of limitations, anticipating the popular saying in the nineteen-eighties when many Americans viewed the accumulation of wealth as the greatest of all values, "He who dies with the most toys wins." Punishment cannot reach into the grave, Job emphasizes. We all come to the same end. The innocent and wicked alike lie in the dust and are covered with worms. What justice can this represent?

Eliphaz's Third Statement: Job Has Failed to Act Justly

Eliphaz opens the third round of dialogue with brief but challenging questions delivered like stinging jabs from a skilled boxer:

Can a man be of use to God,
A wise man benefit him?
Does Shaddai gain if you are righteous?
Does He profit if your conduct is blameless? (Job 22:2-3)

If God derives no gain from humanity's right behavior, what Eliphaz leaves unsaid must equally be true. God cannot be injured by wickedness. Therefore God has no personal stake in judgment. His rewards and punishments are objective and altogether just.

Believing he has cleared God's name, Eliphaz then pursues another line of thought. Like a boxer behind in the point count, he swings a wild knockout blow. Job deserves punishment because he really has done wrong. He has exacted pledges from his fellows and left the naked stripped of their clothes. Keeping the collateral of debtors violates the Law detailed in Exodus 22 and Deuteronomy 24, texts never mentioned in the narrative. But neither Eliphaz, Bildad nor Zophar has ever offered proof that Job has done such things.

Continuing the boxing analogy, Eliphaz dodges and weaves to force his opponent's punches to miss. Job also has received his just desserts, he states, for what he has *not* done.

> You do not give the thirsty water to drink;
> You deny bread to the hungry.
> The land belongs to the strong;
> The privileged occupy it.
> You have sent away widows empty-handed;
> The strength of the fatherless is broken. (Job 22:7-9)

These accusations involve errors of omission rather than commission, echoing specific commandments in the Torah regarding the implementation of social justice. Deuteronomy 27:19, for example, curses anyone who "subverts the rights of the stranger, the fatherless, and the widow." Job later refutes the accusations in chapter 31.

As to Job's belief that God is removed from human concepts of justice, Eliphaz disagrees. The heavenly heights and the dense clouds that cover the earth prove no barrier to His scrutiny and punishment. Then Eliphaz, as in his first response, again holds out a ray of hope. "Be close to Him and wholehearted; / Good things will come to you thereby" (Job 22:21).

All is not lost. Job need only return to God and, in doing so, cast aside his former interest in material things. "Regard treasure as dirt," Eliphaz advises the man who once possessed massive wealth (Job 22:24). If Job lives humbly and acknowledges his misdeeds, he will be delivered.

Job's Eighth Complaint: God Cannot Be Approached

Job has been hit hard, but he refuses to yield. Countering Eliphaz, he replies that if only he could present his case to God, he would be cleared, because,

> I have followed in His tracks,
> Kept His way without swerving,
> I have not deviated from what His lips commanded;
> I have treasured His words more than my daily bread. (Job 23:12)

Job will not allow his reputation to be sullied. He insists that he is not the impious man Eliphaz makes him out to be. Neither has Eliphaz any right to associate wealth with wrongdoing—a view that runs counter to mainstream Jewish thought, which places wealth in perspective, hailing the fruits of labor while upholding the pursuit of social justice.

Job's response presents yet another puzzle. Does Job's mention of "His way" and the words God has commanded refer to the Noahide laws passed down after the Flood? Or do they refer to the Torah of the Israelites? Both sets of laws are valid—the former for the nations and the latter for Israel. Whichever the answer, the Job narrative suggests an author who frames the story within Israel's religious belief system. But Job's Uzzite identity and our inability to answer this question support the universality of his argument. This in turn leads us to conclude that all human beings are duty-bound to live according to whichever set of God's laws may be applicable to them.

Job's vehement protestations leave him frustrated. Upstanding though he may be, he realizes that his day in court can never come. God cannot be approached like an earthly judge. He cannot even be found. And even if He could, Job declares in all his pessimism, He could not be dissuaded. Job remains "terrified at His presence" (Job

23:15). But yielding is out of the question. He rails against those who do evil and the God who fails to respond.

> Men groan in the city;
> The souls of the dying cry out;
> Yet God does not regard it as a reproach. (Job 24:12)

"Surely," Job concludes, "no one can confute me" (Job 24:25).

Bildad's Third and Final Reply: All the World is Impure

In his concluding speech of only six verses—which may be only a surviving fragment of his third discourse—Bildad counters, "How can man be in the right before God?" (Job 25:4). Nothing in the world—not even the moon and stars—is pure. "How much less man, a worm, / The son-of-man, a maggot" (Job 25:6).

With these words, the three friends conclude their argument.

Job's Final Reply: I Remain Right

We can practically see the frustrated Job throwing up his hands in despair—if he has any remaining strength. Eliphaz, Bildad and Zophar, he replies, have been of no comfort at all. Job acknowledges God's greatness but with a caveat: God may have organized the heavens, but earth is in chaos. The friends, he says, do not grasp that God's ways are unknowable and therefore not necessarily just. If he suffers, Job suggests, it is not because he has done anything wrong. Human wisdom is simply too limited to understand God's ways.

Job then renews his theme of being in the right in a long complaint that will go unanswered by the friends. He will not speak out against God, he states, but, "I persist in my righteousness and will not yield; / I shall be free of reproach as long as I live" (Job 27:6). Job's insistence, comments Yehezkel Kaufmann, provides ample proof that he is a man of principle. His sense of righteousness—of being right—remains an intrinsic value even though he has no hope of reward. (Glatzer, 67)

Then Job appears to turn the tables on us. He replaces his previous complaint—the wicked prosper—with a new statement: God *does* punish the evil man (Job 27:13-23). His wealth will disappear, terror will overtake him and the east wind will carry him off. What's more, the evil man's sons also will be punished. Without question, this speech seems out of character. According to Victor Reichert, it more accurately reflects Zophar or Eliphaz. (Soncino/Job, 114) Robert Gordis believes it to be a small fragment of a lost speech by Zophar. (Gordis, 291) On the other hand, Job could be quoting back to the friends their own argument to ridicule it. The explanation, alas, will likely elude us.

The Hymn to Wisdom: So Near and Yet So Far

Chapter 28 presents a poem known as the Hymn to Wisdom, a work that may seem something of a digression. Robert Gordis considers this to be a separate work of the Job poet later added to the Job material. N.H. Tur-Sinai considers it to be part of the original but the climax of God's speeches that follow later in chapters 38–41. Other modern commentators believe the Hymn to be the work of a different poet. Stephen Mitchell takes this latter position and leaves it out of his modern translation altogether.

The Hymn focuses on the difficulty of attaining wisdom—what Maimonides terms the recognition of those truths that lead to the knowledge of God. Men, Job says, dig into the farthest recesses of the earth where no falcon's eye has gazed and no beast has explored. They overturn mountains and dam up rivers to find silver, gold, iron, copper and sapphires. "But where can wisdom be found; / Where is the source of understanding?" (Job 28:12).[82]

Earthly riches, no matter how deeply buried, are far easier to obtain than wisdom, which "cannot be found in the land of the living" (Job 28:13). Moreover, if wisdom *could* be found, it could not be purchased with silver, gold or other precious materials being so far beyond them in value that "a pouch of wisdom is better than

82 Proverbs 8:22ff presents a parallel in which Wisdom reveals itself to be one of God's earliest creations, "the first of His works of old."

rubies" (Job 28:18). Fortunately, wisdom is not out of humanity's reach. God has revealed it: "See! Fear of the Lord is wisdom; / To shun evil is understanding" (Job 28:28).[83]

We cannot understand why God's creation is as it is, but we can understand what God expects of us. If Job's words now seem familiar, it is because they are. The Book of Proverbs advises, "The fear of the Lord is the beginning of knowledge" (Prov. 1:7). Such fear—*yirah* in Hebrew—does not necessarily mean dread, however, but rather humility and awe of God.

Job's Final Speech: His Humiliation Knows No Limits

In chapter 29, Job resumes his lament for his past wealth and glory "in the days when God watched over me" (Job 29:2). He has been laid low and humiliated. Younger men, "whose fathers I would have disdained to put among my sheep dogs," deride him (Job 30:1). Job also has been laid waste physically. "By night my bones feel gnawed; / My sinews never rest," he complains (Job 30:17). In this he echoes Lamentations, which equates a conquered Jerusalem to a man enduring his suffering at God's command: "He has worn away my flesh and skin; / He has shattered my bones" (Lam. 3:4). Job then again appeals to God. "I cry out to You, but You do not answer me; / I wait, but You do [not] consider me" (Job 30:20).

Job suffers, and the narrative spares no earthy detail. "My bowels are in turmoil without respite," he cries (Job 30:27). Job concludes his complaint by referring to his standing as *tamim*. He has been pure not just in deed but also in thought. "I have covenanted with my eyes / Not to gaze on a maiden" (Job 31:1).

This language of sexual purity—of the strictest moral conduct—reflects a critical component of the Torah's instruction. The Torah does not propose or prize asceticism; God tells Adam and Eve to "be fertile and increase" (Gen. 1:28), and Job himself has fathered ten children. Rather, Exodus 20 forbids adultery (the Seventh

83 The poet uses the word Adonai rather than YHVH, thus "Lord" is printed in upper and lower case rather than with small caps as "Lord."

Commandment), and Leviticus 18 offers a detailed list of forbidden sexual relationships.[84]

Job then refutes earlier accusations of wrongdoing with a rhetorical question: "Have I walked with worthless men, / Or my feet hurried to deceit?" (Job 31:5).

Finally, he returns to the purity of his thoughts, relating that he has never coveted another man's wife (the Tenth Commandment).[85] Had Job ever had impure thoughts, he concedes, no punishment would be too severe.

> If my heart was ravished by the wife of my neighbor,
> And I lay in wait at his door,
> May my wife grind for another,
> May others kneel over her. (Job 31:9-10)

Job pulls no punches. His language is graphic because no shame would be too great had he committed such an offense. But he has not. And so he calls on his friends to respond to the forcefulness of his denial.

Additional, and more concrete, evidence attests to his righteousness, Job asserts. He has treated even his servants well, alluding to the commandment to "Love your fellow as yourself" (Lev. 19:18). And he has never performed idolatry—a violation of the Second Commandment.

> If I ever saw the light shining,
> The moon on its course in full glory,
> And I secretly succumbed,
> And my hand touched my mouth in a kiss,
> That, too would have been a criminal offense,
> For I would have denied God above. (Job 31:26-28)

---

84 Adultery, defined as a married woman having sex with a man other than her husband, represents so serious a violation that the Torah (Deut. 22:22) condemns both the woman and the man to death.

85 Judaism delineates the Tenth Commandment as forbidding coveting one's neighbor's house, wife, slave, domestic animals or any other possessions. The Catholic and Lutheran churches divide this into two commandments.

His protestations having run their course, Job maintains his insistence that God grant him a hearing. If he has done anything wrong, he will accept his punishment. And with this, Job's words of complaint and his defense before Eliphaz, Bildad and Zophar come to an end. But we have not come to the end of the story.

The Appearance of Elihu: God Warns the Proud Man

Suddenly, another man—much younger than the friends—appears. Elihu, son of Barachel the Buzite, now speaks. From where has Elihu come? We don't know. Only now, in chapter 32, is he first mentioned. The narrative provides no prior hint of another friend or associate visiting Job.

Elihu's sudden appearance suggests to some modern scholars that his speech is a later addition by another author. N.H. Tur-Sinai believes that the "Elihu portion was written in Hebrew in Palestine after the translation of the main part of the book [into Aramaic—DP]." (Tur-Sinai, XXXVIII) Solomon Freehof points out that the Elihu passages contain many more Aramaic words than the rest of the Book of Job. Why was the character of Elihu added? "Some editor or reader was dissatisfied with the state of the argument in which Job had evidently vanquished and silenced the friends," Freehof posits. "To this editor it was intolerable that Job should be successful." (Freehof, 204) Other commentators believe Elihu's speeches to be an integral part of the book.

As to Elihu's nationality, we cannot be sure. Elihu—"He is my God"—is a Hebrew/Israelite name. Elihu, son of Tohu, rates a mention in 1 Samuel 1:1 as an ancestor of Samuel. On the other hand, Buzites descend from Buz, brother of Uz and a nephew of Abraham. Some blood relationship may exist with the Israelites, but no certain identification can be made. How does Elihu know Job? Victor Reichert offers the speculation that because Elihu frequently addresses Job by name—which the friends do not—he may be a relative. Rabbinic interpretation sees Job, the friends and Elihu all as descendants of Abraham. (Soncino/Job, 169)

We don't know, then, whether Elihu, as the critic Leslie Fiedler writes, is "an afterthought, a last desperate attempt on the part of the poet who gave the Book of Job its final form to defend orthodoxy against Job's subversive challenge." (Rosenberg, D., 334) What we *do* know is that Elihu is one angry young man. The three friends' failure to overcome Job's argument makes him furious. But what stirs his wrath is Job's condemnation of God's justice rather than an assumption of Job's wickedness. A clever young man, Elihu launches a preemptive attack on any attempt of the friends—or Job—to silence him. He is young, he admits, but young men also are competent to speak because...

> ...it is the spirit in men,
> The breath of Shaddai, that gives them understanding.
> It is not the aged who are wise,
> The elders who understand how to judge. (Job 32:8-9)

Bursting with words, Elihu demands relief. He will speak the truth regardless of the positions taken by Job and the other men. In a statement echoing Leviticus 19:15 and Deuteronomy 1:17, which command courts to judge everyone—the wealthy and poor, the high and low—without favoritism or sympathy, he affirms, "I would not show regard for any man, / Or temper my speech for anyone's sake..." (Job 32:21).

As to justice—God, Elihu contends, *does* reply to man's charges. In fact, God speaks regularly, although man does not always perceive it:

> In a dream, a night vision,
> When deep sleep falls on men,
> While they slumber in their beds. (Job 33:15)

Job suffers for a reason—but not the reason he claims—Elihu insists. God disciplines the proud man—as opposed to the wicked one—to prompt him away from potential evil actions.

He is reproved by pains on his bed,
And the trembling in his bones is constant.
He detests food;
Fine food [is repulsive] to him.
His flesh wastes away till it cannot be seen,
And his bones are rubbed away till they are invisible.
(Job 33:19-21)

In this light, the Talmud (Berachot 5a) later admonishes, "If a man sees suffering coming upon him, let him scrutinize his actions."

But Job's ills represent no more than warning shots fired across the bow of a ship that has strayed off course. Hope abounds. If a man has but one advocate in the heavens, Elihu states, God will grant him mercy. The advocate may be an angel or, according to Malbim, a good deed that the warned man has performed. (Freehof, 214) No innocent man suffers because, "Shaddai does not pervert justice" (Job 34:12). God chastises whom He will when He will only to prod repentance. In short, says Elihu, God is just by definition and always impartial. Job can offer no better system of justice.

Elihu's words may suggest encouragement, but his anger doesn't abate. Job must be tried without sympathy, the outraged Elihu insists, since his railings against God reflect the answers of sinful men and only serve to increase his transgression. Echoing Eliphaz in Job 22:2-3, Elihu emphasizes that Job is at fault for imagining that by not sinning he should gain something.

If you are righteous,
What do you give Him;
What does He receive from your hand? (Job 35:7)

Wickedness and righteousness alike affect only mortals. Oppressed people may cry out, but if they understand properly, they do not ask where God is. God, in turn, does not offer an immediate response to their dilemmas. However, God *does* take note of their sufferings—even if Job denies this—out of concern for His creatures. God perfectly well knows what Job is enduring and will respond in His own good time.

Elihu continues to pour out his anger in chapter 36. "I will justify my Maker," he announces (Job 36:3). God does indeed punish the wicked and grants justice to the lowly. Repeating his position that suffering is God's warning to the haughty, Elihu emphasizes that, "He declares to them what they have done, / And that their transgressions are excessive" (Job 36:9).

Such a declaration takes the form of assistance rather than punishment. Discipline and distress open the wicked to understanding. Rashi agrees: "Worry not about the afflictions if thou art righteous, because they are for thy good." (Soncino/Job, 186) If the wicked repent, Elihu says, they will spend their days in happiness. A different fate awaits those who rebel against God because of their lack of understanding. "They shall perish by the sword, / Die for lack of understanding" (Job 36:12). Solomon Freehof cites an earlier JPS translation of this verse: "And they shall die without knowledge." This would have Elihu say, "The real tragedy is to suffer and learn no lesson at all from the failure, thwartings, and sorrows that come to us." (Freehof, 224)

No one can bring God—the Creator and manipulator of the heavens—to task for what He does. Thunder, snow, rain, wind, cold, ice—all may be a scourge or a blessing based solely on God's intent. Argument and protestation prove fruitless for even the most wise.

Enter God

Job, the friends and Elihu have all sought to interpret God's actions. But only God can explain Himself—providing that He is willing to do so. And He is: "Then the Lord replied to Job out of the tempest [others "whirlwind"]… (Job 38:1). Job has yearned for this confrontation. Now he has it. This, William Safire suggests, gives Job a victory. Having forced God to present Himself, Job has gained "an inkling of divine accountability." (Safire, 149)

There can be no dispute about which of these opponents wields more power. The tempest provides God with not only a dramatic entry but a fitting one as well. God is, after all, the Creator of the universe and master of its physical forces. The tempest suggests the *ruach* or wind—interpreted by Christians as the Holy Spirit—from God that sweeps over the waters of the yet unformed earth in Genesis 1:2. It also recalls God's blowing the breath of life into Adam's nostrils as well as the thunder and lightning preceding God's revelation at Sinai.

Nonetheless, God's appearance out of a destructive and frightening phenomenon suggests—in addition to creative power, life giving and law—a great anger, even combativeness, in response to Job's presumption. God's initial words match that image.

> Who is this who darkens counsel,
> Speaking without knowledge?
> Gird your loins like a man;
> I will ask and you will inform Me. (Job 38:2-3)

Throughout two chapters, God challenges Job with rhetorical questions designed to impress on him his puniness as a human being. "Where were you when I laid the earth's foundations?" God asks (Job 38:4). And, he continues some verses later, who causes it,

> To rain down on uninhabited land
> On the wilderness where no man is,
> To saturate the desolate wasteland,
> And make the crop of grass sprout forth? (Job 38:26-27)

The image of rain falling on uninhabited areas rings true with our modern concept of the earth as an integrated ecosystem, but proves something of a shock in Job's era. Adam and Eve may be the crowns of God's earthly creation, but man is not the measure of all things. God directs precious rain where He chooses even if that rain provides no usefulness to human beings. The subtext suggests that Job has lost perspective. Are all the wealthy and contented years of his life to be ignored because he now suffers?

God cannot be questioned because He, not man, creates.

> Does the rain have a father?
> Who begot the dewdrops?

From whose belly came forth the ice?
Who gave birth to the frost of heaven? (Job 38:28-29)

A lengthy series of questions regarding the wonders of nature—including a variety of animals that survive and thrive with only their God-given instincts—serves to clearly separate God from His creations.

God's questions also separate His justice from humanity's, according to Maimonides, who emphasizes that "as there is a difference between works of nature and productions of human handicraft, so there is a difference between God's rule, providence, and intention in reference to all natural forces, and our rule, providence, and intention in reference to things which are the objects of our rule, providence, and intention." God occupies a completely separate plane. "This lesson is the principal object of the whole Book of Job," Maimonides writes. Understanding this makes "everything that may befall us easy to bear." (Maimonides, 3:23)

Job is humbled. God's questions, according to G.K. Chesterton, turn rationalism against itself. They "fling down and flatten out all conceivable questioners." (Glatzer/Job, 233) Job can only meekly reply: "See, I am of small worth; what can I answer You? / I clap my hand to my mouth" (Job 40:4).

Job's day in court seems to evaporate under the heat of God's ferocity. But let us not be misled by simple assumptions. In actuality, God may be granting all that Job could possibly wish for under the circumstances. God's very appearance, according to Alan Segal, "is actually meant to be an act of supererogatory grace... He owes Job an explanation, which is exactly what Job receives, even though neither he nor we can fully understand it." (Segal, 149) Moreover, Job's yielding does not necessarily mean that he accepts that he is wrong. Robert Gordis suggests the opposite. Job makes no concession but rather "sets forth his weakness and insignificance and his determination to remain silent." (Gordis, 466) Looking at his situation pragmatically, Job simply concludes that no other course of action remains available.

Yet even if God's overwhelming power stuns Job, it does not necessarily condemn him. On the other hand, Job's silence fails to appease God, Who again speaks out of the tempest and repeats His challenge:

> Gird your loins like a man;
> I will ask, and you will inform me.
> Would you impugn My justice?
> Would you condemn Me that you may be right? (Job 40:7-8)

God then hurls a new challenge. If Job can bring every proud (wicked) man low and into obscurity, then He will praise Job. Of course, this is a set-up. God does not gamble—except, perhaps, with the Adversary, which has led to Job's current state. As God has explained, Job's strength cannot match His own. Yet in spite of God's strength, proud men still exist. If God cannot—or perhaps will not—bring low the proud and the evildoer, who is the puny Job to speak of justice?

God is not finished with comparisons, however. To further demonstrate Job's insignificance, He asks if Job can capture and subjugate behemoth—often cited as the hippopotamus although termed a "fanged beast" in Deut. 32:24—or pull Leviathan—generally considered to be the crocodile but held to be the whale by the scholar G.R. Driver—from the water with a fishhook. Chapters 40 and 41 present both monsters, whose origins lie in ancient Semitic mythology, as frightening symbols of divine creation beyond human control.[86]

> See, any hope [of capturing] him must be disappointed;
> One is prostrated by the very sight of him.
> There is no one so fierce as to rouse him;
> Who then can stand up to Me? (Job 41:1-2)

---

86 Leviathan with its terrifying teeth, protective scales, sneezes that flash lightning, eyes "like the glimmering of dawn," firebrands that stream from his mouth, nostrils that emit smoke and breath that ignites coals seems the forebear of the dragons of medieval tales. Nachmanides, on the other hand, characterizes behemoth and Leviathan as any huge beast or big fish. (Soncino/Job, 211)

Job is overmatched by God's own creations, and the implication is clear. No matter how much knowledge we humans acquire, the physical world lies beyond our comprehension. How then can we hope to fully comprehend the moral order God has established? Look at the big picture, God tells Job in so many words. The world as a whole works quite well, thank you, even if it does not always satisfy some—or even many—human beings who, after all, constitute only part of creation.

And so Job surrenders.

> Indeed, I spoke without understanding
> Of things beyond me, which I did not know.
> Hear now, and I will speak;
> I will ask, and You will inform me.
> I had heard You with my ears,
> But now I see You with my eyes;
> Therefore, I recant and relent,
> Being but dust and ashes. (Job 42:2-6)[87]

Let us now put off Job's yielding his anger for a moment to ponder a mystery: When Job sees God with his eyes, *what* does he see? The narrative presents God appearing *within* the tempest. This parallels events in Exodus. Moses sees the burning bush on Mount Horeb rather than God Himself. God's post-Sinai presence in the wilderness remains concealed from the Israelites within a pillar of cloud by day and of fire by night. God, as Jewish tradition maintains, *cannot* be seen. Who tells us this? God Himself. He informs Moses atop Sinai that, "you cannot see My face, for man may not see Me and live" (Ex. 33:20). God permits Moses to see His Glory, but only when God hides him in a cleft in a rock, revealing His back after His presence passes by. It is through *words,* along with wonders, that God reveals Himself—words that in the Book of Genesis create the world and in the Book of Job convey the enormity and complexity of that creation. What then does Job actually see of God? Stephen Mitchell offers that

87 Job's self-description of "being but dust and ashes" recalls Abraham's words in Genesis 18:27 prior to his bargaining with God on behalf of the proposed innocent minority in Sodom and Gomorrah.

God's words create images so intense that Job does not hear them at all but actually *sees* them in a vision. (Mitchell, xx) Perhaps God can only be *experienced*—"seen" in a dimension with which perhaps only the patriarchs and prophets have familiarity.

As to Job's surrender: He experiences the ironic truth of the old adage that warns to be careful what you wish for—you might get it. Facing God, his bravado melts into helplessness. Job recognizes that he is way out of his league. He cannot reconcile God's power with His apparent lack of justice.

Job seems to embrace a new sense of peace, however, by becoming a detached observer of the Divine. "Job discovers a new joy, a new meaning to existence," Rabbi David Hartman comments, "when he perceives the world from the theocentric focus. His new perception of reality does not explain his suffering, but it enables him to see it in a different proportion and thus to bear it." (Hartman, 128) Yehezkel Kaufmann similarly suggests that Job satisfies himself with God's revelation rather than with wisdom. It is not what God does but the fact that God *is* that counts, providing "the distinctive Israelite feature of the book." (Glatzer/Job, 70)

But does might make right? Robert Gordis points out that, "Contrary to a widely held but mistaken view, Job does not concede that he is mistaken in any of his arguments." (Gordis, 566) The writer and teacher Jack Miles concurs. God's concluding speeches only cloak the issue at hand because "…Job has never called the Lord's power into question. It is his justice of which Job has demanded an accounting." (Miles, 314-15) In turn, God questions Job's ability to call Him to account but never tells Job that he is wrong. Job at last recognizes the truth: God's justice and human perceptions of justice do not align with each other.

The Sages offer sympathy to Job even if they don't share his position. Job deserves God's rebuke, they comment, but not punishment. Thus the Talmud (Bava Batra 16b) offers, "No man is taken to account for what he speaks in his distress; because of his dire affliction Job spoke as he did"

After all is said and done, according to Alan Segal, God's appearance before Job represents an extraordinary gesture. "God is far more merciful than any ancient Near Eastern monarch. Unlike the other ancient Near Eastern heavenly voyagers, God comes to Job. And so, even though Job has been frightened and awed by God's power, he leaves court vindicated." (Segal, 153)

Others dissent. Rabbi Arthur Green refuses to let God off the hook. God's speeches in Job may be "among the most elevated religious documents of all time," but they do not defend God as just within the human experience. "Job is given no reason for his suffering, no explanation of his children's deaths, or his own affliction. Rather, he is shown the magnificence of God's universe, the great and wondrous creatures that extend far beyond human reach or human understanding.... It is in seeing these, and realizing both his own smallness and his own place within a vast and glorious cosmos, that God's challenger finds his consolation." (Green, 69-70)

Job's resignation may disappoint some modern readers because he *is* guiltless. Our modern sense of justice demands redress. We cannot bear that Job yield. If he is to suffer defeat, we prefer that he go down with the ship rather than even hint at compromise. Here, the critic Leslie Fiedler offers Job support. Seeing God suggests to Job "not merely that God is beyond good and evil, but that He reveals Himself only to one willing to maintain this unpalatable truth over the objections of the pious." (Rosenberg, D., 335) Give God credit. His very appearance vindicates Job before his errant friends.

Of course, if God does vindicate Job, another question must be addressed. Why does God respond to the Adversary's challenge in the first place? Or is it possible, as Fiedler suggests, that Satan does not exist at all? To Fiedler, ha-Satan is another aspect of God's personality—His own "Other Side." God has doubts as we do, Fiedler posits, and so He bets against Himself that Job will not disappoint Him. (Rosenberg, D., 345)

The Epilogue: (Almost) Everything is Made Right

It is entirely possible that ancient listeners and hearers of the Job story were equally frustrated by Job's suffering. How to appease them—and us? The story's conclusion offers Job a reward for his endurance and, perhaps, obstinacy. The prose epilogue seemingly ties up all our loose ends. God upbraids Eliphaz, along with Bildad and Zophar, "for you have not spoken the truth about Me as did My servant Job" (Job 42:7). Job *is* innocent, and God's early reference to his being *tam* resonates. God is not upset when humanity questions apparent injustice, even if such injustice is beyond human understanding. Indeed, God may expect or even *demand* such questioning, which, as has been previously mentioned in reference to Sodom and Gomorrah, is central to Abraham's character.

The friends, according to the Swiss Protestant theologian Leonhard Ragaz, are no more than "unauthorized pious advocates" whose defense of God is an insult to Him. (Glatzer/Job 129) God condemns them, writes Jonathan Sacks, "because He asks of us *not* to take his part but to be human, the essence of which is acknowledging that we are not God." (Sacks/Heal, 26) Through all his tribulations, Job has remained God's *servant*—a word God repeats four times in His rebuke.

The young upstart Elihu disappears from the narrative altogether. God never addresses him in the epilogue—perhaps because Elihu never accuses Job of being wicked but instead castigates him for failing to recognize the unknowable nature of God's justice. Or, as N.H. Tur-Sinai proposes, Elihu is a later addition to the original poem. As to Eliphaz, Bildad and Zophar, they must do penance by offering God seven bulls and seven rams. The offering reflects the book's Israelite influence. The Levites make a similar offering when they carry the Ark of the Lord to Jerusalem under David's command (1 Chron. 15:26). Further, King Hezekiah and the nobles of Judah offer seven bulls and seven rams when they restore the Temple (2 Chron. 29:21).

And what of the Adversary? His role in the story has long since ended. We may assume that he has lost the wager, but this no longer seems important. No reference to the Adversary or the wager appears. Ultimately, the Adversary proves no more than a dramatic necessity whose sole task is to prompt God's testing of Job. The essence of the story lies in the confrontation between Job and God rather than any between the Adversary and God.

Job, on his part, proves magnanimous. He forgives his friends and accepts their offering, leading God to make amends. "The LORD restored Job's fortunes when he prayed on behalf of his friends, and the LORD gave Job twice what he had before" (Job 42:10). Job receives double his lost wealth, consistent with the Torah's penalties for theft (Ex. 22:3, 6 and 8)—even if God permitted all of Job's losses. Moreover, Job fathers seven new sons and three new daughters, although Robert Gordis calls the JPS and other translations into question. Gordis translates the Hebrew *shiveanah* not as a variant of "seven" but as an archaism consistent with the doubling of Job's other property. Job, he comments, has not seven but fourteen new sons. The number of new daughters—three—remains unchallenged. Because girls were viewed as less valuable in the ancient Near East, no double restoration was required. (Gordis, 498)

Job also lives happily ever after for another 140 years—210 in all. Here, a doubling of the standard biblical life span of 70 is added to his age. This might indicate that Job was already 70 when he was afflicted. Or it may tell us that he reached age 70 at the point when all of his new children had been born or matured into adulthood, and his wealth was fully restored.[88] Job is further blessed with four generations of sons and grandsons, double the expected number. "So Job died old and contented" (Job 42:17)—also translated as "old and full of years"—a phrase that describes the deaths of Abraham and Isaac.

Since we all love happy endings, the conclusion of the Book of Job should leave us contented. But this is unlikely. Among many objections, at least one forces its way into our discussion. It involves Job's children. The plain text informs us that Job propagates a second set of sons and daughters who provide him with great joy. In fact, the daughters so please Job that he goes so far as to give estates to them as well as to his sons. This takes him beyond the requirements of

88 Methuselah sets the Bible's longevity record at 962 years followed by Jared (962), Noah (950), Adam (930), Seth (912), Kenan (910) and Enosh (905). All were part of the first ten generations of humans. Abraham, in contrast, lived to 175 and Moses to 120. Genesis makes no mention of Eve's longevity or of corresponding women in the first ten generations, although informing us that Sarah lives to 127.

the Law, which arise from the story of the daughters of Zelophehad in Numbers 27:1-11, who demand their father's property as an inheritance since he had no son—and get it. Against what then might we protest? Job says nothing about his first generation of children. Nor does God offer words of consolation. The children seem entirely forgotten. And so we may ask, what kind of parent considers a child as a commodity? Job's other wealth—cattle and gold—are replaceable. But from our perspective, his servants, and certainly his children, are not.

Finding ourselves echoing Job, we also are likely to ask what kind of God ultimately allows such suffering? God will not, or perhaps cannot, bring the dead back to life. Job's children are gone for good and along with them, Jack Miles insists, God's own innocence. (Miles, 328)

If there is comfort, we may find it in the fact that our concerns go back many generations. Nachmanides rejects the pessimism engendered by Job's replacement children. He considers Job's original sons and daughters to have been returned from captivity by Satan rather than having died. Job simply gives his daughters new names. (Soncino/Job, 221-22) Our contemporary, Stephen Mitchell, also believes the "new" children to be Job's existing sons and daughters "sprung back to life as gracefully as the bones of a murdered child in a Grimms' tale." (Mitchell, xxix)

The discussion has proven timeless. The American philosopher Paul Weiss complains of "the inhumanity of the author (or of his God, if one prefers)" and draws a parallel with those who comment on the book but fail to abhor what God has done. Weiss also levels criticism at Job as a man troubled more by his physical suffering than by the deaths of his children. "Our modern torturers know better. They know that the core of a decent man can be more readily and vitally touched by killing his dependents than by making him sick or weakening him with pain." (Glatzer/Job, 183)

Elie Wiesel finds no comfort in Job's restoration to wealth. "Much as I admired Job's passionate rebellion, I am deeply troubled by his hasty abdication. He appeared to me more human when he was cursed and grief-stricken, more dignified than after he rebuilt his lavish residences under the sign of his newly found faith in divine glory and mercy." Wiesel prefers to believe that the real ending was lost, "That Job died without having repented, without having humiliated himself; that he succumbed to his grief an uncompromising and whole man." Job's immediate acceptance of God's unknowable justice is a decoy, Wiesel concludes. "Job personified man's eternal quest for justice and truth—he did not choose resignation. Thus he did not suffer in vain; thanks to him, we know that it is given to man to transform divine justice into human justice and compassion." (Wiesel, 246-48)

So What Does It All Mean?

Had the Book of Job either rigidly maintained or condemned orthodoxy regarding reward and punishment, it may never have earned inclusion in the canon. A mindless defense or bitter diatribe would have added little to the biblical discussion. It is Job's questioning that places the book squarely in the Jewish tradition in which debate and exploration are valued highly as ends in themselves and not merely as means. Thus the English writer Seton Pollock suggests that the importance of the Book of Job lies not in the answers it offers but in the questions it poses. "Job was right to doubt his creed, however well established it was, when he found that it did not square with the facts, for God is better pleased with honest heresy than with fraudulent piety; and although the outworks of his faith were sorely shaken, his ultimate faith in God weathered the tempest of doubt triumphantly." (Glatzer, 270)

Those questions abound, tormenting and humbling us. Does the doubling of Job's wealth assure us that goodness will be rewarded if only we will ourselves to endure? Certainly, our life experience—like Job's—informs us that not everyone who suffers ultimately comes to an earthly reward or restoration. Or is the "happy ending" only a sop offered in deference to older, more traditional religious views? G.K. Chesterton posts a warning: "If prosperity is regarded as the reward of virtue it will be regarded as the *symptom* [italics mine—DP] of virtue." (Glatzer, 236) The most corrupt among us may be viewed as the most virtuous. The Bible presents a superb example of this in Omri, King of Israel, who "did what was displeasing to the Lord; he was worse than all who preceded him" (1 Kings 16:25). Yet Omri apparently died in peace.

If, then, good people can expect no reward and the wicked do prosper, how shall we lead our lives? Will a false north continually misdirect our moral compasses? The Torah's blessings and curses, along with the prophetic teachings, offer a sense of certainty, but they do so on the communal and national levels. The Sages saw the individual human condition quite differently. Thus the Midrash (Bereshit Rabba 76) informs us that righteous people enjoy no guaranty of reward or safekeeping in this world. The *yetzer hatov* (good inclination) and the *yetzer hara* (bad inclination) remain in continual conflict while nature itself both nurtures and threatens.

Yet the existence of evil does not deny the inherent pattern of good in the world. "On the contrary," Robert Gordis emphasizes, "the harmony and beauty of the natural order support the faith that there is a similar pattern of meaning in the moral sphere, since both emanate from the One God. Sustained by this faith, man can bear the burden of suffering and yet find life a joyous experience, secure in the knowledge that God's world is basically good." (Gordis, 566)

Maintaining such faith poses no small challenge, writes H.H. Rowley from the Christian tradition, but humanity has no other choice. As Rowley explains, "There are mysteries of experience that neither theology nor philosophy can fully elucidate; but this does not mean that the human spirit should not wrestle with the problems. But what the Book of Job says is that there is something more fundamental than the intellectual solution of life's mysteries." (Glatzer, 124) Gaining new insights beyond those offered by the intellect can be rewarding but is not without considerable difficulty. Faith, notes the scholar Marvin Pope, "is not achieved without moral struggle and spiritual agony." (Glatzer, 277)

It is the struggle rather than the victory that counts, according to Walter Kaufmann. Judaism utters a ceaseless cry in the night against what Ecclesiastes 4:1 terms "all the oppression that goes on under the sun." Retaining its faith in spite of such oppression, Judaism maintains its outcry rather than retreating into complacence. Attempting to fashion something from suffering and endure defeats *without* resentment, Kaufmann assures us, "is compatible with the faith of a heretic." (Glatzer, 244-5)

The outcry persists even when—*especially* when—the goal appears unattainable. "Justice, justice shall you pursue," Deuteronomy 16:20 commands. We must *pursue* justice, but we are not necessarily expected to achieve it. Perfect justice may well be beyond the reach of humanity, but such an ideal is no less worthy because it is unattainable.

Nonetheless, our angst as moderns continues. The Holocaust and similar horrors—manmade and natural alike—have not merely challenged the faith of many people but shattered it. We cannot easily dismiss such questions as why God allowed such carnage, and whether the Holocaust served as the collective punishment of an errant Jewish people.

The first question often expressed in response to the Holocaust is, where was God—has the God of History permanently withdrawn from Israel and, for that matter, from all of humanity? Reflective of what Job has to teach us, Elie Wiesel counters, "Where was man?" God's justice may indeed be established on a higher plane beyond our understanding, which reinforces the requirement that humanity take responsibility for itself.

The second question finds some—but fortunately few—Jews and others answering that the Holocaust really did serve as God's chastisement of Israel, of a European Jewry gone astray. Whenever an ultra-orthodox rabbi or commentator in Israel condemns the victims—which happens periodically—a great uproar reaches from Jerusalem and Tel Aviv around the world. Few people believe that all of the victims could have been guilty of transgressing against God. The Bible presents two critical stories that shed light on this question. In the case of Sodom and Gomorrah, as few as ten righteous men could not be found, and so those evil cities were destroyed in spite of Abraham's call for justice. Guilt was punished because virtually every inhabitant *was* guilty. In the case of Nineveh, God's response to Jonah's desire for the city's punishment demonstrates that He will not strike down those who repent as well as those who are innocent in the first place (see *Kings and Commoners*). God asks, "And should I not care about Nineveh, that great city, in which there are more than a hundred and twenty thousand persons who do not yet know their right hand from their left, and many beasts as well!" (Jonah 4:11) The Holocaust consumed as many as a million or more children who did not yet know their right hand from their left—children innocent by definition since Jewish tradition makes parents responsible for the religious failings of those under age thirteen.[89]

Let me make it clear, however, that we cannot fall back on easy answers. The Bible also presents us with the slaying of the Egyptian first-born males, which ranges from old men, who have enjoyed many years in which to sin, to newborns. The Sages, medieval commentators and modern commentators all have struggled with this. It is their—and our—discomfort that speaks out for the world's innocents, refusing to condemn them for the evils that befall them.

All this being stated, the Holocaust still poses at least one more agonizing question in relation to Job. It regards the mitigation of Job's suffering by his doubled wealth and new set of children, and how this relates to contemporary Israel. The groundwork for the State of Israel had been laid well before the rise of the Nazis and the beginning of the Second World War. Yet Germany's defeat and the disclosures of the Holocaust that followed doubtless increased the support of Jews inside and outside Palestine—as well as of many other nations and individuals—for a Jewish state. From the Jewish perspective—no attempt is being made here to discuss the Israel-Palestine situation, which remains unsettled as I write—Israel represents a necessary good. While World War Two may have slowed the formation of the Jewish state, exposure of the Holocaust probably sped it up in the post-War world, although by how many years no one can say. But statehood in no way justifies or diminishes the suffering of Jews who endured the death camps or fought, hid

---

89 At bar- and bat-mitzvah age, thirteen for boys and girls outside Israel, twelve for girls in Israel, a child becomes a religious adult responsible for upholding the commandments.

and survived outside them. No quid pro quo can be imagined. Israel's declaration of statehood in 1948 cannot be seen as compensation for the Holocaust. Monetary and other compensation can assist survivors, but it cannot wipe away the tortuous memory of suffering and death. And so we ask more questions. Can an individual who survives a tragedy and builds a new life—even achieves wealth and/or fame—truly be made whole? Does time really heal all wounds?

If we can never wholly reconcile the suffering we have experienced or the suffering of others—if time heals wounds but does not conceal scars—we must assume a different perspective that integrates suffering into our lives rather than foolishly attempts to ignore it. Thus Job's living to a contented old age does not require him to be oblivious to what he has experienced. The text does not tell us that Job forgot his original children, his servants and his suffering. Rather, Job endures. He again embraces life as he retains his faith in God. That he does so may result not from of a faulty memory but in spite of a clear one.

Endurance, suggests Viktor Frankl, a psychoanalyst who survived Auschwitz among a number of camps, is possible because "...everything can be taken from a man but one thing: the last of the human freedoms—to choose one's attitude in any given set of circumstances, to choose one's own way." (Frankl/Meaning, 86) Can suffering be ennobling? "The right kind of suffering—facing your fate without flinching—is the highest achievement that has been granted to man," Frankl offers. (Frankl/Soul, xii) The challenge is frightening. Few of us wish to undergo suffering. Being realists, however, we understand that we cannot always avoid it. What strength can we find when we must? Frankl cites Dostoevsky: "There is only one thing that I dread: not to be worthy of my sufferings." (Frankl/Meaning, 87) We rebuild our shattered lives to the best of our abilities and live on. This, according to Frankl, requires only a sense of purpose, whatever it may be. "A man who becomes conscious of the responsibility he bears towards a human being who affectionately waits for him, or to an unfinished work, will never be able to throw away his life. He knows the 'why' for his existence, and will be able to bear almost any 'how.'" (Frankl/Meaning, 101)

We must, then, yield to the life force. "The moral of the Job story is not, as most people think, that we cannot understand the ways of God," Rabbi Arthur Hertzberg writes. Rather it is that Job remarried, had additional children and "forged a useful life." According to Hertzberg, "No matter how mighty the obstacles we encounter on our journey, we Jews will do as the Prophet Ezekiel advised after the destruction of the First Temple: 'Build houses, cultivate vineyards, and wait for the day your fortunes will be revived.'" (Ezekiel 28:26) (Hertzberg, 57)

Solomon Freehof suggests another, complementary approach. Humanity must get to work improving our world. God's speeches about the forces of nature are meant to urge us to reduce our ignorance and thus reduce the misery in our lives. "The progress of human knowledge, the extension of human power over nature, is a mandate from God and a means to the conquest of much of suffering." (Freehof, 32)

If the ultimate message is "continue on," the Book of Job takes a particularly Jewish point of view. It affirms Moses' guidance to the Israelites in Deuteronomy 30:19 as they conclude forty years in the wilderness and prepare to enter Canaan. Truly in the manner of so much Jewish discussion, it tantalizes us by reflecting the reward-and-punishment theme that the Book of Job calls into question while emphasizing individual and communal responsibility. "I call heaven and earth to witness against you this day: I have put before you life and death, blessing and curse. Choose life."

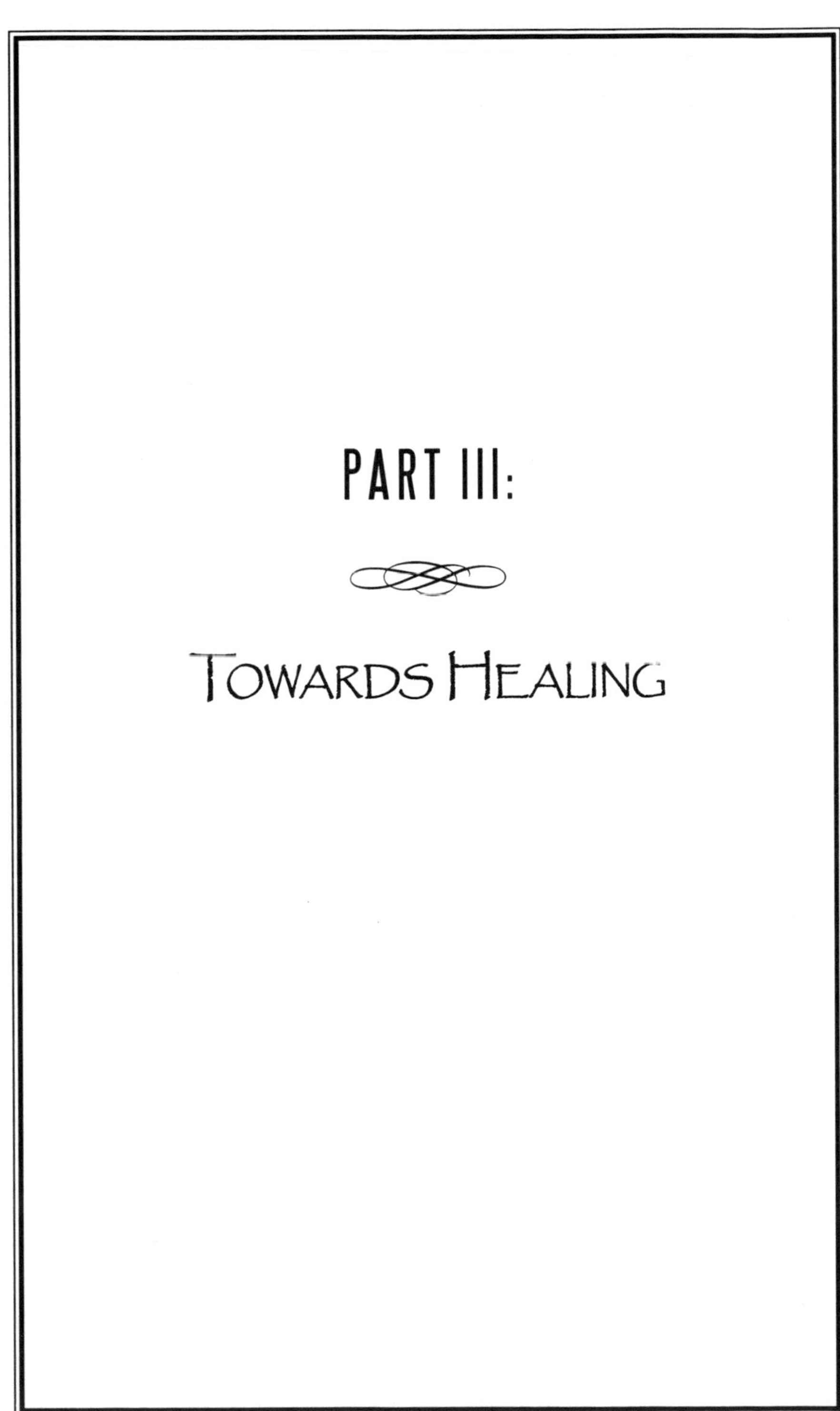

PART III:

Towards Healing

9

Beyond Tolerance: The Challenging Path to Respect

Love your fellow [neighbor] as yourself.
Leviticus 19:18

Who is a wise man? He who learns from all men.
Mishnah: Avot 4:1

The stories of "God's others" can stand by themselves in any volume. Yet leaving those encounters without a final comment would do a grave injustice to these non-Israelite characters, the Bible's authors and to this book's readers. The history of both Western and global religious conflict compels us to seek a solution—or, more realistically perhaps, steps leading towards a solution—to the hostilities that continue to plague us. The encounters of non-Israelites with the God of Israel provide a sound platform for brief thoughts that offer Jews, Christians and Muslims of good faith—as well as followers of Eastern religions, agnostics and atheists—opportunities to take more gracious approaches to each other.

Many adherents of the three Abrahamic religions increasingly cry out for tolerance. And indeed, the West in particular has produced more tolerant societies following the Second World War and the

Holocaust. Yet the very concept of tolerance impedes our progress. To many people, tolerance implies a willingness to accept—and even celebrate—differing ethnicities, cultures and religious beliefs. Jonathan Sacks terms this willingness "the dignity of difference." Regrettably, tolerance has a "dark side." It suggests that we merely put up with that which we believe to be disagreeable or even wrong for the sake of achieving a reasonable, if limited, degree of peace and harmony. This may resemble, for example, tolerating the unwanted symptoms of a chronic illness because we cannot make them disappear. We do so as a practical approach to managing our condition—but only grudgingly. In this respect, tolerance fails to engender a respect for difference. Tolerance may help to delay and even prevent hostile confrontations, but it does not necessarily change our opinion that others' differences cause them to miss the mark, that those who are different fail to meet higher standards of belief and practice as we have defined them.

Tolerance thus becomes a necessary evil—one we practice selectively. George Bernard Shaw in his play, *Saint Joan*, offers, "The degree of tolerance attainable at any moment depends on the strain under which society is maintaining its cohesion." Tolerance thus represents a problematic stance by which we accommodate differences rather than accept—let alone embrace—them. It covers over, rather than removes, sources of animosity. The potential for violence may be moderated for a while only to risk rising again just as water boiling on a stove may be stilled by turning the flame down then quickly reheated to bubble up and over.

Moreover, tolerance may serve a group's purpose only so long as the group believes that it does not have the upper hand and cannot force others to think and act as it does, or that the risks of confronting others outweigh the opportunities. Ultimately, tolerance proposes that differences must inevitably create barriers between peoples—barriers that cannot be ignored but only endured. Thus tolerance more resembles the willingness to establish an armistice that halts hostilities temporarily rather than a treaty that ends them permanently. As such, tolerance may often be helpful but ultimately proves fragile and insufficient.

In this light, the German poet Goethe aptly comments, "Tolerance should really be only a temporary attitude; it must lead to recognition. To tolerate means to offend." George Washington, in his 1790 letter to Moses Seixas of the Hebrew Community of Newport, Rhode Island, takes a similar stand regarding citizens of the newly formed United States. "All possess alike liberty of conscience and immunities of citizenship. It is now no more that toleration is spoken of, as if it was by the indulgence of one class of people that another enjoyed the exercise of their inherent natural rights. For happily the Government of the United States, which gives to bigotry no sanction, to persecution no assistance, requires only that they who live under its protection, should demean themselves as good citizens."

In our day, the historian Bernard Lewis notes that Washington's concept of tolerance as indulgence remains in practice. "The degree of tolerance accorded in the different societies that practise it varies from minimal to maximal. Even at best, it remains a revocable concession, granted by a dominant group to a subordinate group." (Lewis, 198)

Humanity's challenge in the religious sphere—particularly, but not exclusively, relating to Judaism, Christianity and Islam—is to go beyond tolerance, to view beliefs that are different simply *as different* rather than as wrong, and to accept the legitimacy of others holding different religious positions while maintaining the integrity of their own. This is exactly the point of the Noahide laws discussed in chapter two, *Monotheism: Humanity's Natural Religious State*. We must acknowledge that many paths towards God exist even when we choose to follow our own very specific path.

Recognizing the Other

In spite of vociferous contemporary critics espousing the moral superiority of atheism, religion is here to stay. We will be better off if, rather than antagonizing people of faith or, just as aptly, those of *other* faiths, we seek common ground in our essential humanity—a meeting place in which no one coerces or devalues the other. To arrive there, we must speak *with*, rather than *at*, each other. As the theologian Martin Marty proposes, "*Conversation* is not the same as argument. *Argument* is guided by the answers, not the questions. If you have the answers about the divine, the sacred, the mysteries, God and power, you either have to convert me, humiliate me, exile me, or kill me. Conversation is guided by the questions, not the answers. Each of us, as individuals and as parties, can bring our commitments, and learn to respect those of others." (Ahmed, 188)

"God's others" help point the way. Because the Hebrew Bible serves as the foundation text of Jewish, Christian and Muslim scripture, we must acknowledge the relationships God establishes with people from a variety of cultures and religious perspectives along with others' capacity to encounter God in their own ways. Failing to do so promises nothing but additional strife. As Jonathan Sacks emphasizes, "Until the great faiths not merely tolerate but find positive value in the diversity of the human condition, we will have wars, and their cost in human lives will continue to rise." (Sacks/Dignity, 200)

We understand, of course, that our differing religions, ethnicities and cultures often divide us into discrete and mutually distrustful communities. The Book of Genesis acknowledges this in the story of the Tower of Babel. Humans seek to build a tower of bricks to the very heavens. God foils the plan by toppling the tower and turning their common language into many tongues. In doing so, He creates numerous nations from one. But our focus must shift from what separates us to the common humanity that unites us. We all have multiple identities—religious, political, familial and other—but these need not stand in the way of maintaining a parallel universal human identity. Akbar Ahmed, writing from a Muslim perspective, comments, "We need to build the idea of *asabiyya* or group loyalty that encompasses global society or all mankind, not just the tribe or the nation." (Ahmed, 164)

At the same time, we must understand that the concept of global *asabiyya*, which complements Jonathan Sacks' "dignity of difference," does not require us to incorporate others' beliefs into our own. Jews may respect Christian love and charity, and embrace a common humanity with Christians, without accepting Jesus as the Messiah. Christians may acknowledge the validity of Jewish law and Jews' very humanity without adhering to the *mitzvot*. Jews and Christians may recognize the legitimacy of Islamic monotheism and their common humanity with Muslims while not accepting the Quran as God's revelation or praying in the direction of Mecca. And Muslims need not add Yom Kippur and Easter to their religious calendar to view Judaism and Christianity not as errant antecedents but as monotheisms of truly equal validity, and Jews and Christians as fully developed religious individuals. Maintaining the specifics of our own faith need not conflict with respecting others' right to maintain their own.

At the same time, let us recognize that legitimizing those with different points of view while not accepting their beliefs is easier said than done. For many individuals, this goal may remain beyond reach as an intellectual concept to which they can pay lip service but not internalize.

And so I propose that what is most important is the effort we make rather than the result we achieve. Our attempts to create a true sense of openness and respect may fall short of perfection, but we can attain greater openness and respect as long as these efforts, no matter how imperfect, continue. The old adage of the nineteen-sixties, "It's the journey, not the destination," really does apply.

A New Language

To go beyond tolerance, we must alter our language and frame of reference. This calls for abandoning what Bernard Lewis calls the triumphalist attitude towards others, whether explicit or implicit: "I'm right, you're wrong, go to Hell." (Lewis, 198-99) Therefore I urge replacing the statement that "What you believe is not true" with "That is not in my belief system."

Terming others' beliefs untrue not only negates those beliefs but also places the believers on the defensive. Rather than focusing on our own faith or beliefs, we cast aspersions on those of others, and careen down a very slippery slope. Considering others to be wrong about God, we inevitably view them as offending God. And how can we, if we are strong in our faith, fail to defend God? "Not true" becomes a value judgment that vilifies others and encourages enmity, persecution and violence. Taken to its extreme, such a position may lead to prosecuting others for waging war against God as did an Iranian court, which issued a death sentence to a supporter of reform presidential candidate Mir Hussein Moussavi, according to the International Herald Tribune on March 4, 2010.

Opinions can and do differ as to what is true and what is not. We must recognize, however, that such opinions are based on faith rather than demonstrable observation. More flexible, open-ended language leads us to understand that truth often refers to belief—a perspective that is subjective rather than objective. More accommodating language can enable people with beliefs in differing truths not only to co-exist but also to thrive together. When Rabbi Abraham Joshua Heschel, one of twentieth-century Judaism's intellectual/spiritual giants, marched with Martin Luther King in Selma, Alabama to promote civil rights, both men agreed upon the "truth" that all Americans were entitled to equal justice and treatment. Their shared convictions sprang from mutual belief in human dignity rather than a common theology.

Elliot Dorff urges us to take a more modest approach to attaining religious truth. "The claim to absolute knowledge of God's will, then, amounts to a theologically improper egotism and/or idolatry. People certainly have the right to their convictions; indeed, I would argue that we all have the *duty* to think through what we believe and commit our lives to. But we must all acknowledge that our convictions are what I (or we) *think* is the truth, given our history, values, fears, hopes, personalities, associations, and perspectives." (Dorff/Right, 59)

Surely, we can express our own religious faith without denigrating the faiths of others. When we state, "That is not in my belief system," we affirm our own beliefs without passing judgment on those of others. We acknowledge the existence of other beliefs as valid *for those who honor them* without suggesting that our own beliefs lack validity. We see the other as offering a point of view that is different rather than threatening. We also find ourselves more capable of living up to our most deeply professed beliefs.

Defining the Neighbor We are Commanded to Love

Adherents of the three Abrahamic faiths share a familiarity with the biblical injunction to "Love your neighbor ["fellow"—JPS] as yourself" (Lev. 19:18). Yet this seemingly simple verse poses a potent challenge. Just who are our neighbors? Are they those with whom we share physical proximity? Or are they the people closest to us genetically and/or religiously? At what point do people whose beliefs differ from our own distance themselves from us so that we do not share their concerns? Or should we take a more universal—as opposed to universalistic—view and think of all human beings as our neighbors?

Rabbi Abraham Cohen addresses the question from the Jewish perspective. The Talmud defines "neighbor" as an Israelite to the exclusion of Gentiles, which stems from the Sages' understanding of the scriptural text: the Torah speaks to Jews about Jews. And it must be emphasized that Jews today practice (or reject) rabbinic Judaism, which interprets the Torah through the Oral Law and layers of commentary rather than read it literally with no other frame of reference.

Yet modern readers, as the Sages, maintain an awareness of the commandment following shortly after "love thy neighbor":

> When a stranger resides with you in your land, you shall not wrong him. The stranger who resides with you shall be to you as one of your citizens; you shall love him as yourself, for you were strangers in the land of Egypt; I the LORD am your God. (Lev. 19:33-34)

The stranger (*ger*), literally sojourner, may be viewed not only as a convert, as the Sages interpret the word, but in its plain sense as a non-Jew living or sojourning in the midst of or near Jews. Thus, Cohen points out, the Sages take a more global view of Jews' responsibilities to others. "It cannot be logically or justly deduced from this fact that the Rabbis advocated the practice of ethical principles in connection with none but co-religionists." (Cohen, A., 213) Admittedly, the Sages of the Talmud make negative comments about non-Jews—the result of frequent persecution and suffering. For this reason, medieval and later commentators did not always speak kindly of their neighbors in the Christian West either. Yet today, the Jewish mainstream in all its forms embraces all human beings as neighbors sharing a common humanity on a single planet. A great many non-Jews espouse this principle, as well. But do we—can we—translate the wider concept of neighborliness into action?

Extending the concept of neighbor beyond our circle of family, friends and co-religionists is no simple feat. But we must rise to the challenge regardless of the significant degree of difficulty. If we choose to live in a world in which Jews love only Jews, Christians love only Christians and Muslims love only Muslims—and we further define acceptable relationships as those among people of the same stream, denomination or sect within each religion—tensions and violence will continue. The bloodshed we witnessed on and following 9/11 clearly informs us that this is a state of affairs that we cannot and should not abide.

Knowing what we know about "God's others," we must each bear responsibility for acknowledging not only others' differences but the legitimacy of those differences and leaving them in peace in spite of our own most passionate beliefs. "The duty to love our neighbors is a precept of both the Christian and Jewish traditions," Stephen Carter reminds us, "and the duty is not lessened because we happen to think our neighbor is wrong about a few things." (Carter, 23)

Challenges abound as we seek to widen our circle of acceptable human beings and love all of our neighbors. How do we define what being "wrong about a few things" means? More pointedly, must we define "different" as "wrong" in the first place? While I posit that different should be considered only as different, we too easily conclude that those who are not with us are against us. Civility urges us to refrain from attacking those whom we consider wrong in matters of belief. Carter cites the sociologist John Murray Cuddihy's position that civility allows us "to live with unknown others without transforming them into either brothers or enemies." (Carter, 58)

Loving our neighbors—*all* of our neighbors—includes respecting, rather than adopting, minority opinions. The Talmud offers a worthy example. While providing the generally accepted opinions of the majority on a wide variety of legal topics, the Talmud takes pains to include minority reports and cite the Sages who present them. For example, the Talmud deals extensively with the competing opinions of the school of Hillel, generally more liberal in its interpretation of the Law, and the conservative school of Shammai. The school of Hillel continually wins out, but the school of Shammai always is heard from. Indeed, the Talmud (Makkot 1:10) offers a marked example of including the minority report in a discussion of capital punishment, mandated by the Torah for three-dozen offenses. Rabbi Eleazar b. Azariah, Rabbi Tarphon and Rabbi Akiba all decry even a single execution. But Rabbi Simeon b. Gamaliel's minority opinion follows that such refusal to execute murderers will "multiply shedders of blood in Israel." The majority exercises influence while accepting the right—indeed, the necessity—of the minority to be heard. The minority, in turn, forms a loyal opposition, dissenting from the majority but accepting the majority right to make and uphold decisions in disputed matters.

Today, regrettably, the minority often finds itself under increasing pressure within its own frame of religious reference. The phrases "un-Jewish," "un-Christian" and "un-Muslim"—explicit or implicit—are offered up with alarming frequency. Those who proclaim that only one way exists deny the validity of the dissenting report and sometimes, conversely, the legitimacy of the majority.

Yet difference of opinion need not spur hostility. Again, the Talmud provides a stirring example of respect and concern for others. A legend (Megillah 10b) tells of the angels celebrating Israel's freedom as Pharaoh's army—the force that held Israel in slavery—drowns in the Reed Sea. God responds, "My children are drowning in the sea, and you are singing songs!"

Let us recognize then that loving one's neighbor does not compel groups and individuals to accept their neighbors' religious—or social or political—beliefs and practices. Likewise, stating positions that differ from our own need not—and should not be—interpreted as antagonism and threat. And so I propose that we examine the commandment to "Love your neighbor as yourself" with a more critical—and open—sensibility:

• *Love:* Actions, not just words, prove the real measure of our intentions. We must treat all human beings equitably rather than pay lip service to the phrase "all God's children."

• *Your:* The neighbors to whom Leviticus refers are *ours*, not someone else's. We each must take personal responsibility for the way we deal with others.

• *Neighbor:* It is crucial that we expand our definition from those nearest to us—family, friends, the people living on our street, co-religionists—to those we do not know and even those we do not agree with. Extending a sense of neighborliness follows naturally from our belief in a single Creator and our common descent from Adam and Eve.

• *As yourself:* We cannot treat others harshly unless *we* wish to be treated harshly. "That which is hateful to you do not do to others," Hillel taught. We cannot complain of hatred and violence inflicted on us if we are willing to devalue, hate or persecute anyone else.

Given the narrow definition of neighbor that has set religions and their various sects at each other's throats with disturbing frequency, can Jews, Christians and Muslims truly expect to live in harmony? The impact of long standing hostilities should not be underestimated. But the will of individuals to overcome them should not be taken lightly. Person by person, step by step, each of us can make a difference. In 2002, during some of the most trying days of the Second Intifada, which presented Palestinians and Israelis with a harsh new cycle of violence, individuals of different backgrounds demonstrated goodwill that may yet help overcome long-held hatreds. Palestinian doctors found an abandoned Palestinian girl, only ten months old. Nuns cared for her and Israeli surgeons repaired her heart. (Keyser) All involved demonstrably broadened the definition of neighbor for the entire world.

Such willingness to respect others also can be found with Billy Graham, the United States' foremost Christian evangelist of the second half of the twentieth century, who championed true love of *all* his neighbors in his later years. Asked whether Jews, Muslims, Hindus and other non-Christians could enter heaven, he replied, "Those are decisions only the Lord will make. It would be foolish for me to speculate on who will be there and who won't..." (Meacham)

We are All God's Others

The encounters of "God's others" demonstrate that no human being may deny God the right to define the ways in which He will reveal Himself to us or, by extension, how human beings will interpret those revelations. When we focus on the meaningfulness of our own beliefs rather than the perceived falseness of others' beliefs, we demonstrate our ultimate respect for God. Displaying that respect by extending respect to all other human beings will continue to challenge us, of course. And no matter how worthy the goal, it may well be out of reach. But as the Mishnah (Avot 2:16) advises, "You are not required to complete the work, but you are not free to abandon it." Maintaining that work, even if we can take only one small step at a time, is not only desirable, it is necessary if Jews, Christians and Muslims are to put into practice their commonly stated value of peace. At the end of the day, we must acknowledge Genesis' message that God created all humanity in His image, and that no one can claim an exclusive relationship with God without actually rejecting Him.

As Karen Armstrong, a self-described "freelance monotheist" with connections to all three Abrahamic religions aptly admonishes readers: "Our task now is to mend our broken world; if religion cannot do that, it is worthless. And what our world needs now is not belief, not certainty, but compassionate action and practically expressed respect for the sacred value of all human beings, even our enemies." (Armstrong/Spiral, 304)

Let us look appropriately to the Bible for our conclusion. Exodus 23:9 instructs Israel, "You shall not oppress a stranger, for you know the feelings of the stranger, having yourselves been strangers in the land of Egypt." Because the Israelites in Egypt were a people of a different religion and culture than their hosts, the Bible informs us that the stranger we are to protect is, indeed, someone from outside our family or religious group—someone who is truly an "other." But refraining from oppressing the stranger, while praiseworthy, is not sufficient. The Torah adds, "You must befriend the stranger, for you were strangers in the land of Egypt" (Deut. 10:19). We must welcome rather than reject our neighbor regardless of our religious or cultural differences. Only by taking such action do we fulfill the commandment to "Love your neighbor as yourself."

Each of us, like "God's others," must encounter God in our own way. When we allow our neighbors the same privilege we expect for ourselves—when we acknowledge different as being just that rather than wrong—we go beyond tolerance to establish a world in which we are all neighbors and all loved—indeed, all "God's own."

Bibliography

Primary Scriptures

JPS Hebrew-English Tanakh, The Traditional Hebrew Text and the New JPS Translation — Second Edition. Philadelphia: The Jewish Publication Society, 1999.

The New American Bible. Online at www.Vatican.va/archive/ENG0839.

The Koran, Fourth revised edition. N.J. Dawood, trans. New York: Penguin Books, 1974.

Scripture Commentaries

Alter, Robert. *The Five Books of Moses.* New York: W.W. Norton & Company, Inc., 2004.

The Anchor Bible: Ruth, A New Translation with Introduction and Commentary by Edward F. Campbell, Jr. New York: Doubleday & Company, Inc., 1975.

Book of Job, A Commentary, Freehof, Solomon B., D.D., ed. New York: Union of American Hebrew Congregations, 1958.

Buttenwieser, Moses, Ph.D. *The Book of Job.* New York: The Macmillan Company, 1922.

The Chumash: The Artscroll Series®/Stone Edition, Rabbi Nosson Scherman, ed. Brooklyn: Mesorah Publications Limited, 1998, 2000.

Book of Kings 1: A Commentary. Dr. Leo L. Honor, ed. New York: Union of American Hebrew Congregations, 1955.

Etz Hayim, Torah and Commentary, Senior Editor: David L. Lieber. New York: The Rabbinical Assembly, The United Synagogue of Conservative Judaism, 2001.
- Rembaum, Joel. "Dealing With Strangers: Relations With Gentiles At Home and Abroad," pp. 1377-82.

The Five Scrolls. Israel Bettan, D.D., ed. Cincinnati: Union of American Hebrew Congregations, 1950.

Friedman, Richard Elliott. *Commentary on the Torah.* New York: HarperCollins, 2001.

Gordis, Robert. *The Book of Job: Commentary, New Translation and Special Studies.* New York: The Jewish Theological Seminary of America, 1978.

The Interpreter's Bible. George Arthur Buttrick, commentary ed. Nashville: Abingdon Press, 1954.

Job: A New English Translation. Translation of text, Rashi and commentary by Rabbi A.J. Rosenberg. New York: The Judaica Press Inc., 1989.

Jonah. Translation and Commentary by Rabbi Meir Zlotowitz. Brooklyn: Mesorah Publications, Ltd., 1978, 1980.

The JPS Torah Commentary

- *Exodus: The Traditional Hebrew Text with the New JPS Translation, Commentary by Nahum M. Sarna.* Philadelphia: The Jewish Publication Society, 1991.
- *Genesis: The Traditional Hebrew Text with the New JPS Translation, Commentary by Nahum M. Sarna.* Philadelphia: The Jewish Publication Society, 1989.
- *Jonah, Commentary by Uriel Simon.* Philadelphia: The Jewish Publication Society, 1999.

Leibowitz, Nehama. *New Studies in Bamidbar (Numbers).* Jerusalem: Eliner Library, Department for Torah Education and Culture in the Diaspora, The World Zionist Education, 1993.

—. *New Studies in Bereshit (Genesis).* Jerusalem: Eliner Library, Department for Torah Education and Culture in the Diaspora, The World Zionist Education [no pub. date].

—. *New Studies in Shemot (Exodus).* Jerusalem: Eliner Library, Department for Torah Education and Culture in the Diaspora, The World Zionist Education, 1993.

The Pentateuch, Volume II, Exodus (3rd edition). Translated & explained by Samson Raphael Hirsch. London: Isaac Levy (Translator & Publisher), 1967.

The Schocken Bible: Volume I, Five Books of Moses: Genesis, Exodus, Leviticus, Numbers, and Deuteronomy, A New Translation With Introductions, Commentary and Notes by Everett Fox. New York: Shocken Books, 1995.

The Soncino Books of the Bible

- *Daniel/Ezra/Nehemiah*. Rev. Dr. A Cohen, ed. London and New York: The Soncino Press, 8th edition, 1985.
- *Job*. Rabbi Dr. Victor E. Reichert, ed., revised by Rabbi A.J. Rosenberg. London/Jerusalem/New York, The Soncino Press, revised edition, 1985.
- *Joshua-Judges*. Rabbi Dr. A. Cohen, ed., revised by Rabbi A.J. Rosenberg. London/Jerusalem/New York: The Soncino Press, revised edition, 1982.
- *Kings*. Rabbi Dr. A. Cohen, ed. London/Jerusalem/New York: The Soncino Press, Revised Edition, 1983.
- *The Five Megilloth*. Rabbi Dr. A. Cohen, ed. London/Jerusalem/New York: The Soncino Press, revised edition 1983.
- *The Twelve Prophets*. Rev. Dr. A. Cohen, ed. London-New York: Soncino Press, 1985.
- *Samuel*. Rabbi Dr. A. Cohen, ed. London/Jerusalem/New York: The Soncino Press, revised edition, 1983.

The Torah, a Modern Commentary, Edited by W. Gunther Plaut. New York: The Union of American Hebrew Congregations, 1981.

The Torah: A Woman's Commentary, Tamara Cohn Eskenazi, editor; Andrea L. Weiss, associate editor. New York: URJ Press, 2008.

Tur-Sinai (Torczyner), N.H. *The Book of Job: A New Commentary*. Jerusalem: Kiryath Sepher Ltd., 1967.

The Women's Torah Commentary: New Insights from Women Rabbis on the 54 Weekly Torah Portions. Rabbi Elyse Goldstein, ed. Woodstock, Vermont: Jewish Lights Publishing, 2000.

- Alpert, Rebecca T. "Shmot (1:1-6:1): Rediscovering Tziporah," 121-26.
- Shekel, Rabbi Michal. "Lech Lecha (12:1–17:27): What's in a Name?" 57-62.

Sources

Ahmed, Akbar and Forst, Brian, editors. *After Terror: Promoting Dialogue Among Civilizations*. Malden, Mass: Polity Press, 2005.

- Marty, Martin. "Risking Hospitality," 186-190.

Alshich, Rabbi Moshe. *The Voyage of the Visionary: The Commentary of Rabbi Moshe Alshich on the Book of Jonah*, translated by Ravi Shahar. Spring Valley, New York: Feldheim Publishers, 1992.

Armstrong, Karen. *The Battle for God.* New York: The Ballantine Publishing Group, 2000.

—. *Muhammad: A Biography of the Prophet.* New York: HarperSanFrancisco, A Division of HarperCollins Publishers, 1992.

—. *The Spiral Staircase.* New York: Anchor Books, 2004.

Bialik, Hayim Nahman and Ravnitzky, Yehoshua Hana, editors; William G. Braude, trans. *The Book of Legends (Sefer Ha-Aggadah): Legends from the Talmud and Midrash.* New York: Schocken Books, 1992.

Cahill, Thomas. *The Gifts of the Jews.* New York: Nan A. Talese, 1998.

Caroll, James. *Constantine's Sword: The Church and the Jews.* New York: Houghton Mifflin, 2001.

Carter, Stephen L. *Civility, Manners, Morals, and the Etiquette of Democracy.* New York: Basic Books, 1998.

Cohen, Rabbi Abraham. *Everyman's Talmud: The Major Teachings of the Rabbinic Sages.* New York: Schocken Books, 1975.

Cohen, Shaye J.D. *The Beginnings of Jewishness: Boundaries, Varieties, Uncertainties.* Berkeley and Los Angeles: University of California Press, 1999.

Coogan, Michael D., ed. *The Oxford History of the Biblical World.* New York & Oxford: Oxford University Press, 1998.

- Cogan, Mordechai. "Into Exile: From the Assyrian Conquest of Israel to the Fall of Babylon," 321-65.

- Leith, Mary Joan Winn, "Israel among the Nations: The Persian Period," 367-419.

- Stager, Lawrence E., "Forging an Identity: The Emergence of Ancient Israel," 123-175.

Dorff, Elliot. *To Do the Right and Good: A Jewish Approach to Modern Social Ethics.* Philadelphia: The Jewish Publication Society, 2002.

Finegan, Jack. *Let My People Go: a journey through Exodus.* New York: Harper & Row, Publishers, 1963.

Finkelstein, Israel and Silberman, Neil Asher. *The Bible Unearthed: Archaeology's New Vision of Ancient Israel and the Origin of Its Sacred Texts.* New York: Simon and Schuster, 2001.

Firestone, Reuven, Ph.D. *Who are the* Real *Chosen People?: The Meaning of Chosenness in Judaism, Christianity and Islam.* Woodstock, Vermont: Skylight Paths Publishing, 2008.

Frankl, Victor E., M.D. *Man's Search for Meaning,* Revised and Updated. Boston: Washington Square Press, 1985.

—. *The Doctor and the Soul: from psychotherapy to logotherapy.* New York: Alfred A. Knopf, 1955.

Freeman, Charles. *The Closing of the Western Mind: The Rise of Faith and the Fall of Reason.* New York: Vintage Books, a Division of Random House, 2005.

Friedman, Richard Elliott. *Who Wrote the Bible?* (Second Edition). New York: HarperSanFrancisco, 1997.

Ginzberg, Lewis. *Legends of the Jews.* Philadelphia: Jewish Publication Society of America, 1968.

Glatzer, Nahum M., ed. *The Dimensions of Job: A Study in Selected Readings.* New York: Schocken Books, 1969.

- Chesterton, G.K. "Man is Most Comforted by Paradoxes," 228-37.
- Kallen, Horace M. "Job the Humanist," 175-81.
- Kaufmann, Walter. "An Uncanny World," 237-45.
- Kaufmann, Yehezkel. "Job the Righteous Man and Job the Sage," 65-70.
- Herder, Johann Gottfried. "God and Nature in the Book of Job," 141-56.
- Pollock, Seton. "God and a Heretic," 268-72.
- Pope, Marvin H. "Viewed as a Whole," 276-77.
- Ragaz, Leonhard. "God Himself is the Answer," 128-31.
- Roth, Leon. "Job and Jonah," 71-74.
- Rowley, H.H. "The Intellectual versus the Spiritual Solution," 123-29.
- Weiss, Paul. "God, Job, and Evil," 181-93.

Goldin, Judah, ed. *The Jewish Expression, Edited and with an Introduction by Judah Goldin.* New York: Bantam, 1970.

- Speiser, E.A. "The Biblical Idea of History in Its Common Near Eastern Setting," 1-17.

Green, Rabbi Arthur. *Seek My Face, Speak My Name: A Contemporary Jewish Theology.* Northvale, New Jersey: Jason Aronson Inc., 1992.

Hartman, David. *A Living Covenant: The Innovative Spirit in Traditional Judaism.* Woodstock, Vermont: Jewish Lights Publishing, 1997.

Heschel, Abraham Joshua. *The Prophets.* Philadelphia: The Jewish Publication Society of America, 1962.

Hourani, Albert. *A History of the Arab Peoples.* New York: Warner Books, 1991.

Johnson, Paul. *A History of the Jews.* New York: Harper & Row, Publishers, 1987.

Kates, Judith A. and Twersky Reimer, Gail, editors. *Reading Ruth: Contemporary Women Reclaim a Sacred Story.* New York: Ballantine Books, 1994.

- Aschkenasy, Nehama, "Language as Female Empowerment in Ruth," 111ff.
- Kates, Ruth, "Women at the Center," 187ff.
- Feld, Merle, "At the Crossroads," 166ff.
- Frankiel, Tamar, "Ruth and the Messiah," 321ff.
- Twersky Reimer, Gail, "Her Mother's House," 97ff.
- Zornberg, Avivah, "The Concealed Alternative," 65ff.

Kaufmann, Yehezkel. *The Religion of Israel.* Translated and abridged by Moshe Greenberg. Chicago: University of Chicago Press, 1966.

Lewis, Bernard. *From Babel to Dragomans: Interpreting the Middle East.* New York: Oxford University Press, 2004.

Maimonides, Moses. *The Guide for the Perplexed*, translated from the original Arabic text by M. Friedlander, Ph.D. New York: Dover Publications, 1956.

Menzies, Gavin. *1421: The Year China Discover America.* London: Transworld Publishers, 2002; New York: Harper Collins (Perennial edition), 2004.

Miles, Jack. *God: A Biography.* New York: Alfred A. Knopf, Inc., 1995.

Mitchell, Stephen. *The Book of JOB.* New York: HarperPerennial, 1992.

Niditch, Susan. *Underdogs and Tricksters: A Prelude to Biblical Folklore.* San Francisco: Harper & Row, 1987.

Rosenberg, David, ed. *Congregation: Contemporary Writers Read the Jewish Bible.* San Diego, New York: Harcourt Brace Jovanovich, Publishers, 1987.

- Fiedler, Leslie. "Job," 331-45.
- Ozick, Cynthia. "Ruth," 361-82.
- Schwartz, Sharon Lynne. "Daniel," 418-34.

Rubenstein, Richard E. *Aristotle's Children: How Christians, Muslims, and Jews Rediscovered Ancient Wisdom and Illuminated the Middle Ages*. Orlando: Harcourt, Inc. (A Harvest Book), 2004.

Sacks, Rabbi Jonathan. *The Dignity of Difference: How to Avoid the Clash of Civilizations*. London and New York: Continuum, 2002, 2003.

—. *To Heal a Fractured World: The Ethics of Responsibility*. New York: Schocken Books, a Division of Random House, 2005.

Safire, William. *The First Dissident: The Book of Job in Today's Politics*. New York: Random House, 1992.

Segal, Alan F. *Life After Death: A History of the Afterlife in Western Religion*. New York: Doubleday, 2004.

Spinoza, Baruch. *Theological-Political Treatise* (Gebhardt Edition), translated by Samuel Shirley. Indianapolis/Cambridge: Hackett Publishing Company, 1925.

Stern, Rabbi Chaim. *Pirké Avot: Wisdom of the Jewish Sages*. Hoboken, New Jersey: Ktav Publishing House, Inc., 1997.

Telushkin, Rabbi Joseph. *Jewish Literacy. The Most Important Things to Know About the Jewish Religion, Its People, and Its History*. New York: William Morrow and Company, Inc., 1991.

Wiesel, Elie. *Messengers of God: Biblical Portraits & Legends*. New York: Random House, 1976.

Zornberg, Avivah Gottlieb. *The Particulars of Rapture: Reflections on Exodus*. New York: Doubleday, 2001.

Articles, Web Citations and Conversations

Blow, Charles M. "Heaven for the Godless?" New York Times, December 26, 2008.

Cohn Eskenazi, Tamara. Private conversation, December 16, 2005.

Goethe, Johann Wolfgang Von. *Sayings in Prose*. Cited www.bartleby.com/66 (Columbia World of Quotations, #25307).

Hertzberg, Arthur. "2025: The Next Generation." Reform Judaism, Fall 2002.

Keyser, Jason. "Jews, Christians, Muslims save abandoned baby." Associated Press—The Jerusalem Post: Online/www.jpost.com, February 25, 2002.

Meacham, Jon. "Pilgrim's Progress." Newsweek, August 14, 2006.

INDEX

B

C

D

E

F

G

H

K

N

O

P

Q

R

S

T

U

V

W

Y

Z

CPSIA information can be obtained at www.ICGtesting.com
224671LV00005BA/18/P

9 781450 222785